LATIN AMERICA'S
ECONOMIC DEVELOPMENT

The Countries
of
Latin America

LATIN AMERICA'S ECONOMIC DEVELOPMENT
Institutionalist and Structuralist Perspectives

Edited by
JAMES L. DIETZ &
JAMES H. STREET

Lynne Rienner Publishers   Boulder & London

Frontispiece map from Cathryn Lombardi and John
Lombardi, *Latin American History: A Teaching Atlas*
(Madison: University of Wisconsin Press, 1984). Reprinted
with permission.

Published in the United States of America in 1987 by
Lynne Rienner Publishers, Inc.
948 North Street, Boulder, Colorado 80302

and in the United Kingdom by
Lynne Rienner Publishers, Inc.
3 Henrietta Street, Covent Garden, London WC2E 8LU

Library of Congress Cataloging-in-Publication Data

Latin America's economic development.

   Includes index.
   Bibliography: p.
   1. Latin America—Economic policy.   2. Latin
America—Economic conditions—1945–
I. Dietz, James L., 1947–   .   II. Street, James H.
(James Harry), 1915–   .
HC125.L3536   1987   338.98   87-10046
ISBN 1-55587-067-8 (lib. bdg.)
ISBN 1-55587-068-6 (pbk.)

Printed and bound in the United States of America

The paper used in this publication meets the
requirements of the American National Standard
for Permanence of Paper for Printed Library
Materials Z39.48-1984. ∞

Contents

Tables and Figures

Acronyms

A	amortization of debt
AAUP	American Association of University Professors
ABDIB	Associação Brasileira pelo Desenvolvimento de Industria de Base
BEFIEX	Export Fiscal Benefits
CAPES	Coordinação do Aperfeiçoamento de Pessoal de Nível Superior
CIEPLAN	Corporación de Investigaciones Económicas para América Latina
CIMMYT	Centro Internacional para el Mejoramiento de Maíz y Trigo
CN	consumer nondurables
CONICET	National Council of Scientific and Technical Research
DC	developed country
DFI	direct foreign investment
ECLA	United Nations Economic Commission for Latin America (CEPAL in Spanish)
ECLAC	United Nations Economic Commission for Latin America and the Caribbean
FLASCO	Latin American Faculty of the Social Sciences
FY	foreign income outflow
GDP	gross domestic product
GNP	gross national product
IMF	International Monetary Fund
IMIT	Instituto Mexicano de Investigaciones Tecnológicas
IPADE	Instituto Panamericano de Alta Dirección de Empresa
ISI	import substitution industrialization
LDC	less developed country
LIBOR	London Inter-Bank Borrowers Rate

MTB	merchandise trade balance
NFS	balance of nonfactor services
NIC	newly industrialized country
OECD	Organization for Economic Cooperation and Development
OPEC	Organization of Petroleum Exporting Countries
PES	primary export substitution
PIS	primary import substitution
PREALC	Regional Employment Program for Latin America and the Caribbean
SAM	Mexican Alimentation System
SIC	semi-industrialized country
SUDENE	Superintendency of Development of the Northeast
TNC	transnational corporation
UNAM	Universidad Autonoma de México
UNESCO	United Nations Educational, Scientific, and Cultural Organization

Preface

To the student: Each section of readings begins with an introduction that identifies the main contributions of each article and can help you better understand the significance of each reading. The introductions are integral to the text, so do not skip them. They are there to help you and to raise important issues, not just to take up space!

We hope you will find that the book presents a persuasive analysis of the challenges facing Latin America's development. As noted in the readings that follow, the structuralist perspective has become the dominant mode of thinking among Latin American economists. It is important for North Americans to understand how Latin Americans think about themselves, their history, and their hopes for the future. If you are an economics major, this may be your first extensive exposure to an alternative to neoclassical economic thinking. If so, and regardless of whether you ultimately find it convincing, we sincerely hope that the structuralist and institutionalist alternatives have caused you to rethink, and better understand, your own economic perspective. If you found the structuralist/institutionalist view useful, or would like to read further, you can consult the two major journals representing each school of thought: the *CEPAL Review* and the *Journal of Economic Issues.* Also recommended is *Challenge,* a bimonthly magazine that often includes institutional perspectives as well as those of other heterodox economists, especially post-Keynesians.

There is one particularly good source of current information on political, economic, and social events in Latin America besides your daily newspaper: the *Latin America Weekly Report.* It contains excellent, up-to-date, short articles and news items. It is well worth a look, particularly if you have to write a research paper.

Lastly, we invite your comments on the book and will take seriously any suggestions you may have to improve it. We will try to answer your questions. Please write to us at the Department of Economics, California State University, Fullerton, CA 92634. We look forward to hearing from you!

To the professor: We have designed this book so that it can stand alone in a course on the economic development problems of Latin America and the Caribbean, particularly for those who have taught the course in the past and have a body of notes on key topics, not all of which, of course, can be discussed fully here as they would be in a textbook. There are, at this writing, less than a handful of such texts in print. This reader complements any of the existing texts on Latin America's economic development (C. Furtado, *Economic Development of Latin America*; J. Swift, *Economic Development in Latin America*; B. Kadar, *Problems of Economic Growth in Latin America*) and adds important insights and depth not included in those books. We also have used the reader in tandem with J. Hunter and J. Foley, *Economic Problems of Latin America,* now out of print, but which, with permission from the authors and publisher, we have used in a photocopy reprinting.

We have found that contrasting the structuralist and institutionalist perspectives with orthodox economic analysis is a pedagogically useful way, whatever one's own theoretical perspective, to make clear the essential differences, strengths, and weaknesses of competing economic theories. Students learn to think more critically and analytically. They also learn that there are not necessarily any accepted "truths" in economics. Of course this reader aims to advance the structuralist and institutionalist perspectives, a view the editors share, but we believe that more orthodox economists will find that the reader challenges their students in positive ways. As educators, regardless of our own theoretical predisposition, this is a goal upon which we can all agree.

We invite you, as we invited our student readers, to write to us if you have comments, criticisms, or suggestions for improving the book. Are there significant articles we have overlooked? We would be pleased to provide course outlines, reading lists, study questions, and examinations we have used to assist you in course preparation and in making the best possible use of the reader. Write to us at the address at the end of the student section. We will answer personally and promptly. Good reading and teaching!

J.L.D.
J.H.S.

LATIN AMERICA'S
ECONOMIC DEVELOPMENT

part one

An Overview

The first chapter, by James Dietz and James Street, provides a brief history of Latin America's economic development from the conquest to the present. Latin America's contemporary development problems derive from two sources. First in importance are external factors resulting from unequal relations between the advanced center countries—Spain and Portugal during the colonial period, and the United States, Western Europe, and Japan today—and the Latin American periphery. Second, internal institutional and structural constraints, such as extreme disparities in income distribution, the absence of political and economic democracy, and the failure to make use of technological advances, have prevented Latin America from achieving more rapid and more just economic development. During some periods the external forces have outweighed the internal barriers to economic progress, but undoubtedly and always the internal constraints have been extremely resistant to progressive change.

As will become clearer from other chapters in this volume, however, Latin America's path of economic development has tended to be shaped more by international forces than domestic considerations. Changes in economic strategy have resulted from balance-of-payments crises; these crises have forced governments to adjust their economies to compensate for, but without always correcting, past deficiencies. In a general sense, it is reasonable to suggest that, at root, Latin America has suffered from outward-oriented dependence regardless of the particular economic strategy pursued.

No discussion of Latin America can avoid addressing the role of import substitution industrialization (ISI), the basis of the expansion of the manufacturing sector in the region. A discussion of ISI and other critical issues are included in this introductory chapter and are taken up in even greater detail in the remainder of the readings.

1

Latin America's Economic Development

James L. Dietz
James H. Street

Latin America, including the Caribbean, is a region diverse in culture, language, and geography. Spanish, of course, is most commonly spoken, but nearly one third of all Latin Americans—Brazilians—speak Portuguese; in the Caribbean region, besides Spanish in Puerto Rico and Cuba, English, French, Dutch, Papamento, and Creole are official languages. In many countries—Peru, Bolivia, Guatemala, and Mexico, for example—indigenous populations remain quite large, and Indian languages are the daily, and often the only, communication of this neglected and still abused segment of the population. Of the approximately forty countries that make up the region, population size ranges from the smallest, including Antigua, St. Kitts-Nevis, and Dominica in the Caribbean, each with populations of less than 80,000, to the giants, such as Mexico with 77 million and Brazil with 133 million people.

South America alone is about the size of the continental United States and Canada, and the region has some of the world's most diverse and essential resources: bauxite, gold, nickel, tin, copper, petroleum, and, of course, abundant land. Yet, despite its apparent wealth, Latin America remains part of the underdeveloped Third World, although most countries—Haiti is a glaring exception—fall into the World Bank's low-middle or middle income categories (see Table 1 in the Statistical Appendix). In 1985, per capita incomes ranged from $2,248 in Mexico to $320 in Haiti (Brazil, $1,852; Guatemala, $1,216). For most countries, these incomes are less than those of a decade earlier, which is due, in most cases, to the adverse impact of the debt crisis and world recession. These, in turn, were brought on largely by U.S. domestic measures to control inflation through induced economic contraction, which adversely affected Latin American trade, finance, and investment (see Chapter 18).

Even these income levels give a distorted perspective on living standards for the majority of Latin Americans. Most countries suffer from an ex-

2

tremely unequal distribution of income (although disparities are not so great in Costa Rica, Cuba, and Puerto Rico). Per capita income levels, which are simple averages, are poor indicators of actual income levels for the majority of the population. For example, while the top 20 percent of income earners in Brazil received 67 percent of the economy's total income, the poorest 60 percent shared but 16.4 percent of total income in 1972, the last year with reliable data. Income distribution was little better in most other countries—in Mexico the top 20 percent received 58 percent of total income in 1977 while the poorest 60 percent received 21.9 percent; in Peru the top 20 percent obtained 61 percent of all income in 1972, and the poorest 60 percent obtained 18 percent (World Bank 1986: Table 24, 226-227).

Table 1 in the Statistical Appendix provides some evidence of the relatively poor living conditions facing most Latin American and Caribbean people: low literacy levels, high infant mortality, and low life expectancy (the last line of the table includes figures for the United States to facilitate comparison). Latin America's top-heavy income distribution not only has social and health consequences; it also has important economic implications. The existing income distribution limits the size of the market—that is, the demand for domestically produced goods—but more significantly, this distribution reflects a hierarchical socioeconomic structure and a limited economic and political democracy, which act as structural and institutional barriers to the development process. The impact of these barriers and their causal relation to the relative lack of economic dynamism in Latin America are important themes in this volume.

Understanding Latin America's Development Problems

Why is Latin America poor relative to the United States, Western Europe, and Japan? This is the obvious question that must be confronted and answered. To do so adequately, it is necessary to consider the region's historical development.

After the Spanish conquest of the Americas in the sixteenth century, Spain treated its colonies as little more than lucrative treasure chests to be raided (Stein and Stein 1970 are excellent in describing this period). At first gold and later, in much greater and more significant quantities, silver were appropriated and mined, using indigenous slave labor, and shipped to Spain to finance the sumptuous lifestyle of the royalty and merchant class. Spaniards, Portuguese, and other foreigners who emigrated to the "New World" did not go to work in the fields but came to enrich themselves as quickly as possible so as to return home as "gentlemen." Those not involved directly in the mining operations often founded haciendas based on royal land grants, which included the labor of resident Indians to work the property. These semifeudal haciendas prospered by producing food and other products for the workers in the mines, and soon small stores, cantinas (saloons), brothels, and other related establishments appeared in small settlements around the mining regions, which acted as growth poles for such complementary production (see Furtado 1976). This privileged class of Spanish immigrants imported manufactured and other luxury goods directly from Spain for their personal consumption, while saving for their eventual return to Europe to live from the wealth "earned" on the backs of exploited Indian and other forced labor.

Ironically, the large flow of precious metals extracted from the New World after the conquest did not contribute to the ongoing development of Spain. In fact, easy access to such liquid wealth by elite groups severely retarded Spanish economic progress by making expanded production unnecessary for the attainment of high levels of consumption. It was enough to profit by position or by commerce, as the bulk of the gold and silver, perhaps two thirds, simply passed through Spain on its way to other parts of Europe, particularly England, which produced the greater part of the manufactured goods consumed in Spain or transshipped to the colonies. Consumption goods thus flowed from Europe to Spain and then on to the colonies; precious metals flowed in the other direction. Spain functioned as little more than an intermediary for all this trafficking as its domestic industry crumbled from the competition. In effect, Spain's easy wealth, plundered from its colonies, delayed the arrival in Spain of the industrial revolution that was sweeping across the rest of Europe, propelled forward by the colonial wealth that only passed through Spanish hands. Spain thus remained a predominately feudal economy held back by its adherence to mercantilist economic policies, while the rest of Europe was in the throes of the transition to capitalism with its vastly expanded production possibilities. This failure to enter the modern economic world was reflected in the colonies, which failed to be transformed significantly in either institutions or modes of production under Spanish rule.

Spanish economic backwardness produced anachronistic colonial policy. Pure-blooded Spanish immigrants (*peninsulares*) were accorded privileges in commerce and colonial administration not open to *criollos* (their children born in Latin America), a form of favoritism that created mounting tensions as the *criollo* class grew in size and self-consciousness. This was particularly true after the silver mines had been depleted (roughly, after 1650) and were replaced by agricultural products for export, from plantation enclaves in Brazil and the Caribbean and *haciendas* elsewhere, as the primary sources of rapid wealth accumulation. *Criollos* found their emerging economic and political ambitions—limited by colonial edict to small land ownership, petty trade, and the lower administrative posts in each colony—blocked by a corrupt and self-serving foreign colonial administration bent on preserving its position at all costs. The frustration of nationalist aspirations characteristic of the maturation of the new domestic *criollo* elite class erupted into the wars of independence beginning in 1809-1810. Spain, locked in the Napoleonic wars on the Continent at the time, was unable either to defend militarily its back door in the colonies or to muster the political foresight to grant the *criollos* greater autonomy within the colonial structure, a move that might have won their allegiance. By the mid-1820s, all of Spain's former colonies in Latin America, except Cuba and Puerto Rico, had won their political freedom, but only after much blood had been spilled.

Breaking the colonial bonds, however, did not lead to a full rupture with the past. Factions within the new creole elite fought among themselves for political control for another half century, and split into independent nations that mirrored the separated colonial viceroyalties that had kept the colonies divided from each other for so long. Moreover, the creole elite classes were not interested in, or were not capable of, transforming their newly independent countries along the path that had been followed in Europe and the United States, that is, a dynamic capitalist and industrial revolution. Rather, the goals of these new elite classes were relatively limited. They wished only to gain the class privileges Spanish (and Portuguese) colonial policy had for so long reserved exclusively for *peninsulares*. Such a backward-looking elite could perpetuate only the unprogressive productive and political structures it had inherited from Spain. This elite was content to continue the pattern of exporting primary commodities begun under Spanish rule, for as the new dominant class of large landowners, merchants, and politicians, the creole elite was certain to enrich itself through the expansion of such exports.

As chance would have it, the demand and prices for Latin America's minerals and agricultural products were high in the second half of the nineteenth century due to rapidly rising world incomes. Trade with the advanced center countries permitted *criollo* leaders to import the manufactured luxury goods to which they aspired as displays of their class position. With easy access to vast reaches of land, much of it taken by expropriation from holdings of the Catholic church and native Indians, the *criollo* elite was able to prosper by producing in the same old ways on more land (extensive production) rather than being forced to utilize the latest technological advances in an effort to make each unit of land more productive (intensive production). The lag in developing Latin America's essential infrastructure, such as banks, communication systems, and roads, simply reinforced the lag in modernization by making new methods and techniques of production more expensive for any who might have wished to become more technologically adaptive. It was in this period after the 1870s or so, then, that Latin America's pernicious pattern of limited export diversity of primary commodities was consolidated, in some countries manifesting itself as classic monocultural production, with all the attendant dangers such a limited array of exports brings.

Of course, the economic ideology prevalent in Europe at the time—free trade liberalism—exerted a powerful influence on a creole elite anxious to consume not only foreign goods but foreign ideas as well. The vaunted benefits of production according to the doctrine of comparative advantage and of free trade among nations, espoused by English economists in particular (see Chapter 6), kept the newly independent governments from taking steps to develop their own manufacturing industries through trade limitations and tariff protection to replace similar imports. Not surprisingly, the free trade doctrine coincided perfectly with the needs of English importers of tropical primary products and exporters of manufactures—who supplied some two-thirds of the world market in the last half of the nineteenth century—but at the expense of reinforcing limited production diversity in Latin America and the Caribbean.

Thus from the beginning of independence, the newly established Latin American republics suffered from internecine economic warfare that cost at least fifty years of progress as former colonial rivalries were reproduced among the new nation states. Further, the weak central governments that resulted were captives of a foreign ideology that served best the growing power of English manufacturers and merchants and but poorly Latin Americans, particularly the disenfranchised masses. A productive structure deriving from the colonial period was reinforced by the limited goals of the new creole elites and the prevailing economic orthodoxy. All this left Latin America to supply the world market with the least lucrative outputs made in the least productive ways (although the creole exporting elite and merchants of course did gain for a time). This international division of labor, in which manufactured goods for export were produced in the center countries and primary products in the periphery, was to become one of the key elements of structuralist criticism of the organization of the world economy (see Chapters 6 and 7). It is important to recognize, however, that Latin America's productive structure was the result of internal class conflict and weaknesses intensified by external factors, especially the rapidly expanding role of British world trade.

By the end of the nineteenth century, then, most Latin American and Caribbean countries had outward-oriented economic structures. Domestic economic growth, income, and wealth accumulation depended on such external factors as favorable demand and prices for Latin America's primary exports. While the world economy was growing, as it did from about 1880 to 1910, the Latin American economies tended to grow; but when exports lagged, or their prices declined, as happened beginning even before the onset of World War I in 1914, domestic economic growth, income, and accumulation were affected adversely. The center countries, like the United States or England, meanwhile, had economies and productive structures that were inward oriented. The dynamic industrialization and economic growth of the center countries depended upon the application of new technology to domestic production and a consequent growth in domestic consumption. This did not mean that the center economies were self-sufficient or that external factors had no impact, but it did mean that these economies exercised substantially more control over their own patterns of development than did the technologically stagnant, outward-oriented economies of Latin America and the Caribbean. These economies were affected profoundly by, but did not substantially influence, the center countries that were their major trade partners.

The Crisis of Outward-Oriented Dependence

Latin America's outward-oriented economic model provided the domestic agricultural and commercial elites in Latin America with substantial success prior to World War I. Economic growth was rapid, and in some countries like Argentina, the elite standard of living rivaled that of many Western European countries as well as the United States. However, this success was transitory, based as it was on primary product export growth, which began to reach its limits even before 1914. Engel's Law shows a statistical relationship demonstrating that the demand for primary agricultural products tends to have a low response to increases in income (technically, an income elasticity less than 1); the growth of Latin America's export demand slowed considerably, thereby causing domestic imbalances. Successive shocks, beginning with World War I, followed soon after by the Great Depression of 1929-1933 and then World War II, caused the Latin American economies to enter into a severe and prolonged economic crisis.

The international economic collapse of the Great Depression was magnified in Latin America by its excessive dependency on export and import markets. Unable to sell their exports and to earn sufficient income to purchase the former level of imports, the Latin American countries suffered from a succession of balance-of-payments crises that necessitated a rethinking and reorientation of the conventional belief in free trade and forced the adoption of a new growth strategy (see Chapter 11 for the examples of Brazil and Mexico).

For the larger countries with some existing industry, the new model was based on the expansion and promotion of a particular type of industrialization, import substitution industrialization or, more simply, ISI (Cardoso and Pérez 1979 are good on this transition). During the 1930s, the emphasis was on "easy," or horizontal, ISI—that is, the domestic production of simple manufactured consumer goods that had been formerly imported (see Chapters 8, 9, and 11). In essence, the Great Depression acted in the same way that tariff protection does by providing the shield from external competition required to initiate industrial production in diverse sectors. In Latin American, then, industrialization via import substitution was begun following the isolation from the world markets resulting from war and depression.

This structural shift toward industry had a far-reaching impact on Latin America's institutional and power structure. ISI diversified the domestic productive structure, created a trend in the direction of more inward-oriented growth, and generally strengthened the position of the incipient industrial capitalist class relative to the landed oligarchy because the agricultural sector was neglected as a result. Nevertheless, the transfer of power was not complete in any of the countries. Further, in all cases of ISI, state initiative was fundamental in setting in motion and redirecting the new process of domestic production and accumulation. The expanded participation of the Latin American states in their economies thus can be dated from the 1930s. There is little doubt that the shift toward ISI and the enlarged role of the state in the economy made the larger Latin American countries structurally less dependent on the world market than they had been prior to 1914, at least for a time. These changes in Latin America's development pattern can be summarized in Figure 1.1.

The Crisis of ISI

Easy, horizontal ISI, nevertheless, suffered from internal contradictions and limitations given Latin America's existing institutional structure. In particular, the size of the market for consumer goods produced in each country was limited by low incomes, their unequal distribution, and the neglect of agriculture (see Chapter 8). In the second stage of industrialization (by the 1960s), the larger countries—Mexico, Brazil, and Argentina—turned to vertical ISI, as they began to produce more of their own intermediate and capital goods, the imports of which had grown to some 80 percent or more of all imports under the previous horizontal ISI strategy. In fact, the growing need for intermediate and capital good imports had reinforced, rather than relieved, Latin America's dependence on export markets to earn foreign exchange. Only now, rather than luxury consumer good imports, the success of the horizontal ISI strategy required the purchase of a growing level of the imported inputs essential to the new industries. Latin America's exports, however, for the most part continued to be primary products. Vertical ISI, although more difficult because of the additional technology and capital required, could help to ease this secondary import dependence.

Vertical ISI brought with it a further problem, however—intermediate and capital goods production was characterized by the use of capital-

Figure 1.1   Stages of Latin America's Development, 1500-1945

Mineral extraction; colonial plunder; growth poles	→	Hacienda production; *criollo* control; greater trade	→	Regional fragmentation; export orientation; U.S. investment	→	Easy ISI; industrialization; inward orientation
1500-1700		1700-1810		1825-1914		1915-1945

1810-1824
Wars of Independence

intensive techniques of production that only exacerbated Latin America's growing employment problem (see Chapters 14 and 15). Further, the capital and technology required for such sophisticated production very often could be attained only through greater transnational corporate investment. Direct foreign investment (DFI—the control of productive facilities), especially from the United States, had been growing in Latin America since the 1870s (see Cardoso and Pérez:115; and Hunter and Foley 1974:215-217, for details), but it accelerated with particular rapidity in the 1960s. In 1929, the book value of U.S. DFI was $3.5 billion, rising to $4.4 billion 1950, $12.3 billion in 1970, and $38.9 billion in 1981.

DFI can provide important inputs to underdeveloped countries like those in Latin America and can be the source of more productive technology and finance capital, which can spur economic growth.[1] Foreign investment, whether portfolio or direct, provides an inflow on the capital account of the balance of payments that helps to finance expenditures for imports on the current account (a rudimentary knowledge of the balance-of-payments accounts is essential in understanding many of Latin America's problems in changing trade and investment flows and in the strategy of development). However, DFI comes with strings attached that ultimately can make any substantial dependence on external financing very costly (see Chapter 12); economic sovereignty is restricted, and profit, dividend, and interest repatriation by transnational subsidiaries to their parent companies creates a drain of income outside the country. This income repatriation, which the debt crisis of the 1980s has exacerbated, creates a growing divergence between gross domestic product (GDP) and gross national product (GNP) that is reflected in an outflow on the current account of the balance of payments as "factor service payments." Such outflows easily can swamp whatever positive inflow DFI originally generated.

Direct foreign investment by transnationals also can bring other complications in its wake. First, as Gereffi and Evans show (Chapter 11), most transnational investment in Mexico and Brazil has been manifested as takeovers of existing enterprises formerly owned by domestic capitalists. Thus, rather than contributing new capital to the development process, such transnational investment has resulted in the denationalization of the investment process; in many key sectors this process is dominated by foreign-owned companies acting as foreign capital substitutes for, rather than complements to, domestic ownership and production.

Further, transnational investment can block, rather than stimulate, linkages to firms that might supply inputs to the local transnational subsidiary. For a variety of reasons (Dietz 1985), transnationals often choose to supply their own inputs through imports from other subsidiaries within the international transnational corporate structure, thus limiting the extent of backward linkages to domestic suppliers and the stimulative impact on development of the transnational investment within the local economy. The weakness of linkages in the local economy often results in transnational subsidiaries becoming virtual enclaves, much like the mining and plantation export enclaves of the colonial era.

The Institutionalist and Structuralist Perspectives

The readings in this book have been chosen and are organized to present an interpretation of Latin America's development problems consistent with the predominant, although not unchallenged, economic theory in Latin America: structuralism. Structuralist theory is a truly indigenous creation of Latin American intellectuals that has had an impact on development thinking around the world; both dependency analysis and the equity-with-growth, basic needs strategies (discussed in Chapter 3) are related to Latin American structuralism.

Structuralist theory emerged as a reaction to the failure of orthodox neoclassical theories to offer acceptable explanations for Latin America's continuing development lag or to offer feasible suggestions for alleviating the growing income gap relative to the advanced center countries (see Chapters 6 and 7). Given the existing structural problems, such as incomplete markets, in which supply and demand do not respond in the usual fashion; unequal trade relations with the advanced center countries; the dominance of primary product exports; and wide disparities in internal income and power relations, structuralist economists argue that the orthodox recommendation to rely on market forces only can reinforce and widen Latin America's development lag. For structuralist economists, much more conscious state activism, including development planning, is required to reduce and eventually overcome the most serious barriers to the development process plaguing Latin America. These structural problems, both internal and external, are not of the "marginal" sort with which neoclassical tools are best equipped to deal, and hence structuralists have attempted to create new, innovative solutions to Latin America's existing realities. In a sense, the effort to create a new economics more appropriate to the underdeveloped Latin American periphery has a parallel in the history of economic doctrines. The macroeconomic theories developed by John Maynard Keynes in the 1930s were necessitated by the inadequacies of classical macroeconomic theory in explaining how advanced, oligopolistic capitalist structures functioned. In a like manner, structuralism can be understood as an attempt to develop theories and policies appropriate to less developed capitalist structures in the periphery dominated by the world system.

Institutionalist theory is much more a North American product. The original founders of the American Economic Association were chiefly institutionalists, although they quickly were displaced by practitioners of the new marginalist orthodoxy that began to dominate economic thinking in the last third of the nineteenth century. In an important sense, all institutionalist thinking is about development. Institutionalist economics focuses on the societal barriers that prevent socioeconomic systems from reaching their full potential, whether the problem is full employment in labor markets, the concentration of industrial production, or the problems of underdeveloped nations. For institutionalists, the framework of analysis involves an examination of the tensions between the dynamic force that promotes economic growth and development—technological progress—and the retarding, "past-binding" institutions, socioeconomic structures, and their associated behavior and thinking patterns—ceremonialism—that tend to slow technological adaptation and block economic development. Institutionalist analysis thus is fundamentally qualitative and concerned with the larger picture of the movement of irreversible economic processes. Institutionalism is essentially dynamic and interactive. Neoclassical economics, by contrast, is basically quantitative and static and is concerned not with the larger picture, but with the smaller, with infinitesimal nonsystemic changes in a timeless, reversible framework. One further way to comprehend the differences between the institutional and neoclassical economic perspectives is to note that institutionalist analysis is essentially Darwinian and evolutionary (that is, historical), while neoclassical economic analysis is Newtonian and mechanical (that is, ahistorical).

In recent years, Latin American structuralists and North American institutionalists have come together in complementary fashion to provide a more complete explanation of the development process in Third World countries. The Third World is seen not as a static system subject to universal, invariable, and repetitive rules, but as a product of an evolutionary process in which the structural characteristics of the economy and society are in constant flux and in which there is no assurance that adjustments to disequilibrium conditions will be automatic or equilibrating. Growth is undoubtedly a painful process, often lopsided and subject to obstructive bottlenecks that require collective intervention by democratic societies in order to break and surmount. Yet this view, which is more realistic than a simple trust that "things will work out," is not inherently fatalistic. It offers ground for hope that with the application of collective intelligence and cooperative effort, the growth process can be made less costly in human terms and more steadily directed toward social progress. This is the optimistic, constructive orientation of the writers represented in this book.

Notes

1. This might be a good point to note an important difference between orthodox and institutionalist thinking on the investment process. Typically, neoclassical economics posits the following sequence: saving→investment→income and economic growth→more saving, and so on. Thus saving, or the current sacrifice of con-

sumption, is required for investment to take place and economic growth to occur, which results in an even higher level of saving, more investment, more growth, and so on. The problem of the underdeveloped countries is often posed as a low level of saving, which results in low growth. To escape from this "low equilibrium growth trap," foreign saving (equals foreign investment) can be substituted. Unfortunately, fifty years after the Keynesian revolution in economics, this myth of the priority of saving persists. Keynesian analysis confirmed that the actual sequence is the following: investment→income and economic growth (which generates sufficient saving to finance the investment)→more investment→. . . . Typically, government had to oversee the macroeconomic variables in order to maintain the desired level of investment—that is, to reach the full employment level of production. When "investment" is defined to include "human capital" accumulation and technological progress, this view is perfectly consistent with the institutionalist and structuralist perspective, particularly if the emphasis is placed on the quality of human resources.

References

Cardoso, Ciro F. S., and Héctor Pérez Brignoli. 1979. *Historia económica de américa latina.* Vol. 2. Barcelona: Ed. Crítica.

Dietz, James L. 1985. "Export-Enclave Economies, International Corporations, and Development." *Journal of Economic Issues* 19 (June): 513-522.

Furtado, Celso. 1976. *Economic Development of Latin America.* 2d ed. New York: Cambridge University Press.

Hunter, James, and John Foley. 1974. *Economic Problems of Latin America.* Boston: Houghton Mifflin.

Stein, Stanley, and Barbara Stein. 1970. *The Colonial Heritage of Latin America.* New York: Oxford University Press.

World Bank. 1986. *World Development Report 1986.* New York: Oxford University Press.

part two

Economic Ideologies, Growth, and Development

James Street, in Chapter 2, provides valuable insight into the daily realities of abuse and intolerance that, until recently, characterized much of Latin America and, unfortunately, continue to be far too common. In addition to the personal suffering resulting from human rights violations, Street singles out two basic economic impacts for examination.

First, the ubiquitous intervention by governments into universities and research institutes for political reasons—basically, to protect existing power relations—has stifled academic freedom and impeded open-ended inquiry, which is the sine qua non of successful development. This in turn has seriously impeded the stimulation of an indigenous capacity for and control of technological innovation and progress, thereby forcing the Latin American countries to rely on outside sources of technology in industry and agriculture. Interference with academic freedom and disruption of ongoing research thus has "effectively depriv[ed] their nations of essential long-term sources of innovation, skills, and trained workers necessary to solve increasingly complex problems of rapidly changing societies." The resulting technological dependence has drained income from these countries to pay for imported technology and has forced Latin America to accept higher levels of direct investment from transnational corporations, which, not surprisingly, control much of the available modern technology.

Second, Street criticizes orthodox economics, particularly monetarism, for its failure to answer successfully the challenge of Latin

America's compelling development problems. Monetarist policies since the 1970s have brought recession, austerity, and more difficult living conditions for the majority of Latin Americans. Moreover, Street suggests that monetarist economic policies, which were introduced as an alternative to the structuralist and institutionalist policies advocated in this book, have been utilized deliberately by repressive governments to restore traditional patterns of unequal income distribution. There is a sad irony in this because monetarists of the Chicago School, who profess a profound belief in political and economic freedom, may be able to see their prescriptions fully implemented only under conditions of political authoritarianism and dictatorship. It is in this sense that Street refers to the "poverty of [orthodox] economic doctrine" and offers a challenge to institutionalist and structuralist economists to develop new policies that again can promote growth, development, and social justice in Latin America.

Paul Streeten's contribution (Chapter 3) provides an excellent overview of the "growth versus development" debate. Early development economists and other policymakers measured the success of a country's development efforts by noting the pace of growth in its per capita income (or gross national product, GNP). A larger income pie certainly seemed preferable to a smaller one, as there was more to be divided among society's members. However, in many underdeveloped countries, growing GNP did not result in marked improvement in living conditions for the poor. Streeten points out that this was due both to the failure of income to "trickle down" the income pyramid as it had in the more highly developed countries and to the failure of governments in underdeveloped countries to take steps to correct the income concentrating tendency of existing institutions and markets. Nor did increasing relative (and, sometimes, absolute) inequality seem to be overcome as a country's income rose (the famous Kuznets U-shaped curve of income distribution over time). On the contrary, a "certain type of economic growth" (Streeten) in the underdeveloped countries tends to concentrate income and economic power rather than disperse them as the gross national product rises.

The World Bank has estimated that at least one-quarter of the world's population lives in absolute poverty. Given the gravity of this condition, one division of the bank in the 1970s proposed a new development strategy to replace the yardstick of the traditional, and increasingly inadequate, GNP growth criterion. This became known as the "basic needs strategy." The goal of this strategy is to assure that specific goods and services, in the form of housing, food, education, and health care, are delivered to the poorest 40 percent of society. In the basic needs approach, these goods and services are not considered charitable distributions (although, of course, they do immediately improve the living conditions of the poor); instead such goods and services are viewed as investments in deprived human beings and in society in general. Healthier, better educated adults with a more complete diet tend to have fewer children and are themselves more productive contributors to society and the economy when they are at work. Further, there are linkages between the better nutrition of the poor and reduced health expenditures as well as between better education and better health care. In effect, basic needs expenditures provide the possibility for substantial gains in productivity *and* for savings in other aspects of the economy, all of which make the actual cost of the basic needs strategy less than its apparent cost. Technically, it can be argued that the basic needs strategy combines important and compelling aspects of a public good with substantial positive externalities for society. Of course, there is the strong moral component of the basic needs strategy; its goal is to create directly and immediately a more just economic and social system in which the traditionally dispossessed become important parts of, and contributors to, society.

chapter two

The Reality of Power and the Poverty of Economic Doctrine

James H. Street

When Thorstein Veblen published *The Higher Learning in America, A Memorandum on the Conduct of Universities by Businessmen* in 1918, he was 61 and had never gained full professorial rank or academic tenure in any of the universities where he taught over a period of twenty-six years.[1] Bitter experience convinced him at last that there was no secure place in the academic community for the dissident who chose to lead his own life and to conduct unorthodox analyses of prevailing doctrine and practice.

It was not that he had failed as a publishing scholar—two of his six previously published books received widespread attention at home and abroad. Rather he had published too much that was a biting indictment of his society and of those in control. Universities, as he had come to know them, were governed by boards of wealthy businessmen and subservient presidents all too willing to deny tenure to a perennial troublemaker. And rarely would other members of an academic faculty come to the defense of a colleague whose views were under attack.

We have come a long way since that day, thanks to those who later became victims of gross violations of freedom of expression and association in the eras of the Dies Committee on Un-American Activities and the personal witch-hunt conducted by Senator Joseph McCarthy, and thanks to those who had the courage to fight back. Ultimately these defenders of academic freedom became effective through the American Association of University Professors (AAUP) and its successful instrument, Committee A on Academic Freedom and Tenure, which now serves to protect (or at least assist) all who have attained tenure.

Reprinted from the *Journal of Economic Issues* 17 (June 1983) by special permission of the copyright holder, the Association for Evolutionary Economics.

Yet the threat to academic freedom persists. It operates in grossly repressive forms in many parts of the world, including several formerly open countries in which I have had the opportunity to work as a development economist. By a strange twist of the reins of control, academic freedom is also under duress in subtle and sometimes overt ways in some of the major universities of this free and enlightened country. Nowadays, it is often academics, rather than businessmen, legislatures, or military rulers, who seek to exclude the ideas of some of their university colleagues. As in Veblen's day, ideas are feared for their "corrupting" influence on the young and for the harm they may do to prevailing power structures.

Economics, as a field, is peculiarly prone to this internal suppression of ideas. Despite the widely acknowledged disorderly state of economic theory in relation to a disordered world economy, insistent efforts are made in the universities, both North and South, to define and isolate a "mainstream" and to cut off the tributaries and eddies that might replenish the flow of useful ideas. Inquiry into the nature and causes of the modern growth process becomes a search for a universal dogma. Efforts to apply universal dogma to complex, dissimilar problems convert economic policy into doctrine—doctrine whose poverty is soon revealed in practical failure. As Veblen well understood, the exercise of power is a universal reality; but even the most unrelenting and skillful use of power cannot sustain an economic orthodoxy whose poverty is demonstrated in its application.

The Reality of Power

I learned the reality of raw power during my first foreign teaching assignment, at the National University of Asunción in Paraguay in 1955. The standard textbook then in use was a compendium of neoclassical thought by Charles Gide that had last been revised in 1913![2] A class of graduating seniors in the Faculty of Economic Sciences requested that as their first visiting professor from the United States I conduct a seminar in contemporary economics, a task I was happy to undertake.

The course came to an abrupt end, however, after a class on the unfamiliar concepts of John Maynard Keynes. I learned that students who had betrayed undue curiosity about such subversive ideas had been rounded up and taken to the headquarters of the secret police, where they were savagely whipped. I was shocked when these students privately showed me, with some pride in their own fortitude, their raw and bleeding backs. My sense of shock was compounded when I realized that these members of my class had been fully aware that there were informers in every classroom, and that they had anticipated the probable consequences of their questions.

Nevertheless, in their desire to know, they had taken the risk.

Paraguay remains largely shut off from outside intellectual contact, a country the world prefers to ignore. General Alfredo Stroessner, the military dictator who was there in 1955, is still in virtual totalitarian control twenty-seven years later [and, in 1987, he continues to be in power]. The government has long invoked martial law as justification for arbitrary arrests and detention without trial. Seventeen officially sanctioned assassinations have been reported within the past two years [1980-1982].[3]

I imagine it is difficult for someone who has not worked in the Latin American region to appreciate the enormity of what has befallen the formerly free universities of the Southern Cone with the return of military rule to Argentina, Chile, and Uruguay in the 1970s. Political intervention in the public universities and scientific institutes, and even in some of the private ones, has become deeply institutionalized. Because interference is not confined to the social sciences, political control has seriously affected scientific and technological progress necessary to the development of the countries affected.

The present governments of Argentina, Chile, Paraguay, and Uruguay tend to regard their universities as centers of political agitation, rather than as establishments for the production of useful knowledge and skilled human resources. In each country, when there is political unrest teachers are subjected to tests of loyalty to the regime in power, kept in a state of economic insecurity and career uncertainty, and sometimes jailed and tortured, exiled, or killed. So ingrained are these reactions that they are sometimes practiced by civilian as well as military governments, whether of the right or the left.

One consequence has been a steady brain drain of intellectuals and technicians in a period of acute need for specialized skills and competent leadership to solve domestic problems. Colonies of expatriates in other countries await the day when they can return home, restore democratic institutions, and work to rebuild their own societies.

The pattern of institutionalized intervention is now well defined. When a Latin American university is "intervened," it typically means that the system of autonomous governance established throughout the region by the Argentine University Reform movement of 1918 is set aside, and an official *interventor* is installed as rector with the specific task of establishing firm control over faculty and students. Often a retired military officer is assigned this role, and deans of faculties and professional schools are also replaced with colonels or others considered completely loyal to the regime. Faculty and students are screened to eliminate agitators; many are barred from classes, and textbooks are examined for political content. The interventor is charged particularly with making sure that if student elections, which nearly always reflect national issues, are held, they do not embarrass the government in power.

The Case of Argentina

Modern institutionalized intervention may be traced to policies adopted by the Argentine government in the 1940s, when ideological influences from Fascist Italy and Nazi Germany were strong.[4] The government of General Pedro Ramírez in 1943 undertook a sweeping overhaul of the entire educational system, restoring religious instruction in violation of the constitution, and seeking to impose a system of national thought control.

In response, a group of 150 prominent Argentinians, including university professors, signed a manifesto objecting to the government's efforts to impose a fascist regime and calling for a restoration of effective democracy. The professors were summarily dismissed and replaced in their classes by official spokesmen.

Among those removed in 1943 was Bernardo Houssay, a distinguished member of the medical faculty of the National University of Buenos Aires and later a Nobel laureate. Because of his reputation as a scientist, he was reinstated two years later, but he remained an outspoken critic of the government and was dismissed again in 1946 by President Juan Domingo Perón. He bade farewell to his students with the much-quoted words: "And now I have delivered my last lecture; the next will be given by a colonel."[5]

From this time on, the Argentine universities have been regularly subjected to a political housecleaning with every major change of government. In his first term in office, President Perón used armed police to quell the protests of professors and students, and by May of 1946 had sent into early retirement or dismissed 70 percent of the members of university faculties. Many intellectuals were forced to leave the country. Among them was Raúl Prebisch, who later became executive secretary of the United Nations Economic Commission for Latin America and founder of the Structuralist School of economic thought. Perón's influence was felt for thirteen years, until he was driven from office in 1955, by which time the universities and scientific institutes that had given distinction to Argentina throughout the region were in shambles.

After the overthrow of Perón, a conservative reaction set in and the universities were again forcibly "purified" by the interim governments of General Eduardo Lonardi and General Pedro Eugenio Aramburu. Only after President Arturo Frondizi took office in May 1958, following a free election, was it possible to restore autonomy to the universities and rebuild academic standards. Both President Frondizi and his brother Risieri, who became rector of the University of Buenos Aires, were staunch defenders of academic freedom, and for nearly a decade Argentine higher education showed marked improvement. During this period I was privileged to work closely with the Faculty of Economic Sciences in Buenos Aires under its eminent dean, William Leslie Chapman, who directed an exchange program between the Argentine universities and my own university. For the first time in many years, young Argentine scholars were permitted to go abroad to catch up in their fields, while a pronounced shift in university enrollment took place in the direction of the basic sciences, agronomy, veterinary science, and economics as students turned to the tasks of national recovery.

In July 1966, however, a military government headed by President Juan Carlos Onganía once more took over the educational system. Four rectors of the eight national universities were obliged to resign, and hundreds of faculty members were deprived of their positions throughout the university network. About one hundred physicists, including entire research teams, migrated from Argentina during this period. Thousands of students were driven from their classrooms as politically unacceptable.

Another upheaval in a contrary ideological direction took place under President Héctor J. Cámpora in May 1973. Cámpora was a caretaker president who prepared the way for the return of Juan Domingo Perón to the presidency a few months later, and he made a determined effort to rid the universities of all possible political opposition, a policy that Perón himself continued relentlessly. In the name of popular education, entrance examinations were abolished and the doors of the universities thrown open to students without a secondary school diploma. Within a year the student enrollment in the University of Buenos Aires doubled and the national university enrollment increased from about 300,000 to 450,000 students.

Again professors of genuine professional distinction, especially those trained in foreign universities, were removed or forbidden to enter the classroom for fear of contaminating students with alien or "technocratic" ideas. In the Faculty of Economic Sciences of the University of Buenos Aires alone, fourteen tenured professors were dismissed while some three hundred new teachers were hired, few with academic credentials, to staff the crowded classrooms. An eminent economic historian, who had studied at Göttingen and the Sorbonne and who held an Oxford Ph.D., was forbidden to set foot in a classroom on pain of expulsion from the university.

During a period of a year and a half, the turbulent university was headed by five successive state-appointed rectors ranging in political identification from the extreme left to the extreme right of the Peronist spectrum. With abrupt haste, academic and scientific programs that had been painfully built up over the previous decade were reduced to chaos and graduate instruction virtually ceased to exist in the universities.

President Perón died in July 1974 and within two years another military takeover took place. General Jorge Rafael Videla, who had been active in suppressing left-wing terrorist groups, became president as leader of a military junta, and immediately undertook a major reorganization of the Argentine educational system. Ricardo Bruera was appointed Minister of Education and announced that the university authorities would no longer be permitted to decide academic policy or make faculty appointments. The national law governing the universities, which provided for a tripartite system of administration by councils of professors, students, and alumni, was rewritten to transfer control to the central government.

In August 1976, Videla and Bruera purged the University of Bahía Blanca, arresting a former rector and sixteen other professors, chiefly economists, and charging them with subversion. Minister Bruera announced at this time with evident pride that he had dismissed about 3,000 academics, administrators, and teaching assistants from Argentine universities and secondary schools since the Videla government had come to power.

In September 1976, President Videla announced that the situation in the universities had "stabilized." He promised to restore academic freedom and autonomy of governance to the universities. Yet a few weeks later, Minister Bruera issued a decree eliminating ninety-five career fields from the universities, including most of the social sciences and such newer scientific fields (in the Argentine system) as ecological studies and oceanography.

It must be noted that these political changes in the educational system were made in a general atmosphere of terrorism, kidnappings, sudden arrests, and disappearances that made life in the universities chaotic and exceedingly dangerous. University administrators and professors spent much of their time in hiding, rather than conducting classes, and students were occupied in clandestine meetings in fragmented groups. When apprehended by the police, they were frequently tortured and some were executed. It is impossible to document the number of Argentine *desaparecidos,* which certainly exceeds the 5,818 reported missing, but it is known to include sixty scientists identified by name.[6]

The Argentine junta also extended its political control to scientific institutes outside the universities. Precise numbers of persons affected cannot be verified, but a group of Mexican scientists and intellectuals protested to President Videla in 1976 that nearly one hundred research scientists supported by the Argentine National Council of Scientific and Technological Research (CONICET) had been dismissed, and that more than six hundred others had been fired from other government research institutions, including the National Research Institute for Agriculture and Cattle Breeding, the National Institute for Industrial Technology, the National Physics and Technology Institute, and the National Atomic Energy Commission. Among those dismissed were research associates of Luis A. Leloir, an Argentine Nobel laureate in chemistry. One-fourth of the members of the Argentine Physics Society lost their jobs in the purge.

The state arrested at least eight scientists employed by the National Atomic Energy Commission, and subjected some of them to torture while in prison. They included Antonio Misetich, a physicist who took his Ph.D. at the Massachusetts Institute of Technology and who had been a member of the

M.I.T. faculty. The Argentine government at first acknowledged his arrest, but later disclaimed knowledge of his whereabouts.

At the same time these dismissals took place, the regime drastically cut funds for research as a form of political punishment. A number of Argentine nuclear physicists who could obtain permission to leave found positions in Iran (before the collapse of Shah Mohammed Reza Pahlavi's government in 1979). Ironically, these departures occurred at the time when the Argentine economy was undergoing a severe energy crisis and the government was seeking to build a second nuclear power plant to augment the one just come on stream at Atucha.

In addition to physicists, the Argentine authorities singled out psychiatrists, physicians, and social workers for mass dismissal and, in some cases, for arrest and torture. After the Argentine Federation of Psychiatrists had voiced concern about the effects of detention on the mental health of some prisoners, military leaders began to associate psychiatry with subversion and suspended the organization. The regime subjected students as well as professors and practicing professionals to police harassment and unexpected arrest or abduction; under these conditions it was virtually impossible to carry on scientific research or to train graduate students in these fields.

José Westerkamp, an internationally known Argentine physicist, who was dismissed in 1980 from his teaching post in the National University of Buenos Aires, and whose son, Gustavo, has been imprisoned for seven years [since 1975] without charge, describes the university atmosphere in Argentina as follows:

> They are universities in name only. Fear is the only thing that predominates and makes the professors and teaching staff docile. The reprisals taken against certain faculties have completed their mission: to sow fear among those professors who remain, even if they can still think freely, and to strengthen the authoritarian tendencies among those professors who are authoritarian by nature.[7]

The Case of Chile

Political intervention in the universities has not been confined to Argentina. [Argentina's] case has been cited in detail because it is well documented and because Argentina nearly a century ago assumed leadership in higher education and scientific research in Latin America, a reputation now in eclipse. However, Santiago, the capital of Chile, was also long known as a cosmopolitan center of free expression. In the 1950s it attracted a number of internationally supported research institutes, and they provided a base for the structuralist movement that was ultimately to have a powerful influence on heterodox economic thought and on international economic policy.

After the election of a Marxist government headed by Salvador Allende Gossens in September 1970, the Chilean universities became intensely politicized and riots broke out between Marxist and anti-Marxist students over control of faculty appointments in the University of Chile. In 1971 President Allende ordered criminal prosecution of Edgardo Boenninger, rector of the university, who headed a group opposed to making the institution a political instrument of the government. In an election held the following year, however, anti-Marxist forces regained control of the university.

Political intervention became egregious in scope and severity in 1973, when a military group headed by General Augusto Pinochet overthrew the Allende regime. Determined to eradicate all remnants of the previous Christian Democratic as well as Marxist political movements, the Pinochet government took direct control of the entire educational system, from kindergarten to university, and revised all courses of instruction with heavy emphasis on patriotic dogma. It virtually eliminated the social sciences except for an officially approved version of economics derived from the Chicago School.

The government replaced elected rectors in all the universities with *rectores delegados* selected for their military background. Even the rector of the Catholic University, long known for its academic excellence and educational independence, was obliged to resign and was replaced by Jorge Swett, a retired admiral. A year later, in a dispute over Admiral Swett's repressive policies, Cardinal Raúl Silva Henríquez, the grand chancellor of the university, also resigned. In August 1975, the Catholic University's entire political science department was eliminated, and a number of prominent economists retired to private activity.

The national universities sustained massive dismissals of professors in the purge of 1973. Exact figures for each institution are difficult to obtain, but it is estimated that the Pinochet government expelled 18,000 people at all levels from the universities, including 30 to 35 percent of the teaching faculties.[8] The government barred thousands of students from classes, abruptly terminated their careers, and threw many into prison, where they were tortured, or simply eliminated.[9]

Even internationally supported and supposedly independent institutions in Chile were affected. The Latin American Faculty of the Social Sciences (FLACSO), organized by UNESCO as a regional center for graduate study and research and supported by the Inter-American Development Bank, suspended its academic activities in September 1973 after fourteen people connected with the school were arrested. Among them were two Bolivian students who died in the custody of the secret police. FLACSO eventually dispersed its principal teaching activities to other locations in Mexico, Ecuador, and, for a time, Argentina.

Subsequent to the educational purge, the Pinochet government in 1981 restructured the entire Chilean system of higher education under a new university law that reduced the number of national universities to four essentially professional schools, cut the higher education budget in half, and limited the enrollment in the University of Chile to one-third the number of students who attended in 1980. In February 1980 the government dismissed seventy professors in anticipation of these changes, and has since further reduced the staff.

As in Argentina, the government has done more than destroy academic freedom in Chile. Under a new constitution, it has prohibited all political activity during a continuing "state of emergency" and under an even harsher "state of perturbation" provision renewed every six months. The police routinely subject detainees to electric shock treatment; the courts may banish prisoners to internal exile in a remote part of the country, or expel them from Chile. A leading Roman Catholic educator recently commented, "The most grave thing in Chile today is that the abuse of human rights has become institutionalized."[10]

The Cases of Uruguay and Paraguay

Alone among the nations of the Southern Cone, Uruguay has a single national university in Montevideo, which was completely shut down in October 1973 while the newly installed military government waged a campaign to suppress a terrorist group known as the Tupamaro movement. Even after it had wiped out that movement, the government dismissed 80 percent of the teachers and research staff in the School of Agronomy, and discharged sixty-one people in the School of Medicine, terminated the contracts of another 183, and charged thirty-five more with criminal offenses.[11] Between 1973 and 1982, the government imprisoned eighty-six physicians, and the police severely tortured many of them in an attempt to exact the whereabouts of fugitives they may have treated.

Among the university faculty detained was Professor José Luis Massera, an internationally known mathematician and a prominent Marxist member of the Uruguayan congress. At the time of his arrest in 1975, he was brutally beaten and has since suffered repeated torture in prison. At 66 years of age, he remains in the infamous prison ironically named "La Libertad," where most political prisoners are held.

The government allowed the university to reopen, faculty by faculty, some two years after the intervention, only after a thorough revision of the curriculum. Advanced students in the School of Medicine were suddenly informed that two years of work had been cancelled and must be repeated under a new curriculum.

In Paraguay, the National University of Asunción has been under political control continuously since General Alfredo Stroessner came to power in

1954; intelligence agents keep it under close surveillance. A few years ago when the Stroessner administration decided that social research being conducted at the Colegio Cristo Rey, a branch of the Catholic University, had become too critical of social conditions in the country, it expelled the leading Jesuit professors, most of them holding doctorates from North American universities.[12]

Governments in the Southern Cone that have imposed draconian measures on their universities invariably assert that they are not really centers of learning but rather breeding grounds of subversion and terrorism that justify the most severe means of control. In their indiscriminate repressions, however, they are effectively depriving their nations of essential long-term sources of innovation, skills, and trained workers necessary to solve the increasingly complex problems of rapidly changing societies.

Attempts to organize university professors nationally or regionally to promote career security generally have been ineffective. There is no Latin American organization comparable to the American Association of University Professors, with its vigilant Committee A on Academic Freedom and Tenure. In cases of violation of academic freedom the individuals affected may have the support of their associates, but they have no contractual basis for asserting their rights, something virtually all U.S. universities have accepted contractually or voluntarily in recognition of the 1940 AAUP statement of principles on academic freedom and tenure.

The AAUP's success in achieving its goals, facilitated by its use of a nationally disseminated list of censured administrations applied against the few offending institutions, was possible only in the milieu of a liberal democratic society. Latin American academics who take strong positions on academic freedom in the Southern Cone must constantly bear in mind the reality that they face not only dismissal but possible jail terms, physical torture, and exile.

The Poverty of Economic Doctrine

Studies of the policies of the military governments of the Southern Cone have revealed that they are rendering their respective societies increasingly dependent on outside sources of the technology necessary to their continued growth.[13] In many cases the forms of technology available from abroad may not be appropriate to the peculiar requirements of domestic development.

If economic theory may serve a similar instrumental function in development, the governments of Argentina, Chile, Paraguay, and Uruguay have likewise rendered themselves unduly dependent on a single set of ideas that have not served them well. It is quite remarkable that so extensive a part of the world as the Southern Cone should have come to rely so exclusively on the economic theories of Milton Friedman and Arnold C. Harberger, as those ideas have been transmitted through their former students at the University of Chicago—and with such disastrous results.

The Chicago School's monetarist conception of the economy has, of course, been reinforced by the conventional wisdom of the experts of the International Monetary Fund (IMF), who prescribe the constraints of "conditionality" that developing countries must meet in order to obtain international financial assistance. Over the years these constraints have displayed a consistent bias toward contractionary rather than expansionary strategy, a pronounced preference for austerity over growth.

As a condition for granting stand-by credits, the IMF has usually required that borrowing governments reduce their budgetary deficits, limit the issuance of money and credit by the banking system, and remove controls on exchange rates. It has looked with favor on the elimination of tariffs and other restrictions on foreign trade and on the imposition of official ceilings on wage increases.

Groups in the borrowing country—both constitutional governments which regard them as interferences with their freedom to make fundamental political decisions, and labor groups, who believe they cause the burden of economic adjustments to fall most heavily on the working class—often deeply resent such conditions. Economists of the Structuralist School have also criticized IMF restraints on the use of money and credit as depriving domestic industry of necessary funds for growth and job creation.

As Prebisch observed long ago, there is a strong moralizing tone in the advice given by monetarists, who see in the stresses of the Latin American growth problem no more than a popular insistence on living beyond one's means. "Those," he said, "who profess [orthodox] . . . anti-inflationary policy—both those who suggest it from outside and those who live in the midst of this harsh and hazardous reality of Latin America—sometimes entertain the esoteric notion that sin can be redeemed by sacrifice."[14]

In the Southern Cone, the moral view that the economic problems of developing countries essentially are rooted in unbridled consumption by the masses goes hand-in-hand with the military juntas' strong contempt for democracy and political process as a way of solving social problems, to which they attribute the current crisis. Thus, as Adolfo Gurrieri remarks, "the justification of political authoritarianism arises from this crisis: the procurement of economic development, it is claimed, requires firm, well-ordered, and prolonged leadership, which cannot be provided by these weak and ineffective [elected] regimes, but rather by strong governments capable of overcoming the inevitable economic and political contradictions."[15]

Thus it is not surprising that military governments in the Southern Cone have been exceptionally receptive to the stabilization programs advocated by the "Chicago boys" (as they are known in Chile) and the financial experts of the IMF. These governments have indeed shown more zeal in holding down wages by state decree and by the forcible detention of labor leaders and workers engaged in outlawed work stoppages than perhaps the IMF experts would formally recommend.

However, the purely theoretical content of monetarist doctrine cannot be wholly divorced from the ruthless manner used to apply stabilization policies. Close observers have expressed the belief that only the methods of the police state have kept recent austerity measures in Argentina, Chile, and Uruguay in place.[16] Certainly no Western European or North American government would be able to utilize such measures to achieve economic stability.

Shortly before his assassination by agents of the Pinochet government in Washington, D.C. in 1976, the Chilean economist and former Foreign Minister Orlando Letelier pointed out the irony that the austerity measures imposed in the name of establishing a "free market" are most effectively applied by highly interventionist governments.[17] Members of the working class are well aware that the privileges of a free market have been denied to them when there are no free labor organizations, no free press to report their complaints, and no free political institutions through which to seek redress.

Although difficult to document with reliable wage and income data, the social effect has been evident.[18] While monetarist policies have at times been able to check tendencies toward hyperinflation in highly disorganized economies, wage increases permitted by the ministries of labor invariably have fallen substantially below the rising cost of living. The outcome has been a continuous decline in real wages and a restructuring of income distribution in favor of the propertied and business classes who have found ways to capitalize on inflation.

The failure of monetarist policies to promote growth and development among the less developed countries is now inescapable. In the great laboratory of practical affairs, monetarism has proved a catastrophe.[19]

As dismal as they are, official measures of performance in Argentina, Chile, and Uruguay are no longer considered reliable.[20] At great personal risk a group of highly competent independent economists associated with the private Corporación de Investigaciones Económicas para América Latina (CIEPLAN) in Santiago has undertaken a series of studies to provide trustworthy empirical data on the actual achievements of the much-touted stabilization programs carried out by ministries exclusively staffed with "Chicago boys" and supported by ample loans from foreign commercial banks, the United States government, and the IMF.[21]

The Pinochet government considers these factual reports, recently published in Chile, so damaging to its public image that it sought to recall and destroy the entire edition of 2,000 copies after the volume had reached the booksellers.[22]

What these studies, and evidence from other sources, reveal are similar patterns of extreme economic disorder in Argentina, Chile, and Uruguay: low rates of economic growth, high rates of inflation, large numbers of plant shutdowns, business failures, and banking collapses, and heavy destruction of domestic industries built up during previous periods of import substitution, with resultant rates of unemployment never before experienced in the region. The international aspects of these economies are also in advanced stages of deterioration: unprecedented deficits in the current account and the balance of payments are associated with disappearing monetary reserves, falling exchange rates, and staggering debt burdens requiring an increasing share of export earnings to service them, if this can be accomplished at all without extraordinary international rescue efforts.[23] Argentina is currently the economic basket case of Latin America: under monetarist policies, the economy has shown negative rates of growth in four of the last seven years.[24] The rise in the official consumer price index will exceed 200 percent in 1982, and the monetary unit has been quoted as low as 59,000 pesos to the dollar, at the official rate.

"The Invisible Hand Encased in the Iron Glove"
In a spectacular blitz of television and letterpress promotion, Milton Friedman and his wife Rose have recently drawn the attention of the world to the universally desired "freedom to choose" afforded by an unquestioning faith in the market system.[25] With a singular choice of language, Friedman, while lecturing in Chile with his colleague Arnold Harberger in March of 1975, prescribed a "shock treatment" requiring a drastic rise in unemployment among Chilean workers. He was quoted in *El Mercurio,* the leading newspaper, as saying that "the social economy of the market is the only medicine. Absolutely. There is no other. There is no other long-term solution."[26]

Harberger added, "I am in agreement with my colleague that there is no other medicine possible. I do not see any alternative other than the social economy of the market."

Advocates of unqualified neoclassical ideology in its monetarist form must surely raise and earnestly consider the question, Is it really necessary and socially defensible to use mass jailings, officially sanctioned torture, and extralegal executions to achieve the degree of economic freedom and stability now visible in the Southern Cone? René Villarreal has aptly characterized this association of means and ends as "the invisible hand encased in the iron glove."[27]

The evidence strongly indicates that the real aim of the present military governments in the Southern Cone, utilizing a rationale provided by the "Chicago boys," is to re-establish an elitist social structure with the power of command as the fundamental organizing principle, and justifying *any* degree of human repression to insure a desired class differential in the distribution of income.

We must also raise the question, Is it either necessary or desirable in the universities and research centers of the Southern Cone to suppress the flow of all economic ideas that do not conform to the Chicago School? The great tragedy implicit in the events of the 1970s in Argentina, Chile, and Uruguay is not only that the structure of democratic decision making has been effectively dismantled, but that the sources of alternative strategies of development, which can emanate only from the most intelligent minds of the universities and the other institutes of investigation, have been likewise effectively obliterated from public consideration.

The ordinary people of these countries *do* desire freedom of choice. A phrase commonly heard among those searching for an answer is, "Ni Moscú ni Chicago": Neither Moscow nor Chicago. Somewhere there must be a strategy of development that lies between broken-down Marxism and the visible failures of monetarism.

This, of course, is the challenge to North American institutionalism and Latin American structuralism, as some of us (alas too few) have tried to point out over the years. This is the urgency of formulating development strategies superior to those of conventional doctrine. Twenty years have gone by in which the goals of expansion and development should have replaced the aims of contraction and stagnation.

Coda: Academic Freedom in America

Alfred S. Eichner has described the economics profession in the United States and in the United Kingdom as a social system, whose institutional characteristics operate powerfully to promote at the highest theoretical levels an economic orthodoxy at core not grounded in scientific method.[28]

While the profession is perhaps less rigidly organized than he describes it, and many outlets exist for the dissemination of unorthodox ideas, there is a large element of truth in his observations, as there was in Veblen's observations concerning the institutional suppression of heterodoxy in his day. Evolutionary economists have seen a significant number of instances where students were discouraged from pursuing alternative lines of inquiry simply because they were not in the intellectual "mainstream" and have witnessed cases where younger faculty members failed to receive promotion and tenure for similar departures from orthodoxy.

Today's process of academic promotion, set in a highly competitive environment, places a premium on publishing early and in only the most prestigious journals (if indeed the number of outlets will permit). At the same time, the demands of mathematical rigor and acquaintance with the most advanced levels of theory limit the degree to which the graduate student and the assistant professor can ruminate about the state of the art before their convictions congeal. When personnel committees are particularly exacting in demanding an early attachment to the mainstream, they risk excluding from the profession the late bloomers and the idly curious who cannot conform to these specifications.

I think we in higher education should ask ourselves whether there is qualitatively any essential difference between excluding from the profession our own mavericks and carrying out the gross violations of academic freedom I have tried to describe in this essay, and that nearly everyone can deplore. There is nothing so painful for me to witness as my junior colleagues excluding from their midst, in the name of maintaining high standards of academic excellence and preserving the purity of the mainstream, their fellows with whom their differences are clearly ideological. The reality of power can be abused at many levels; when it is used intolerantly in even the most genteel of atmospheres, it contributes nevertheless to the impoverishment of our field.

Yet I remain an optimist. As Clarence Ayres used to say, "Even the poorly informed can describe where it hurts. And that is the beginning of wisdom."

Notes

1. *The Higher Learning in America* (New York: Viking Press, 1918) was completed shortly before Veblen left the University of Missouri to enter the field of editing and publishing. Although tendered the presidency of the American Economic Association in 1925, a distinction he refused, Veblen was disappointed in his last stint as a lecturer in the newly organized New School for Social Research and considered himself an academic failure.

2. Charles Gide, *Cours d'économie politique,* 3d ed., rev. and augm. (Paris: L. Larose et L. Tenin, 1913).

3. *Mbareté: Two Years Later, May 1980-May 1982, An Updated Report on Human Rights Abuses in Paraguay* (New York: International League for Human Rights, June 1982), 20.

4. The historical account that follows is drawn from James H. Street, "Political Intervention and Science in Latin America," *The Bulletin of the Atomic Scientists* 37 (February 1981):14-23. Documentation is provided in this article and in a rejoinder to a comment by William Glade, "On Academic Freedom in Latin America," *The Bulletin of the Atomic Scientists* 37 (August/September 1981):57-58.

5. Hubert Herring, *A History of Latin America: From the Beginnings to the Present,* 2d ed., rev. (New York: Alfred A. Knopf, 1961), 678-679.

6. Inter-American Commission on Human Rights, *Report on the Situation of Human Rights in Argentina* (Washington, D.C.: General Secretariat, Organization of American States, 1980), 136. Eric Stover and Kathie McCleskey, *Human Rights and Scientific Cooperation,* AAAS Workshop Report (Washington, D.C.: American Association for the Advancement of Science, 1981), 93-95.

7. José Westerkamp, "La situación universitaria," *El Socialista Argentino* (November 1980). Quoted in translation in Stover and McCleskey, Human Rights, 82. See also Committee on Scientific Freedom and Responsibility, *Scientists and Human Rights in Argentina Since 1976* (Washington, D.C.: American Association for the Advancement of Science, June 1981).

8. Jaime Ruíz-Tagle P., "Universidades: De las purgas a la privatización," *Mensaje* (Santiago, Chile) 29 (April 1980):92-95.

9. Bulé (pseud.), "Elements for a Critical Analysis of the Present Cultural System," in *Chile at the Turning Point: Lessons of the Socialist Years, 1970-1973,* Federico G. Gil, Ricardo Lagos, and Henry A. Landsberger, eds. (Philadelphia: Institute for the Study of Social Issues, 1979), 359-398; Richard Fagen and Patricia Weiss Fagen, "The University Situation in Chile," *LASA Newsletter* 5 (September 1974):30-37.

10. The statement is by Msgr. Juan de Castro Reyes, head of the Solidarity Vicariate of the Roman Catholic church in Santiago. Edward Schumacher, "Chile Rights Abuses Persist, Monitors in Country Report," *New York Times,* 6 December 1982, A1, 13.

11. Mario Otero, "Oppression in Uruguay," *The Bulletin of the Atomic Scientists* 37 (February 1981):29-31; Joel R. Primack, "Human Rights in the Southern Cone," *The Bulletin of the Atomic Scientists* 37 (February 1981):24-29; Richard Goldstein and Alfred Gellhorn, *Human Rights and the Medical Profession in Uruguay Since 1972* (Washington, D.C.: American Association for the Advancement of Science, August 1982).

12. James H. Street, "Social Science Research in Paraguay: Current Status and Future Opportunities," in *Responsibilities of the Foreign Scholar to the Local Scholarly Community,* Richard N. Adams, ed. (New York: Education and World Affairs and Latin American Studies Association, 1969), 95-96; "Jesuit Declares Paraguay Has Stepped Up Repression," *New York Times,* 12 April 1969, 4; Jonathan Kandell, "Paraguay's Oppressed Suffer Behind a Wall of Silence," *New York Times,* 11 June 1976, 1-3.

13. See references cited in Dilmus D. James, James H. Street, and Allen D. Jedlicka, "Issues in Indigenous Research and Development in Third World Countries," *Social Science Quarterly* 60 (March 1980):588-603.

14. Raúl Prebisch, "Economic Development or Monetary Stability: The False Dilemma," *Economic Bulletin for Latin America* 6 (March 1961):1.

15. Adolfo Gurrieri, "Technical Progress and Its Fruits: The Idea of Development in the Works of Raúl Prebisch," *Journal of Economic Issues* 17 (June 1983):389-396.

16. René Villarreal, "Monetarismo e ideología: de la 'mano invisible' a la *manu militari,*" *Comercio Exterior* (México, D.F.) 32 (October 1982):1059-1070.

17. Orlando Letelier, "The 'Chicago Boys' in Chile: Economic 'Freedom's' Awful Toll," *The Nation* 223 (28 August 1976):137-142.

18. Official indices of unemployment, price levels, and wages have become increasingly suspect as governments of the Southern Cone recognize that undoctored statistics may prove too revealing as indicators of poor economic performance. See René Cortázar, "Distribución del ingreso, empleo, y remuneraciones reales en Chile, 1970-1978," *Colección Estudios CIEPLAN* (Santiago, Chile) 3 (June 1980):5-24.

19. Rudiger Dornbusch, "Stabilization Policies in Developing Countries: What Have We Learned?" *World Development* 10, no. 9 (1982):701-708.

20. Reference to Paraguay is omitted here because its relative isolation permits both greater economic control and manipulation of published data by the government, and because the country is beginning to enjoy the economic bonanza of hydropower development on its Brazilian frontier, which has greatly alleviated the energy crisis and its effects on the balance of payments.

21. Alejandro Foxley, "Experimentos neoliberales en América Latina," *Colección Estudios CIEPLAN* 8 (July 1982):5-170. See also Foxley, "Hacia una economía de libre mercado: Chile: 1970-1978"; Ricardo Ffrench-Davis, "Liberalización de importaciones: La experiencia chilena en 1973-1979"; Pilar Vergara, "Apertura externa y desarrollo industrial en Chile: 1974-1978"; José Pablo Arellano, "Sistemas alternativos de seguridad social: Un análisis de la experiencia chilena"; and René Cortázar and Jorge Marshall, "Indice de precios al consumidor en Chile: 1970-1978," *Colección Estudios CIEPLAN* 4 (1980):5-201.

22. The suppressed work is by José Pablo Arellano and others, *Modelo económico chileno: Trayectoria de una crítica* (Santiago: Editorial Aconcagua, 1982). The Chilean Ministry of the Interior's suppression of the book is described in "Libertad de expresión: Censura al ataque," *Hoy* (Santiago, Chile) 6 (14-21 September 1982):13-14. See also Stephen Dobyns, "The Perishing of Publishing," Letter from Chile, *Washington Post Book World* 13 (2 January 1983):14-15.

23. The official data are extensively reported in recent annual reports of the Inter-American Development Bank. See, for example, *Economic and Social Progress in Latin America: 1982 Report* (Washington, D.C.: Inter-American Development Bank, 1982), *passim*.

24. The exogenous shocks of the OPEC crisis in 1973-1974 and 1979-1980 and the associated world recessions have had their impacts on Argentina, as has the ill-fated military venture against Great Britain in the South Atlantic. Nevertheless, the economic failures of recent Argentine governments are clearly identified with monetarist policies in which it was difficult to detect any long-term strategy for growth that would offset adverse outside influences.

25. Milton Friedman and Rose D. Friedman, *Free to Choose: A Personal Statement* (New York: Harcourt Brace Jovanovich, 1980). See also their earlier work: Milton Friedman (with the assistance of Rose D. Friedman), *Capitalism and Freedom* (Chicago: University of Chicago Press, 1962).

26. All Chileans were familiar with the *picana,* or electric cattle prod, used by the DINA, the national secret police, to shock prisoners. "Arnold Harberger y Milton Friedman: Economía social de mercado: Unica vía," *El Mercurio* (Santiago, Chile) 23 March 1975, 29, 35; "Formula de 'shock' económico: Friedman sugirió reducción del 20% de gastos fiscales," *El Mercurio,* 27 March 1975, 19. Later, in defense of his role in Chile, Friedman insisted that he was only offering technical advice as an economist: "Despite my sharp disagreement with the authoritarian political system in Chile, I do not regard it as evil for an economist to render technical economic advice to the Chilean government to help end the plague of inflation, any more than I would regard it as evil for a physician to give technical medical advice to the Chilean government to help end a medical plague." "Advising Chile," *Newsweek* 87 (14 June 1976):5, 8. One recalls that in Nazi Germany both physicians and economists had no qualms about serving Adolph Hitler, since in their own minds they were without doubt merely performing technical services.

27. I have tried to provide an idiomatic translation of Villarreal's cogent phrase, "de la 'mano invisible' a la *manu militari,*" "Monetarismo e ideología," 1067.

28. Alfred S. Eichner, "Why Economics Is Not Yet a Science," *Journal of Economic Issues* 17 (June 1983):507-520.

chapter three

From Growth to Basic Needs

Paul Streeten

How is it that, in spite of growing hostility and misconceptions, the concept of "basic human needs" has been so widely accepted as the principal objective of development policies? Among the advocates of a basic needs approach to development are not only bilateral and multilateral donor agencies, but also thinkers from the Third World whose views are expressed in documents such as *The Declaration of Cocoyoc* (1974), *What Now— Another Development* (1975), prepared by the Dag Hammarskjöld Foundation, *Catastrophe or New Society?* (1976), prepared by the Bariloche Foundation in Argentina, and *Reshaping the International Order* (1976).

In order to understand the wide appeal of this approach, it is helpful to reflect on how the concept has evolved and on the way in which accumulating experience has called for changes in the approaches adopted by development policymakers. Otherwise we might be tempted to say that the international development community takes up, from time to time, new fads and fashions, or that we are acting out a comedy of errors. Basic needs is not just another fad. (Nor, of course, is it the revelation of ultimate truth.) It is no more, but also no less, than a stage in the thinking and responses to the challenges presented by development over the last twenty to twenty-five years.

If, in the following pages, the deficiencies of the prebasic needs approaches are stressed and the virtues of the basic needs approach overstressed, this is done in order to bring out sharply its distinctive features. It is not intended to imply either that the previous approaches have not taught us much that is still valuable, or that the basic needs approach is not subject to many of the objections raised to earlier approaches, and some additional ones.

Reprinted with permission from *Finance and Development* 16 (September 1979).

Basic needs is concerned with removing mass deprivation. The approach can be defined briefly as one which is designed to improve, first, the income earning opportunities for the poor; second, the public services that reach the poor; third, the flow of goods and services to meet the needs of all members of the household; and fourth, participation of the poor in the ways in which their needs are met. All four pillars must be built on a sustainable basis. In addition, basic needs must be met in a shorter period and at lower levels of earned income per capita than has generally been true in the past, or than would have been achieved via the income expansion associated with growth alone.

The early discussions of development in the 1950s had the same concern with deprivation. But, strongly influenced by Sir Arthur Lewis and others, these discussions concentrated on economic growth as the most effective way of eradicating poverty. It was on the growth of incomes, especially in modern, organized, large-scale industrial activity, that the hope for improvement in basic welfare was built. At this early stage, it was quite clear (in spite of what is now often said in a caricature of past thinking) that growth was not an end in itself but merely a performance test or an indicator of development.

There were three types of justification for the emphasis on a country's economic growth as the principal performance test. One was the belief that the gains from economic growth would automatically "trickle down" to the poor and their benefits would spread through market forces, raising demand for labor, raising its productivity, and raising wages, or lowering prices. There were, of course, even in the early days, some skeptics who said that the process of growth tends to give to those who already have, not to spread its fruits widely.

Alternatively, the assumption was made that governments are democratic, or at any rate concerned with the fate of the poor, and will extend the benefits of growth by policies such as progressive taxation or social services. If, in fact, market forces did concentrate benefits, governments would correct them.

The third justification was the more hardheaded belief that in the early stages of development the fate of the poor must not be a major concern. The best way to help them, it was argued, was first to build up the capital, infrastructure, and productive capacity of an economy. For a period of time—and it can be quite a long period—the poor might even have to go through a process of belt tightening, while the benefits from development would go mainly to the rich. But if the rewards of the rich are used to provide incentives to innovate, to adapt, to save, and to invest, the accumulated wealth will eventually benefit the poor.

This view was supported by analysis based on the U-shaped so-called Kuznets curve, which has strongly influenced thinking about development.

According to this model, the early stages of growth are accompanied by growing inequality. Only at an income of about $600 per capita (in 1973 dollars) is further growth associated with reduced inequality (measured by the share of the lowest 20 percent of the population).

Dualism and Unemployment

Each of these three assumptions turned out to be wrong, or at least not to be universally confirmed, as we gathered more experience. Income did not automatically trickle down to the poor, except possibly in a few countries, with special initial conditions and policies; nor did governments (not surprisingly) always take corrective action to reduce poverty; and it certainly was not true that a period of increasing poverty or inequality was needed in order to accumulate capital and stimulate entrepreneurship. It was found that small farmers saved at least as high a proportion of their income as big landlords, and were actually more productive in terms of yield per acre, and that entrepreneurial talent was widespread and not confined to large or foreign firms.

Judging by economic growth, the development process of the last twenty-five years was a spectacular, unprecedented, and unexpected success. But judged by poverty reduction, it was much less successful. Growth was often accompanied by increasing dualism—the expansion of the modern, urban, large-scale manufacturing sector alongside slow growth or stagnation in the rest of the economy. Despite high rates of growth of industrial production and continued general economic growth, not much employment was created. Nor were the benefits spreading to the poor. In 1954, Sir Arthur Lewis had predicted that subsistence farmers and landless laborers would move from the countryside to the higher-income, urban, modern industries. This would increase inequality in the early stages of growth (as long as rural inequalities were not substantially greater than urban inequalities), but when all the rural poor were absorbed in modern industry, the golden age would be ushered in, when growth would be married to equality.

The Lewis predictions, which dominated not only academic thought but also political action in the early days of development, did not turn out to be true for three reasons. (1) The differences between rural and urban incomes were much greater than Lewis had assumed, owing partly to trade union action on wages, partly to minimum wage legislation, and partly to income differentials inherited from colonial days. (2) The rates of growth of the population and of the labor force were much larger than expected. (3) The technology transferred from the rich countries to the urban industrial sector was labor saving and did better at raising labor productivity than at creating jobs.

The reaction to the growing dualism that had resulted from modern, industrial growth was to turn to the need to create employment. Since 1969, work by the International Labor Organization's missions to seven countries has shown that "employment" and "unemployment," as these are defined in the industrial world, are not illuminating concepts for a strategy to reach the poor in the developing world. Experience in many countries showed that "unemployment" can coexist with considerable labor shortages and capital underutilization. (Gunnar Myrdal had criticized the employment approach in *Asian Drama* earlier.)

"Employment" and "unemployment" only make sense in an industrialized society where there are employment exchanges, organized and informed labor markets, and social security benefits for the unemployed who are trained workers, willing and able to work, but temporarily without a job.

There are none of these institutions in many developing countries. The root problem of poverty in the developing countries is not unemployment. It is very hard work and long hours of work at unremunerative, unproductive forms of activity. This discovery has drawn attention to the informal sector in the towns: the blacksmiths, the carpenters, the sandal makers, the builders, and the lamp makers—all those who often work extremely hard, are self-employed, or are employed by their family, and are very poor. And it has drawn attention to the women who, in some cultures, perform hard tasks and work long hours without even being counted as members of the labor force. The problem then was redefined as that of the "working poor." Not only labor but also capital are grossly underutilized in many developing countries, which suggests that causes other than surplus labor in relation to scarce capital are at work. There are three types of causes of low labor utilization in developing countries, none of which is captured by the conventional employment concept, but all of which are important if development is to mobilize fully the abundant factor—labor. These can be classified under (1) consumption and levels of living; (2) attitudes; and (3) institutions.

Nutrition, health, and education—aspects of the level of living—are important for fuller labor utilization. But they have been neglected because in rich societies they count as consumption, which (except for some forms of education) has no effect on human productivity (or possibly a negative one, like four-martini lunches). In poor countries, better nutrition, health, and education can increase production. They constitute forms of investment in human resources. (This is one thread that goes into the fabric of the basic needs approach.)

Attitudes also make a difference to what jobs people will accept. In Sri Lanka, for example, a large part of unemployment is the result of the aspirations of the educated, who, as a result of their education, are not prepared to accept manual, "dirty" jobs.

The third dimension is the absence or weakness of such institutions as labor exchanges, credit institutions, and an appropriate system of land ownership or favorable tenancy laws. As a result, labor is underutilized.

For reasons such as these, an approach to poverty which runs in terms of unemployment and underemployment, in which levels of living, attitudes, and institutions are assumed to be adapted to full labor utilization (as they are in industrial countries), or automatically adaptable (as they are in Marxist theory, though not in Marxist practice), has turned out to be largely a dead end.

Moreover, and this brings us closer to basic needs, perhaps 80 percent of the population of developing countries are members of households, so that one might, by raising the income of the head of the household, presume to benefit them. (Some qualifications are discussed below.) But there are perhaps 20 percent outside these households. These are not the unemployed but the unemployables: the old, the infirm, the crippled, and orphaned children. If we wish to meet basic needs, we ought to be concerned also with those for whom productive and remunerative work is not an option and who do not benefit from being members of a family.

Inequality

With the concern for the "working poor," the attention then switched from dualism and employment to income distribution and equality. The book published in 1974 by the World Bank and the Sussex Institute of Development Studies, entitled *Redistribution with Growth,* was concerned with redistribution. This concern arose from two sets of questions. (1) How can we make the small-scale, labor-intensive, informal sector more productive? How can we remove discrimination against this sector and improve its access to credit, information, and markets? How does redistribution affect efficiency and growth? Does helping the "working poor" mean sacrificing productivity, or is helping the small firm and the small farm an efficient way of promoting growth? (2) How does economic growth affect income distribution? In Bangladesh, India, Indonesia, Pakistan, the Sahel of Africa, and Sri Lanka growth (of a certain type) is necessary to eradicate poverty. But economic growth in some countries—for example, Brazil and Mexico—reinforced and entrenched existing inequalities in incomes, assets, and power. Therefore, not surprisingly, a certain type of growth, beginning with an unequal land and power distribution, made it more difficult either to redistribute income or to eradicate poverty.

It is an empirical question to ask how economic growth affects inequality and poverty, and how both in turn affect economic growth. The answers to these questions will vary from country to country and will depend in large measure upon the initial distribution of assets, the policies pursued by the government, available technologies, foreign trade opportunities, and the rate of population growth. It is another empirical question to ask how policies aimed at reducing inequality and meeting basic needs affect individual freedom. But we also asked ourselves the question: Which objective is more important—to reduce inequality through redistribution or to meet basic needs?

In societies in which many people's levels of living are low, the goal of meeting basic needs may have a higher priority than reducing inequality—for two main reasons. First, most people would, rightly, regard meeting basic needs as more important than equality. Equality per se is of no great concern to people, other than to utilitarian philosophers and ideologues. Second, implementing basic needs is a more operational goal than equality. Equality is a highly complex, abstract objective, open to many different interpretations, and it is, therefore, difficult to know what are the criteria for achieving it, quite apart from the difficulties of implementation. On the other hand, meeting the basic needs of deprived groups, like removing malnutrition in children, preventing disease, or educating girls, are concrete, specific achievements judged by clear criteria. If we judge policies by the evident reduction of suffering, the criterion of basic needs scores higher than that of reduced inequality.

Basic Human Needs

The current emphasis on "basic human needs" is a logical step along the path of development thinking. The evolution from a concern with growth, employment, and redistribution to basic needs shows that our concepts have become less abstract and more disaggregated, concrete, and specific.

The basic needs approach is concerned with particular goods and services directed at particular, identified human beings. Another advantage of the basic needs approach is that it is a more positive concept than the double negatives of eliminating or reducing unemployment, alleviating poverty, or reducing inequality. The basic needs approach spells out in considerable detail human needs in terms of health, food, education, water, shelter, transport, simple household goods, as well as nonmaterial needs like participation, cultural identity, and a sense of purpose in life and work, which interact with the material needs.

Moreover, basic needs have a broad appeal, politically and intellectually. Because of the political appeal, they are capable of mobilizing resources, which vaguer objectives, like raising growth rates or contributing 0.7 percent of GNP or redistributing for greater equality, lack. Intellectually, they provide a key to the solution of a number of apparently separate, but on inspection related, problems. Urbanization, the protection of the environment, equality, international and intra–Third World trade, appropriate technology, the role of the transnational enterprise, the relation between rural development and industrialization, rural-urban migration, domination, and dependence all appear in a new light and are seen to be related, once meeting the basic needs of men and women becomes the center of our concern.

Income Approach and Basic Needs

Does, then, the basic needs approach represent an improvement on the earlier approaches, which advocated raising the productivity, incomes, and purchasing power of the poor? There are several reasons for thinking that it does. An improvement in only the productivity of, say, poor farmers may not raise their earnings. It may be reflected only in lower food prices and benefit urban food consumers. But even when higher productivity is fully registered in higher earnings, the income approach has serious limitations. Personal income which is earned by an employed worker or self-employed farmer or artisan is sometimes an inefficient way of meeting basic needs and may even reduce the amount spent on necessities. The expenditure pattern of subsistence farmers who switch from growing their own food to cash crops, or are employed in dairy farming, often changes from coarser, more nutritious, to finer, less nutritious, cereals or from food to nonfood items. Nutritional and health standards fall, even though income has risen.

Similarly, when women go out to work and cease to breast-feed their children, incomes rise but health standards fall. We have to see how we can achieve appropriate medical, biological, and physiological standards of nutrition because the methods by which higher incomes are generated may interfere with the availability of nutritious food. There is also the neglected question of the intrahousehold distribution of goods and services. In our surveys we often assume that if the head of the household receives adequate income the other members of the family are also looked after. But the male head of the household often benefits at the expense of the women and children. In these cases simply increasing incomes does not help the deprived "target groups."

Another criticism of the income approach is that, while it may provide adequate personal income to buy needed goods and services in the market, some basic needs cannot be met at all or cannot be met efficiently by private purchases. Such needs as health, education, safe water, and sewerage can only, or more efficiently, be provided for through public efforts. (A minimum private income is, however, often necessary for gaining access to free goods and services: first, to cover the costs of foregone income—of children sent to school who would otherwise have worked on the farm, for example—and second, to cover out-of-pocket expenses, such as transport, clothes, or books.)

Other limitations of the income approach are that it ignores those who are incapable of earning an income—the unemployables—and that it ignores nonmaterial needs. Participation in the design and implementation of projects affecting the poor, a sense of purpose in life and work, and a sense of national and cultural identity built on indigenous values are essential.

The role of nonmaterial basic needs, both as ends in their own right and as means to meeting material needs that reduce costs and improve impact, is a crucial aspect of the basic needs approach. Nonmaterial needs interact in a complex and underexplored way with material needs, but are quite distinct in that they normally do not require the allocation of scarce resources and, therefore, cannot readily be dispensed by the state. But any proper definition of basic needs must encompass a whole range of needs that cannot be met simply by supplying goods to the needy.

The essence of the case for the basic needs approach is that it enables us to achieve a widely agreed-upon, high-priority objective in a shorter period, and with fewer resources, than if we took the roundabout route of only raising employment and incomes, and waiting for basic needs to be satisfied. This is clearly illustrated by the experience of Sri Lanka and the state of Kerala in India, where, at extremely low income levels, life expectancy, literacy, and infant mortality have reached levels comparable to those in the most advanced countries. The basic needs approach achieves this objective by economizing on the resources required and by increasing the available resources.

The required resources are reduced because the basic needs approach economizes on resources devoted to nonbasic needs. For example, it replaces expensive, urban, curative health services, by low-cost, replicative, preventive, rural health services. It also economizes by using linkages between sector programs, such as improving nutrition, and thereby reducing health expenditure, improving health (by eliminating parasitic diseases, for example) and thus reducing both health and nutritional expenditures. In Sri Lanka, for example, the right kind of education has made possible economies in the provision of safe water, because the people know when to boil unsafe water. Finally, it economizes on required resources by reducing fertility rates. When infant morality is reduced and more children survive, when women are better educated, and when the community takes care of the old and disabled, the need and the desire for large families are reduced. Resources can then be devoted to improving the quality of life of smaller families.

The available resources are increased because a sustained basic needs approach makes for a healthier, more vigorous, better skilled, better educated, better motivated labor force, both now and later when the present generation of children enters the labor force, because it mobilizes previously underutilized labor (and local materials) and because it makes use of capital-saving techniques. Costa Rica, South Korea, Singapore, Taiwan, and Yugoslavia illustrate this.

Basic needs is therefore thrice blessed. It is an end in itself, not in need of any further justification. But it is also a form of human resource mobilization, it harnesses the factor in abundant supply in the poor countries, and, by reducing population growth, it economizes in the use of resources and improves the quality of labor.

If this effective and concerted attack on hunger, malnutrition, ignorance, and ill health also mobilizes more international resources, by making meeting basic needs a first charge on our aid budgets, it would testify to the fact that we have begun to acknowledge our membership in the human family.

part three

The Institutionalist Perspective on Development

As a successor to Thorstein Veblen, Clarence Ayres is perhaps the best known and most quoted of the North American institutional economists. The Foreword to Ayres's *The Theory of Economic Progress* (Chapter 4) provides a succinct overview of the foundations of the institutionalist analysis of development. Ayres asserts that economic development is the result of the successful triumph of technology over ceremonialism. Technology (which includes not only tools but, and inseparably, the human skills to use them) is a cumulative and evolutionary process in which new technologies build upon past knowledge. Ayres argues, however, that the pace of technological progress, and hence of economic development, can be retarded by "past-binding" ceremonial behavior and by an inappropriate institutional structure. Such a structure usually includes a complex system of social stratification, beliefs, and customs that gives privileges to some classes and conditions people to resist change.

In the institutionalist perspective, the level of development of a country is intimately related to its level of technological progress, which itself is affected by the extent of retarding ceremonial behavior and institutions in the economy. One objective of the institutional development economist is to study the nature of the institutions and ceremonial obstructions in underdeveloped countries that block the creation, spread, and adaptation of new technology. In Latin America, such institutions include the extreme concentration of land ownership and income in the hands of a relative few; monopoly power lodged in transnational corporations; authoritarian power structures, such as military dictatorships; and deficiencies in the educational system. Development requires a revamping of these institutions and the behavioral patterns that accompany them, so that the technological process can move forward. As already noted in Chapter 2 by Street, control of the technological process, and not just access to foreign technology, is essential to successful development, which is a complex interaction between technological expansion and appropriate, facilitating institutions.

It bears repeating, as Ayres emphasizes, that "the most important factor in the economic life of any people is the educational level . . . of the community," for this is a thread that runs through institutionalist thinking. Adding more physical capital without the appropriate level of "human capital" may be useless or wasteful. Thus the orthodox economic prescription that underdeveloped countries simply need more capital in order to develop is deemed inadequate, and perhaps positively harmful, by institutionalists. The problem is not one of inadequate financial saving, but of an inadequate institutional structure dominated by ceremonial behavior that blocks technological advance, including the spread of human skills, thus slowing and distorting the process of economic development.

In Chapter 5, James Street shows how the Ayresian perspective can be applied fruitfully to understanding Latin America's development problems, as exemplified by the case of Argentina. Prior to World War I, Argentina's development placed it among the ten leading nations of the world in terms of GNP per person. Yet the nation's growth could not be sustained after the Great Depression because the rigidity of the institutional structure increasingly stifled the production process and blocked further technological advance. This case study provides verification of the institutionalist emphasis on technology as the motive force of development and on the importance of an appropriate institutional climate within which technical innovation can flourish. Street also introduces a potentially useful concept, technological fusion, which is a critical mass of technological development that can help to explain rapid bursts of development. Together, the Ayres and Street readings provide introductions to the theory and practical application of the institutionalist analysis to the development process.

chapter four

Economic Development:
An Institutionalist Perspective

C. E. Ayres

Human progress consists in finding out how to do things, finding out how to do more things, and finding out how to do all things better. If the question is asked whether some things are not better left unlearned, the answer is No; and the reason is, all things are related—causally related. Learning to kill people might perhaps be thought of as a lesson better left unlearned. But not only is the art of killing people exactly the same as the art of killing animals for food (an activity which goes back not only to the dawn of human culture but even to our zoological predecessors); the art of killing people is indissociable from the art of keeping people alive. Doctors know best how to kill people, unless perhaps physicists know even better.

In using such comparatives as "more" and "better" it may seem as though I am prejudging the whole matter. What do "more" and "better" mean? The answer is, the meaning of such terms is implicit in the process. In both cases it is a processual, or operational, meaning. The meaning "more" is implicit in the meaning "amount," whatever may be quantified. Any quantity implies moreness and lessness; and the same is true of "better." This is an activity word. Any and every doing implies betterness and worseness, and in every doing the significance of "better" and "worse" is implicit in what is being done.

Moreover, all these meanings are aggregative—and this is the most important point of all. They are so because that is the way the world is. Everything anyone does affects his other doings and also the doings of other people. The temptation is strong to think of certain things and acts as intrinsically good, and of others as intrinsically bad, as though each were suffused with good magic or bad magic. Indeed, the inveterate addiction of mankind

---

Reprinted with permission from C.E. Ayres, "Foreword—1962," *The Theory of Economic Progress,* 3rd ed. (Kalamazoo MI: New Issues Press, 1978).

to belief in magic is the source of our temptation. But the simple truth is that nothing exists by itself. No act is performed by itself. All are causally related, and can be known and judged only as aggregates.

Thus progress is an aggregative term. There can be small aggregates as well as large ones, of course. We can speak intelligibly of a single individual's progress in learning to swim, or of a whole community's progress in physical fitness. By the same token, we can speak of human progress in general, meaning the broadest possible aggregate of all human activities.

Technology and Ceremonialism

At this point, however, a serious difficulty arises. Are all human activities alike in the sense of being parts of the same aggregate? The answer to this question assuredly is No. All are alike in the sense of being human. But through all human activities there runs a deep cleavage—or perhaps it would be better to say a sort of polarity, since at all times we are to some degree subject to opposing influences. Two forces seem to be present in all human behavior in all ages: one progressive, dynamic, productive of cumulative change; the other counterprogressive, static, inhibitory of change.

Our common tongue contains no satisfactory terms with which to designate these forces. The terms used [here]—technology and ceremonialism— derive from Thorstein Veblen, who pioneered the study of the interaction of these forces. Each must be understood as being used in a very broad and also a very special sense. Thus "technology" must be understood to include all human activities involving the use of tools—all sorts of tools: the simplest striking stones of primeval man as well as the atom-splitting bevatrons of present-day physicists, written language, books, and the symbols mathematicians manipulate, as well as marks in the sand, notches on a stick, or the fire built around the trunk of a tree to fell it.

But tools are not technology. The two commonest mistakes people make with regard to technology are (1) thinking of it as nonhuman tools, and (2) thinking of it as human skill. Both misconceptions make it impossible to understand how technology develops. The former leads to the presumption that technology is a feature of the setting in which human beings carry on their activities, part of the physical environment of mankind; and this suggests that it is static and inert. But the other conception of technology as human skill likewise fails us, since we know that human beings are no brighter, no more apt, today than a hundred thousand years ago.

This dilemma can be resolved and the technological process can be understood only by recognizing that human skills and the tools by which and on which they are exercised are logically inseparable. Skills *always* employ tools, and tools are such *always* by virtue of being employed in acts of skill by human beings. Once the dual character of the technological process is understood, the explanation of its dynamism is obvious. Technology advances by virtue of inventions and discoveries being made—by men, of course. But all inventions and discoveries result from the combining of hitherto separate tools, instruments, materials, and the like. These are capable of combination by virtue of their physical existence. The combining is of course performed by man, and especially by bright and restless men. But no one ever made a combination without there being something to combine. Furthermore, the more there is to combine in any given situation the more likely inventions and discoveries become—unless the inveterate restlessness of human hands and brains is severely curbed.

It is what Veblen called ceremonialism that provides the curb. This type or mode of behavior manifests itself in various ways, particularly these five ways. For one thing, the social stratification which seems to occur in all societies is such a manifestation. Second, this stratification (or hierarchy, or status system) is defined and sustained by a system of conventions which delimit and prescribe the behavior that is proper to persons of every social rank. These are commonly known as mores. Third, both status and mores are further sustained by an ideology, or system of tribal beliefs, which purports to explain the magic potency which distinguishes people of higher ranks and the awful consequences which are believed to follow infractions of the mores. Fourth, the members of every community are emotionally conditioned to acceptance of the beliefs in question, observance of the mores, and respect for lines of caste and status by systems of indoctrination which begin in infancy. And fifth, all these patterns of behavior are defined, codified, and intensified in mystic rites and ceremonies. It is by virtue of sacred ceremonies that persons of various ranks have imparted to them the mysterious powers—the "ceremonial adequacy," as Veblen called it—of their particular ranks; the ceremonies define the mores; they reenact what people believe to be their tribal history; and they are above all solemn, awe-inspiring, fear-inducing, and generally emotion-conditioning.

This system of behavior is static and inhibitory of change, such as technological activities promote, for a very obvious reason. In all its manifestations the ceremonial system is past-binding. The ceremonies are reenactments of what is presumed to be tribal history—the more ancient the better; hence their emotional impact. Tribal beliefs resist change because they are presumed to have been laid down in the remote past, and the same is true of mores and status systems. Sacred commandments do not change, nor does the authority of ceremonially invested rank. The overall effect of this whole system of behavior is to keep things as they are—and, presumably, always have been.

Thus what happens to any society is determined jointly by the forward urging of its technology and the backward pressure of its ceremonial system. A well-known study of social change in a great number of primitive societies has established a positive correlation between change and movement. When peoples move around they come in contact with other peoples, and changes result from those contacts. This raises a further question. Why do peoples move around? The answer to this question would seem to be: people move when they have the technical means of doing so, if they are not prevented by recognized authority, moral law, and emotional attachments.

The question may still be asked, What motivates such movement? In all cases the answer is the same. People climb a mountain to see what is on the other side—or, in the words of a celebrated mountain climber who lost his life on Mount Everest: "Because it's there." These very words are being quoted today by astronauts. In short, the motive is implicit in the process. This is true of both processes. Ancestor worshippers do not decide to oppose change. They oppose change only because they hate it, and they hate it because they love "the old ways." Scientists do not seek knowledge because they are dissatisfied with the knowledge they already have. As has been said thousands of times by thousands of scientists, every discovery raises more questions than it answers. In short, the motive is implicit in the process. Mount Everest was eventually climbed by use of improved techniques for bottling oxygen in portable tanks. Thus it is literally true that what led to the climbing of Mount Everest was the bottling of oxygen.

Veblen did not schematize his basic principles quite as I have done. But he did show their applicability to all societies, including our own. Such is the import of one of his most celebrated dicta.

> History records more frequent and more spectacular instances of the triumph of imbecile institutions over life and culture than of peoples who have . . . saved themselves alive out of a desperately precarious institutional situation, such, for instance, as now faces the peoples of Christendom.

These words appear in *The Instinct of Workmanship,* which was published in March, 1914: six months before the assassin of Sarajevo triggered the wars of the twentieth century. But they are even more pertinent today than when they were written. Science and technology are now advancing faster than ever. We can do things now that were not even dreamed of in 1914. And our institutional situation is more desperately precarious than ever.

. . .

Basic Principles of Economic Development

The first of these [principles] is that the process of economic development is indivisible and irresistible. If we consider it country by country, or invention by invention, there have already been many industrial revolutions. But in a much more significant sense all have been incidents in a general process which began in Western Europe at the dawn of modern times (thereby marking the onset of modern times) and has been spreading throughout the world ever since.

The propelling force of this vast cultural revolution has been technological. But this does not mean that institutional circumstances have not been a causal factor of equal importance. In the centuries that followed "the fall of Rome" (that is, the separation of "All Gaul" from the Empire), Western Europe manifested a unique combination of technological continuity and institutional detachment. The former meant that the technical possibility of invention and discovery was as great here as anywhere in the world, and the latter meant that Europeans enjoyed a greater freedom to bring such possibilities to fruition than did the inhabitants of any ancient center of civilization.

The "breakthrough" occurred during the fifteenth century. What was broken through was feudalism, the manorial-agricultural economy, the medieval world view, the absolute spiritual authority of the Roman Catholic church, and European isolation. The forces which became manifest during this century had of course been operative for many centuries. A revolution in land transport had already been brought about by horse shoes and the horse collar, and the germs of powered machinery had been introduced in the form of windmills and water wheels and medieval clocks. The Arabic numerals and Chinese printing had been introduced, and gunpowder had been invented. By the end of the fifteenth century printing from movable types had been invented, and (bibliophiles calculate) twenty million books had been printed and, for the first time in human history, were spreading literacy throughout the entire community. Ships, and the arts of navigation, had been developed to carry Europeans equipped with arms vastly superior to those of any other people to the shores of all the continents. The Copernican revolution was imminent, and cracks in the monolithic structure of the church were beginning to appear. In short, Western Europe was launched upon a "takeoff" from which there was no turning back.

The second basic principle of economic development is that the technological revolution spreads in inverse proportion to institutional resistance. The irresistible dynamism of the technological revolution which became manifest in Western Europe during the fifteenth century does not mean that no resistance was offered. Ceremonial traditions always resist change. They have done so in Western Europe from medieval times onward, though with steadily diminishing force; and they do so everywhere else, with results that still remain to be determined.

Since the technological revolution made it possible, Europeans have penetrated to all parts of the world. Their motives for doing so have been extremely various and on that account alone may be safely disregarded. The determining factor in all cases has been their ability to do so. Moreover, wherever they have gone, Europeans have taken their tools and know-how with them. Where they have encountered no effective resistance from alien cultures, technological development has continued and has even spurted ahead faster than in the [European] countries, where despite all change a considerable "residue" of ancient ceremonialism still persists. That is why the United States, Canada, and Australia now stand among the most advanced industrial countries in the world today. But wherever ancient cultures prevail, and most especially among a dense population, resistance to change is correspondingly great.

Such resistance is both passive and active: passive in the sense that illiteracy is more difficult to cope with in large masses than in small ones, active in the sense that teaching people to read and write almost inevitably involves interfering with their traditional way of life and may even involve drastically modifying the language habits of a thousand years—all of which people bitterly and even violently resist. What language should the people of India be taught to read and write?

In this matter of institutional resistance the practitioners of total revolution enjoy a tremendous advantage. During the colonial period Europeans made it a matter of deliberate policy not to "interfere" with "native" cultures. They did so partly as a matter of snobbery by holding themselves aloof from the indigenous population, and partly out of respect for the human rights of the "subject" peoples as a matter of humanitarian conviction. Revolutionists scorn both these motives, and so make the extirpation of the indigenous culture their first order of business, following which the introduction of industrial technology is relatively easy. This is the secret of the astonishing rapidity with which the Soviet Union has been catching up with the West. To be sure, revolutionaries may be afflicted with traditions of their own which act as a brake on the developmental process. The compulsive collectivization of agriculture may be such an institutional liability.

Short of total revolution, what is to be the outcome of the confrontation of the irresistible force of the technological process by the seemingly immovable obstacle of a population that is vast and dense and saturated with a preindustrial culture? Can such a mass of human beings be transformed without resort to violence? We do not know. None has been yet. But we do know the principle by which alone such a transformation must be governed.

This the third principle of economic development: that of the creation of human capital. The nature of human capital and its significance for economic development have never been more clearly stated than by Thorstein Veblen in his two essays "On the Nature of Capital," first published in the *Quarterly Journal of Economics* in 1908, and reprinted in *The Place of Science in Modern Civilization and Other Essays* in 1919. His argument was of course based on his conception of technology. Granted that technology is human skills and know-how and the complement of tools and equipment in which such skills and know-how are embodied and through which they are exercised; the equipment is useless without the know-how. But given the skills and know-how, equipment can be reproduced. Hence the most important factor in the economic life of any people is the educational level, as we now call it, of the community. A technically sophisticated community can and will equip itself with the instrumentalities of an industrial economy. There is no instance of any such community having failed to do so. Conversely, an ignorant and unskilled community cannot advance except by acquiring knowledge and skills.

Obvious as these propositions are, they have been obscured by the "conventional wisdom." We have traditionally conceived capital both as industrial plant and as accumulated funds, and in both guises have supposed it to be indispensable to economic growth. Consequently both of these conceptions have seemed quite plausible when applied to the development of the less industrialized peoples.

Thus it seems to stand to reason that lack of funds is the decisive impediment to economic growth, and vast efforts have been made to supply a flow of funds to regions in which such development is being fostered. This presumption is based in part on what is quite generally taken to be the actual experience of countries such as the United States in which very considerable and very rapid growth has indeed taken place. It is commonly assumed that such development was made possible by the advancement of funds by older and wealthier countries. But in a paper entitled "The Contribution of Foreign Investments: A Case Study of United States Foreign Investment History," published in the spring, 1961 issue of *Inter-American Economic Affairs,* my colleague Professor Wendell Gordon has showed conclusively that such was not the case. Using figures most carefully compiled by the National Bureau of Economic Research he shows "that for the period 1790 to 1900 (or 1914) net earnings on foreign investments in the United States substantially exceeded net increase in United States indebtedness. And this relation prevailed generally throughout the whole 125-year period." In short, the hardy bands of men and women who first landed on these shores were quite capable of instituting a viable economy from the very start, and of paying for whatever imports they required with their own exports. This, and not a supply of funds from abroad, is the explanation of the growth of the American economy.

It is nevertheless true, as Professor Gordon himself remarks, that this demonstration "does not question the importance of capital equipment. Capital equipment, the shipment of which is financed by outright purchase in the supplying country, may make quite a contribution." The question is, To what? Students of economic development have been much troubled in recent years by a phenomenon they speak of as "economic dualism." This is the coexistence of islands of industrial enterprise in the midst of relatively primitive economies of oceanic proportions. In some cases the industrial islands have not only been financed by foreign interests but have been built and continue to be operated by the human capital of the initiating power. In other cases the industrial islands are, or have become, largely indigenous. The industrial cities of India offer the most conspicuous example of such development. They are surrounded by rural India, where a population mass of some 350 million people lives virtually untouched by the worldwide technological revolution. In short, capital equipment will work anywhere. But it will affect the lives only of those who are in direct contact with it. It does not automatically bring economic development to a whole people.

Only education can do that: hence my emphasis on the role of literacy in the "takeoff" of the Western peoples. Reading and writing (and, of course, ciphering) are basic skills. As such they are even more fundamental to the process of industrialization than basic industries. To qualify for even the most "unskilled" industrial employment one must be able to "read the directions" and to keep a simple record. The industrialization of Japan dates, as everyone knows, from the Meiji revolution. What is not so widely appreciated is that the Meiji revolution not only transformed the power structure and class system of Japanese society. It was an educational revolution which brought literacy to the Japanese people and so laid a solid foundation for the industrialization that followed. The same was true of the Russian Revolution. Bolshevik seizure of power was immediately followed by a massive educational effort: "Every one teach one." Without such an effort Soviet industrial achievements would have been impossible.

This is the culture-area in which the "big push" must be made. As development experts speak of it, the "big push" means setting an industrial complex going of such magnitude that its momentum will draw the whole community in its wake in an accelerating process of "sustained growth." But if it is not to be island growth—if the rest of the community is not to be left behind on "reservations," however populous, such as those of the American Indians—the big push must be applied to the entire community. Only education (by whatever name it is called) can do that.

Whether success is possible in any given case remains to be determined. No doubt Hindu priests and Mohammedan mullahs will resist the enlightenment of their people with all the wiles at their command, just as the Christian church resisted the translation of the Bible from Latin into the various regional dialects. According to their lights, they will be right in doing so; for—we must face it—technological revolution brings its own values to fruition, to the detriment of all local and tribal value systems.

This is the fourth, and perhaps consummatory, principle of economic development. The values which are engendered in the technological process are universal values. Science, the intellectual aspect of technology, assumes and requires a commitment to the discovery of truth, and science prescribes its own conception of truth. It is a processual, or operational, or instrumental—tool-defined—conception of truth.

This conception of truth and of human values generally is at variance with all tribal legends and all tribal authority; and since the technological revolution is itself irresistible, the arbitrary authority and irrational values of prescientific, preindustrial cultures are doomed. Three alternatives confront the partisans of tribal values and beliefs. Resistance, if sufficiently effective, though it cannot save the tribal values, can bring on total revolution. Or ineffective resistance may lead to sequestration like that of the American Indians. The only remaining alternative is that of intelligent, voluntary acceptance of the industrial way of life and all the values that go with it.

We need make no apology for recommending such a course. Industrial society is the most successful way of life mankind has ever known. Not only do our people eat better, sleep better, live in more comfortable dwellings, get around more and in far greater comfort, and—not withstanding all the manifold dangers of the industrial way of life—live longer than men have ever done before. Our people are also better informed than ever before. In addition to listening to radio and watching television, they read more books, see more pictures, and hear more music than any previous generation or any other people ever has. At the height of the technological revolution we are now living in a golden age of scientific enlightenment and artistic achievement.

For all who achieve economic development profound cultural change is inevitable. But the rewards are considerable.

chapter five ====================================

The Ayres-Kuznets Framework
and Argentine Dependency

James H. Street

The evolution of the Argentine economy during the past century represents
a curious case of a relatively primitive society that was suddenly transformed
into an advanced agricultural and commercial system and that subsequently
fell into a condition of persistent unsatisfactory growth. This condition often
has been described as "economic stagnation," and although there have been
intervals of apparent improvement, the generally sluggish trend of the economy has been evident long enough to exhibit pronounced secular characteristics.[1] More recently, writers influenced by the Dependency School and
the neo-Marxist concept of underdevelopment have tended to treat Argentina as a case of international economic dependency, stressing its critical reliance on foreign sources of investment funds, foreign exchange, and
technology.[2]

A study of the country's history since its political independence indicates that the Argentine problem best can be understood in light of a theoretical framework derived from the work of C. E. Ayres and Simon Kuznets.
Ayres, following Thorstein Veblen, clearly identified the cumulative process
of technological innovation and its impact upon social institutions as the
prime source of economic progress through the course of human development. He drew particular attention to the evaluative judgments that distinguish technological from institutional behavior.[3]

While differing with Ayres regarding the causal interplay between
technology and institutions, Kuznets, in his extensive empirical studies of
modern development, nevertheless strongly reinforces the basic concept
that a country's economic growth is "based on advancing technology and
the institutional and ideological adjustments that it demands."[4] His major

Reprinted from the *Journal of Economic Issues* 8 (December 1974) by special
permission of the copyright holder, the Association for Evolutionary Economics.

contribution has been to generalize and support empirically the structural changes that typically ensue when modern economic development begins.[5]

Viewed in the Ayres-Kuznets framework, Argentine development—notwithstanding occasional exogenous shocks—has been powerfully shaped by technological forces and institutional resistances. When Ayres speaks of "institutions" and Kuznets of "institutions and ideology," it is clear that both are concerned not solely with formal structures, such as the policymaking agencies of government, the educational system, and business firms. They also are concerned with conditioned attitudes and values that informally characterize the work ethic, inventive activity, and managerial practice, elusive as such attitudes and values may be to isolate. Institutional behavior, although altered by new experience, is unavoidably conditioned by past cultural influence.

The larger study upon which this article is based raises two questions: Why did the Argentine economy grow so rapidly during the period from 1870 to 1914? Why did it thereafter show a chronic and increasingly widespread tendency toward long-term stagnation and technological dependency? The answers to the second question are strongly conditioned by the answers to the first.

In contrast with a number of other explanations, the present study does not consider a high growth rate as a normal or inherent path from which the Argentine economy has departed; rather, such growth is an exceptional occurrence requiring specific explanation. The failure to maintain the dynamic growth process which emerged for half a century under exceptionally favorable conditions therefore is interpreted as a lapse into social attitudes and habits deeply embedded in the Argentine culture which impede the positive actions required to promote a continuous transformation into an industrial economy. These social forces are widely pervasive in Argentine society and are not confined to a particular social class. They do not reflect a general lack of intelligence, but, rather, a cultural predisposition to behave in ways not fully consistent with the functional requirements of an industrial society. Because this cultural predisposition is highly *institutionalized,* it rarely receives conscious critical examination.

Evidence of Stagnation and Dependency

Economic historians generally agree that the period of most vigorous economic growth in Argentina occurred from about 1870 to the beginning of World War I in 1914. Statistics based on contemporary data are lacking, but Carlos F. Díaz Alejandro has estimated that the real gross domestic product grew at an average annual rate of at least 5 percent during the half century preceding World War I, which he describes as "one of the highest growth rates in the world for such a prolonged period of time."[6]

Growth accelerated during the latter part of this period. The Economic Commission for Latin America has estimated that during the period 1900–1914 the Argentine gross domestic product expanded at an annual rate of 6.3 percent, while the population also was growing at a high rate of 3.5 percent. Thus there was a 2.8 percent annual increase in per capita output at the height of the dynamic period.[7]

In contrast with the commonly recognized dynamic period, subsequent history has been subject to widely differing interpretations. Alejandro Bunge, who first applied the term *stagnation* to Argentina, believed that the economy began to stagnate when railroad building came to an end in 1914.[8] Although Alvin Hansen's stagnation thesis regarding the roles of the closing land frontier, declining population growth, and the cessation of massive innovations (such as the railroads) in the United States did not emerge until the 1930s, in retrospect it seems to have some application to Argentina.[9]

Díaz Alejandro dates the beginning of stagnation to 1930, when a severe foreign exchange bottleneck occurred as a result of the world depression. From 1925 to 1965 the overall rate of growth in gross domestic product averaged 2.7 percent per year, and the per capita growth rate was only 0.8 percent.[10] The rural sector (agriculture and livestock), which had expanded at an annual rate of 3.5 percent during the first three decades of the century, grew at only slightly more than 1 percent after 1930.[11]

Rostow, on the other hand, considered that Argentina had entered the takeoff to self-sustaining industrial growth during the 1930s. His students, Guido di Tella and Manuel Zymelman, initially accepted this view, but later they concluded that the apparent acceleration of the 1940s was arrested by the domestic economic crisis of 1952, when a high rate of investment began to yield relatively low increments of output.[12] Aldo Ferrer selects 1948, during the first regime of Juan Perón, as the beginning of stagnation, associating it with a decline in per capita product and the beginning of chronic inflation.[13]

Raúl Prebisch and his ECLA team regarded the period 1954–1957, when per capita output leveled off, as the onset of stagnation, but their investigation revealed evidences of sluggish growth and specific sectorial lags that antedated the Perón period.[14] Other analysts have applied the concept of stagnation to the recent period of "stop-go cycles," treating them as a technical trap from which a succession of governments has been unable to lift Argentina to a new growth path.[15]

This review indicates that stagnation is a very imprecise term, but its persistent use suggests that the Argentine economy long has been subject to unsatisfactory performance in one aspect or another. In recent years Argentina seems to have reached a plateau of development affording a moderately high standard of living but with only sporadic improvements in the quantity and variety of goods available for consumption. The forces of applied technology have had, and continue to have, a powerful effect in preventing a general deterioration of the economy; yet the influence of prevailing social institutions is to limit the effect of these forces, prevent the formation of a fully integrated industrial economy, and create social tensions which erupt in periodic political crises. Indeed, it is doubtful, as some have believed, that Argentina as a diversified economy has ever entered a period of continuous, self-sustaining growth. While some parts of the industrial sector, in a protected environment, continue to support growth, early achievements in agriculture and in petroleum production seem to have lost their vitality, while other elements, such as the railroads, port system, and power and communications networks, have been allowed to deteriorate, thus undermining the productive substructure that had been laid down.

Conventional Explanations and Remedies

A great diversity of explanations of and suggested remedies for the Argentine stagnation problem have been advanced, but many of these involve exogenous forces largely beyond the control of domestic policy. Prebisch, for example, blamed the basic Argentine problem on foreign trade "strangulation," as Díaz Alejandro emphasized the chronic shortage of foreign exchange, but both recognized domestic failures in policy and performance.

Within Argentina, unsatisfactory growth has led to a bitter struggle to redistribute the shares of income. In this respect the Argentine problem appears to have much in common with that of other countries in Latin America, some of which are at lower stages of development.

The present study departs from much current discussion of the problems of Latin America in that the basic difficulty is seen not primarily as a function of the maldistribution of income but of an inability to produce enough goods and services to supply a burgeoning urban population and the failure of technical efficiency and managerial organization which this represents. This is a problem of production, rather than distribution. Questions concerning the distribution of the shares of output are significant, but they are secondary to the solution of the growth problem.

The tendency to define the problem of Latin American development as one requiring primarily a redistribution of income stems from three principal sources. It is, of course, associated with the widespread poverty that always has characterized the region and which was conspicuously aggravated by the growth of wealth among the elite groups who were the chief beneficiaries of early development epochs. These widening social inequities usually resulted from the intense exploitation of a single mineral or agricultural product in what proved to be short-lived booms, but in which income disparities were greatly magnified. Brazil has had at least six such booms that did not lead to ongoing growth, and the dynamic period of Argentine growth until 1930 begins to look in retrospect like such an episode. The poor and the newly emerging middle classes always have felt aggrieved in such periods, and the traditional political parties, as well as more recent labor and white-collar interests ranging the entire spectrum of political shadings, have patterned their strategies on the effort to achieve a more satisfactory share for the groups they represent.

In the modern period of import substitution strategy and the application of income and investment models stemming from the Keynesian revolution in the advanced industrial countries, the redistribution of income has taken on a new significance. At some point import substitution strategy commonly runs into a failure of domestic demand for the products of the new industrial sector, and money income redistribution seems to be an obvious way to relieve the market bottleneck. However, this diagnosis tends to neglect the inability of large segments of the population in the dualistic economies of Latin America to generate sufficient *real* income to participate effectively in the economic growth process. This is at heart a production— and a productivity—problem. While Argentina is less polarized than most Latin American countries, it is far from an integrated society. The existence of a general failure of demand in the urban sector is belied by a chronic and apparently uncontrollable inflation that has averaged more than 20 percent per year in recent times and that could well be worsened by a vigorous redistribution of income in advance of the formation of a productive base.[16]

A third intellectual influence tending to define the Latin American dilemma as an income distribution problem is derived from the neo-Marxist analysis of social exploitation and historical development. Insofar as this thesis is not simply an additional complaint against the extremes of inequality in capitalist society (as it tends to be among uneducated workers and peasants), the argument for a redistribution of income shares in favor of the working classes is that they alone produce the output which forms the basis for current consumption and they alone provide the domestic technological motor for future development. In the view of Paul A. Baran and André Gunder Frank, underdevelopment is a necessary concomitant of development in the advanced capitalist countries. Hence in Latin America the working classes are systematically deprived by their foreign and domestic exploiters not only of the Marxian surplus above subsistence that they produce, but also of the *potential* surplus that an unimpeded native growth process *would* have produced.[17] Thus a redistribution of income by social class is essential to realize the true developmental capacity of the countries subjected to underdevelopment.

This analysis rests upon two questionable premises. It implies that less developed countries normally contain inherent domestic growth impulses that would surge forward if not held in check by dominant foreign and national groups. The historical and anthropological evidence, however, suggests that most underdeveloped societies tend to remain static and traditional until disturbed by outside forces, which may be either destructive or growth fomenting.

The second premise is that the source of increased output ("surplus value") that is the distinguishing mark of modern economic growth is chiefly a forcible extraction from the routine effort ("labor power") of workers held to subsistence wages; furthermore, the introduction of new technology by employers tends to dry up the source of this surplus. On the contrary, historical evidence suggests that the source of increased output per worker with *less* effort is precisely the application of new and advanced methods of production which make possible a higher average real output per capita. How this output is shared is, of course, a function of social institutions, but how the new methods of production are generated and introduced is a function of the technological process.

Technological Fusion and Accelerated Growth

Why did the Argentine economy grow so rapidly from 1870 to 1914? The chief factor was a process of "technological fusion" represented by the introduction of a complex of technological innovations, engineering and managerial skills, and educational methods that were almost wholly novel to the prevailing Latin American culture. These changes were introduced into a geographic region that was both endowed with exceptional natural resources and singularly receptive to development by virtue of institutional and demographic circumstance.

The term *technological fusion* as used here is akin to Kuznets's concept of "epochal innovation"; it has been substituted for the earlier term *technological combination,* adopted by Ayres, which does not seem to this writer to convey the important element of a novel outcome.[18] "Technological explosion" also has been used but is less satisfactory because it suggests a destructive process, while "fusion" may be the forerunner of constructive development.

Technological fusion is defined as the coming together of a sufficient number of new technical elements to form a critical mass, with a resultant dynamic effect on economic growth and development. Prominent earlier examples have been the invention of printing in the mid-fifteenth century, the synthesis of the oceangoing sailing ship later in the same century, the Industrial Revolution of the eighteenth century, and the mechanization of agriculture in the nineteenth and twentieth centuries.[19]

In the mid-nineteenth century the technological basis of Argentine life remained quite primitive. The interior economy of the pampas depended upon the most rudimentary of technological devices—the *gaucho*'s saddlehorse, his knife, and his *boleadoras,* a rawhide hunting snare.[20] The remaining technological complement—oxcarts, sugar mills, wine presses, and handlooms—were derived mainly from [Spain] in the colonial period or, in some cases, from indigenous sources. Few productive innovations were added after the colonial period, and the rural population remained largely illiterate and custom-bound. There was little foreign trade except in mules, salted hides, and jerked beef, and Buenos Aires was a small, relatively insignificant port whose estuary oceangoing ships could enter only with difficulty. Internally the country was beset by continual warfare among rival *gaucho* chieftains (*caudillos*) and indigenous tribes.

The principal cultural and technological innovations stimulating the Argentine transformation entered the country from abroad in a succession of waves primarily affecting the agricultural, commercial, and transport sectors. English breeds of sheep imported by immigrant ranchers from the British Isles began to replace the poor native flocks and made wool the major export product in the 1870s and 1880s. This stage was followed by the upgrading of cattle, also with English breeding stock, the installation of cheap barbed wire fencing and steel windmills of British or North American design, and the introduction of clover and alfalfa, which increased the carrying capacity of the Argentine cattle ranges and permitted meat exports to take the lead.[21]

At the same time the construction of railroads, port facilities, and packing houses utilizing European engineering techniques transformed the Litoral of the Río de la Plata and the Pampa into an integrated production zone highly complementary to the British economy. Argentina acquired a railway network (the first in Latin America) larger than that of the British Isles during this period, but as Bunge complained, its effects were largely confined to the agricultural and commercial sectors. Few market towns and regional industries came into being.

The key innovations of the period—methods of processing and shipping meat long distances under refrigeration—were the results of extensive experimentation in France, England, the United States, and Australia, with many attendant failures.[22] The discovery that beef could be chilled, rather than frozen, and shipped across the tropics to arrive in England in good condition opened up a vast new Argentine market for a preferred (price and income elastic) good. This stimulated the construction of *frigoríficos* (packing houses equipped with mechanical refrigeration) and the technical perfection of efficient refrigerated steamships. By 1905 Argentina had displaced the United States as the chief exporter of fresh beef and mutton to the British market.

The cereals phase of agricultural development dominated by wheat production followed. By World War I wheat growing became increasingly mechanized with imported machinery. Grain exports were facilitated by the application of Dutch techniques of dredging and diking in developing the great grain port of Rosario and in improving the artificial port of Buenos

Aires. Urban settlement of the Litoral and the consequent stimulation of construction, urban transport (including the building of a subway system in Buenos Aires), and the use of thermal electric power fed the growth process. Little, however, was done to create an infrastructure for basic industry, except for the forward-looking program of Domingo Faustino Sarmiento, who was president of the republic from 1868 to 1874 and later national director of schools.

Sarmiento had an exceptionally keen insight into the development needs of his country. He encouraged railway construction and free immigration, but his most significant achievements were the establishment of a national system of popular education and the creation of new institutes of scientific investigation.[23] The recruitment initiated by Mary Mann, the widow of Horace Mann, of sixty-five young North American women to establish normal schools throughout the interior was to have a profound effect on Argentine literacy. Both school facilities and enrollment almost doubled during Sarmiento's term, reaching 1,645 schools and over 100,000 pupils.[24] School attendance was made compulsory through the age of fourteen; although this rule was often violated, the national illiteracy rate fell from more than two-thirds in the census of 1869 to one-third by 1914.[25] Improvements in the structure of the universities placed Argentina clearly in the lead in Latin American higher education; as a consequence, Buenos Aires became the region's cultural center in such fields as newspaper and book publishing, serious music, and stage and motion picture arts.

Institutional circumstances that facilitated the early growth process were the political unification of the country and the establishment of a national fiscal system by President Bartolomé Mitre in 1862. The customs receipts of Buenos Aires at last became the revenue of the nation, interior trade barriers were reduced, and a national monetary system and a national postal system gradually emerged. These organizational changes laid the institutional basis for an integrated national economy for the first time.

Ayres has emphasized the role of the frontier in loosening the hold of encrusted institutions and permitting cultural cross-fertilization to take place.[26] In Argentina the existence of a frontier culture had both positive and negative effects. The country escaped a neocolonial plantation economy mainly because its products, except for cane sugar and cotton in the north, neither required nor justified the use of masses of resident farm hands. Slavery, being unprofitable, disappeared and with it potential problems of racial dualism that have affected many other Latin American countries as well as the United States. However, the absence of a public domain and the uncontrolled speculative distribution of land prevented the emergence of a class of yeoman farmers, and landholdings soon became heavily concentrated. Immigrant tenant farmers were permitted to grow field crops only on short three- to five-year rental contracts and on condition that they would leave the land in improved alfalfa pastures for conversion to cattle ranges when their contracts were up.

As the export trade grew, the availability of cheap return passage in empty cattle and grain ships fostered heavy immigration. The newly arriving colonists were unable to take up desirable land except as small tenants and thus joined the migratory labor force or settled in the cities of the Litoral. Some handicraft industries were introduced by these immigrants, but most of the new arrivals did not come from the industrial zones of Western Europe. They became the packing house workers, small tradesmen, and domestic servants of a growing metropolis. While the frontier provided opportunities for individual enterprise, free trade discouraged the growth of domestic manufactures.

The integration of Argentina into the British trading community gave the country the advantages of an established commercial system, access to European financial markets, and a stable gold-based currency, but it also created a relationship of administrative dependency. A significant feature of nineteenth-century international financial institutions was that they provided, through the limited liability of the joint stock company and legal bankruptcy, for the liquidation of unsuccessful ventures. The Argentine economy began to lose the advantages of this arrangement when the government accepted the responsibility for guaranteeing essentially private investment, thus converting business failures into a funded public debt burden. However, commercial and investment credit remained functionally separated during this period, so that a temporary crisis on current account neither undermined the usefulness of long-term financing nor seriously interrupted access to the international capital market. In general, although income flowed heavily to the landed *estanciero* class, Argentine investors were willing to take few risks on new enterprises during the growth period, preferring to use their profits to acquire more land and mortgages. It was not for lack of local financial resources that industrial investments remained in foreign hands and under foreign managerial direction.

In summary, an examination of the promotive forces in Argentine growth during the dynamic phase reveals the crucial role of borrowed technology and a remarkably passive role played by *criollo* entrepreneurship throughout the period.

Institutional Rigidity and Stagnation

Why did a chronic and widespread tendency toward economic stagnation and technological dependency set in after World War I in most parts of the Argentine economy? Two related factors seem to be chiefly accountable: the inability to domesticate and propagate a technological process derived from outside sources and the resumption of cultural attitudes and habits embodied in institutions not suited to the promotion of an ongoing diversified economy.

Notwithstanding an auspicious beginning, the technological culture represented by innovations introduced from abroad remained largely alien to Argentine behavior patterns, except as the new practices could be adopted by a few native *criollo* groups and by an increasing inflow of European immigrants from areas where the culture was already familiar. Moreover, the utilization of the new practices remained to a remarkable degree imitative (as in Japan following the Meiji Restoration) and in few respects became truly innovative (as it later did in Japan). Argentine society never succeeded in wholly adapting the foreign technological process necessary to permit economic development to become an internally generated transformation, and this deficiency became acute when the country was thrown increasingly upon its own resources after the world economic crisis of 1930 and particularly when, after 1946, the government attempted wholly autarchical development. An insufficient basis had been laid for the internal generation of the ongoing functional components of growth (as was done, by contrast, in the Soviet Union, Japan, and Israel).

The economic symbiosis of Argentina and Great Britain was dealt severe shocks by World War I and the Great Depression, but only the latter was sufficiently critical to lead Argentina to revise its policy of domestic development. Di Tella and Zymelman have identified the "Great Delay" from 1914 to 1933 that prevented Argentina from beginning a process of industrialization until the conditions for successful import substitution were perhaps at their least propitious, in the depths of the Great Depression.[27] Meanwhile, the opportunity to lay an educational foundation and to develop the necessary technical leadership and skilled manpower for the transition to a new stage of development largely had been missed.

It has been argued that a dominant social class such as the Argentine landed oligarchy hardly could be expected to foresee its own demise and plan for its succession, yet the question goes beyond deliberate choice and conscious motivation. As Ayres so effectively demonstrated, it is a matter of social conditioning. H. S. Ferns, in his pathbreaking study, *Britain and Argentina in the Nineteenth Century,* remarks that the history of nineteenth-century Argentina "commences with men but it ends with processes."[28]

In a sufficiently fluid and evolving society, the emerging educational opportunities and pragmatic experiences may bring forth a process of social trial-and-error that will result in increasing technical sophistication and thus have a growth effect. In the case of Argentina this possibility was only partly realized.[29]

The *estancieros* who came to dominate Argentine society during the early part of this century were direct products of *criollo* society, which meant in most instances the rudimentary *gaucho* culture. They had little appreciation for the significance of invention, discovery, and adaptation nor for education as part of the process of industrial growth, although as they became the beneficiaries of the export bonanza they rapidly adopted the modes of conspicuous consumption inspired by contact with Victorian and Edwardian England. The wealthiest of them sent their sons—the notorious *niños bien* with their retainers and strings of polo ponies—to the Sorbonne and to Madrid rather than to foreign institutes of agronomy, veterinary science, and engineering. Their concept of education, as Osvaldo Sunkel has said, was ornamental rather than functional. (Thorstein Veblen might have said ceremonial rather than workmanlike.)

The vitality of the system of public education laid down by Sarmiento and continued by his energetic protégé and minister of education, Nicolás Avellaneda (who succeeded him as president), rested in large part on the experimental and socially relevant methods of education introduced by the sixty-five North American "daughters of Sarmiento." After Sarmiento's passing, however, the innovative stimulus seems to have declined, both as to method and content. Neither the contemporary functional education movement introduced by Enrique C. Rébsamen to the limited zone of Xalapa in Mexico nor the later educational revolution precipitated by John Dewey in the United States caught on in Argentina, with the result that rote instruction given in half-day classes became the prevailing mode of elementary education. The expenditure of funds increasingly was concentrated in Buenos Aires, and children of the lower class in the interior cities and towns rarely completed more than two years of instruction. Access to the secondary schools and universities became the privilege of the children of the landed elite and the urban middle class. Law and medicine, the routes to professional status and wealth, became the approved university fields, while agronomy, animal husbandry, and viniculture were taught only in secondary institutes.[30]

The newly founded scientific centers were poorly supported, except in such fields as natural history and medicine, and in the former area continued to carry on routine taxonomic investigations while the fruits of Darwin's discoveries (some of them made in Argentina) were inspiring novel investigations in genetics and anthropology elsewhere. The attitude of wealthy Argentines seems to have been: Why invest in scientific research, with its uncertain benefits, when the most advanced technology of the world or its products can be bought with the sterling proceeds of cattle and wheat?

Even the continuance of this source of wealth began to be affected. Many landowners moved to townhouses in Buenos Aires and left their *estancias* in charge of majordomos, to the neglect of soil conservation, local improvements, and interior communications. Only stockbreeding captured their interest and continued to advance.

Military engineering, so important in the development of North American waterways and harbors and hence in the basic transport system, was chiefly confined to naval operations. When later called upon by President Perón to provide direction for mining and manufacturing, military technicians proved severely deficient in training.

The electoral reforms which permitted the Radical party to come to power in 1916 provided an opportunity for a change of direction. However (as David Rock has shown[31]), the middle class *criollos* and working class immigrants who formed the basis of the party upheld essentially the same values as the *estanciero* oligarchy they had temporarily displaced. Hipólito Yrigoyen, their mystical leader, had essentially no program for an economic transition (much less a takeoff) and soon began to suppress the very workers who had helped to bring him to power. Until the crisis of 1930 Argentina continued the policies of the "Great Delay" and made little progress toward structural transformation.

Only the University Reform of 1918, which began in Córdoba, emerges from this period as a positive change in the direction of providing the human capital needed for development. Unprogressive professors were replaced, university government was made more representative, and access to higher education was widened. Yet the fields of pure and applied sciences, except for medicine, were neglected, and there are few indications that invention and discovery (or their later forms, research and development) were actively promoted, either in the universities, in the public institutes, or in business. As a consequence, and on the basis of available evidence, the technological innovations that Argentina has given to the world must be regarded as negligible.[32]

Exogenous Shocks and the Failure to Take Off

In an illuminating analysis of the Puerto Rican growth experience, Luz Torruellas has pointed out that dependent economies sometimes receive severe exogenous shocks, which may take a negative or a positive form.[33] The Great Depression was a negative shock of great moment to Argentina. It drastically reduced the export market, which had taken the bulk of the production of the pampa before 1929, and therewith slashed the country's normal inflow of equipment and preferred consumer goods. The Argentine government was forced to adopt a policy of import substitution at a time when the advanced countries were "exporting unemployment" as never before. Many "penetration industries" established during this period, although characteristically highly competitive and self-sustaining, required continuous protection and never became independently viable. Entrepreneurial history is deficient, yet it indicates that oligopolistic practices entered Argentina almost at the outset of the new era of industrialization.

World War II, which isolated Argentina from normal commercial contact with the advanced countries, permitted the managerial inefficiencies of the 1930s to become standard practice and provided the country with neither the incentives nor the capacity for intense technological activity that the war engendered among the principal belligerents. As the ECLA study was later to reveal, managerial inertia and plant obsolescence reduced the ordinarily dynamic character of petroleum and electrical energy production, rail and road transport, and commercial agriculture during this period, while a marked shift of the labor force toward less productive forms of employment began to occur.[34]

The end of World War II fortuitously provided Argentina with the only opportunity for a strong positive shock of this century. The rapid accumulation of exchange reserves made possible by the resumption of demand for food in Europe and the existence of large unsold stocks in Argentina could have provided the "seed corn" for extensive development. In a much discussed model, President Juan Perón and his consort, Eva, made spectacular changes in social policy, but despite their aspirations for an independently developing country that could be strongly influential throughout Latin America, they exemplified the very institutional behavior that had previously obstructed growth. Their errors of judgment with respect to development only can be suggested here. These included a systematic depletion of resources ("decapitalization") of the agricultural sector, the use of large foreign balances to purchase a railway system already installed but in disrepair, the failure to admit imports of standby equipment for essential power production, the neglect of petroleum exploration and development, the mismanagement by military administrators of industrial plants that had been declared alien property, the commitment of public funds to monumental construction projects of little productive use and the failure to extend the highway system or to provide motor transport as the railways fell into unreliable operation.

The effect of the Perón administration on labor utilization and human capital formation is particularly noteworthy. The normal flow of population from rural to urban areas was accelerated to a degree that, together with the unavailability of machinery, forced farm operators to return to less labor-intensive methods of production.

Under similar circumstances in the United States, the loss of farm workers facilitated mechanization, both in the wheat and cotton regions. By contrast, Argentine landlords returned to cattle production or allowed their land to lie idle and grow up in thistles. Much of the labor released from the land was absorbed in a pronounced overstaffing of the railroads and the administrative services. The government encouraged higher rates of consumption at the same time the productive base was being eroded, and this policy was no doubt a contributing factor to the subsequent persistent inflation.

Most of the advantages of the University Reform of 1918 were undone after 1943. Under the doctrine of *"Alpargatas sí, libros no!"* the most distinguished university professors were obliged to resign en masse (a procedure that has been repeated by subsequent governments), political indoctrination became obligatory, standards of admission were reduced, and examination procedures were corrupted.[35] Not only was the quality of a university degree significantly lowered but also the conduct of technical studies became subject to political intervention.[36] To its subsequent embarrassment, the Perón government invested heavily in an abortive project to develop the peaceful uses of atomic energy which proved to be headed by a scientific charlatan.

At the elementary and secondary levels instruction also was heavily politicized, and teachers were placed under the surveillance of their own pupils. Thus the effects of educational intervention were transmitted to a new generation.

It is difficult to magnify the structural damage to the Argentine economy that occurred during the first Perón period, although its historical roots extend farther back. An alternating succession of elected and military governments has since been unable for the most part to correct the critical sectorial lags. Some of the experience, however, has been instructive. In a sharp reversal of policy in 1959, President Arturo Frondizi allowed a group of foreign oil companies, with outside engineers and equipment, to apply their skills to the Argentine petroleum fields. The action was construed as an ideological betrayal and later reversed, yet the temporary outcome demonstrated conclusively that the problem of petroleum production was essentially technological and managerial and that Argentina had the capability for becoming self-sufficient in this resource.

The foregoing analysis, which must be pursued in far greater detail, seeks to explain the sluggishness of important sectors of the Argentine economy—and hence the phenomenon of stagnation—as a result of institutional obstacles that prevented Argentina from availing itself of a fully domesticated technological process and that produced policies inappropriate to promote the accelerated growth required for a takeoff. It is necessary, however to account for the fact that Argentina, notwithstanding all its problems, remains the country in Latin America with the highest *general* standard of living (as distinguished from the highest average per capita income, attained by Venezuela). This is not merely a heritage from the past, nor is it wholly attributable to a more equitable distribution of income.

The growth of Argentina in the last four decades has been quite lopsided. Some sectors have shown considerable dynamism, while others have lagged, and it was particularly the growth of manufacturing industry as a "leading sector" in the 1930s that led Rostow, Di Tella, and Zymelman to conclude that Argentina was approaching a takeoff.

Kuznets, in a passage that might have been written about Argentina, has explained in general terms that such a process may be misleading.

> At any given time in the history of a country's economy some dynamic "leading" sectors are the loci of dynamic growth which, through various linkages, induce growth elsewhere in the economy. But unless the relation between changes in these modern "leading" sectors and the rest of the economy is significant, stable, and general, a marked rise in these modern sectors may have little effect on the persistently stagnating remainder of the economy of some countries and thus on their overall growth.[37]

The progress in manufacturing and related productive sectors has not been sufficient to lift Argentina to an accelerated growth path except for short intervals, yet it has enabled the economy to operate at a fairly sustained and moderately high level that merits explanation. Díaz Alejandro has attempted to measure the differential contributions of major sectors to growth from the period 1927–1929 to 1963–1965 by comparing their net additions to gross domestic product. Manufacturing stands out as making the major contribution to growth during this period.[38] Other major contributors are the transport and government service sectors, while the rural, oil and mining, construction, and communications sectors lag notably. In part, the increases in transport and government services are explained by a relatively heavy flow of manpower to these sectors induced by policies of the earlier Perón regime and also by the statistical limitation that "the contribution of most services to Argentine output is measured by quantifying their *inputs* (e.g., government services essentially measure employment), without looking too closely at changes in the quality of these services. The high proportion in the increase of GDP between 1927–1929 and 1963–1965 accounted for by all services . . . plus the generalized impression that the quality of many services has deteriorated, strengthens doubts as to the extent of real growth during the last thirty-six years."[39]

Nevertheless, the growth of industry is more than a statistical illusion. It rests upon the exceptional access to the international transfer of technology that characterizes this sector. At times, as during the Frondizi administration, import restrictions are relaxed and a flood of new equipment enters the country as industrialists take advantage of an opportunity for which they have been waiting and often accumulating foreign bank balances. Even when the decision to allow capital goods imports is not wholly rational, as in permitting ten new firms at once to begin producing automobiles for a protected market estimated to have an absorptive capacity of only 200,000 vehicles a year, the machine tools, once in the country, are adaptable to other uses.

International companies also find ways to supply their subsidiaries with new techniques, new product lines, and the necessary financial support. Private domestic manufacturers, through trade fairs, product licensing, franchise agreements, and similar sources, tend to have more contact with new products and processes than do state enterprises in the transportation, petroleum, electricity, and communications fields, as well as private agricultural enterprises dependent on deficient public research agencies. Job changes by managers and engineers who move from firm to firm also have produced innumerable side effects in transferring industrial know-how throughout the private sector. The "spread effects" are probably greater than heretofore suspected.

In a recent study, Jorge M. Katz found that while the gross domestic product of Argentina rose at an annual cumulative rate of 3.3 percent between 1960 and 1968, cumulative growth in the manufacturing sector reached 4.4 percent. Within this sector the 200 largest manufacturing plants in nine branches of industry had an annual growth rate for the same period of 9 percent, or double the annual growth rate of the industrial sector as a whole.[40] The plants with the highest rates of growth in output were those with the highest rates of growth in capital stock per worker and those with the highest rates of technical progress, as measured by the rate of growth of overall factor productivity. The most dynamic firms in this regard were concentrated in the metallurgical, electrical, and chemical industries—those with strong links to foreign sources of technology.

Much of the recent discussion of the role of the multinational corporation in dominating and controlling the spread of advanced technology deplores the resulting "dependence" of the less developed countries that must receive their innovations and improved techniques in this way, often at costs that seem unconscionably high. This complaint overlooks the fact that in the short run such countries really have no alternative if they wish to gain access to the rapidly changing international stock of useful knowledge. Having developed no internal sources of technology, these countries must perforce depend on outside sources.

Moreover, contrary to Katz's conclusion, the evidence of increased productivity suggests that however expensive the acquired techniques may seem, they pay off. Argentine users of borrowed technology may consider that they are in a poor bargaining position, but the results more than warrant the costs when there are no domestic alternatives.

The Prospects for Technological Independence

While it is not yet possible to give a secure empirical foundation to the conclusions advanced in this article, if it is indeed true that the basic causes of the extended Argentine stagnation problem are deeply cultural and involve failure to internalize the technological modes of behavior common to the advanced countries, serious policy implications are raised. The inference may be drawn that it will require a profound cultural reorientation to restore the earlier growth conditions, and a new strategy of development would have to seek out systematically the deficiencies in present practices and the means of repairing them. This cannot be accomplished overnight, but the reversal of policy must be made if Argentina is to have any hope of overcoming technological dependency.

The failure of Argentina to maintain the growth path it embarked upon a century ago is the more disquieting, especially to Argentines, as they witness developments now taking place in the industrial zones of Brazil and Mexico, their principal rivals in leadership for the longer range integration of the entire Latin American region that is under way. Neither Mexico nor Brazil has been so well endowed as Argentina with fertile, well-watered agricultural lands, a temperate climate, an integrative network of railways and other interior communications, a high standard of literacy, and early access to international capital markets. How is it possible, Argentines ask, for such countries to forge ahead? The answer in simplest terms is that they are learning to draw on the world storehouse of useful knowledge in ways appropriate to their own aims. The cases of Mexico and Brazil also merit investigation within the Ayres-Kuznets framework!

Moreover, with the passage of time, productive processes and market relationships become more complicated and sophisticated, and the race to catch up in technique becomes more difficult. Individual invention no longer suffices, and collectively organized research and development become essential. Meanwhile, old habit patterns become ingrained and political frustrations mount.

Given the widespread Argentine desire for economic independence, any government that comes to power must take responsibility for redirecting development policy. Recent indications have not been very promising.

Before his death, President Perón reaffirmed his earlier objective of "recovering economic independence by demolishing foreign financial, technological and commercial control" over Argentina's economy.[41] His "Plan for National Reconstruction and Liberation 1974–1977" calls for almost doubling the overall rate of economic growth within the extremely short period of three years.[42] In light of past performance, this goal can be accomplished only by statistical manipulation or by borrowing from the future at the cost of another severe "stop-go" cycle. The plan emphasizes heavy domestic savings and investment, increased productivity, and a strong expansion in exports without indicating how these are to be achieved or sustained in real terms. In addition there will be extensive redistribution of income and the promotion of social welfare, although the resources of the post–World War II period are no longer there.

Legislation already has been put into effect placing restrictions on new foreign capital investments (excepting technology, transport, and insurance operations) and invoking exchange controls as a means of concealing the increasing costs of imported components of production.[43] These are essentially defensive measures, and in common with recent thinking of the Dependency School such policies seem to define Argentina's basic problem as one of exploitation imposed by outside forces.

Whatever merit there may be in this view, it overlooks the very serious deficiencies in the preparation of Argentines to control and advance their own destiny. Once more the Argentine universities have been subjected to a political overhaul, and leading scholars have been obliged to join the brain drain that perennially bleeds the country. The domestication of the technological process begins with the formation and retention of human capital, and as the developed countries have long since discovered, freedom to think, to explore, and to experiment is essential to that activity.[44] Moreover, the creation of institutions that foster free inquiry and its applied fruits, from the nursery school to the advanced scientific institutes, from the experiment stations to the extension service, from the vocational school to on-the-job training, is vital to nurture the growth process. No one understood this better than Sarmiento, and Argentines might take a leaf from their own history.

Notes

1. The principal analyses of the Argentine stagnation problem have been made by Raúl Prebisch and a team of the United Nations Economic Commission for Latin America (ECLA), *El desarrollo económico de la argentina* (Santiago, Chile: ECLA, 1957–1958, mimeo) and *Análisis y proyecciones del desarrollo económico. V. El desarrollo económico de la argentina* (México, D.F.: U.N. Department of Economic and Social Affairs, 1959); Aldo Ferrer, *The Argentine Economy* (Berkeley: University of California Press, 1967); Guido Di Tella and Manuel Zymelman, *Las etapas del desarrollo económico argentino* (Buenos Aires: Editorial Universitaria de Buenos Aires, 1967); and Carlos F. Díaz Alejandro, *Essays on the Economic History of the Argentine Republic* (New Haven: Yale University Press, 1970). The profession is enormously indebted to Professor Díaz Alejandro for assembling and refining the basic data for the Argentine economy to 1965.

2. Francisco C. Secovich, "Dependencia tecnológica en la industria argentina," *Desarrollo Económico* (Buenos Aires) 14 (April-June 1974):33-67; and Jorge M. Katz, "Industrial Growth, Royalty Payments and Local Expenditures on Research and Development," in *Latin America in the International Economy*, Victor L. Urquidi and Rosemary Thorp, eds. (London: Macmillan, 1973), 197-224.

3. C. E. Ayres, *The Theory of Economic Progress*, 2d ed. (New York: Schocken Books, 1962). See especially Chaps. 5-11. See Chapter 4, this volume.

4. Simon Kuznets, "Modern Economic Growth: Findings and Reflections," *American Economic Review* 63 (June 1973):247.

5. See especially Simon Kuznets, *Modern Economic Growth: Rate, Structure, and Spread* (New Haven: Yale University Press, 1966).

6. Díaz Alejandro, *Essays*, 2-3.

7. ECLA, *Análisis y proyecciones*, 4, 400. Cited by Díaz Alejandro, *Essays*, 6, 8.

8. Alejandro E. Bunge, *Las industrias del norte* (Buenos Aires: 1922), vol. 1, 159. Compare Díaz Alejandro, *Essays*, 53n.

9. Alvin Hansen, *Full Recovery or Stagnation?* (New York: W. W. Norton, 1938), 279-280, 288-289.

10. Díaz Alejandro, *Essays*, 67-69.

11. Ibid., 71.

12. Di Tella and Zymelman, *Las etapas*, 22-32, 142.

13. Ferrer, *Argentine Economy*, 174-175, 185.

14. ECLA, *Análisis y proyecciones*, 3 and *passim*.

15. Oscar Braun and Leonard Joy, "A Model of Economic Stagnation—A Case Study of the Argentine Economy," *Economic Journal* 78 (December 1968):868-887; and Reinaldo F. Bajraj, "Some Notes on the Argentinian Economy" (unpublished paper presented at the University of Cambridge, England, 14 December 1972).

16. The average annual rise in the cost of living in Buenos Aires reached 39 percent during the period 1955-1959 and 23 percent in 1960-1964. Díaz Alejandro, *Essays*, 365. For the year 1972 the cost of living rose 54 percent. *Bolsa Review* 7 (November 1973):578.

17. André Gunder Frank, *Capitalism and Underdevelopment in Latin America: Historical Studies of Chile and Brazil* (New York: Modern Reader Paperbacks, 1969), 108.

18. Ayres, *Economic Progress*, 112-124. "An epochal innovation may be described as a major addition to the stock of human knowledge which provides a potential for sustained economic growth—an addition so major that its exploitation and utilization absorb the energies of human societies and dominate their growth for a period long enough to constitute an epoch in economic history." Kuznets, *Modern Economic Growth*, 2.

19. Ayres, *Economic Progress*, 127-152; Kuznets, *Economic Growth*, 1-16. See also James H. Street, *The New Revolution in the Cotton Economy: Mechanization and Its Consequences* (Chapel Hill: University of North Carolina Press, 1957), 91-156.

20. James R. Scobie, *Argentina, A City and a Nation* (New York: Oxford University Press, 1964), 67-68.

21. Simon G. Hanson, *Argentine Meat and the British Market* (Stanford: Stanford University Press, 1938), 11-16, 100-101, 117-118. The British breeds of sheep and cattle must be regarded as "technological" innovations as they represented the products of generations of controlled breeding, a process completely unknown to the *gaucho*.

22. Ibid., 18-47.

23. Hubert Herring, *A History of Latin America from the Beginnings to the Present*, 2d rev. ed. (New York: Alfred A. Knopf, 1961), 650-655. See also Alice Houston Luiggi, *65 Valiants* (Gainesville: University of Florida Press, 1965).

24. Herring, *History*, 654.

25. Arthur P. Whitaker, *Argentina* (Englewood Cliffs: Prentice Hall, 1964), 41.

26. Ayres, *Economic Progress*, 133-154.

27. Di Tella and Zymelman, *Las etapas,* 71-101.

28. Henry S. Ferns, *Britain and Argentina in the Nineteenth Century* (Oxford: Oxford University Press, 1960), x.

29. The indispensable nature of scientific and technical education in advancing economic development is emphasized by both Ayres in *The Theory of Economic Progress,* xxi and *passim,* and Kuznets in *Modern Economic Growth,* 289-293.

30. Alejandro E. Bunge described the aristocratic elitism and lack of attention to technical studies that came to dominate Argentine education by 1916. "Argentine instruction, through the ends that it sought, the mere diploma, presumed a country already formed. Yet far short of that, barren and poor, the country became populated by lawyers." *Las industrias del norte,* 173 (my translation).

31. David Rock, "The Rise of the Argentine Radical Party (the Union Cívica Radical), 1891 - 1916," Unpublished Working Papers 7 (Centre of Latin American Studies, University of Cambridge, n.d.).

32. It is not, of course, necessary for an advancing industrial country to generate all of its own technology, as O. J. Firestone has shown for the case of Canada, where only about 5 percent of the patents currently in use are of domestic origin. See his *Economic Implications of Patents* (Ottawa: University of Ottawa Press, 1971), especially chapter 7. However, in the long run a considerable price is paid by countries that do not enter the stream of world innovative practice as active participants.

33. Luz M. Torruellas, "Some Theoretical Insights into Puerto Rico's Recent Economic Growth" (Unpublished paper presented at Rutgers University on 30 November 1962).

34. ECLA, *Análisis y proyecciones,* 19-39.

35. The slogan translates loosely as "Up with the workers, down with the intellectuals!"

36. The disdain for and frequent expulsion of skilled technical workers extended beyond the universities to other centers of investigation. The Pergamino agricultural research station, one of the few in Argentina, had 14 professionals in 1949 but lost half of them shortly afterward. Antonio Mauro, an Argentine plant breeder, had developed two promising hybrid varieties of corn, but his efforts were ignored because of his political views. Díaz Alejandro, *Essays,* 190.

37. Kuznets, *Modern Economic Growth,* 25.

38. Díaz Alejandro, *Essays,* 73.

39. Ibid., 73-74 (his italics).

40. Katz, "Industrial Growth," 203-204.

41. The statement by President Perón is quoted in the *New York Times,* 22 December 1973, 2.

42. República Argentina, Poder Ejecutivo Nacional, *Plan trienal para la reconstrucción y la liberación nacional 1974 - 1977* (Buenos Aires: December 1973).

43. Ibid., 20-23.

44. The question whether economic development can be achieved under totalitarian institutions requires separate treatment and hinges critically on how *development* is defined.

part four

Latin American Structuralism

The United Nations Economic Commission for Latin American (ECLA, now ECLAC for "and the Caribbean") has been the intellectual center for the development of structuralist economic thinking in Latin America, and Raúl Prebisch, the first head of ECLA, who died on April 29, 1986, was indisputably the "father" of structuralism. In Chapter 6, Joseph Love traces the origins of Prebisch's seminal contribution to understanding the nature and persistence of Latin American's underdevelopment, which in turn laid the basis for the structuralist school of thought.

Prebisch analyzed the relations between nations at unequal levels of development, using the spatial imagery of center and periphery. In this perspective, the more advanced center countries normally reap the bulk of the gains from international trade and investment at the expense of the weaker, underdeveloped periphery. Indeed, trade relations between the center and periphery tend to reinforce development in the center while intensifying underdevelopment and poverty in the periphery. This, of course, is the opposite of the orthodox economic argument that the pursuit of comparative advantage in international trade will benefit all participating nations and that, in time, income levels between different regions should tend toward equality.

Prebisch's conclusion that the relations between the center and the periphery are antagonistic and detrimental has three bases. First, Prebisch argued that the application of technology to traded goods—predominately manufactured goods in the center and primary products in the periphery—has quite different impacts in each case. The advanced center countries are dominated by oligopolistic industries with a substantial degree of control over the prices of their products, and unions and social convention dictate that rising worker productivity be rewarded with higher incomes. In the periphery, on the other hand, primary products—agricultural goods and minerals—face substantial domestic and international competition so that the supply price is difficult to control. Labor is generally in surplus in the periphery, thus putting downward pressure on wages, and unions and social convention, particularly in the primary sector, are not strong.

Prebisch argued (as did Hans Singer, another development economist, at about the same time) that the application of new, cost saving technology in the center would continue to result in greater worker productivity and higher wages, but without any tendency for price decreases to reflect falling unit costs, due to oligopolistic pricing as corporations increased their profit share. In the periphery, however, where something closer to the competitive "ideal" is common in many primary product industries, the introduction of new technology results in falling output prices and stagnant, and perhaps declining, wages. Thus, according to the Prebisch-Singer hypothesis, the center gains doubly from new technology and trade with the periphery, while the periphery becomes worse off as the terms of trade (an index that measures the prices of imports relative to the prices of exports) worsen. In effect, the center is able to buy the periphery's cheaper imported primary products with its own higher-profit manufacturing exports, while the periphery finds that new technology only forces the prices of its exports down on the world market, thus requiring more of them to buy the relatively more expensive manufactured imports from the center. This view of the differential impact of technology led Prebisch and the structuralists to push for an expansion of Latin America's manufacturing sector to counteract this effect, which results from the existing pattern of trade and thus reflects the international division of labor.

Second, Prebisch argued that the differences in the income elasticities of manufactured versus primary commodities, especially agricultural goods, worked over time to the detriment of the periphery. In essence, as world income grows, the demand for manufactured goods rises faster than the demand for agricultural products (an expression of Engels Law), thus resulting in a secular (that is, long-term) deterioration of the terms of trade for the periphery. This reinforces the need for peripheral industrialization (as suggested by the Prebisch-Singer hypothesis), a policy proposal that was a theme of structuralist writings throughout the 1950s and 1960s, along with the need for international commodity agreements and regional integration.

The third basis of Prebisch's center-periphery critique touched upon the lower level of the import coefficient in the United States than in Great Britain. As the United States replaced Great Britain as Latin America's most important trading partner, this suggested the difficulty of continuing to expand exports to purchase manufactured imports, again supporting the argument for expanded industrialization in the region.

James Street (Chapter 7) compares aspects of structuralist and institutionalist views on Latin America, pointing out that the "inertia of institutions" that is integral to institutionalist thinking also finds its way into structuralist thinking. From Street's description, it is clear that it is possible to speak in the singular of an institutionalist and structuralist perspective on development.

Besides providing a positive introduction to the structuralist analysis of Latin America's development problems, both chapters suggest a very different way of comprehending economic processes. The center and periphery have conflicting interests under the current institutional arrangements. Conflict and unequally wielded economic power are fundamental to the institutionalist and structuralist analysis of Latin America. Orthodox economics, on the other hand, begins with the premise that relations among individuals and nations are voluntary, harmonious, and mutually beneficial. The concepts of center and periphery have no functional place in neoclassical economics, but are key to the structuralist and institutionalist analysis.

chapter six

Raúl Prebisch and the Origins of the Doctrine of Unequal Exchange

Joseph L. Love

The perception of the international economic system as one of industrial center and agrarian periphery, in which the former dominates the latter, has had a tremendous influence in the analysis of underdevelopment; the significance of the idea is impossible to gauge because its acceptance is still expanding. Raúl Prebisch's analytical terms, and the concomitant theory of trade relations, now known as unequal exchange, have been adopted not only by the followers of a dependency theory tradition in Latin America, stemming directly from Prebisch, but also by non-Latin American writers (assuredly, with extensive modifications) such as Arghiri Emmanuel, André Gunder Frank, Immanuel Wallerstein, Johan Galtung, and Samir Amin.[1]

In the realm of economic planning, Prebisch's influence has likewise been enormous, not only in the U.N. Economic Commission for Latin America (ECLA, or in Spanish, CEPAL) and the U.N. Conference on Trade and Development—agencies which he headed—but also in the Latin American Free Trade Association, the Central American Common Market, the Alliance for Progress, and in the development programs of several Latin American governments, such as the Kubitschek administration in Brazil (1956-61).[2]

In the underdeveloped world, center-periphery terminology has been widely accepted—often by governments which welcome the entry of foreign capital, as well as those which do not. At the Conference on International Economic Cooperation (the "North-South dialogue") in Paris in June 1977, the Brazilian foreign minister, representing a regime known for its economic neo-orthodoxy and its divergence from ECLA precepts, nonetheless called for a "substantial transfer of resources from the center to the periphery" of the world economic system.[3]

Abridged and reprinted with permission from Joseph L. Love, "Raúl Prebisch and the Origins of Unequal Exchange," *Latin American Research Review* 15, no. 3 (1980):45-72.

Prebisch's center-periphery thesis, first formulated in the 1940s, sug-gested a point of view that most economists in the United States and Western Europe still find difficult to accept. It implied a hegemonic relationship be-tween two discrete elements in a single economic system, even if "primary" and "secondary" centers changed relative positions. Not only that; the elabo-ration of the idea of unequal exchange between the two elements led to the conclusion that the center derived part of its wealth from the periphery (but not all, in Prebisch's version, because of the technological progress gener-ated by the center). Furthermore, implicit in the original scheme was the idea that the relationship was an enduring one. The formation of new cen-ters by peripheral areas was possible only by breaking away from the old center. Many of Prebisch's critics on the left differed with him more on the paths toward that break than on the nature of the international system.

The problem examined in this essay is how and why Prebisch formu-lated his initial thesis, which became that of ECLA; this is part of a larger prob-lem of how and why the Third World came into existence after 1945. Like all theories, this one has some forerunners—most of which were not geneti-cally related—but the Prebisch thesis in any event is probably the most in-fluential idea about economy and society ever to come out of Latin America.

Although this paper belongs to this history of economic doctrines, and in a broader sense to the history of ideologies, I will argue that much of Pre-bisch's reasoning was based on empirical observation and experimentation. Therefore, we must begin with Prebisch's biography and the economic his-tory of Argentina in the second quarter of the twentieth century.

Born in the city of Tucumán in 1901, Raúl Prebisch studied at the Univer-sity of Buenos Aires, whose Department (Facultad) of Economics at the time was probably the best school for economic theory in Latin America.[4] Pre-bisch gave clear promise of a distinguished career within Argentina's eco-nomic establishment, as an insider's insider. In 1923, upon completing a master's degree in economics, he was asked to join the staff at the university.[5] In 1922, i.e., before Prebisch's graduation, Enrique Uriburu, on behalf of the elite Sociedad Rural, the powerful stockbreeders' association, appointed the young man director of the Rural's statistical office. Two years later the Sociedad Rural sent Prebisch to Australia, where he studied statistical methods related to stockraising, and presumably, he also obtained a broader perspective on Argentina's position in the international economy.[6] By 1925 he was both a teacher at the university and an official in the Argentine gov-ernment's Department of Statistics. In 1928 he was again working part-time for the Sociedad Rural, compiling a statistical yearbook for the organization. Its president, Luis Duhau, noted in his preface to the compendium that "the marked interdependence of our ranching and agricultural activities and the world market explains . . . the broad coverage the *Anual* gives to interna-tional data."[7] Thus, from his earliest professional activities, Prebisch gained an appreciation of the international economic system.

Furthermore, Prebisch was intensely interested in policy issues from the outset of his career.[8] In 1928 he assumed the editorship of the *Revista Económica,* a journal published by the government-directed Banco de la Nación Argentina; it was concerned not only with pressing monetary matters, but also with problems of stockraising, agriculture, and international trade—not with theoretical issues in economics. In the early 1930s Prebisch was an economic advisor to the Argentine government's Ministries of Finance and Agriculture, and proposed the creation of a central bank (with powers to control the interest rate and money supply) to the government of General José Uriburu, who had seized power in 1930. Finance Minister Alberto Hueyo contracted Sir Otto Niemeyer, the British financial expert, to revise the project Prebisch and others had drawn up in 1931. The final version of the law was, however, again modified extensively by Prebisch and other Argentine economists and statesmen. The Banco Central was in fact the nation's first true central bank, and from its inception in 1935 until 1943, Prebisch served as its director-general.[9]

In many respects, Prebisch and his colleagues in the 1930s were treading in doctrinal terra incognita. Before the Depression it was believed that Argentina had prospered according to the theory of comparative advantage in international trade. This doctrine, originated by David Ricardo (1819), and elaborated by John Stuart Mill (1848), Alfred Marshall (1879), Eli Hecksher (1919) and Bertil Ohlin (1933), can be summarized as follows:

1. Given an absence of commerce between two countries, if the relative prices of two commodities differ between them, both can profit by trading such commodities at an intermediate price ratio. That is, both can gain even if one country produces both traded goods more efficiently than the other.
2. Countries export commodities whose production requires relatively intensive use of factors found in relative abundance within their boundaries.
3. Commodity trade reduces (if it does not eliminate) international differences in wages, rents, and other returns to factors of production.
4. Among other things, the theory assumes the absence of monopoly power and the spread of the benefits of technological progress across the whole trading system.[10]

In Argentina, the benefits of export-led growth, based on an international division of labor, made the theory of comparative advantage a near-sacrosanct doctrine (at least down to the Great Depression). In the words of Carlos Díaz Alejandro, "From 1860 to 1930 Argentina grew at a rate that has few parallels in economic history, perhaps comparable only to the performance during the same period of other countries of recent settlement."[11]

Not only did powerful export groups espouse comparative advantage, but the Argentine Socialist party—viewing itself as the defender of worker and consumer interests—vigorously opposed industrial protectionism in the 1920s.[12]

That decade, however, was a period of disequilibrium as well as expansion in world trade, and though Argentina prospered, the country experienced the same problems as a number of other primary-producing nations in the final years before the October 1929 crash—namely, falling prices, rising stocks, and debt payment difficulties. Argentina was in fact the first nation in the world to abandon the gold standard in the Great Depression, in December 1929. In October 1931 its authorities introduced exchange controls to try to stem the outflow of capital and facilitate the repayment of loans negotiated in hard currencies. Prebisch later wrote that "exchange control was not the result of a theory but was imposed by circumstances."[13] The Depression thus brought about the abandonment of many hallowed economic doctrines and practices.

In the crisis, Great Britain exploited [its] monopsonist position against [its] many suppliers. In general [Great Britain] attempted to purchase less abroad, and thereby got [its] imports cheaper, despite Britain's own devaluation in 1931.[14] In the case of Argentina, Britain's trading power was magnified by the South American nation's loss of dollar investments. The United States had become a major supplier to Argentina in the mid-1920s, but the latter country, of course, had chronic difficulties in paying directly for U.S. imports with [its] own noncomplementary exports. Therefore Argentina had depended on U.S. capital exports, but during the Depression, North American lenders disinvested in Argentina.[15] Excluded from the U.S. market by high tariffs and other regulations, and cut off from continental markets as well in the early thirties, Argentine statesmen feared above all the loss of the British market—already partly closed by the Ottawa Conference agreement (1932) among Great Britain and its dominions, several of which were Argentina's export competitors.[16] Britain's trading power was further enhanced by the fact that in these years [it] bought much more from Argentina than [it] sold to [Argentina]: in the four years 1930–1933, Britain took over 40 percent of Argentina's exports, but supplied only about 20 percent of Argentina's imports.[17]

Consequently Argentine statesmen and government economists—among them Raúl Prebisch—were willing to enter into the Roca-Runciman Pact of 1933, an arrangement more to Britain's advantage than Argentina's, whereby the U.K. agreed to keep up a certain level of meat purchases in exchange for regular debt service payments and tariff reductions for British manufacturers. Thus beef exports, the traditional preserve of the Argentine oligarchy, were favored over wheat.[18] An agreement in 1936, according to the Argentine economic historians Fodor and O'Connell, was even more favorable to British interests. After war broke out in 1939, the British government played its monopsonistic position to yet greater advantage, in negotiations between the Bank of England and Argentina's Central Bank, led by Raúl Prebisch.[19] One can easily surmise that Argentina's protracted and notorious dependency on [its] major trading partner left a lasting impression on Prebisch.

It is also worth recalling that the Argentine government made great sacrifices to retain its credit rating by paying its debts; perhaps Argentine statesmen were overly influenced by the smashing success, before the Depression, of export-driven growth. In any case debt payment policies put the country in an unlikely camp. Argentina was one of only three countries in Latin America not to default on international debts during the Depression, and the other two, Haiti and the Dominican Republic, were under direct U.S. fiscal supervision.[20] (In later years, Prebisch, who bore partial responsibility in this matter, defended Argentina's debt payment record, indicating that debt repayment affected the availability of credit in the future—or so it seemed in the 1930s.)[21]

The Depression not only brought about bilateral negotiations, but a series of international economic meetings as well. In 1933 Prebisch, as an invitee of the Council of the League of Nations, attended a gathering of the Preparatory Committee of the Second International Monetary Conference in Geneva. From Switzerland Prebisch reported to the *Revista Económica* that the assembled monetary experts believed that one basic blockage in the international economic system derived from the facts that the United States had replaced Great Britain as the world's chief creditor country, and that high American tariff schedules (especially Smoot-Hawley, 1930) did not permit other countries to repay U.S. loans with exports. Consequently the rest of the world tended to send gold to the United States, and the bullion was not recirculated in the international monetary system.[22]

Prebisch then went to London to help negotiate the Roca-Runciman Pact as a technical advisor; later that year, he attended the World Monetary Conference in the same city. By his own account, Prebisch was influenced by John Maynard Keynes's proposals for that meeting. Keynes, in a set of articles for the London *Times,* recommended his "pump-priming" remedies of deficit spending to increase national income, and thereby to increase employment. Keynes also proposed the creation of an international monetary authority to resuscitate credit for world trade, and it is noteworthy that he made Argentina one of seven countries that would have qualified for the maximum loan of 450 million dollars. (In the next few years Prebisch would become an enthusiastic Keynesian, an influence from which he later sought to free himself.)[23] But the World Monetary Conference broke up in failure, and the tendency toward bilateralism in world trade continued.

Back in Argentina, Prebisch sought to understand another vexing problem wrought by the Depression—declining terms of trade. In 1934 he published an article pointing out that "agricultural prices have fallen more profoundly than those of manufactured goods," and that in 1933 Argentina had to sell 73 percent more than before the Depression to obtain the same quantity of (manufactured) imports. Prebisch furthermore pointed out that in the previous year the nation had to pay double the amount in terms of gold on its fixed foreign debt obligations as it did in 1928, an additional and considerable disadvantage to adverse changes in the country's terms of trade. (In the same article Prebisch attacked as "scholastic" the orthodox equilibrium theories of his senior colleague at the University of Buenos Aires, Professor Luis Gondra, because such doctrines ignored the stubborn fact of sustained depression.)[24]

Prebisch was a member of an economic "team" groping with the crisis, and recent economic historiography has emphasized that the policies of Federico Pinedo (finance minister, 1933-1935 and 1940-1941) and his collaborators, including Prebisch, involved extensive governmental intervention in the economy; such innovation occurred despite the oligarchic political cast of the regime from 1930 to 1943 (the "infamous decade" of political history). Not only did the state reform the monetary and banking system through the creation of a central bank and the introduction of exchange controls, but it also intervened in the processing and marketing of Argentine exports, i.e., beef and grain.[25] This novel and vigorous activity by the state may have had corporatist as well as neoliberal sources of inspiration, but in this endeavor Argentina was clearly in step with [its] neoprotectionist trading partner, Great Britain.

At the international level, the state also chose an interventionist course, and in 1933 Prebisch, at Geneva and London, played a leading role in convincing policy makers of the other three major wheat-exporting countries—the United States, Canada, and Australia—to agree to a plan to cut back production, on terms especially advantageous to Argentina, since it had to make no reduction in acreage sown. But the brief history of the arrangement showed the fragility of such efforts: Argentina, Canada, and the United States all broke the terms of the plan before the end of 1933.[26]

The return of severe depression in 1937-1938, a problem originating in the United States, had its major spread effects in the less-developed agricultural- and mineral-export areas of the world, because Europe and Japan were "pump-priming" through their armaments programs. Wheat was one of the commodities for which prices fell sharply in 1937.[27] As other countries introduced new trade controls, so did Argentina, in 1938, in the form of quantitative restrictions on imports. In the next two years, Argentina's banking officials, among whom was Raúl Prebisch, were trying to keep international credits and debits in balance "in the strictest short-run sense." Thus trade policy was not yet consciously used to foster industrialization.[28]

Nevertheless, with sharply restricted export earnings throughout the Depression—the dollar value of Argentine exports in 1933 was one-third the 1929 figure—self-sufficiency in industry was a policy of necessity. Manufacturing in Argentina grew impressively in the 1930s and early 1940s, a fact that was recognized by contemporaries at home and abroad. In particular, the Central Bank's *Revista Económica* noted an increase in output of 85 percent (by value) between the industrial census of 1913 and that of 1934-1935.[29] Argentina was experiencing a phrase of industrial development common to southern South America, where Chile and Brazil also found themselves in similar situations with the collapse of their export sales. By 1935, a North American economist thought that "there is probably no major section of the world in which there is greater industrial activity relative to pre-depression years than in temperate South America" (i.e., Argentina, southern Brazil, and Chile).[30] Industrialization in the face of the Great Depression was a response of agricultural-exporting nations elsewhere too, notably in Eastern Europe. In any case, Argentina's Central Bank made a sharp break with the past in 1942 by championing industrialization. The bank's annual report for that year, reflecting Prebisch's views, argued that exports and industrial development were by no means incompatible; rather, the issue was to change the composition of imports from consumer to capital goods.[31]

Prebisch the policymaker interests us less than Prebisch the emerging economic theorist, though the two are hard to separate. In the latter capacity he was beginning to formulate his theory of unequal exchange by 1937. In that year the *Revista Económica* noted:

> Manufacturing industries, and therefore industrial nations, can efficaciously control production, thereby maintaining the value of their products at desired levels. This is not the case with agricultural and livestock countries for, as is well known, their production is inelastic on account of the nature [of production] as well as the lack of organization amongst agricultural producers.
>
> In the last depression these differences manifested themselves in a sharp fall in agricultural prices and in a much smaller decline in the prices of manufactured articles. The agrarian countries lost part of their purchasing power, with the resultant effect on the balance of payments and on the volume of their imports.[32]

The emphasis was thus on the elasticity of supply of industrial production, and implicitly on monopoly, and not on wage contracts in the industrial countries, which was later to be a focal point of Prebisch's analysis.

In the same comment the *Revista* noted that Argentina's industrial complex made its greatest gains in two periods, World War I, and during "the worldwide recrudescence of the policy of economic self-sufficiency during the years 1929–1936."[33] Thus Prebisch seemed to be nearing the view that export-led growth was no longer a viable path to economic development.

Prebisch was also intensively interested in the trade cycle in Argentina. The Central Bank began its effort to conduct countercyclical monetary policy in 1937, by decreasing the public's purchasing power through the sale of bonds in that boom year; in the following period of contraction, it would attempt to expand purchasing power by lowering the rediscount rate.[34] In 1939, in its annual report for the previous year, the Central Bank—representing Prebisch's thinking on the matter—argued that the nation's trade cycles were primarily a reflection of those of its principal (industrialized) trading partners. It also held that Argentina's heavy import requirements, combined with internal credit expansion which was triggered by an initial export surplus and which resulted in additional demand for imports, produced a balance-of-payments crisis that occurred repeatedly in the history of the Argentine business cycle.[35]

After his dismissal from the Central Bank in 1943, Prebisch began to read widely in the recent economic literature.[36] Returning for the moment to teaching, he prepared a series of lectures in 1944 in which he referred, for the first time, to "center" and "periphery." He developed a historical argument, with Britain as the nineteenth century center of the trading and monetary system based on the gold standard. (Clearly, this was a better model for the first half of the century than the second half, but Britain as center for the whole period fit Argentina's situation well enough.) Under Britain's leadership as the cycle-generating center, Prebisch argued, the world economic system had equilibrated gold flows and the balance of payments over the course of the cycle for both center and periphery. "Gold tended to leave Great Britain, the center of the system, and to enter countries of the periphery in the upswing of the cycle." Then it returned in the downswing. A problem for peripheral countries was that when gold departed in the downswing, "there was no way to diminish the gold flow except by contracting credit. . . . No one could conceive of . . . the possibility of raising the rediscount rate in competition with the monetary center in London." Thus overall monetary stability was only maintained at the cost of economic contraction in the periphery. "The gold standard was therefore an automatic system for the countries of the periphery, but not for the center," where the rediscount rate could be adjusted for domestic needs.

Passing on to the post–World War I years, Prebisch concluded that New York bankers in the 1920s and 1930s did not have the knowledge or experience of the "British financial oligarchy," though of course the world situation was dramatically different after the war. By 1930 the United States had sucked up the world's gold. Consequently, "the rest of the world, including our country, [is] forced to seek a means of inward-directed development (*crecer hacia adentro*)"[37]—a phrase that ECLA would later make famous.

The Argentine business cycle had depended on exogenous factors operating through the balance of payments. In the upswing exports and foreign investment produced an influx of gold and exchange credits, creating new money and therefore imports. Such changes also expanded credit to the agricultural and pastoral industries; but because of inelastic supply, during the downswing, credit was immobilized in the rural sector. Additional imports were paid for with reserves, producing a monetary crisis.[38]

In seeking a solution to Argentina's problems, Prebisch began to think in more general terms about Latin America and its relations with the United States; his first concern in that area had involved a plan in 1940 (probably drafted by Prebisch, but presented to congress by Finance Minister Pinedo) "to link the Argentine economy to the surging power of the United States and to growing Latin American markets," in part by exporting manufactures.[39]

After his dismissal from the Central Bank, Prebisch was twice in Mexico during the mid-forties at the invitation of Mexico's central bank (Banco de México), which he helped organize. On both occasions he participated in international meetings: once in 1944 at a gathering of intellectuals from Latin America at the Colegio de México on problems the region would face in the postwar era,[40] and again in Mexico City at an inter-American meeting of central bankers in 1946.

Prebisch's interest in industrialization as a solution to Latin America's economic problems originally arose from a desire, shared by many other Argentine contemporaries, to make Argentina less economically "vulnerable," a vulnerability painfully evident for the whole period 1930–1945. As noted above, the Argentine Central Bank, under Prebisch's leadership, had begun to advocate industrialization in its 1942 report. By implication Prebisch was recommending the same policy for other Latin American countries in his Colegio de México lecture in 1944.[41] In his "Conversations" at the Banco de México in the same year, Prebisch again noted that the period of greatest industrial development in Argentina had been the Great Depression and times of world war, periods in which the nation had to produce for itself what it could not import.[42] Later, ECLA theorists would elaborate extensively on this proposition, as they developed the concept of "inward-directed development."

In a 1944 article in Mexico's *Trimestre Económico,* Prebisch noted that the United States, unlike Argentina, had a low propensity to import (defined as the change in the value of imports generated by a given change in the national product). Since other countries, he implied, had high propensities to import, and the U.S. had replaced Britain as the chief industrial trading partner of the Latin American states, Prebisch expanded on the League experts' argument in 1933 and warned that the postwar international trading system faced the danger of permanent disequilibrium.[43]

Prebisch first used the terminology center-periphery in print in 1946, at the second meeting mentioned above, that of the hemisphere's central bankers, who convened at the invitation of the Banco de México. Prebisch now identified the United States as the "cyclical center" and Latin America as the "periphery of the economic system." The emphasis, as indicated, was on the trade cycle, whose rhythms the U.S. economy set for the whole international system. Fiscal and monetary authorities in the United States could pursue a policy of full employment without producing monetary instability, Prebisch argued; furthermore, such authorities did not need to be especially concerned about the impact of full employment policies on the exchange rate of the dollar in other currencies. By contrast, Prebisch asserted, the nations of the periphery could not apply the same monetary tools as the center. Extrapolating from his 1944 argument with reference to Argentina, Prebisch contended that the money supply in peripheral countries could not be expanded in pursuit of full employment, because such a measure would quickly exhaust foreign exchange (implicitly because the new money put too great a pressure on imports, assuming no devaluation).

This 1946 statement and previous writings of Prebisch implied that peripheral countries faced three options, all with unacceptable consequences: they could have strong currencies and maintain high levels of imports at the cost of high unemployment; they could fight unemployment with an expansionist monetary policy but would thereby create inflation and decrease their ability to import, because of a fall in the exchange value of their currencies; or, if they used monetary policy to maintain high levels of employment, but failed to devalue, their reserves would disappear. When prices of the periphery's products fell during the downswing of the cycle, furthermore, governments of peripheral countries, at least in isolation, could not affect world prices for their goods as the center could for its goods. Thus equilibrium theories in international trade were not acceptable.[44] This was a direct assault on the "economic science" of the industrialized countries.

Back in the classroom in Buenos Aires in 1948, Prebisch specifically attacked the theory of comparative advantage, and noted that its precepts were repeatedly violated by the industrialized nations, whose economists nonetheless used classical trade theory as an ideological weapon. He also implied that industrial countries acted as monopolists against agricultural countries in the trading process. Prebisch then asserted that historically, in both the United States and Britain, technological progress did not result in a decrease in prices, but in an increase in wages. "The fruit of technical progress tend[ed] to remain in Great Britain" in the nineteenth century; yet, because Britain had sacrificed its agriculture, part of the benefits of technological progress had been transferred to the "new countries" in the form of higher land values. Britain's nineteenth-century import coefficient (defined as the value of imports divided by real income) was estimated by Prebisch as 30-35 percent, whereas that of the U.S. in the 1930s was only about 5 percent. All of this implied a blockage to growth for the agricultural-exporting periphery under the new largely self-sufficient center.[45]

This center-periphery theory even *in nuce* implied a single system, hegemonically organized. Though the term hegemony did not appear in this early use of center-periphery terminology, Prebisch himself, years later, would specifically employ the word to characterize relations between the two elements of the world economy.[46] To appreciate the significance of the terms we should bear in mind that the idea that there was something fundamentally different about the economies of the "retarded regions"[47] was still novel in the 1940s. The concept of "underdevelopment" as a syndrome was only elaborated in that decade, chiefly after the creation of specialized United Nations agencies in 1947–1948. The euphemisms "developing countries" and "less developed countries," were still in the future.[48] While a few Marxists and others preferred to employ "backward" rather than "underdeveloped," even "backward" among these non-center-periphery terms did not in itself imply hegemony; nor did "backward" necessarily put the central emphasis on the international capitalist system. Rather, such a concept could imply that the problem was largely one of leads and lags—the modernization thesis in its ahistorical setting.[49]

Despite the fact that some of the key ideas of Prebisch's later analysis were set forth in international meetings in 1944 and 1946, there was no discussion on these occasions of an Economic Commission for Latin America, the U.N. agency that was subsequently to be Prebisch's principal theoretical and ideological vehicle. Rather, it resulted from a Chilean initiative in 1947 at U.N. headquarters in Lake Success, New York. The founding of ECLA and the struggles involved in that effort have been related in several places,[50] and need not detain us here. The agency was approved by the U.N. Economic and Social Council in February 1948, and ECLA held its first meeting in Santiago, Chile, in June of that year. Alberto Baltra Cortés, the Chilean minister of the economy, presided at the occasion. At the opening session Baltra stressed Latin America's need to industrialize, an attitude to which representatives of the United States and the European colonial powers professed not to object. Prebisch's ideas were already familiar to the Chilean leaders, and for the future of ECLA, or at least its most famous thesis, the chief outcome of the meeting was a resolution calling for a study of Latin America's terms of trade.[51]

But ECLA was not yet ECLA, without Prebisch's leadership. His personality, theses, and programs so dominated the agency in its formative phase that it stood in sharp relief to the Economic Commission for Asia and the Far East (established in 1947) and the Economic Commission for Africa (1958), agencies with more purely technical orientations.[52] The year of ECLA's founding,

1948, seemed propitious for obtaining Prebisch's services: in Perón's Argentina he was excluded from official posts, perhaps because of his long and close association with the nation's traditional economic elite.[53] Meanwhile, his reputation as an economist in Latin America had been enhanced by the publication in Mexico of his *Introducción a Keynes* (1947).

Prebisch turned down the first offer to direct ECLA in 1948, because he feared an international organization like the U.N. would not permit underdeveloped countries to analyze economic problems from their own perspectives; in this regard, he had in mind the League of Nations' lack of interest in underdeveloped areas.[54] A few months later, however, he was again invited to go to Santiago to work on special assignment as editor and author of the introduction to an economic report on Latin America, authorized at the initial ECLA meeting. In Santiago, Prebisch also elaborated his theses on the deterioration of the terms of trade in the *Economic Development of Latin America and Its Principal Problems,* published in Spanish in May 1949, and dubbed the "ECLA Manifesto," in an obvious allusion to the Communist Manifesto, by economist Albert Hirschman.[55] Prebisch implicitly already had his opinions about the direction of Latin America's long-range terms of trade, since he had argued in the classroom in 1948 that the benefits of technological progress were absorbed by the center. Now, a new study by the U.N. Department of Economic Affairs, *Relative Prices of Exports and Imports of Underdeveloped Countries,* provided an empirical foundation for his thesis. This work was an examination of long-term trends in relative prices in the goods traded by industrialized and raw materials-producing countries, and concluded that the terms of trade from the late nineteenth century till the eve of World War II had been moving against the exporters of agricultural goods and in favor of the exporters of industrial products: "On the average, a given quantity of primary exports would pay, at the end of this period, for only 60 percent of the quantity of manufactured goods which it could buy at the beginning of the period."[56]

ECLA explained this finding in part by arguing that gains in productivity over the period in question were greater in industrial than in primary products, thus challenging basic assumptions of the theory of comparative advantage. If prices of industrial goods had fallen, this development would have spread the effects of technical progress over the entire center-periphery system, and one would expect the terms of trade for agricultural goods to have improved. They did not do so; and the significance of this fact, ECLA asserted, had to be understood in terms of trade cycles. During the upswing, the prices of primary goods rise more sharply than those of industrial goods, but they fall more steeply during the downswing. In the upswing the working class of the center absorbs real economic gains, but wages do not fall proportionately during the downswing. Because workers are not well organized in the periphery (least of all in agriculture), the periphery absorbs more of the system's income contraction than does the center.[57]

Another initial ECLA argument grew out of Prebisch's observations on Argentina's import problems in the 1930s. The United States, the principal cyclical center, had a much lower import coefficient than export coefficient, and the former was also much lower than those of the Latin American countries. The U.S. tended to sell more to Latin America than it bought from the region, exhausting Latin American reserves and creating a tendency toward permanent disequilibrium. Such a tendency had not existed, ECLA averred, during the time in which import-hungry Great Britain had been the principal center.[58]

In an article published in 1950, the year after the ECLA manifesto, another United Nations economist, Hans Singer, argued that technical progress in manufacturing was shown in a rise in incomes in developed countries, while that in the production of food and raw materials in underdeveloped countries was expressed in a fall in prices. He explained the differential effects of technical progress in terms of different income elasticities of demand for primary and industrial goods—an extrapolation of Ernst Engel's law that the proportion of income spent on foods falls as income rises—and in terms of the "absence of pressure of producers for higher incomes" in underdeveloped countries. Since consumers of manufactured goods in world trade tended to live in underdeveloped countries and the contrary was true for consumers of raw materials, Singer continued, the latter group had the best of both worlds while the former had the worst.[59] This idea was linked to Prebisch's and the two men's theories were quickly dubbed the Prebisch-Singer thesis, though both economists state that there was no direct exchange of ideas at the time the related sets of propositions, based on the same U.N. data, were developed.[60] (Prebisch of course was in Santiago, and Singer in New York.) Since ECLA's *Economic Development* appeared in print in May 1949, more than six months before Singer presented his American Economic Association paper (published in 1950). Prebisch clearly seems to have reached his position earlier than Singer; in fact, the U.N. study simply bolstered conclusions he had already reached.

By 1951, the year that ECLA became a permanent organ of the United Nations, the agency's emphasis had shifted from import coefficients to disparities in income elasticities of demand at the center for primary products, and those at the periphery for industrial goods.[61] This adoption of Hans Singer's terms was significant, because it dealt with the center countries as a group and not just the United States, which had unusually low import requirements because of its tremendous agricultural output.

But Prebisch and the ECLA team he organized were also interested in another dimension of the problem—monopolistic pricing at the center. The original analysis in 1949–1950 laid much more emphasis on the rigidity of wages in the downward phase of the cycle than on monopolistic pricing as such, but the latter argument was there.[62] In any event, both phenomena were assumed to be nonexistent in neoclassical trade theory. Peripheral countries did not have monopolies on the goods they offered in the world market (with rare and temporary exceptions) just as they lacked well-organized rural labor forces that would resist the fall in wages during the downswing of the cycle.

Samir Amin sees the emphasis on the rigidity of the center's wage bill as a significant difference between the arguments of Prebisch and Singer, who focused on the differences in demand for agricultural and industrial products. Amin immediately follows up his approval of Prebisch's thesis on wages by adding to it the argument that "it was monopoly (after 1880-1890) that made possible the rise in wages" in the industrialized center.[63]

Attacking the international division of labor, as ECLA did from 1949 on, entailed a call for the rapid industrialization of the periphery, but ECLA's "manifesto"—admittedly, without elaboration—also called for international agreements for price protection for primary products during the downswing of the trade cycle.[64] In this regard ECLA followed a recent U.N. effort to establish an International Trade Organization. The idea of commodity price stabilization at the international level had been discussed at the Bretton Woods Conference (1944), a meeting which resulted in the creation of the International Bank for Reconstruction and Development and the International Monetary Fund. In 1947-1948 a special U.N. conference at Havana established an International Trade Organization, whose principles included intergovernmental action to prevent violent price fluctuations in primary commodities. The U.S. Congress ultimately failed to approve the ITO, which consequently did not become part of the international monetary system.[65] Thus a program of price stabilization for primary commodities, which implicitly included the idea of countermonopoly against the industrialized countries, was taken up by ECLA in 1949. (This was a line of argument that would be elaborated by the U.N. Conference on Trade and Development after Prebisch became its first director in 1963.)

. . .

ECLA's theses, from their initial appearance in 1949, were hotly contested by neoclassical trade theorists, such as Jacob Viner. As Albert Hirschman has recently pointed out, the economics profession had just been treated to a formal demonstration by Paul Samuelson in 1948-1949 that, under certain conventional (but unrealistic) assumptions, trade could serve as a complete substitute for the movement of factors of production from one country to another, indicating that international trade could potentially equalize incomes among nations. Thus the less rigorous (but much more realistic) arguments of Prebisch and Singer burst upon the scene just after Samuelson had raised neoclassical trade theory to new heights of elegance, and against this theory the new ideas would have to struggle. [66] Looking back on the problem in the late 1970s, and possibly referring to Viner, Prebisch recalled "a sense of arrogance toward those poor underdeveloped economists of the periphery."[67] In particular, ECLA's intellectual adversaries attacked the idea of a long-term deterioration of the terms of trade for primary producers. Although Prebisch's original data base (the U.N. study, *Relative Prices*) has been largely discredited, this debate is still very much alive.[68]

Meanwhile, since its birth in the 1940s, the influence of Prebisch's center-periphery analysis has been vast and diffuse. Elsewhere I have tried to show, in brief compass, how ECLA helped shape the radical theses of unequal exchange in the work of André Gunder Frank, and partly through him, the work of Samir Amin.[69] Of Prebisch himself, Amin wrote, at the end of *Accumulation on a World Scale*:

> There can be no doubt that the first edition [of this work] did not do justice to the debt I owe, along with all concerned with nonapologetic study of underdevelopment, to the Latin American writers on the subject. Raúl Prebisch took the lead in this field, and I have shown in this book that the theory of unequal exchange was founded by him, even if the conjunctural context in which he set it, in his first version, has lost its significance. It is also to the United Nations Economic Commission for Latin America, of which he was the moving spirit, that I owe the essence of the critical theory to which I adhere, for it was this Commission that led the way in the reflections from which all the present currents in Latin American thinking on these matters have developed.[70]

In *Accumulation,* Amin repeatedly condemns "economism," an indifference in Western economic analysis to social and political contexts at a theoretical level; and it is interesting that a recent internal history of ECLA makes a similar point about its own work, even though the agency's "structural" analysis went far beyond its "monetarist" opponents in distinguishing the unique features of peripheral economies.[71] This is a criticism that Prebisch himself has taken seriously in recent writings; he notes, for example, that the interests of the upper strata of the periphery are closely linked to those of the center—a point the Comintern had made, in different phraseology, half a century earlier. Prebisch's current analysis hardly converges with that of more radical theorists, but it does seem closer: he makes clear his belief that the center(s) exploit the periphery, and he now speaks of an economic surplus which the periphery in part exports to the center. He places more emphasis on inherent monopolistic relationships than he formerly did, arguing that "some price relationships have always been unfavorable, ever since the periphery was incorporated into the international economy."[72] This judgment clearly demotes the trade cycle as a mechanism for withdrawing income from the periphery. Prebisch now rejects the consumption-oriented society of the "center type" in favor of "democratization" of peripheral areas, a process which depends on a sharp increase in capital accumulation and a "modification" (but not transformation?) of the distribution of income.[73] Yet Prebisch still has little to say, it seems, about the political means whereby the world economic system might be restructured.

In this chapter I have described how Raúl Prebisch formulated a thesis of unequal exchange over the course of two decades of involvement in economic and financial policy. I have shown that Prebisch came to reject the thesis of comparative advantage via his partial rejection, in the context of peripheral economies, of the monetary and banking policies of Keynes. I have argued that relatively little of the center-periphery thesis was derived or borrowed from other writings, and that it owed more to empirical observation and experimentation than to Prebisch's reading of other theorists—Marxist, corporatist, Keynesian, or neoclassical. Not paradoxically, I hope, I have also argued that Prebisch had formulated the elements of his thesis before the appearance, in 1949, of the empirical base on which the thesis rested in its first published form—the U.N. study, *Relative Prices*.

Although there were a few other economists from the Third World who made important contributions to development theory in the early postwar years (e.g., Hla Myint and Arthur Lewis), Prebisch was probably the only one exclusively trained in, and residing in, a Third World area; he was also the only one directing an institutional forum that could be construed as a distinctive Third World voice. Thirty years later Prebisch's views are still evolving; but whatever his final position, he has surely won himself a place of eminence in the history of the theory of imperialism—even if "imperialism" is not part of the ECLA vocabulary.

Notes

1. See Arghiri Emmanuel, *Unequal Exchange: A Study of the Imperialism of Trade* (New York: Monthly Review Press, 1972), 263 ("center-periphery"); André Gunder Frank, *Capitalism and Underdevelopment in Latin America: Historical Studies of Chile and Brazil,* rev. ed. (New York: Monthly Review Press, 1969), 8 ("metropolis-satellite"); Immanuel Wallerstein, "The Rise and Future Demise of the World Capitalist System: Concepts for Comparative Analysis," *Comparative Studies in Society and History* 16, no. 4 (Sept. 1974), 401 ("core-semiperiphery-periphery"); Johan Galtung, "A Structural Theory of Imperialism," *Journal of Peace Research,* no. 2 (1971), 81 ("center-periphery").

2. Celso Furtado, *Economic Development of Latin America: A Survey from Colonial Times to the Cuban Revolution,* tr. Suzette Macedo (Cambridge: Cambridge University Press, 1970), 192 (CACM), 208 (Kubitschek); Luis di Marco, "Introduction," in di Marco, ed., *International Economics and Development: Essays in Honor of Raúl Prebisch* (New York: Academic Press, 1972), 11 (LAFTA); Jerome Levinson and Juan de Onís, *The Alliance that Lost Its Way* (Chicago: Quadrangle, 1970), 39-40, 72 (Alliance). Furthermore, in 1954 the *cepalista* economist Celso Furtado applied

Prebisch's argument on international terms of trade to problems of interregional trade in Brazil, and thereby helped justify the creation of the Superintendency of Development of the Northeast (SUDENE). A similar analysis of the Northeast's terms of trade was made independently and more or less simultaneously by Hans W. Singer, whose theories on international trade paralleled Prebisch's (see below).

3. Brazilian Embassy, Washington, D.C., *Boletim Especial,* no. 31, 21 June 1977, 1.

4. In 1918, Luis Gondra introduced South America's first course in mathematical economics at the University of Buenos Aires. Gondra et al., *El pensamiento económico latinoamericano* (México: Fondo de Cultura Económica, 1945), 32.

5. Prebisch interview, Washington, D.C., 10 July 1978.

6. Prebisch, *Anotaciones demográficas a propósito de los movimientos de la población* (Buenos Aires: n. pub., 1926), 3.

7. Duhau, "Prólogo," in Prebisch, ed., *Anuario de la Sociedad Rural Argentina,* no. 1 (Buenos Aires: Gotelli, 1928), vii.

8. Among other works, Prebisch's articles in the 1920s published in the *Revista de Ciencias Económicas* include "1° conferencia financiera internacional de Bruselas" (1921); "Anotaciones sobre nuestro medio circulante" (1921-1922); "Anotaciones sobre la crisis ganadera" (1922); "La caja internacional de conversión" (1923); and "El régimen de pool en el comercio de carnes" (1927).

9. *Who's Who in the United Nations and Related Agencies* (New York: Arno Press, 1975), 455-456; Prebisch, "Versión taquigráfica de la conferencia de prensa ... 15 de noviembre de 1955," 23-24 (Prebisch file, ECLA, Santiago, Chile); Carlos F. Díaz Alejandro, *Essays on the Economic History of the Argentine Republic* (New Haven, Conn.: Yale University Press, 1970), 97; Banco Central de la Republica Argentina, *La creación del Banco Central y la experiencia monetaria argentina entre los años 1935-1943* (Buenos Aires: Banco Central, 1972), 1:267 et seq. The last named work details the differences in the Niemeyer plan and that actually adopted by the Argentine government. (Niemeyer was also an advisor to Brazil, another major recipient of British capital, and played a similar role on the east coast of South America that the American financial advisor, Edwin Kemmerer, did on the west coast—where U.S. investment predominated.)

10. For example, see Richard E. Caves and Ronald W. Jones, *World Trade and Payments: An Introduction,* 2d ed. (Boston: Little, Brown, 1977), 12, 109. For another summary, see Fernando H. Cardoso, "The Originality of a Copy: CEPAL and the Idea of Development," *CEPAL Review* (2d half of 1977), 4:9-10.

11. Díaz Alejandro, *Essays,* 2.

12. Rodolfo Puiggros, *Historia crítica de los partidos políticos argentinos* (Buenos Aires: Editorial Argumentos, 1956), 276; Peter H. Smith, *Politics and Beef in Argentina: Patterns of Conflict and Change* (New York: Columbia University Press, 1969), 52, 74-75. As late as 1940, Finance Minister Federico Pinedo had to defend the promotion of industrial production before the Argentine Senate by distinguishing between "natural" industries, for which the nation had the necessary raw materials, and "artificial" industries, for which it lacked inputs. Javier Villanueva, "Economic Development," in Mark Falcoff and Ronald H. Dolkart, eds., *Prologue to Perón: Argentina in Depression and War: 1930-1943* (Berkeley: University of California Press, 1975), 78. All the same, the country's tariff structure was so complex (con-

fused?) that Díaz Alejandro believes that "on balance protectionist and revenue considerations prevailed" over free trade sentiment between 1906 and 1940 (*Essays,* 307). Perhaps no one in the period understood the net effects of the tariff system; in any event, revenue may have been the primary motive for tariff levels, and from 1916 to 1930, Radical governments favored the Sociedad Rural over other groups in their tariff policy. (On the last point, see Carl Solberg, "The Tariff and Politics in Argentina: 1916-1930," *Hispanic American Historical Review* 53, no. 2 [May 1973], 284.)

13. Charles P. Kindleberger, *The World Depression: 1929-1939* (London: Penguin, 1973), 102, 104; ECLA, *The Economic Development of Latin America and Its Principal Problems* (Lake Success, N.Y.: United Nations, 1950), 29.

14. Kindleberger, *World Depression,* 181.

15. Jorge Fodor and Arturo A. O'Connell, "La Argentina y la economica atlántica en la primera mitad del siglo XX," *Desarrollo Económico* 13, no. 9 (April-June, 1973), 18, 30.

16. D. M. Phelps, "Industrial Expansion in Temperate South America," *American Economic Review* 25 (1935), 273-274.

17. Data in Vicente Vásquez-Presedo, *Crisis y retraso: Argentina y la economía international entre las dos guerras* (Buenos Aires: EUDEBA, 1978), 253, 272.

18. Fodor and O'Connell, "La Argentina," 52-54. Britain was to eliminate tariffs on cereal imports, but the emphasis was on beef. Argentina also agreed to spend all sterling sums earned in trade with the United Kingdom. Villanueva, "Economic Development," 65-66. On the negotiations, see Joseph S. Tulchin, "Foreign Policy," in Falcoff and Dolkart, *Prologue to Perón,* 91-98.

19. When the war began in September 1939, a secret pact between the Bank of England and Argentina's Central Bank established that the South American nation would accept sterling for its sales to Britain, and that this money would be used exclusively for paying for British exports to Argentina or to buy back Argentine bonds and purchase British-owned railways. That is, the sterling was held in a blocked account that could not be converted into other currencies, and would constitute payments in a captive export market for British goods after the war. No interest was to be paid on this account, and Britain did not have to use its precious dollars, which Argentina sorely needed. According to Fodor and O'Connell, "During this period [and for a time after the 1943 coup] . . . Argentina did not use its sterling to liquidate its foreign debt nor to buy up [British-owned] railroads, with the result that while Argentina's debts to Britain paid interest, British debts to Argentina did not." (Argentina was apparently willing to accept the lopsided pact of 1939 because of the collapse of cereal prices again at the outset of the war, and the probable loss of her remaining continental markets as the conflict developed.) Even in the postcoup years (i.e., after Prebisch left the Central Bank), the pro-Axis government continued to bow to the economic demands of Britain, for fear of losing its only large market. Foder and O'Connell, "La Argentina," 56 (quotation), 57, 59.

20. ECLA, *External Financing in Latin America* (New York: U.N., 1965), 25. Argentina did default on some of its nonfederal debts.

21. Prebisch, "Versión," 28; Prebisch interview.

22. Prebisch, "La conferencia económica y la crisis mundial," in *Revista Económica* 61, no. 1 (January 1933), 1, 3.

23. Prebisch interview; Keynes, *The Collected Writings of John Maynard Keynes*

9 (London: Macmillan, 1972), 335-366, esp. 360.

24. Prebisch, "La inflación escolástica y la moneda argentina," *Revista de Economía Argentina,* año 17, no. 193 (July 1934), 11-12; no. 194 (August 1934), 60. Later it was discovered that the purchasing power of Argentina's exports fell by about 40 percent between 1925-1929 and 1930-1934. Between these two periods the capital flow was also severely curtailed, so Argentina's capacity to import fell in 1930-1934 to 46 percent of what it had been in the preceding five years. Aldo Ferrer, *The Argentine Economy,* tr. Marjory M. Urquidi (Berkeley: University of California Press, 1967), 162.

25. See Villanueva, "Economic Development"; Díaz Alejandro, *Essays,* 94-105; Vásquez-Presedo, *Crisis y retraso,* 137-186; and in particular, Roger Gravil, "State Intervention in Argentina's Export Trade Between the Wars," *Journal of Latin American Studies* 2, no. 2 (1970), 147-173; and Rafael Olarra Jiménez, *Evolución monetaria argentina* (Buenos Aires: EUDEBA, 1968), 83-99 and *passim.*

26. Gravil, "State Intervention," 171; Wilfred Malenbaum, *The World Wheat Economy: 1885-1939* (Cambridge, Mass.: Harvard University Press, 1953), 205-209. A statement by Prebisch on Argentina's role is found in an interview he gave during the Roca-Runciman negotiations in London. See *La Prensa,* 9 February 1933, 9.

27. Kindleberger, *World Depression* 278-279.

28. Walter Beveraggi-Allende, "Argentine Foreign Trade Under Exchange Control" (Ph.D. thesis, Harvard University, 1952), 219 (quotation), 246.

29. Phelps, "Industrial Expansion," 274; *Economic Review* [i.e., English ed. of *Revista Económica*], series 2, 1, no. 1 (1937), 69.

30. Phelps, "Industrial Expansion," 281.

31. Banco Central de la Republica Argentina, *Memoria . . . 1942* (Buenos Aires: Banco Central, 1943), 30-31.

32. *Economic Review,* series 2, 1, no. 1 (1937), 26-27.

33. Ibid., 69.

34. Olarra Jiménez, *Evolución,* 13.

35. Banco Central, *Memoria . . . 1938* (Buenos Aires: Banco Central, 1939), 5-8; Prebisch to author, Washington, D.C., 9 November 1977. In 1945 the *Federal Reserve Bulletin* came to a similar conclusion about Argentina's recent economic history. Using that country to illustrate Latin America's problems, the *Bulletin* noted the country's rapid industrial expansion between 1940 and 1944 through import substitution; but it also pointed out the high export to national income ratio in Argentina, making the economy sensitive to international cyclical movements. The journal concluded that Latin America's monetary authorities could not control central bank reserves or changes in credit based on them: "Thus every surplus in the balance of payments tended to bring about a multiple expansion, and every deficit a multiple contraction, in the total money supply." See "Monetary Developments in Latin America," *Federal Reserve Bulletin* 31, no. 6 (June 1945), 523-525.

36. Prebisch interview.

37. Prebisch, "La moneda y los ciclos económicos en la Argentina" [class notes by assistant, approved by Prebisch], 1944, 61-65, mimeo. Located at Facultad de Ciencias Económicas, Universidad de Buenos Aires.

38. Prebisch, "La moneda," summarized in Olarra Jiménez, *Evolución,* 76.

39. Villanueva's words quoted, 78. On Prebisch as probable author of Pinedo's plan, see Díaz Alejandro, *Essays,* 105, note 37.

40. At the same time Prebisch gave a series of lectures at the Banco de México on "the Argentine monetary experience (1935-1943)," that is, covering the period in which he was the director-general of the Central Bank. See Banco Central, *La creación* 1:249-588; 2:599-623.

41. "El patrón oro y la vulnerabilidad económica de nuestros paises" (a lecture at the Colegio de México), *Revista de Ciencias Económicas,* año 32, serie 2, no. 272 (March 1944), 234; Banco Central, *Memoria . . . 1942, 30.*

42. Prebisch, "Análisis de la experiencia monetaria argentina (1935–1943)" in Banco Central, *La creación* 1:407.

43. Prebisch, "Observaciones sobre los planes monetarios internacionales," *El Trimestre Económico* 11, no. 2 (July-September 1944), 188, 192-193.

44. Prebisch, "Panorama general de los problemas de regulación monetaria y crediticia en el continente americano: A. América Latina," in Banco de México, *Memoria: Primera reunión de técnicos sobre problemas de banco central del continente americano* (México: Banco de México, 1946), 25-28; "Observaciones," 199.

45. Prebisch, "Apuntes de economía política (Dinámica económica)" [class notes], 1948, 96, 97, mimeo.

46. Prebisch, "A Critique of Peripheral Capitalism," *CEPAL Review* (1st half of 1976), 60.

47. J. Fred Rippy, *British Investments in Latin America, 1822–1949: A Case Study in the Operations of Private Enterprise in Retarded Regions* (Minneapolis: University of Minnesota Press, 1959).

48. See Gunnar Myrdal, "Diplomacy by Terminology" in *An Approach to the Asian Drama: Methodological and Theoretical* (New York: Vintage, 1970), 35-36.

49. For a brief but effective critique of "stages of growth" for individual countries as ahistorical nonsense, see Wallerstein, "The Rise and Future," 387-390.

50. See Hernán Santa Cruz, *Una página de la historia de las Naciones Unidas en sus primeros años* (Santiago: PLA, 1966); John A. Houston, *Latin America in the United Nations* (New York: Carnegie Endowment, 1956); 223-232; David H. Pollock, "Some Changes in United States Attitudes Toward CEPAL Over the Past 30 Years," *CEPAL Review* (2d half of 1978), 57-59.

51. UN ECOSOC E/CN.12/17 (7 June 1948), 2; E/CN.12/28 (11 June 1948), 6; E/CN.12/71 (24 June 1948).

52. Benjamin Higgins, *United Nations and U.S. Foreign Economics Policy* (Homewood, Ill.: Irwin, 1962), 102; C. C. Stewart, "Center-Periphery and Unequal Exchange" [African Section], (Paper presented at the Seventh National Meeting of the Latin American Studies Association/Twentieth Annual Meeting of the African Studies Association, Houston, Texas, November 1977), 4.

53. Aldo Ferrer interview, Buenos Aires, 2 August 1978.

54. Prebisch interview. For support of the League's lack of interest in underdeveloped areas, see H. W. Arndt, "Development Economics Before 1945," in Jagdish Bhagwati and Richard S. Eckaus, eds., *Development and Planning* (Cambridge, Mass.: MIT Press, 1973), 18.

55. Albert O. Hirschman, "Ideologies of Economic Development in Latin America," in Hirschman, ed., *Latin American Issues: Essays and Comments* (New York: Twentieth Century Fund, 1961), 13.

56. United Nations Department of Economic Affairs, *Relative Prices of Exports and Imports of Under-Developed Countries: A Study of Postwar Terms of Trade Be-*

tween Under-Developed and Industrialized Nations (Lake Success, N. Y.: United Nations, 1949), 7.

57. ECLA, *Economic Development,* 8-14.

58. Ibid., 15-16; ECLA, *Economic Survey of Latin America: 1949* (New York: United Nations, 1951), 20, 35-38.

59. Hans W. Singer, "The Distribution of Gains Between Investing and Borrowing Countries," *American Economic Review: Papers and Proceedings* 40, no. 2 (May 1950), 473-485 (quotation from 479). Income elasticity of demand for a good refers to the relative response of demand to a small percentage change in income [$(\Delta q/q) \div (\Delta y/y)$, where q is the quantity demanded, and y is disposable income].

60. Prebisch to author, 29 June 1977; Singer to author, Brighton, England, 21 August 1979.

61. E/CN.12/221 (18 May 1951), 30.

62. ECLA, *Economic Survey 1949,* 59. More ambiguously, *Economic Development* stated that "the income of entrepreneurs and of productive factors" in the center increased faster than did productivity in the center from the 1870s to the 1930s, but in another passage the document placed exclusive emphasis on the role of wages in the center (10, 14).

63. Samir Amin, *Accumulation on a World Scale: A Critique of the Theory of Underdevelopment,* tr. Brian Pierce (New York: Monthly Review Press, 1974), 1:83-84. Celso Furtado, a veteran *cepalista* and one of the most creative minds on Prebisch's team, later offered a different, *marxisant* explanation of labor's role in the "stickiness" of center export prices: in industrial economies, class struggle is the basis for capitalist growth; workers' organizations seek to expand labor's share of the national product, while in underdeveloped countries this does not occur because labor (and especially agricultural labor) is disorganized, and the supply of labor is extremely wage-elastic. *Diagnosis of the Brazilian Crisis,* tr. Suzette Macedo (Berkeley, Calif.: University of California Press, 1965), 48-51, 61. (Presumably ECLA never vigorously promoted rural labor organization because of the immense social and political problems this policy would have encountered, including the probable hostility of many member states of the commission.)

64. ECLA, *Economic Development,* 48.

65. U.S. Department of State, *Havana Charter for an International Trade Organization and Final Act and Related Documents* (Dept. of State pub. 3117, Washington, D.C., n.d.), 39-43; Singer to author, 21 August 1979.

66. Albert Hirschman, "A Generalized Linkage Approach to Development, with Special Reference to Staples," *Economic Development and Cultural Change* 25, (1977) supplement, 68. Samuelson's articles were "International Trade and the Equalisation of Factor Prices," *Economic Journal* 58 (June 1948), 163-184 and "International Factor-Price Equalisation Once Again," *Economic Journal* 59 (June 1949), 181-197.

67. Viner, *International Trade,* especially 61-62; Prebisch to author, 29 June 1977.

68. The data base (for Britain), which showed long-term deterioration of the periphery's terms of trade, was criticized: it allowed for no change in the quality of goods, a process that presumably affected industrial more than agricultural commodities, because of a higher rate of technological progress in the center. Further-

more, P. T. Ellsworth pointed out that the British series included exports F.O.B. but imports C.I.F., and argued that a fall in the prices of primary goods from 1876 to 1905 was largely due to a fall in transportation costs (owing to a combination of advances in steamship and rail networks). But the same writer showed that the evidence for the 1930s supported Prebisch—British export prices did not fall because of resistance to cuts in wages and profits.

Using data for the period 1950–1960, Werner Baer showed that there was substantial evidence that the deterioration of the terms of trade in many parts of the underdeveloped world owed to low income elasticity of demand for its complement's goods at the center, and high elasticity at the periphery. While acknowledging that monopolistic pricing at the center was difficult to prove, Baer found that for 1950–1960 the periphery's export prices tended to decrease or to fluctuate widely. Wages (in constant terms) for the years 1950–1959 rose in selected center countries, while those in peripheral countries fell.

More recently Paul Bairoch has attacked Prebisch's terms-of-trade argument as a long-term phenomenon. Bairoch contends that, contrary to Prebisch, primary goods *benefited* in the secular trends of the terms of trade from 1870 to the early 1950s. To begin with, Bairoch challenges the choice of the terminal year (1938) of the original U.N. study (*Relative Prices*) as an abnormal one. He also cites trade figures for the United States and France (data not available in 1949), which diverge from the trends of the British experience (Robert Lipsey had already shown this for the United States). Furthermore, Bairoch demonstrates that the internal terms of trade for several developed countries moved in favor of agricultural goods in the years 1876–1880 to 1926–1929. Finally, he cites long-term studies of terms of trade for several primary-exporting countries which contradict the U.N.'s findings. Yet Bairoch does think the terms of trade moved against the Third World countries from 1954–1955 to 1962–1963. Among the several causes of this trend was a factor Prebisch had cited—"a difference between the less-developed and the developed countries in the manner in which the gains from increased productivity accrued." Despite Bairoch's forceful arguments on the long-term trends, the dispute about the effects of terms of trade between developed and underdeveloped countries remained very much alive in the year he published (1975).

See Ellsworth, "The Terms of Trade Between Primary Producing and Industrial Countries," *Inter-American Economic Affairs* 10, no. 1 (Summer 1956), 55-57, 63; Baer, "The Economics of Prebisch and ECLA," in Charles T. Nisbet, ed., *Latin America: Problems in Economic Development* (New York: Free Press, 1969), 215-217; Bairoch, *The Economic Development of the Third World Since 1900* (Berkeley: University of California Press, 1975), 111-134, especially 120, 125, 132, 134 (quotation); Robert F. Lipsey, *Price and Quantity Trends in the Foreign Trade of the United States* (Princeton, N.J.: Princeton University Press, 1963), especially 12-17; "Idea of Growing Disparity in World Prices Disputed," *New York Times,* 25 May 1975, 1, 8; Jonathan Power, "Of Raw Materials, Raw Statistics, and Raw Deals," *New York Times,* 31 August 1975, E15.

69. Joseph L. Love, "Centro-Periferia e troca desigual: Origens e crescimento de uma doutrina econômica," *Dado* 19 (1978), 47-62, especially 56-57.

70. Amin, *Accumulation* 2, 609-610.

71. Octavio Rodríguez, "Sobre la concepción del sistema centro-periferia," *Re-*

vista de la CEPAL (1st half of 1977), 240.

72. Prebisch, "A critique," 11-12, 37, 60, 66. Prebisch defines the surplus as the gains in productivity resulting from technological progress, 13.

73. Ibid., 59.

chapter seven

The Latin American Structuralists and the Institutionalists: Convergence in Development Theory

James H. Street

Raúl Prebisch, prime mover among the economists loosely designated as the "structuralists", asserts that from the fluid, often confused state of economic thinking in Latin America a distinct and recognizable body of ideas is emerging. "In the midst of the depression," he observes, "we did not know the true nature of Latin America's difficulties; the dominant idea was simply to return to the past. Fifteen years ago we were already able to attempt to define the set of problems in question and to point with deep conviction to certain basic solutions. And today sufficient progress has been made to work out a system of ideas, a dynamic view of economic and social development leading to practical action. . . . What has to be done is to overcome the ideological poverty that prevails in our countries in this field, the traditional propensity to introduce from abroad nostrums that are largely alien to the real requirements of Latin America's situation."[1]

Some economists doubt that Latin America's problems are so unique that they require a new system of ideas and consider Prebisch's assessment defensive and tinged with regional parochialism. Others share his feeling that while economic doctrine formulated in the more developed countries has not adequately explained current processes nor provided effective formulas for policy, exponents of conventional theory nevertheless assume an attitude of expert knowledge and moral rectitude that is more than irksome to those confronted with the actualities. It becomes coercive when linked to the financial power of outside lending agencies and local interests, all insistent on applying prescriptive remedies where they will not serve.

Reprinted in abridged form from the *Journal of Economic Issues* 1 (June 1967) by special permission of the copyright holder, the Association for Evolutionary Economics.

Roberto Campos, while Brazilian ambassador to the United States, criticized the Anglo-Saxon inclination to regard Latin America's problems from "a moralistic and not a sociological view," adding that "there is little justification for a self-righteous attitude on the part of the lending countries, as if inflation and balance of payment troubles in Latin America were plain lack of guts or love of vice, and not the symptoms of difficult travail in face of adverse winds of trade, impatience of consumers and confused aspirations for the fruits of progress before the tree has matured to yield."[2]

What is the basis for these complaints by Latin American economists? When one seeks a perspective on the bitter exchanges prompted by particular issues such as the terms of trade, inflation, and investment policy, one sees that the structuralists have been suffering much the same experience as befell the institutionalists, their North American counterparts, in an earlier period. Acting independently and apparently with little awareness of the relevant work of Thorstein Veblen, John Dewey, and C. E. Ayres, the Latin American structuralists have attacked identical weaknesses in orthodox theory, though understandably with special reference to their own problems. For a time they also endured the form of academic excommunication described by J. A. Hobson as a "conspiracy of silence," which in part accounts for the fact that institutionalist works are even yet rarely translated and hence infrequently read in Latin America. It also leads some structuralists to feel that more respectable economists in the advanced nations have relegated them to an intellectual doghouse for being hopelessly wrongheaded if not professionally irresponsible.

Yet from the recent work of the structuralists has emerged the outline of a body of positive thought that has much in common with institutionalist growth theory. It will be mutually beneficial for Latin American structuralists and North American evolutionary economists (not all of them, to be sure, institutionalists) to become better informed about their respective contributions to each other's work, remaining gaps in the fabric of thought, and potentials for cross-fertilization of ideas based on differing experiences. "Structures" and "institutions," meaningfully interpreted, have something in common and can form a bridge to a more adequate development theory. It is high time that the communications bridge between related schools of dissident thought surmount problems of distance, language, and environment.

Structuralist Criticisms of Orthodox Theory

Structuralism, like institutionalism, began with an attack on deficiencies in neoclassical economic doctrine or on policies derived from that doctrine. That this controversy should still continue is perhaps surprising, after the upheaval in economic thinking of the 1930s in the more developed countries, but this is in part attributable to the power of old ideas to persist long after new conceptions overtake them. It is also due to the special forms that orthodox theory has taken in the underdeveloped countries, where the problems are of growth more than of cyclical fluctuations, of technological dependence more than industrial unemployment. Even the Keynesian reformulation of neoclassical thought does not seem to meet the requirements of the structuralists.[3]

Structuralist objections to concepts imported from the industrially more advanced countries, though diverse, can usefully be summarized in four points of attack that in their general form will be recognized by students of Veblenian criticism. They question the static analysis of the external growth process, the efficacy of automatic market forces to provide needed external and internal adjustments, the use of conventional measures to correct deep-seated secular problems, and the reduction of the general standard of living as a way of promoting growth.

The Static View of the External Growth Process
To the structuralists, orthodox theory has described essentially static international economic relations and has not explained or provided for dynamic changes over time involving shifts in the use of resources. For Latin America, still emerging from neocolonialism and hence subject to strong outside influences, this criticism first bore upon international trade and investment theory. The key element in the orthodox explanation of growth was the principle of comparative advantage, by which less developed countries had been assured, since at least the time of Adam Smith, a greater share in the wealth of nations if they would specialize and exchange—even with highly industrialized trade partners. This theory, coupled with the understanding that private foreign investment would provide the necessary transfers of industrial know-how and equipment, implied that the less developed countries could only harm themselves by any efforts to regulate the free flow of trade and investment, since both the operation of comparative advantage and the theory of mobility of capital transfers depended upon the absence of market restrictions. These ideas have been little affected by the Keynesian revolution, except insofar as Keynes pointed out that foreign trade may be used in time of depression to export unemployment and thus become exploitative of weaker countries.

Raúl Prebisch, in his seminal essay on "The Economic Development of Latin America and Its Principal Problems" in 1950, challenged the validity of the neoclassical claim that "the benefits of technical progress tend to be distributed alike over the whole [international] community, either by the lowering of prices or the corresponding raising of incomes."[4] Prebisch sought to demonstrate in his now familiar "worsening terms of trade" argument that because the relative prices of manufactured goods produced by the industrialized "center" countries and of primary products supplied by the under-

developed "periphery" countries had tended to run in favor of the industrialized countries, the underdeveloped countries had not obtained the
promised benefits of higher productivity in the center. The industrial countries had resorted to labor organization and administered pricing to raise
their own incomes rather than to lower prices of their export products.
Moreover, the same relative price movements had obliged the weaker
periphery countries, incapable of using similar defensive techniques, to
pass on any gains in their own productivity to the center.

Hans W. Singer pursued a similar argument in an article appearing
about the same time as Prebisch's study.[5] Singer further questioned whether
foreign private investment had actually contributed to the internal development of the capital-receiving countries. Such investment, Singer felt, was too
highly specialized to have general effects. Prebisch later referred to such investment as "characteristic types of foreign enclave which do not spread
technical progress to the internal economy."[6]

The criticisms by Prebisch and Singer of the orthodox explanations of
externally originated growth set off two lines of counterattack—one empirical, the other theoretical—that largely missed the main issue. The question
was, as Prebisch had made clear, how could the benefits of advancing
technology in the more developed countries best be transferred to retarded
economies as they sought to shake off neocolonial limitations? The protracted empirical controversy over the secular deterioration of the terms of
trade has been inconclusive, bogging down on definitional questions and
the interpretation of long waves.[7] Prebisch, conceding that the terms of trade
may fluctuate for particular products and particular countries, has since accepted Gunnar Myrdal's view that differing income elasticities of demand
for raw materials and manufactured goods in the respective export markets
chiefly account for "a cumulative process toward the impoverishment and
stagnation" of raw materials-producing countries.[8] It can hardly be denied
on empirical evidence that the Latin American countries suffer sharp variations in foreign-exchange earnings because they depend on a limited
number of primary-product exports whose prices fluctuate widely in world
markets. These fluctuations in earnings alone are sufficient to impede any
sustained and coherent internal development program.

Efforts to preserve the applicability of the principle of comparative advantage on theoretical grounds also leave the impression that the writers
are less interested in explaining the dynamics of development than in de-
fending the logical unassailability of the theory and its implications for free
trade.[9] These arguments offer little to counter the belief of structuralists that
strict reliance on comparative advantage would condemn the countries of
Latin America to the existing overspecialized and labor-exploitative use of
resources in the face of pressing internal changes, and thus offer no key to a
strategy for progress.

The remaining structuralist criticisms concern internal stimulants to growth. As in the case of external forces, they question the automatic operation of market influences.

Reliance On Free Market Forces for Internal Adjustments
The trust in the free play of the market, which we have so much modified in our own practices, is still one of our principal exports to the developing countries. Professor Gottfried Haberler at a conference in Rio de Janeiro counseled the assembled economists from all parts of the region that to achieve a proper internal diversification of industry, "the simplest method would be for each of the Latin-American countries to adopt a fairly uniform ad valorem import tariff over a wide range of commodities. Then, inside this framework, free enterprise, the forces of demand and supply, would automatically select the industries which would specialize here and there. That, it seems to me, would be the ideal solution."[10]

One need not be a structuralist to find such advice unrealistic in light of the wide disparities in income distribution in Latin America, the persistent tendency for aggregate demand to outrun supply, and the flooding of Latin American markets with superficial "demonstration effect" goods for which modern marketing techniques build an enormous desire.[11] Under these circumstances market demand is hardly a reliable guide to expenditures that will promote maximum development. Structuralists generally accept the need for intervention to correct the pattern of demand, though they are not agreed on the best means of carrying it out. José Figueres, a former president of Costa Rica and architect of major economic reforms in his country, has cautioned that the more successful the Central American Common Market becomes in integrating the economies of its five member countries, the more vulnerable it is to the marketing skills of foreign sellers, who can stimulate demand for nonessential imports much faster than the Common Market can generate domestic productive capacity.[12]

Perhaps what really underlies the yearning for a return to free markets is the belief that the present tangle of pricing arrangements in Latin America is so dominated by special interests and so indefensible on rational grounds that it should be entirely discarded. But few governments can seriously entertain such a possibility. The question is not one of a return to free markets, but how the system of regulation can best be overhauled.

. . .

Positive Contributions of the Structuralists

Because structuralism was born in criticism of received doctrine and has been embroiled in controversy ever since, it was not at first apparent that the school had any positive roots as an organism of its own. The chief claim to originality of the structuralists, aside from their polemic positions, was that they were trying to be more accurately descriptive of the economic system in Latin American than the general theorists with their standard preconceptions. To some, therefore, structuralist analysis, like institutional economics, has become synonymous with "mere description."

Yet, more accurate description is a good place to begin, since it leads to better diagnosis. The structuralists are characterized as a group by their impatience with stereotyped descriptions of Latin American economies. Living in the environment, they see important distinctions between national economic units, available resources, cultural backgrounds, and accidental historical factors that the newcomer to Latin America is likely to overlook or to regard as insignificant. They know that these very differences condition the respective capacities of some countries to make more rapid progress than others. Most of the recognized structuralists are painstakingly empirical in their research, in a region where reliable data are distinguished by their rarity. The statistical output of ECLA, as well as such other agencies as the Getulio Vargas Foundation, while still limited, is becoming an invaluable basis for research on Latin American problems.

Structuralists have tried to be rigorously inductive in their reasoning from the available data. As all economic historians and evolutionary economists know, this procedure is not the easiest of tasks, because the data impose constraints and they do not readily fall into patterns when viewed afresh. Often the most significant facts, being qualitative in nature, are elusive as a basis for tight chains of reasoning and for the quantitative models which the profession now prefers. Although many of the structuralist studies would no doubt be classified by some as more "sociological" than "economic," they are often of a very high order. An example is Sunkel's recent article on "Change and Frustration in Chile," a perceptive account of the very rapid and intense changes that have occurred in Chile during the recent third of a century, while in the final analysis, as he says, "the fundamental elements which determine the generation of the power structure and thus the orientation of economic and social policy have not changed at all."[13]

The related series of studies of the Chilean economy conducted by Aníbal Pinto since 1958 are also an important contribution, particularly as they concern the long-term factors underlying inflation.[14] Unfortunately most of these articles are not yet available in English. Others, associated with the structuralist school, whose major works, principally in the field of economic history, have recently been translated are Aldo Ferrer (Argentina), Víctor Urquidi (Mexico), and Celso Furtado (Brazil).[15]

Raúl Prebisch's work, much of which appeared under the aegis of the Economic Commission for Latin America, is for that reason more familiar to North American readers. Prebisch has been criticized as too "simplistic" in his approach because he has from time to time fastened on one or another of the maladies of Latin America as the "key problem," has occasionally shifted ground, and has offered a variety of solutions. Few economists, however, have revealed a more fertile mind or more consistently pragmatic approach in looking at the problems of Latin America from a fresh point of view, in suggesting new ways of coping with these problems, and in persistently directing attention to the obstacles, often represented by powerful vested interests, standing in the way of change.

Conceptually, the structuralists are best known for their diagnoses of the "structural deficiencies," "bottlenecks," or "internal maladjustments" which they believe account for the lags in Latin American development. Individual members of the school will differ in the relative importance they assign to the respective factors, but all agree that they are basically of two sorts: bottlenecks originating outside the countries concerned, such as the adverse terms of trade and the limited capacity to import; and maladjustments which occur internally, such as accelerated population growth, premature urbanization and expansion of the service sectors of employment, lag in agricultural production, the limited size of domestic markets, ineffective tax systems, and politically significant shifts in class structure. The approach is pragmatic. The structuralists have not come up with a standard list of structural maladjustments or bottlenecks, since circumstances vary from country to country and over time, but the maladies they describe are recurrent.

To the North American economist with an institutionalist background, many of the descriptions of structural problems have a strong "institutional" flavor. While in a significant sense the structural maladjustments are a result of differing rates of historical acceleration among sectors of the economy and thus seem to be uniquely associated with the present epoch of chaotic change in Latin America, they also represent traditional modes of organized behavior that have not been equally responsive to changed conditions. That is to say, they reflect the inertia of *institutions*.

Indeed, it is common to read in the structuralist literature references to structures *and* institutions as obstacles to change, with no differentiation between the two. Thus when Prebisch says, "the social structure prevalent in Latin America constitutes a serious obstacle to technical progress and, consequently, to economic and social development,"[16] the passage might have been written by an institutionalist. This would not be remarkable if it were not for the fact that the bibliographic citations for structuralist literature reveal a striking innocence of acquaintanceship with North American institutionalist writing, whether derived from Veblen, Commons, or Mitchell. Personal conversations with leading structuralists have confirmed that they have arrived at their concern with institutional inertia as a social force by a quite independent and convergent course. "Structures" are indeed "institutions" in some uses of the term, and "structural maladjustment" is often equivalent to "cultural lag" as American sociologists have employed the phrase.

Among the positive achievements of the structuralists, their persistence as critics has probably already had some significant though unacknowledged impact on policy. The International Monetary Fund, for example, has evidently reexamined the larger effects of its monetary and fiscal recommendations on internal economic growth and reveals somewhat greater flexibility in its guidelines. Recently the Fund announced a significant change in lending policy which takes into account the fluctuation in export earnings of member countries as a basis for compensatory financing, thus yielding a point to Prebisch.[17]

Gaps in Structuralist Theory

Areas for fruitful interchange may develop between structuralists and institutionalists (as well as other evolutionary economists) based on the relative emphases they have given to their respective lines of investigation. Institutionalists have particular contributions to make with respect to the nature of technological change, institutional adjustment, and an instrumental system of values.

The structuralists seem to have become aware only recently of the potential significance of technological change in the domestic development process, and this oversight may reflect a cultural hiatus in their own background. In the earlier writings of Prebisch, for example, one detects a feeling that technological innovation is something available exclusively to the center, something to be withheld from the periphery or employed only as an instrument of neocolonial exploitation. When he speaks of "technological enclaves" in the underdeveloped countries, he again implies that the institutional power of the industrial countries has given them exclusive access to the fruits of technology and that these fruits can be tightly contained once they are introduced into the less developed countries. It is doubtful whether such a conclusion is warranted.

There are, of course, no more striking contrasts between North America and Latin America than in the degree of use of technology and in the circumstance that nearly all modern technology in Latin America is borrowed, or alien to [its] culture. This gulf is not easily explained, since in pre-Columbian times both Middle and South America supported rich and inventive cultures and in modern times the region has had continuous contact with European civilization. Why and under what circumstances did the interest in maintaining and elaborating an indigenous process of discovery, invention, and application die? The Spanish conquest and its suffocating institutions no doubt played a major role, yet probably do not constitute a sufficient explanation. Nevertheless, the long absence of a native technological interest has been a key bottleneck in Latin American development worthy of historical study and explanation.

We know from other experience, notably our relations with the Soviet Union, that knowledge of science and technology cannot be withheld from those determined to make use of it. What is clearly needed in Latin America is to domesticate or "internalize" the technological process so that it becomes part of the indigenous culture (or so that Latin America becomes truly part of Western industrial culture, depending on the relative importance attached to other goals). This is what Japan has done, so that [it] is no longer dependent on cultural borrowing, but is innovative in [its] own right. Given modern communications, the stock of technological know-how is not institutionally confined, is accessible, and can become liberating rather than exploitative.

That the integration of modern technology into Latin American civilization has been delayed may be partly attributable to the long orientation of the region to Spain and Portugal, which were similarly retarded, rather than to other parts of Europe and the United States. But it is also probably due to a lack of local exposure to Veblen's "discipline of the machine," for which the paucity of existing industry and the inadequacy of educational substitutes have been responsible.

Countries with relatively high literacy rates, such as Argentina, Chile, and Uruguay, in recent years have had low rates of growth amounting to stagnation. This anomaly suggests that the educational system, though not solely responsible, is not working very well. According to Ayres, "The most important factor in the economic life of any people is the educational level, as we now call it, of the community. A technically sophisticated community can and will equip itself with the instrumentalities of an industrial economy."[18]

It has always seemed to me to be particularly unfortunate that Domingo F. Sarmiento's introduction of popular education into Argentina in the 1870s coincided with the rise of a social class who had no understanding of a technologically based culture (although they benefited handsomely from it) and no interest in mastering the requirements of an industrial system. The *estancieros* of Argentina laid down a pattern for education, especially higher education, that Sunkel has aptly labeled "ornamental rather than functional and technical."[19] In sending their sons to Madrid or to the Sorbonne to acquire the attributes of gentlemen, to the Faculty of Law in preference to Engineering or Agronomy, they implanted a structural defect of enduring influence on the future development of their country. Similar misconceptions of the role of education in relation to development are common in other Latin American countries.

This situation is changing, and the process should be accelerated. Under the impetus of the Alliance for Progress, the construction of urban and rural schools has been stepped up significantly. In Guatemala, for example, where 65 percent of the school-age children have never attended school,[20] the number of classrooms constructed since 1960 exceeds the number built during the entire previous period from the time of the Spanish conquest in 1524.[21] But vastly more important than the building of schools is what is taught in them. Rote instruction by poorly prepared teachers is still common, and anything comparable to the Deweyan revolution in education has yet to touch many parts of Latin America.

In Mexico, where a revolution education is in full swing, leaders of the popular education movement have rediscovered the philosophy of Enrique C. Rébsamen, a Swiss educator who established the first normal school at Jalapa in 1885. Rébsamen's ideas were akin to Dewey's precept of "learning by doing." He believed that children should have a broad exposure to materials and their practical and esthetic uses throughout their learning career. As a result, the state of Vera Cruz, where the Rébsamen movement started, has an exceptionally fine teachers' college, well equipped with shops and laboratories and following a progressive program of instruction. The pattern is extended to numerous rural elementary schools scattered through the state. This is but an instance of the sort of change that will have to occur on a large scale in Latin America if the technical and industrial revolutions are to become part of the basic culture.

The agricultural sector, as the structuralists have repeatedly emphasized, is one of the principal bottlenecks in Latin American growth and becomes more critical as the population surges upward. Lauchlin Currie, a severe critic of the development program inaugurated in Colombia in 1961 under the tutelage of ECLA advisers, asserts that "the chief weakness of the ECLA-Prebisch Approach in Latin America lies in its failure to grasp the significance or potentialities of the technical revolution in agriculture."[22] In view of other constraints prevailing in Colombia the criticism may be unduly harsh, but Currie is correct that to identify a sector as a "bottleneck" is not to concede that it cannot be broken. Special techniques of education which reach rural adults as well as children can wear down the traditional resistance to improved agricultural methods, and as we know from our own experience, an abundance of extension and other informational methods is feasible. The recent remarkable achievements of Mexico in raising agricultural yields and total output through a combination of domestic research and the dissemination of its findings are promising evidence that a concerted effort can overcome this bottleneck. With an estimated two million transistor radios now distributed among the isolated rural people of Latin America, it should be possible to utilize means of communication never before available.

"Technology" is so broad a term as at times to seem an abstraction, and hence a mysterious force available only to the initiated. This conception has often given Latin Americans a sense of hopeless inferiority in the face of the overwhelming technological dominance of the more advanced countries. Actually, however, technology is made up of a multitude of discrete methods and techniques, interrelated to be sure, but accessible "by the piece." This circumstance permits the less developed countries to select their own tools, based upon their peculiar needs at each stage of development and according to their respective complements of resources.

Technology, taken as a whole, is a distinctive way of thinking and acting, and it includes new modes of social organization and managerial skill in which the emphasis is on operational efficiency.[23] The absorption of technology into the culture of less developed countries must therefore proceed at various levels more or less simultaneously. Some of the structuralists have lately begun to investigate the means by which the process can be accelerated. A recent study by Aníbal Pinto examines the reasons for the unbalanced concentration of technical progress which characterizes the dual economies of Latin America and suggests ways that the disparities might be alleviated.[24] A conference on the application of science and technology to Latin American development was held in 1965 in Santiago, Chile, under the joint sponsorship of ECLA and UNESCO, and it recommended that the Latin American countries allocate as much as 1 percent of their national revenue to scientific and technical research. Although this is a much smaller amount than the industrial countries regularly spend on such activities, it would mean a substantial increase over present levels in Latin America.[25]

Institutionalists and structuralists can reinforce each other's investigations in another area. A dynamic program of development requires effective techniques of institutional reform and reconstruction. As Simon Kuznets has said in a particularly lucid passage, "The transformation of an underdeveloped country into a developed country is not merely the mechanical addition of a stock of physical capital; it is a thoroughgoing revolution in the patterns of life and a cardinal change in the relative power and position of various groups in the population. . . . The growth to higher levels of population and per capita income involves a revolutionary change in many aspects of life and must overcome the resistance of a whole complex of established interests and values."[26]

Since the structuralists are dealing with just such aspects of society, their diagnoses and prescriptions are certain to have revolutionary implications. But in what sense are their conclusions revolutionary? While clearly "left of center," structuralist views as a whole are not readily identified with a particular political position in the traditional Latin American spectrum. Their ideology, still in formation, is not cast in the Marxist mold of violent class conflict and is refreshingly free of the sloganizing which has infected most Latin American revolutionary and political reform movements. Yet specific proposals for income redistribution, agricultural reform, and other forms of economic intervention are bound to generate political opposition.

It may be helpful for the structuralists to draw on the problem-solving experience of such figures as John R. Commons, Gardiner C. Means, and Rexford G. Tugwell, whose contributions to administrative and legal reform are well summarized in Allan Gruchy's *Modern Economic Thought: The*

American Contribution.[27] Although these institutionalists were concerned with problems of organizational and political reform in another cultural context, they developed well defined conceptions of the general tactics of induced social change. Another valuable type of investigation is represented by Albert O. Hirschman's *Journeys Toward Progress,* which in three concrete problem situations in Brazil, Chile, and Colombia seeks to unearth successful instances of contrived reforms illustrating tactics which he labels "reformmongering."[28] Hirschman's studies concern the informal political and cultural mechanisms by which economic decisions are actually carried out, or frustrated, and hence go far beyond conventional methods of economic investigation.

Still another area—possibly the most important—in which institutionalists have something to contribute to structuralists is the formulation of a more comprehensive system of values. Institutionalists have long discarded the system of market prices as the ultimate basis of valuation in making normative judgements about the economy. So, it appears, have the structuralists. But many have expressed uneasiness about the lack of a new orientation, once they had cut themselves loose from economic orthodoxy. No doubt this is what Raúl Prebisch has in mind when he complains about the "ideological poverty that prevails in our countries." The same state of mind has often been described in Latin America as a "crisis of confidence." Latin Americans understandably cherish the cultural uniqueness of their civilization, yet many of their intellectual leaders, being products of that culture, seem unable to distinguish purely sentimental and ceremonial values from those that are vital to the evolution of the society.

Celso Furtado, identified with the Brazilian wing of structuralism, explains that this uncertainty is one of the reasons that Marxism has had a wide appeal among the younger generation in Brazil: "Marxism, in any of its varieties, affords a diagnosis of the social reality and a guide to action."[29] By association with these emphases, some structuralists, among them social critics and activists such as Furtado himself, have been charged with being crypto-Communists (an experience not unknown to institutionalists). Furtado, however, explicitly rejects Marxism because in its own way, particularly when applied to agricultural reform, it is a "theory of salvation through punishment" much like orthodox economics. Furtado believes that the new outlook must be rooted in "humanism and optimism concerning the material development of society."[30] What the structuralists may be looking for is the instrumentalist philosophy derived by Ayres from Dewey and illuminatingly applied to economics. Indeed, Sidney Hook has identified Ayres' philosophy as a form of "scientific humanism," though it is more than that term suggests.

. . .

Notes

1. Raúl Prebisch, *Towards a Dynamic Development Policy for Latin America* (New York: United Nations, 1963), 14.

2. Address before Pan American Society, New York, December 19, 1962, *Brazilian Bulletin* 19, no. 424 (January 1, 1963), 6.

3. For an effort in this direction, see Celso Furtado, *Development and Underdevelopment* (Berkeley: University of California Press, 1964), 52-56, 59-60, 72, 115-116.

4. Raúl Prebisch, *The Economic Development of Latin America and Its Principal Problems* (New York: United Nations, 1950), 1.

5. Hans W. Singer, "The Distribution of Gains Between Investing and Borrowing Countries," *American Economic Review* 40, no. 2 (May 1950), 473-485.

6. Raúl Prebisch, *Towards a Dynamic Development Policy*, 7, 53-54.

7. M. K. Atallah, *The Long-term Movement of the Terms of Trade Between Agricultural and Industrial Products* (Rotterdam: Nederlandsche Economische Hoogeschool, 1958).

8. Gunnar Myrdal, *Rich Lands and Poor* (New York: Harper and Brothers, 1957), 52, 101.

9. M. June Flanders, "Prebisch on Protectionism: An Evaluation," *The Economic Journal* 74, no. 294 (June 1964), 305-326. See also Gottfried Haberler, "International Trade and Economic Development," National Bank of Egypt Fiftieth Anniversary Commemoration Lectures, Cairo, 1959, reprinted in Theodore Morgan, George W. Betz, and N. K. Choudhry, eds., *Readings in Economic Development* (Belmont, California: Wadsworth Publishing Co., 1963), 240-249.

10. "Panel: International Policies," *Inflation and Growth in Latin America*, ed. Werner Baer and Isaac Kerstenetzky (Homewood, Illnois: R. D. Irwin, 1964), 465. See also, in English and Spanish editions, *How Low Income Countries Can Advance Their Own Growth* (New York: Committee for Economic Development, September, 1966), 23-29.

11. The income distribution problem is discussed by Prebisch in *Towards a Dynamic Development Policy*, 4-6, and by Osvaldo Sunkel in "The Structural Background of Development Problems in Latin America," *Weltwirtshaftliches Archiv* (Kiel) 97, no. 1 (1966), 45-47.

12. Personal conversation with the author, August 25, 1966.

13. Claudio Véliz, ed., *Obstacles to Change in Latin America* (London: Oxford University Press, 1965), 116-144.

14. The most recent of these is "En torno a Chile—Una economía difícil," *El Trimestre Económico* 33, no. 130 (April-June, 1966), 171-186.

15. Aldo Ferrer, *The Argentine Economy* (Berkeley: University of California Press, 1966); Victor L. Urquidi, *The Challenge of Development in Latin America* (New York: Frederick A. Praeger, 1964); Celso Furtado, *The Economic Growth of Brazil: A Survey from Colonial to Modern Times* (Berkeley: University of California Press, 1963); and Furtado, *Development and Underdevelopment*.

16. *Towards a Dynamic Development Policy*, 4.

17. "Compensatory Financing of Export Fluctuations: Developments in the Fund's Facility," *International Financial News Survey* 18, no. 41 (October 14, 1966),

1. The new policy was first applied to Brazil in 1963, and was announced as a general measure in *The New York Times* on September 24, 1966.

18. See Chapter 4.

19. Sunkel, "Desarrollo económico," notes for a course in economic development (mimeo.), 27.

20. *Economic Development of Central America* (New York: Committee for Economic Development, November, 1964), 34.

21. *Perfiles de progreso en Centroamérica y Panamá* (Guatemala City: U.S. Agency for International Development, 1965), 26-27.

22. L. Currie, *Accelerating Development: The Necessity and Means* (New York: McGraw-Hill, 1966), 60.

23. Cf. C. E. Ayres, *The Industrial Economy* (Boston: Houghton Mifflin, 1952), Chapter 12.

24. Aníbal Pinto, "Concentración del progreso técnico y sus frutos en el desarrollo latioamericano," *El Trimestre Económico* 32, no. 125 (January-March 1965), 3-69.

25. Felipe Herrera, statement at second plenary session of the Inter-American Development Bank, Washington, D.C., April 26, 1966 (mimeo.), 26.

26. Simon Kuznets, "Toward a Theory of Economic Growth," *Economic Growth and Structure* (New York: W. W. Norton, 1965), 30.

27. Allan Gruchy, *Modern Economic Thought: The American Contribution* (New York: Prentice-Hall, 1947).

28. Albert O. Hirschman, *Journeys Toward Progress: Studies of Economic Policy-making in Latin America* (New York: Twentieth Century Fund, 1963).

29. Celso Furtado, "Brazil: What Kind of Revolution?" *Foreign Affairs* 41, no. 3 (April 1963), 527-528.

30. Ibid., 529.

part five

Import Substitution Industrialization: Problems and Promise

Import substitution industrialization (ISI), whereby a country begins to produce goods formerly imported, has been a cornerstone of the structuralist development strategy in Latin America and the Caribbean and one that is constantly attacked by monetarist and orthodox economists for its inward-looking, antiexport bias and its alleged market inefficiency. In Chapter 8, Robert Alexander analyzes the import substitution strategy in terms of its advantages and weaknesses. The early stage of import substitution is referred to as "easy," as there is a known and ready market for the new, domestically produced consumer goods, and producers find profits relatively assured due to the tariff protection that necessarily accompanies the import substitution strategy.

Once this initial phase of ISI is more or less completed—that is, when the size limits of the market have been reached given the existing social, class, and institutional arrangements—firms must become more concerned about expanding their markets and producing goods for more selective and knowledgeable consumers, and this is when the real challenge to ISI begins. The expansion of manufacturing usually is accompanied by the neglect of agriculture, and this results in an unequal distribution of income between the urban and rural population. Marked disparities in land ownership contribute to agricultural backwardness. The relatively limited internal market characteristic of most countries becomes a pressing concern if demand for the products of domestic industry is to continue expanding. Although Alexander wrote his article more than two decades ago, this transition to a new level of general consumption that transcends the social stratification and extreme disparity of income distribution of the past has, in most Latin American countries, yet to be made. Further, Alexander presciently argued for the necessity of a dynamic agricultural transformation (which is yet to be realized), including real agrarian reform, if Latin America is to leave its underdevelopment behind (see Chapters 9 and 18).

In Chapter 9, Gustav Ranis provides an instructive comparison of the East Asian development strategy with that followed by the major Latin American countries. One important lesson is that import substitution was an integral and necessary part of the East Asian growth process and hence cannot be judged per se inappropriate in Latin America, as many orthodox economists have asserted. Nonetheless, Ranis does identify important differences in the evolution of the development processes between the two regions. The East Asian countries, he points out, at first passed from primary import substitution to primary export substitution—that is, they built up their domestic manufacture of previously imported consumer goods until they could export these same goods. These new manufactured exports began to displace primary exports in importance.

Later, the East Asian countries shifted to a type of secondary import substitution combined with secondary export substitution. In this stage, formerly imported durable consumer goods (autos, for example), intermediate, and capital goods began to be produced both for the domestic market and for export, and these exports were substituted for the simple manufactures of the previous stage of ISI. The East Asian economies, in effect, changed the pattern of their exports—from primary agriculture products to simple manufactures to more technologically advanced manufactures—while practicing more sophisticated and more efficient import substitution internally.

The path followed by the Latin American countries was different. They passed from primary import substitution to secondary import substitution without any fundamental change in the pattern of exports such as had accompanied the East Asian transition. In Latin America, primary product exports remained most important despite the capacity to produce manufactured goods, which were produced predominantly for the domestic market. The current stage of the Latin American model is not one of export substitution but of "export promotion," of pushing nontraditional exports on top of the preexisting primary product exports without fundamentally altering the pattern of subsidized, protected production.

Ranis's typology is helpful in understanding some of the differences in success between the two regions and is essential for demystifying some of the criticisms of Latin America's development model emanating from more orthodox economists. The applicability of the East Asian model, and factors explaining why the two experiences have differed, are not taken up by Ranis but are explored in some detail by James Dietz in Chapter 18.

Chapter 10 by Felipe Pazos rounds out the analysis in Part 5 of import substitution. One common criticism of ISI has been that continued high tariff protection for Latin American producers—originally justified by the "infant industry" argument—results in inefficiencies compounded by the oligopolistic structure of most industries operating in markets of relatively limited size. The result, it is argued, has been high prices for consumers, products of poor quality, and a general lack of dynamism on the part of producers, particularly in their ability to penetrate export markets. What Pazos demonstrates is that this argument is not generally valid. In the case of Brazil, for instance, some industries, even though enjoying quite high tariff protection from imports, are extremely competitive on the world market, often to the point of selling at less than world market prices. This is due to the fact that economic growth, even behind tariff protection, has led to internal competition among firms, competition that basically makes tariff protection redundant. Although it would be unwise to use these results to argue that the level of tariff protection is unimportant, they certainly do suggest that there are important internal factors to consider in understanding the level of prices, factors that go beyond the indiscriminate attack on ISI that has characterized much of the debate in the economics literature.

Further, greater competition and attention to demand and markets, which are increasingly important as the ISI strategy matures (see Chapter 8), take place even behind high tariff walls as export production is stimulated. Complacency and inefficiency are not the necessary results of industrial protection. Contrary to Ranis's argument, Pazos suggests that increased Latin American exports have been the result of the maturation of industry, not of subsidies that have artificially pushed export expansion. With the proper technology, Latin American industry can be, and has been, as productive and efficient as industry anywhere in the world.

chapter eight

The Import Substitution Strategy of Economic Development

Robert J. Alexander

The countries which follow the import substitution strategy generally passed first through a phase in which a sector which was modern and was attached to the world economy was developed alongside but separate from a traditional, largely self-sufficient economy. This process began during the last part of the nineteenth century in most Latin American countries—and in many Asian and African ones—and continued, more or less, until the World Depression of 1929. It was stimulated or brought about by the fact that the early industrial countries of Western and Central Europe and of Northern America did not possess within their borders sufficient sources of key raw materials and foodstuffs. They did not have tropical agricultural products; they did not possess sufficient quantities of minerals such as nitrates, copper, zinc, lead, tin and, later, petroleum.

In order to obtain these, the early industrial nations invested large sums in the countries of Latin America, Africa and Asia, which had traditional economies and societies of one kind or another—from those of the Stone Age to the ancient civilizations of India and China. Their investments opened up modern mines and modern plantations. They developed the transportation systems—principally railroads—necessary to get goods to the ports from which they were shipped to Europe or North America. They also built the ports to handle these goods; they likewise provided modern banking systems and commercial enterprises necessary to handle the goods being shipped to the already industrialized nations, as well as handling those commodities brought back in payment.

Reprinted in abridged form from the *Journal of Economic Issues* 1 (December 1967) by special permission of the copyright holder, the Association for Evolutionary Economics.

The net result of all this was the development, alongside the traditional economy and society, of a sector which was modern, both sociologically and economically. This sector was closely tied to the world market, its prosperity depending entirely on whether the one or two major export products of the country could be sold at good prices and in ample quantities. The economy of the modern sector, therefore, became very unstable and highly subject to influences from abroad.

At the same time, this process brought into existence new economic and social classes. It developed a new middle class, tied to the commerce of the modern sector; and it also involved large numbers of white-collar workers in private employment and in the government services which greatly expanded in consequence of the development of the modern sector. Likewise, a new manual working class developed to man the modern mines, the modern plantations, the railroads, the ports, and the incipient new industries which began to emerge as the result of the considerable expansion of the domestic market.

These new social and economic groups were discontented with the *status quo ante.* They were unhappy at the continued control of the society, the economy and politics by the traditional ruling elite—be it native landowners or tribal chiefs, or composed of colonial administrators. However, particularly in countries such as those of Latin America where political colonialism did not exist, these new groups were not powerful enough to challenge effectively the *ancien régime* until the countries had moved substantially into the next phase of development.

The second stage of economic development, in conformity with the import substitution process, arose as a result of interference with the export-import pattern established earlier. The first such shock came during World War I, when it became exceedingly difficult for the economically dependent, or "colonial," countries to obtain the manufactured goods they were by then accustomed to receiving from Europe and the United States. As a result, the people of these nations either had to do without these goods or produce them domestically. In many of the underdeveloped countries, consequently, the process of industrialization really received its first great impetus during World War I.

Once World War I was over, many of these early industries could not meet the competition coming from European and North American manufacturers. However, soon after the war came the Great Depression, during which the same phenomenon occurred as had taken place a decade earlier, only in an exaggerated form. It was the depression which convinced public opinion in the underdeveloped countries which were politically independent that there was need for a conscious policy of industrialization and general economic development.

World War II, following hard on the heels of the depression, confirmed this belief. As former colonies achieved their independence in the postwar period, their leaders were imbued with the same conviction of the need for rapid economic development and, most important of all, for industrialization. Hence, since the Great Depression and particularly since the war, the governments of the underdeveloped nations have been following policies, such as protectionism, the building of social capital and even the financing of new manufacturing industries, which make the import substitution mode of development possible.

Market Situation in Import Substitution Industrialization

The most significant single fact about the import substitution strategy of development, which most underdeveloped countries adopted, consciously or unconsciously, is that as a result of it the size of the market is not a problem of major significance in the first phase of industrialization. A new industry, built to turn out a product which has formerly been imported, possesses from its inception an assured market of predictable size. One set of statistics which even most underdeveloped countries possess is that concerning imports and exports, since most government revenues come, in the early phases of development, from taxes on the country's foreign trade. Hence, it is relatively simple to ascertain the quantity of a given product which has been imported—and therefore the national market for that product which is available when an import substitution industry is established.

Furthermore, the import substitution process tends to expand the market more or less automatically, at least for a while. The workers recruited into these new industries from the nonmarket sectors of the economy, or from employment in which their productivity and income were much smaller than they are in industry, receive a money income on which they principally depend to obtain the goods and services they need, and so serve to expand the market for consumer goods. In addition, the development of consumer industries tends to create a market for some capital goods. Thus, the existence of a sizeable textile industry, for instance, gives rise to a market for textile machinery, or at least replacement parts. In turn, the existence of a textile-machine industry, certain kinds of metallurgical fabricating enterprises, and so forth, may provide the market after a while for a steel industry.

As a result of these circumstances, the entrepreneurs are faced with the happy situation in which, for a time at least, they do not have to be very much preoccupied with the problem of expanding the market for their goods. Their problem is one of meeting the demand which is open to them rather than of generating new markets.

Effects of Market Situation

The fact that new industries being established under the import substitution scheme of development do not have to be preoccupied with trying to augment the number of their customers serves to explain, and make rational, many phenomena which are otherwise difficult to understand in the early phases of industrialization. It helps to explain the relatively little attention paid to such matters as the training of management, the formal training of a labor force, costs of production, quality control and advertising. It also goes far to explain the attitude which leaders of many of the newly industrializing nations have toward the agricultural sector of their economies, and the attitudes which the industrialist class has toward rural problems.

There is relatively little need in the early phases of import substitution industrialization to pay great attention to the development of a highly trained managerial force. Most native industries tend to grow from artisans' workshops or from commercial enterprises which begin to produce some of the things they sell. These entrepreneurs are self-made men who have learned to run an industry by running it and whose methods may be quite unscientific, though sufficiently expert for the needs of the early period of industrialization. The higher costs of production growing out of inefficient management are no great problem because they can easily be passed on to the consumer, who is forced in any case to buy nationally made goods [due to high tariffs].

Similarly, the problem of developing a highly efficient manual labor force does not have the urgency that, *a priori,* one might expect it to have, and for much the same reason. An inefficient worker, learning his skills "on the line" by working alongside an older self-taught employee, undoubtedly makes for relatively high costs of production. But these costs, too, can be passed on more or less easily to the purchaser of the product.

Quality control can also well be overlooked in the first phase of import substitution industrialization. Even though in the abstract the consumer might prefer to buy a foreign-made good the quality of which he could depend upon, he has in fact no such choice. With time, perhaps he even gets used to the varying nature of the products he purchases.

Furthermore, during this phase, there is relatively little need for advertising. Anyone who has spoken with members of advertising firms in the underdeveloped countries will be aware of the difficulty they have in selling local entrepreneurs on the need for advertising and of the fact that most advertising volume comes from foreign firms. This sales resistance is rational, given the circumstances. Again, the readily available markets make heavy advertising unnecessary. Firms which are affiliates of foreign enterprises, particularly [U.S.] ones, may engage in advertising, but they perhaps do it more as a reflection of the experiences of their parent companies than as a function of real need in the developing country.

This situation of lack of concern over the consumer's reactions, in terms of price and quality, is augmented by two other factors which are often, if not usually, present in the developing countries. One of these is the existence of inflation, a generally rising price level, which makes less conspicuous—and hence less damaging to the individual industrialist—the increase in the price of a particular manufactured item. The second is the fact that competition is relatively limited during this phase, there being only a small number of producers who are more engaged in absorbing the purchasing power which is readily available than they are in trying to take markets away from the few competitors who may exist.

The Situation of Agriculture

The market circumstances surrounding import substitution industrialization go far to explain the situation of agriculture during the early phases of the process. It has been widely noted that there is a tendency in the new, industrializing countries more or less to ignore agriculture. It has also been noted that the industrialists tend to be little concerned with the need for agrarian reform, which (other things being equal) appears to be necessary for the continued rapid development of industry itself. Both of these phenomena make sense in the early phases of the development of a country which is using the import substitution process for expansion of its manufacturing and tertiary sectors.

That part of the agricultural sector which has not become involved in producing for export generally remains very backward, technologically and socially, in the underdeveloped countries. In most of these nations (with the possible exception of Black Africa) there exists a system of large landholdings, in which the land is tilled by workers employed under some form of sharecropping or tenant farming or else are engaged at exceedingly low wages. Those who work the land are essentially subsistence farmers with little or no money income. The money income that is generated in this segment of agriculture goes mainly to absentee landlords, living in the urban areas or abroad.

However, there is little pressure to do anything about these conditions of agriculture during the early phases of import substitution industrialization. In the first place, in almost all underdeveloped countries there is a good deal of hidden unemployment or surplus employment in agriculture. It is thus possible to recruit the new industrial labor force from those who are marginally employed in the rural sector. At the same time, their migration into urban areas does not decrease the output of agriculture; it perhaps even results in some increase in productivity and output in the rural part of the economy. In many instances, too, there is some spillover into agriculture from the introduction of new techniques and new capital in the manufacturing sector, which at least for a while may be enough to bring about some increase in agricultural output.

It is true, of course, that the rapid increase in the urban population which accompanies industrialization has a tendency to increase the demand for foodstuffs, while the growth of manufacturing results more or less automatically in an increase of demand for agriculturally produced raw materials. However, for some considerable period of time, this increased demand for foodstuffs and raw materials can be met by imports. The development of domestic industries producing goods which were formerly brought in from outside makes available the foreign exchange which was formerly spent on these manufactured goods and which can now be used to pay for food and raw-material imports.

Thus it is not surprising that in the process of import substitution industrialization there is a tendency to ignore agriculture. Not only is relatively little attention given to raising agricultural output by investment in the rural sector, but little is done to bring about changes in the landholding pattern which might bring a larger portion of the agricultural population into the market.

The fact that the expansion of the available market is not a major problem for new manufacturing enterprises, together with the fact that the foreign exchange which was formerly used to pay for industrial products is now available to bring in food and raw materials, means that in this phase of development there is little pressure from the urban sector for changes in agriculture. The manufacturers and other groups in the cities are loathe to see any appreciable amount of the country's scarce capital resources invested in agriculture, at the expense of industry and its needs. At the same time, the industrialist sees little immediate need for an agrarian reform, which might actually bring large proportions of the rural sharecroppers and tenants into the market for manufactured goods for the first time. At this point, the manufacturer is likely to be more concerned with the general dangers to private property—including his own—which are raised by any suggestion to redistribute large landholdings than he is with any long-run advantages which might accrue to him from converting new small landholders into customers for his products.

In any case, even if industrialists as a group were to favor agrarian reform, it is doubtful that they would have sufficient political influence in most cases to bring about such a change. There is a tendency for the traditional landlords to retain political influence out of all proportion to their numbers and economic power throughout most of the import substitution process.

Nor is there much demand in the rural sector itself for either technological or land tenure change. There is no great demand from either the conservative small peasant or from the very conservative large landowner for the introduction of new methods and hence the investment of sizeable amounts of capital in agriculture. The peasant is satisfied to do things as his ancestors have always done them; in fact, he may not yet have the needs which give him incentive to produce more, even if he becomes convinced that he can do so. The large landowner is satisfied with the living which his present methods give him; he is likely to be engaged in conspicuous consumption and to be spending all or virtually all of his current income. He therefore sees little need to take part of what he is spending on consumption and invest it in new methods and machinery. All the less is he inclined to do so when he still has available large quantities of very cheap labor, which would only be made superfluous by his adopting a more capital-intensive method of production. In fact, an appreciable part of his real income and much of his social prestige arise from the sizeable number of personal retainers he is able to maintain under the traditional conditions of agricultural production.

There is not even likely to be much pressure from the tenant farmers or sharecroppers for agrarian reform in the early phases of import substitution industrialization. The more aggressive members of this class are likely to be siphoned off to the cities to work in the new industries or in tertiary activities. For a long time those who remain behind will not have any feeling that social mobility within the rural structure is a possibility for them; and until they do become convinced that it is possible, they are not likely to demand a change in conditions which seem to have existed virtually forever and to have been determined by the gods.

This lack of significant pressure from either the urban sector or from within agriculture itself for changes in the rural part of the economy during the early phases of import substitution helps to explain one phenomenon which has worried many economists of the already industrialized countries. In spite of the constantly reiterated advice of these foreign experts, the industrializing countries for the most part have stubbornly resisted the suggestion that they need "balanced development," that is, that the growth and diversification of agriculture should accompany the development of industry. Within the conditions of import substitution industrialization, there is for a long period of time no particular incentive, as we have indicated, for government authorities or anyone else to put major emphasis on agricultural development. During this phase, it is quite rational for the public authorities and also the private investors to concentrate their efforts on manufacturing and the services needed to facilitate it, such as electric power and certain transportation facilities. It would involve a misallocation of resources for sizeable quantities to be diverted in this period to the development of the rural economy.

The Crisis of the Import Substitution Strategy

Sooner or later the import substitution strategy of development reaches a point of exhaustion. A point is reached at which an economy has installed virtually all those kinds of industries which can produce commodities formerly imported. At this juncture, the nature of the development problem changes. Instead of being the largely physical one of mounting industries to produce goods for which there is already a market, it becomes one of amplifying existing markets—if the process of development and growth is to continue.

This shift in the nature of the economic-development problem has implications both for the individual enterprise and for the industrial sector as a whole. The individual firm is likely to be faced with a great deal more competition than was previously the case. There will then be only two ways for a firm to expand its sales: either by taking customers away from rival enterprises or by developing customers among those who have not been in the market for its goods at all. If a firm's management, unaccustomed to real competition in the early phases of industrialization, is inclined to continue in its old ways and habits developed in the period when an adequate market could safely be taken for granted, it is likely to run into serious trouble. A more aggressive competitor is apt to begin to take away customers. Furthermore, once the supply of a given industrial product has caught up with the existing demand, the customers are likely to become more selective than was formerly the case.

All of this means that many things which could previously be overlooked now become matters requiring the urgent attention of the management of individual industrial enterprises. One way to increase the market for specific products in a competitive situation is to reduce their prices; thus, entrepreneurs will find themselves forced to become interested in and concerned with the problem of reducing costs and rationalizing their operations. Another method of increasing the individual firm's market will be to assure the customers of a higher degree of uniformity of quality than was formerly the case, and so quality control will assume an importance it did not have in the early phases of import substitution development. Because of these changes in market conditions, firms will be forced to pay more attention to the quality and performance of their management personnel. They will find new incentive to try to develop a better trained and more efficient labor force.

From the point of view of the industrial sector as a whole, new conditions will now demand a new outlook and new policies. With the virtual completion of the import substitution phase of industrialization, it will be to the advantage of the manufacturing firms as a group to bring about an increase in the purchasing power of large segments of consumers who have been in the market but whose incomes have been so low as to permit them to buy only relatively small amounts of goods, and to bring into the market those parts of the population which have hitherto been outside of it.

The first problem will involve particularly the urban wage earners who constitute a substantial proportion of the market for consumer goods. Although their real-income levels have been substantially higher in the import substitution phase than the incomes of most rural workers, they have generally remained well below comparative wages in the older industrialized countries. An increase in their real wages can constitute an important increase in existing markets. The increase in the real purchasing power of this group will require both an increase in their productivity and a rise in their share of the returns from what they produce. The laborers' need for greater productivity makes the increased concern for costs and quality, which we noted as being to the advantage of each individual firm, to the advantage of the industrial sector as a whole. The laborers' need for a larger share of their product will require a change in the psychology of the industrial entrepreneur, who has tended in the import substitution phase of development to stick rather too closely to the habit of the traditional merchant of turning out relatively small amounts of product at a large markup per unit. The psychology of mass production will contribute considerably to the possibility of mass consumption.

The need for bringing into the market those elements which heretofore have been largely out of it will require fundamental changes in agriculture. An agrarian reform now becomes of great importance, both as a means of bringing new consumers into the market—the large numbers of rural workers, sharecroppers, tenant farmers who have not been in the market—and of laying a basis for an increase in domestic agricultural output, thus making it possible for agriculture to produce more adequately the raw materials and foodstuffs required by the urban sector.

In addition, it becomes important at this point to have heavy investment in agriculture, in terms both of providing equipment and machinery, and of developing more adequate marketing and storage facilities and providing fertilizers, credit, extension services, experimental stations and the like. Large investments will also be required to develop adequate transportation facilities, not only in terms of major highways and perhaps occasional railroads, but also neighborhood roads permitting the agriculturalists to get their products to the main transportation arteries.

Applicability of Import Substitution Model

So far, few of the underdeveloped countries have reached the third phase in the import substitution strategy of economic development. Virtually all of the developing countries in Asia and Africa, as well as most of those in Latin America, would seem to be still at a stage in which their industrialization is proceeding on the basis of building industries which can produce import substitutes. However, there are a few Latin American countries—notably Brazil, Chile, Mexico and Argentina, as well perhaps as Venezuela, Colombia and Peru—which have completely or nearly exhausted import substitution possibilities, at least as a major impetus to further development.

The problem faced by these Latin American nations which have reached the end of import substitution indicate that the transition to the post-import-substitution phase is not easy. Chile underwent more than a decade of crisis, during which its economy tended to stagnate, and the political life of the country was marked by a high degree (for Chile) of instability. Brazil has been experiencing a very similar crisis since the exhaustion of import sub-stitution possibilities with the end of the Juscelino Kubitschek administra-tion in 1961. Even Mexico has found it difficult to switch to the emphasis on investment in agriculture which its situation has required.

However, it is noteworthy that certain of the requirements of the third phase of development which we have discussed are being increasingly rec-ognized in these countries. Schools of business, designed to train profes-sional managers, are appearing in increasing numbers. Unaccustomed atten-tion is being given to the training of manual workers in the skills required by the new industrial society. Industrialists in some of the countries have shown a new interest in an agrarian reform, either supporting it or at least remaining neutral on the subject. The governments are increasingly turning their attention to the capital needs as well as to the requirements for reform of the agricultural sector.

We would not suggest that the strategy or model of import substitution industrialization which we have outlined in this article is applicable in every detail to all of the countries which in general are following it. In Mexico, for instance, agrarian reform preceded the main spurt of import substitution industrialization, while in Venezuela the two things have been occurring simultaneously. In some cases, undoubtedly, frequent contacts with United States businessmen have developed an interest in more scientific organiza-tion of individual enterprises considerably before the conditions of the na-tional market would have engendered such interest. Other divergences from the pattern undoubtedly could be found in particular countries.

chapter nine

Challenges and Opportunities Posed by Asia's Superexporters: Implications for Manufactured Exports from Latin America

Gustav Ranis

The process of enhanced differentiation within the developing world in the course of the past two decades has been especially marked by the emergence of the so-called SICs or semi-industrialized countries. The new prominence of this fast growing middle tier of countries, along with the dramatic rise of OPEC, has been instrumental in transforming the landscape within the South, as well as relations between North and South. To the naked eye, moreover, it would appear that the members of this middle class of developing countries have experienced a similar pattern of development over the past two decades—characterized by high overall growth rates and an especially rapid growth of manufacturing, including a rise in manufacturing exports. On closer examination, however, we may become convinced that there really are two very distinct types of SICs to consider, one which may in shorthand—and imperfectly—be called the Latin American type, the second the East Asian type.

This distinction focuses on two important and related dimensions of performance—one having to do with marked differences in the underlying success of their industrial export performance, the other with the internal balance between growth and distributional outcomes. Moreover, I shall examine the causes of the divergence which lie partly in differences in the endowment conditions and partly in the nature of the policy choices made over time in the two subsets of countries.

The East Asian SICs both pose a challenge and present an opportunity to their Latin American counterparts. The challenge is best summarized by their substantially superior industrial export performance over the past two

Reprinted with permission from *The Quarterly Review of Economics and Business* 21 (Champaign, IL: Bureau of Economic and Business Research, University of Illinois, Summer 1981).

decades which has worried not only the developed countries. The opportunity is represented by the extent their example happens to be relevant to current Latin American trade and development objectives.

I

Any effort to "explain" the contrasting export performance of the East Asian and Latin American SICs leads toward the acceptance of the notion that some sort of underlying typological approach to development makes sense. This means that we believe in the existence of a family affinity among some of the Latin American SICs, for example, Argentina, Brazil, Colombia, and Mexico, just as there exists a family affinity among some of the East Asian SICs, for example, Korea, Taiwan, Hong Kong, and Singapore. It clearly does *not* mean that we believe important, and conceptually instructive, differences do not exist within any one subfamily of LDCs; Latin Americans, in particular, will rightly bridle at the notion of "the" Latin American case. Rather, it means that intratypology variances in either endowment or behavior may be less marked than across typologies, and that this methodological approach, while admittedly somewhat casual, may nevertheless be analytically useful.

Developing countries' attempted transitions to modern growth are necessarily circumscribed by their initial conditions, including their colonial heritage, and other economic-geographic factors such as resource endowment, location, and so on. The historical experience we have been able to analyze to date, moreover, permits us to formulate an "evolutionary" view of development, that is, one based on the identification of subphases of transition characterized by somewhat differing structures and changing modes of operation among the three main sectors, agriculture, nonagriculture, and foreign. Such phases, of course, represent a combination of economic progressions and changing policy packages, with a good deal of filling and backing and many "gray areas." In discussing movements between one phase and the next we are, moreover, talking about gradual changes in the way the system is driven rather than anything either abrupt or complete. Nor, I wish to emphasize, is there anything inevitable about any particular sequence of phases. I shall, however, find it useful to contrast the actual Latin American and East Asian SIC experience from this longitudinal vantage point. The interplay between the forces of a dynamically changing endowment picture and the intervention of policies either to accommodate or mute these forces is, of course, an essential element in analyzing these contrasts in phasing and performance.

The family affinity among the Latin American SICs can be summarized in terms of their joint Iberian colonial heritage, a relatively early start for their postcolonial transition growth effort, their fairly large size (on the average), and their endowment which is relatively natural-resources-rich but characterized generally by remaining pockets of a not very literate unskilled labor surplus on the land. At the beginning of serious postcolonial transition growth efforts—whether these are dated more appropriately in the 1880s or the 1930s—we are left with the heritage of a colonial period which focused heavily on extractive primary export activities within a preassigned scheme of the international division of labor.

In contrast, the East Asian SICs are relatively smaller-sized and located in a population-dense and natural-resources-poor region, with favorable levels of literacy for a large labor surplus population and a colonial experience which varied between British entrepôt interests in the (for us) less interesting city states of Hong Kong and Singapore, and heavy Japanese attention to the rural sector and the extraction of food crops in the more relevant cases of Korea and Taiwan.

The two contrasting colonial or pretransition phases may be pictured in panel 1 of Figure 9.1. Under colonialism both the Latin American and the East Asian NICs' agricultural sector A produces the domestic food supply (D_f) for households H plus exportable goods (X_a) which help "finance" the import of nondurable consumer goods (M_{cn}) flowing from the foreign sector F. Given the relative larger size of the typical Latin American case more domestic industries supplying a portion of the domestic market for, say, textiles undoubtedly existed, but large portions of the domestic market for these goods were satisfied via imports in both cases. Another difference, not captured by the chart, resides in the commodity content of the primary export, consisting generally of minerals and raw materials requiring very specific kinds of large-scale infrastructural investments (ports, railways) in the case of Latin America, and of rice and sugar, requiring generally small-scale infrastructural investments (irrigation, roads), as well as organizational innovations (for example, land reform and the creation of farmers' associations) in the case of East Asia.

Both the East Asian and Latin American SICs—as virtually all other LDCs—initiated their transition effort by moving into primary import substitution (PIS) during their respective postindependence periods. According to this pattern, captured in panel 2, an increasing portion of the primary product earnings (X_a) is diverted from the importation of nondurable consumer goods (M_{cn}) and toward the importation of producer goods (M_p) which permit the emergence and growth of so-called primary import substitution industries in the nonagricultural sector NA which is now able to produce these textiles (D_{cn}) to substitute gradually for the previously imported variety (M_{cn}) in the domestic market. It is this subphase of growth, fueled by primary product exports (and, of course, supplemented by foreign capital imports) that entails several statistically observable substitution phenomena, including the gradual reduction of consumer goods imports relative to producer goods imports. Panels (2a) and (2b) are again vir-

Figure 9.1   Transition Phases

	East Asian SICs	Latin-American SICs
1. Pretransition	(1a) Colonial structure	(1b) Colonial structure
2. Initial transition subphase	(2a) PIS growth (1953-63)	(2b) PIS growth (1880-1950) 1930
3. Second transition subphase	(3a) PES growth (1963-72)	(3b) SIS growth (1950-70)
4. Third transition subphase	(4a) SIS/SES growth (1973-present)	(4b) SIS/EP growth (1970-present)

tually equivalent, with one significant exception, that is, there may be need for some net imports of food (M_f), even at this stage, in some of the Latin American SICs.

The overall performance of the two systems during the PIS subphase is not so very different on the surface (see the Appendix Country Statistical Indicator Tables at the end of this chapter). Per capita income growth rates (row 1) were modest, if respectable, with the relative reallocation of the labor force to nonagriculture Θ (row 2) proceeding rapidly in both cases. The economies, even the smaller ones of East Asia, remain basically inward-oriented, as the often-recited interventionist package of protectionist industrial and foreign exchange policies trend the system toward autarky. Saving rates (row 3) are modest, investment rates (row 4) substantial, and distributional indicators, where available (row 5 and 6), heavily influenced by relatively low rates of employment generation, everywhere generally unsatisfactory.

On fuller examination, however, we may note the existence of underlying differences even during this subphase which yield their repercussions on performance later on. One has to do with the relatively better performance of agricultural productivity in the East Asian case, as a consequence of the combination of their better colonial "preparation," and a lesser relative neglect during the primary import substitution phase itself. Second, the level of effective protection was generally lower in the East Asian than in the Latin American case, making its contribution to a somewhat lower temperature in the industrial hothouse. This is important in assessing the more recent experience of these two types of SICs. As traditional land-based entrepreneurs are converted into industrial entrepreneurs, the level of protection and of profit transfer needs to be high enough for infant industry reasons but not so high or persistent as to discourage entrepreneurial maturation.

As is well known, this process of primary import substitution (PIS) growth must inevitably terminate once all nondurable consumer goods imports (M_{cn}) have been substituted for by domestic output (D_{cn}); further industrialization of this type, directed to the domestic market, then has to slow to the pace of population plus per capita income growth. Another indicator of the exhaustion of PIS is the decline of the M_{cn}/M ratio which, as Table 9.1 indicates, reaches a low-level plateau in most cases by the early 1960s. Larger countries as represented by the Latin American SICs may take a longer time to reach domestic market saturation in this sense—witness the fact that Latin America took at least twenty years (1930–1950) to arrive at this point (possibly much longer, 1880–1950) while the East Asian SICs took approximately a decade, 1953–63.

The societal decisions reached to avoid a cul de sac at this point in the transition growth effort may be the most important in explaining the more recent divergence in the performance of our two types of SICs. Once PIS came to its inevitable end, the East Asian SICs moved into primary export substitution as their second transition phase, while their Latin American counterparts continued with import substitution but now of the secondary (or capital and consumer durable goods) type (see Panel 3).

In the East Asian case (Panel 3a) we now encounter the new phenomenon of primary export substitution (PES), that is, the export of the same non-durable consumer goods into world markets. Such penetration is facilitated by the increased ability of the now more experienced industrial entrepreneurs to combine with the abundance of unskilled labor while taking advantage of accommodating changes in the overall economic policy package in the direction of lower protection and increased liberalization in various markets. The emergence of a new type of unskilled-labor-based export (X_{cn}), gradually replacing the traditional primary product export (X_a), is due to both negative and positive factors. Negatively, the basic limitation of natural resources—quite aside from the running out of domestic markets for nondurable consumer goods—will force a change in the structure and operation of the system. Positively, the gradual building up of the system's human resources provides the ingredients for the establishment of efficiency-oriented industries which send labor-embodying manufactured goods to world, especially developed country, markets.

The sustained march of primary export substitution in the East Asian SICs of Korea and Taiwan during the 1960s and early 1970s can be captured by the rapidly rising proportion of total exports which are manufactured (see Appendix Country Statistical Indicators, row 9). Moreover, the rapidly rising overall growth of exports and participation of these systems in the world economy is documented by the growth of total exports (row 10) and of the external orientation ratio X/GNP (row 11), which has reached perhaps the highest levels in the world (50 percent) in Korea and Taiwan.

It is this rapid increase in industrial exports which has earned the East Asian SICs the title of superexporter and which has drawn the attention of

Table 9.1   Primary Import Substitution (M_{cn}/M)[a]

Country	1950	1962	1970	1977
Brazil	4.1(53)	2.52	3.43	2.17
Colombia	12.8(51)	5.37	5.08	6.08(75)
Argentina	14.4	5.21	6.28	3.71(76)
Mexico	5.8	4.30	5.67	4.56(74)
Chile	4.4(52)	4.37	4.53(71)	2.32(74)
Korea	—	8.0	7.4	5.0
Taiwan	17.2(53)[b]	8.1(60)[b]	5.8	2.9

Sources: U.N. *Commodity Trade Statistics, Statistical Papers,* Series D, Taiwan 1977: monthly trade figures, Taiwan Statistical Office. *U.N. Yearbook of International Trade Statistics,* 1950.

[a] Consumer nondurable (*cn*) industries = 61 leather, 65 textiles, 84 clothing, 851 footwear, 892 printed matter, 64 paper, paperboard.
[b] Computation not completely comparable to others due to lack of SITC data.

both the DCs and the Latin American SICs. It is based, of course, on what constitutes a remarkable domestic development performance which has drawn less attention—namely, the ability of the export-oriented industrial sector to absorb quickly its unemployed and underemployed labor at fairly stable real wages. The pursuit of such an employment-sensitive growth path, aided by a strategy of small-scale, rural-oriented industrialization and even faster (than earlier) agricultural productivity change yielded not only extremely rapid rates of per capita income increase but also the achievement of good and improving income distribution performance—even before all the labor surplus was mopped up by the early 1970s. Once the Asian SICs' labor surpluses had run out, first in Taiwan, then in Korea, real wages began to rise and the comparative advantage in labor-intensive manufactured goods gradually disappeared.

As a consequence, the East Asian countries' industrial output mix shifted toward more skilled labor, technology, and capital-intensive goods, both for the domestic and then the export markets. This so-called secondary import cum secondary export substitution phase (see Panel 4a) reinforces elements already present in the earlier subphases, that is, moving along the product cycle in continuing response to gradual changes in the endowment. Capital goods and consumer durables, and so on, are now produced for the home market (D_{cd}) and exported (X_{cd}). A related phenomenon is the more or less complete atrophy over time of the domestic agricultural sector, an activity in which the East Asian SICs do not have a long-run comparative advantage. As a consequence we may note that food imports (M_f) became necessary from the beginning in Hong Kong and Singapore, quite early in Korea (which did less well with its own rural sector), and currently in Taiwan. The international market responsiveness of the East Asian SICs during this period is best demonstrated by their ability to overcome formal and informal quota arrangements in the advanced countries, international recession, inflation, and even the post-1973 OPEC crisis. This is not to say that the current crisis in the world economy is leaving the East Asian SICs entirely unscathed—witness the large foreign debt of Korea, for example—but that an amazing record of growth and export performance has been compiled over the past two decades in spite of all this.

In the case of the Latin American SICs, in contrast, once primary import substitution industrialization ended, around 1950, the system moved directly into a secondary import substitution (SIS) phase (see Panel 3b). This meant the establishment of more skilled labor-, capital-, and technology-intensive industries capable of producing previously imported capital goods and consumer durables and processing raw materials previously processed abroad (D_{cd}). It also meant a continuation of development *hacia adentro,* including the maintenance, if not intensification and broadening—now to include capital goods, and so on—of the protectionist- and controls-oriented policy structure of the previous phase. Table 9.2 indicates the com-

Table 9.2   Effective Protection, Circa 1967

Industry	South Korea 1968		Brazil 1967		Philippines 1965	
	Balassa Measure	Corden Measure	Balassa Measure	Corden Measure	Balassa Measure	Corden Measure
Agriculture, forestry, and fishing	18.5	17.9	10	10	0	0
Processed food	-18.2	-14.2	5.5	40	47	46
Beverages and tobacco	-19.3	-15.5	334	155	15	15
Mining and Energy	4.0	3.5	14	13	-25	-25
Construction materials	-11.5	-8.8	47	29	50	50
Intermediate products I	-25.5	-18.8	—	—	16	16
Intermediate products II	26.1	17.4	—	—	88	85
Nondurable consumer goods	-10.5	-8.0	49	67	55	53
Consumer durables	64.4	39.8	70	101	1,355	1,062
Machinery	44.2	29.5	57	75	112	10.3
Transport equipment	163.5	83.5	47	60	77	75

Sources: S. Korea: Charles R. Frank, Kwang Suk Kim, and Larry E. Westphal, *Foreign Trade Regimes and Economic Development: South Korea* (New York: Columbia University Press, 1975); Brazil and Philippines: Bela Balassa and others, *The Structure of Protection in Developing Countries* (Baltimore: Johns Hopkins Press, 1971).

parative level of effective protection in the mid-1960s for a representative of each of the SIC families as well as for the Philippines (about which more later). The extent of protection on nondurable consumer goods is negative in Korea at this point but substantial elsewhere. With respect to consumer and capital goods, on the other hand, we note much higher effective protection rates in the case of both Brazil and the Philippines. Moving directly into SIS regimes thus meant none of the major shifts in the direction of exchange rate and other market liberalizations which the East Asian SICs had undertaken in the early 1960s.

Another, and closely related, distinguishing feature of the Latin American case is, of course, their continued relative abundance of natural resources, which permits the continued exportation of traditional raw materials and/or the supplementation of traditional by new ones (X_a). Unlike the East Asian case where import substitution, of whatever kind, is necessarily somewhat short-lived, in Latin America it can continue to be fueled even as it becomes more and more "expensive" in terms of possibly increasing deviations from socially optimal industrial output mixes and technologies.

By the late 1960s and early 1970s secondary import substitution in Latin America had generally been modified to include export promotion (see Panel 4b). This, in contrast to export substitution, we define as the selective encouragement of particular industries or even firms by administrative action in order to "push out" exports in the absence of a general change in the structure of protection, or market liberalization. Export promotion requires subsidization either via public sector fiscal transfers, interest rate differentials, tariff rebates, and so on, or alternatively, via private sector subsidization or price discrimination induced or cajoled by assuring the same companies a continuation of high windfall profits in protected domestic markets. The increase in industrial export orientation here is caused not by a product cycle type of evolution resulting from increased entrepreneurial maturation responding to changing resource endowment and accompanied by accommodating changes in general economic policy. Instead, it is the consequence of additional controls and incentives planted "on top of" the existing import substitution superstructure. Domestic content and export targets are imposed, as the overall protective veils on intermediate inputs and on relative prices governing primary inputs are left intact. As industrial exports have become increasingly recognized as a "good thing"—even by Prebisch and his ECLA followers—commodities up the technology and capital intensity ladder have moved into domestic production (D_{cd}) and exports (X_{cd}), most often sequentially, sometimes simultaneously. Automobile assembly is a case in point as increasing domestic component requirements are linked with increased export quotas.

The Latin American SIC development path is clearly much less overall export-oriented (see *X/GNP* in Appendix Country Statistical Indicators, row 11), and with a lower proportion of manufactured exports than the East Asian cases. Note that the proportion of the population in nonagriculture Θ (see row 2) is not that different across the two types of SICs by the mid-1970s, the end of the period; but notice also that the rate of increase in Θ over the past twenty years has been much more pronounced in the East Asian cases—in spite of the relatively higher population growth rates during that period in Latin America.

The relative neglect of food-producing agriculture seems to have continued, perhaps even been exacerbated, during the Secondary Import Substitution/Export Promotion (SIS/EP) phase. As Table 9.3 indicates, the representative East Asian SICs start with somewhat higher cereal yields than the Latin American SICs in 1950 (with other, natural-resource-rich, Asian LDCs somewhat intermediate); but what is most impressive is the divergence in yield growth rates thereafter. Net food imports (M_f) have become an increasingly important factor in these relatively natural-resource-rich Latin American SICs (for example, Mexico) over time. Export cash crops which are generally likely to be less labor-intensive than domestic food crops are favored by a research and relative price intervention system geared to the need to

Table 9.3   Indexes of Major Cereal Crop Yields[a] (annual growth in parentheses)

	1948-52	1952-56	1961	1965	1970	1975	1977
			(Mexico 1950 = 100)				
Taiwan	309	375	427	531	532	529	571
	(5.0)	(2.2)	(5.6)	(0.0)	(-0.1)	(3.9)	
South Korea	483	445	553	513	617	710	904
	(-2.0)	(3.7)	(-1.8)	(4.7)	(2.8)	(12.8)	
Brazil	168	159	175	184	182	208	218
	(-5.3)	(1.6)	(1.3)	(-0.3)	(2.7)	(2.4)	
Mexico	100	108	132	149	162	169	162
	(1.9)	(3.4)	(3.1)	(2.1)	(0.8)	(-2.1)	
Malaysia	220	235	294	294	323	355	361
	(1.7)	(3.8)	(0.0)	(2.3)	(1.9)	(0.8)	
Philippines	157	160	164	175	221	229	261
	(0.4)	(0.4)	(1.6)	(6.0)	(0.7)	(6.8)	
			(1950 yield = 100)				
Taiwan	100	121	138	172	172	171	185
South Korea	100	92	115	106	128	147	187
Brazil	100	94	104	110	108	124	130
Mexico	100	108	132	149	162	169	162
Malaysia	100	107	134	134	147	161	164
Philippines	100	102	104	111	140	146	166

Sources: All figures are from *FAO Production Yearbooks,* 1966, 1970, and 1977, except Taiwan 1975-77, which are estimates based on multiplying 1970 yield by an index of rice yields from Republic of China, *Statistical Yearbook,* 1978.

[a] Figures are the cereal crop to which the most acreage is devoted. For Brazil and Mexico corn yields are used. All other countries' yield statistics are for paddy rice.

continue channeling these export proceeds into import substituting industries. Unskilled industrial real wages are, moreover, likely to increase more in these cases (see Table 9.4), partly as a consequence of the relative rise in the prices of agricultural wage goods and partly as a result of enhanced unionization and minimum wage legislation accompanying prolonged import substitution. As mentioned earlier, Latin American growth and savings rates are generally respectable, if lower than in the East Asian cases (see rows 1 and 3). There is, however, a striking discrepancy in the equity indicators (rows 5 and 6), resulting from the combination of less attention to food-producing agriculture and labor-intensive industries serving international markets.

In summary, what looks superficially like a paler, Latin American version of the same East Asian success story (see Table 9.5a) is actually quite different. As seen in Table 9.5b, the composition of industrial exports was consistently biased against nondurable consumer goods in the Latin American cases, with the exception of Colombia. Only in the 1970s did Korea and Taiwan begin to shift markedly towards more capital-intensive industrial exports. Even when similar categories of goods are being produced in and exported from both sets of SICs the competitiveness at international prices undoubtedly varies markedly, with Latin American intermediate inputs, for

Table 9.4   Real Monthly Wages in Construction (in constant 1970 U.S. $)

	1955	1960	1965	1970	1973	1974	1975	1976	1977
South Korea	81.0	77.2	46.6	73.2	89.7	85.5	95.5	155.0	189.1
Index									
(1955 = 100)	100.0	95.3	57.5	90.9	100.7	105.6	118.4	191.4	233.5
Mexico	51.5	62.6	64.7	84.9	98.4	109.3	104.4	—	—
Index									
(1955 = 100)	100.0	121.6	125.6	164.9	191.1	212.2	202.7	—	—

Source: Swadesh Bose, "Wage Tables for Latin America and the Carribbean Countries,"
(Washington, D.C.: World Bank Development Economics Department, 1979, mimeo).

example, having to be procured domestically, and with primary factor markets considerably more distorted. It is striking, for example (see Table 9.6), that both with respect to the export of all manufactured goods and the export of nondurable consumer goods, there is a tendency for the Latin American SICs to sell a larger and—even more meaningfully—increasing proportion of the total to other LDCs. Sales within the Andean Pact countries, for example, are more like sales in a protected domestic market. Quite the opposite trend is in evidence for the East Asian SICs who are generally increasing their already high sales to the developed countries, especially in the case of the nondurables where their comparative advantage has been presumably highest, at least until 1970. As international trade theory would lead us to expect, a larger proportion of the more labor-intensive exports in the East Asian cases have been destined for the more advanced country markets.

In Latin America, food production and rural industry continue to languish, relative to potential; substantial pockets of unemployment and underemployment persist, as do poverty and worsening levels of income distribution inequality. The question which inevitably arises, from the point of view of Latin American policymakers, is the proximate cause, in nature and in man, of the particular path these economies have taken, and to what extent it is or should be reversible. I intend, finally, to turn attention to these issues.

II

The prior analysis and the necessarily circumstantial evidence presented indicate that the Latin American SICs "skipped" the labor-intensive primary export substitution phase and were, as a consequence, unable to mobilize their cheap unskilled labor effectively en route to economic maturity. It was their relatively abundant land-based exports which permitted them to move directly into the production and export of more sophisticated industrial products. It also permitted them the relative luxury of not fully mobilizing domestic food-producing agriculture and, if necessary, importing food instead.

The underlying relative abundance of natural resources—supplemented, it should be noted, by foreign capital inflows (both of the equity and portfolio variety)—makes its impact felt in two related ways. One, by rendering the system's underlying exchange rate "strong," it effectively discourages labor-intensive exports, ceteris paribus, from being competitive; in its extreme form this is the so-called Kuwait Effect, in the case of the oil-exporting countries. Second, there is the related opiate or cushion effect of ample export proceeds which makes it possible for the system politically to "afford" continued heavy protectionism and moving into more and more "expensive" or capital-intensive areas in which it does not necessarily have a comparative advantage—at least not yet.

The availability of ample natural resources and/or foreign capital can thus be viewed as permitting the system to continue on its old tracks, thus avoiding the political and, at least short-term, economic pain of having to move to a different policy package. Growth rates can in this way be maintained—just by adding more fuel to the engine—and difficult decisions postponed. The contrast with the East Asian cases which, at the end of their PIS phase, could not afford to pay for a prolongation of import substitution, but were forced by necessity to turn to the utilization of their human resources, is clear. While additional resources, in theory, should be able to ease the actual and psychological adjustment pains, they can use, and in the real world are often used, to put off—or entirely avoid—difficult decisions.

In the Latin American SIC cases, in other words, many decades of import substitution growth have led to encrusted habits and strong vested interest groups able to resist reforms or even marginal policy change. The relatively strong natural resources base permitted the society to channel its "windfall" returns both to the workers and the entrepreneurs in the protected industrial enclave. Under such conditions of bilateral oligopoly real industrial wages could be raised, even in the presence of substantial unemployment

Table 9.5   The Growth and Composition of Industrial Exports

	5a				5b		
	Annual Growth Rates (%)				Exports of Consumer Nondurables (% of Total Industrial Exports)		
	Total Manufacturing Exports		Consumer Nondurable Exports				
	1962-70	1970-77	1962-70	1970-77	1962	1970	1977
Brazil	28.6	40.5	41.4	44.7	11.3	24.2	29.8
Chile	13.0	33.4	18.0	29.7	23.3	34.3	31.5
	(62-71)	(71-74)	(62-71)	(71-74)			
Colombia	20.5	38.0	17.8	39.6	48.3	39.2	42.6
		(75)		(75)			
Argentina	24.9	25.6	45.5	22.8	8.8	29.8	26.0
		(76)		(76)			
Mexico	11.8	31.2	5.8	33.9	30.7	20.3	21.4
		(74)		(74)			
Korea	67.0	44.7	75.7	39.5	33.1	49.5	38.3
Taiwan	34.7	32.8	32.6	30.7	46.7	41.2	36.9

Sources: Computed from U.N. *Commodity Trade Statistics, Statistical Papers,* Series D, Taiwan 1977: monthly trade figures, Taiwan Statistical Office.

and the absence of sustained agricultural productivity increases, by means of government-supported union pressure and/or minimum wage legislation (see Table 9.4 for the contrast in wage behavior). Long before substantial pockets of unemployment and underemployment have been eliminated by labor absorption and growth, higher wages thus encourage the substantial "skipping" of the labor-intensive export phase. Higher-than-normal entrepreneurial returns and higher-than-normal wages for elite workers result. To the extent sectoral clashes on distribution occur, these may result in inflation, but the availability of ample land-based exports and/or foreign capital are bound to cushion such clashes and permit the system to continue on its path.

With some zigs and zags, this has been the general Latin American SIC experience. The only events likely to bring it to an end are either the ultimate running out of a sufficiently large natural resources base, for example, Brazil in the face of rising oil import requirements, or Mexico (a couple of years ago) having difficulty in attracting the customary volume of commercial capital flows; or, on the other hand, the population's unwillingness to permit the continued nonparticipation of substantial portions of economic actors and the resulting inequities in the distribution of income. The most recent economic policy changes in Brazil may represent a mixture of both these pressures coming to the fore and forcing a reassessment of policies.

Whether a strong desire really exists, beyond the rhetorical level, to respond to employment and distributional problems in the typical Latin American SIC is a subject of some controversy which I am ill-equipped to deal with. However, the extent to which the Latin American SICs have, in fact, lost opportunities, and the extent to which such losses are reversible inevitably represent relevant issues of importance to policymakers and need to be addressed.

Table 9.6   **Exports of Manufacturing, Total and Consumer Nondurables (CNs), by Destination (Percentage)[a]**

	1962 Total		1970 Total		1977 Total		1962 CNs		1970 CNs		1977 CNs	
	DCs	LDCs	DCs	LDCs	DCs	LDCs	DCs	LDCs	DCs	LDCs	DCs	LDCs
Brazil	63.2	36.6	54.7	43.4	55.7	43.1	75.7	20.6	78.3	16.4	74.7	19.2
Colombia	50.5	49.4	42.4	57.0	42.9	56.6	47.9	51.8	60.2	38.1	70.7	28.4
Argentina	65.7	31.4	44.6	51.9	33.4	62.5	75.0	21.0	67.9	23.1	68.0	19.2
Mexico	78.3	21.6	76.0	23.5	73.8	25.6	68.8	31.0	72.0	28.0	87.4	10.1
Chile	41.7	57.4	33.4	66.8	24.5	71.3	—	99.9	1.1	97.9	—	99.6
Hong Kong	83.3	15.6	84.0	15.9	82.2	17.0	75.8	24.0	84.3	15.4	84.4	14.1
Singapore	3.4	96.5	27.4	72.1	50.3	48.6	2.2	97.6	27.4	71.3	49.6	47.7
Korea	83.3	15.6	87.3	12.7	73.3	26.6	98.4	—	85.5	14.4	78.9	20.8
Taiwan	42.0	58.0	68.7	31.3	n.a.	n.a.	42.8	56.7	68.1	31.9	n.a.	n.a.

Source: Computed from U.N. *Commodity Trade Statistics, Statistical Papers*, Series D.

a   Nonmarket economies not included.

Table 9.7   Manufactured Exports—Market Shares

	Share of World Exports			Share of LDC Total Exports		
	1960	1970	1975	1960	1970	1975
2 East Asian SICs	0.19	0.57	1.59	3.44	10.37	22.87
5 Latin American SICs	1.23	1.07	1.26	22.24	16.31	18.11
South Korea	.01	.32	.80	.18	4.88	11.51
Taiwan	.18	.36	.79	3.26	5.49	11.36
Brazil	.05	.18	.43	.90	2.74	6.18
Argentina	.08	.12	.19	1.45	1.83	2.73
Mexico	.33	.24	.21	5.97	3.66	3.02
Chile	.65	.50	.37	11.75	7.62	5.32
Colombia	.12	.03	.06	2.17	0.49	0.86

Sources: U.N., *Yearbook of International Trade* for country statistics; UNCTAD, *Handbook of International Trade and Development Statistics* for world and total developing country statistics, except Taiwan, 1975: Monthly Trade Figures, Taiwan Statistical Office.

One way of establishing an upper-bound estimate of "what might have been" had the Latin American SICs not decided to skip the PES phase, is to estimate the value of manufactured exports for each had it maintained its base-year, say 1960, market share. In that base year, the beginning of the rapid PES subphase in Asia, the two Asian SICs had 0.19 percent of the world market in industrial exports, compared with 1.2 percent of Latin American counterparts. By 1975, however (see Table 9.7) the global market share of the East Asians had increased eight times while that of the Latin Americans had remained about constant. Looking at individual countries, note that both Taiwan and Korea vastly expanded their market share, while those of Chile, Mexico, and Colombia declined, with only Brazil as an outstanding exception. It is, moreover, important to note that even in the LDC market in which they are relatively favored, the Latin Americans SICs have been losing market shares.

Even in the most difficult, post-1973 years, I should point out, the East Asian SICs have been able to maintain—or better, restore—healthy industrial export growth rates from an already high base, in spite of the combination of energy price rises, global inflation, recession, and increased DC protectionism, which has been devastating for non-oil LDCs generally. The growth rate of DC-manufactured imports from LDCs, for example, fell from 23.3 percent in 1973–1974 to .3 percent in 1974–1975 but recovered to 39.8 percent by 1975–1976. Similarly, Korean manufactured exports rate of growth dropped to 9.5 percent in 1974–1975 from 39 percent in 1973–1974 but recovered to 63 percent by 1975–1976.

In spite of the increased DC-protectionist response which has accompanied the superexporters' success in recent years, it should be noted, of course, that LDC-manufactured exports still constitute only a tiny, if growing, fraction of global industrial exports; in 1955, for example, the developed market economies bought only 4 percent of their imported manufactures from LDCs; by 1976 this proportion, however, had almost doubled to 7.8 percent. The annual growth rates, even in the comparatively "difficult" 1970–1976 period, were 29 percent for DC purchases from LDCs versus 18 percent from the DCs. Similarly, there has been substantial growth, if from a low base, in intra-LDC manufactured trade, with LDC imports from other LDCs growing by a 27 percent annual average during 1970–1976 versus 26 percent for such imports from DCs. The continued contrast in growth rate of manufactured exports between the specific two sets of countries, in spite of the large difference in the initial base already established by the time of the first OPEC crisis, is vividly demonstrated in the empirical record.

The really important question is, of course, to what extent Latin Americans should consider the divergent East Asian experience as a "natural" consequence of different endowment conditions, and to what extent of different policy choices which might be reversible. As with most important questions, this one is rather difficult to answer definitively. What we can and will do, instead, is once again appeal to comparative historical analysis to shed some light on the question.

Societies in some sense act like individuals and are likely to take the road of lesser resistance if they can "get away with it." Thus, the relative natural resources abundance of Colombia, Mexico, and Brazil clearly biased their transition growth phasing toward the Latin American type as I have outlined it. More natural resources and/or more foreign capital inflows can clearly be used to help ease the transition from one policy regime to another but, just as easily, they can be used to avoid what for some interest groups represent unpleasant changes, for example, the need to seek earned profits in manufactured exports as a replacement of windfall profits in manufacturing for domestic markets. In an odd Toynbeeian sense the problem of the East Asian SICs was indeed easier. There were no real alternatives; the agricultural sector could be viewed as a temporary, if important, source of fuel, but the system's long-run comparative advantage had to be sought for elsewhere, that is, in the system's human resources, first unskilled, then skilled.

To some extent clearly, the "skipping" of the primary export substitution phase in Latin America was thus a politically convenient decision rather than the simple consequence of resources and exchange rates. Protectionist devices were generally maintained and reinforced; agricultural productivity neglected; real wage rates raised; and selective industrial export subsidies administered. But many of these policies can also be reversed, and currently existing substantial pockets of unskilled surplus labor productively absorbed. The dubious benefit arising from temporary natural resource bonanzas can be controlled by running a surplus and trying to sterilize the inflows, as Chile (and the UK) is attempting to do. Minimum wages—and the power of unions—can be permitted to lag in real terms. And rural sectors can be given some real attention for the first time, both in terms of a shift to smaller-scale infrastructural investments and better internal terms of trade. Given the relatively larger size of the Latin American SICs, larger attention to domestic balanced growth as part of the strategy is probably indicated. Most of all, a reversal of development strategies requires a redress of the neglect of food-producing agriculture as is currently under way in both South Korea and some of the Latin American SICs, particularly Brazil (see Table 9.3).

Real world economies, of course, move in ambiguous nonmonotonic paths, lurching forward in one direction one year, partly retracing their steps the next. Moreover, as pointed out earlier, they are too complicated to be packaged into neat typologies or transition phases. In fact, it is that very grayness and ambiguity which also support the positive argument for substantial residual flexibility within any given system at any given point in time.

This point is perhaps best demonstrated by pointing out that Korea and Brazil have been deviating sufficiently from their own "families" in recent years to have several elements in common. There can be little doubt that there have been substantial elements of export promotion along with export substitution in the Korean situation, especially since 1968—witness the setting of firm export targets combined with substantial arm-twisting or implied threats concerning the withdrawal of other favors. Korea's relative early neglect of agriculture (with respect to its own reference group, see Table 9.3) combined with a rapid primary export substitution drive in the 1960s meant foreign capital had to be relied on much more heavily than, say, in Taiwan, both to help finance food imports and rapid industrial expansion. Similarly, Brazil's performance, particularly between 1963 and 1973—and perhaps again currently—contains substantial elements of export substitution, yielding a burst in shoe and textile production and exports. While it is too early to tell, indications are, moreover, that Brazil may be seriously concerned with mobilizing the domestic balanced growth blade of such a strategy with the required help of a spurt in the hitherto neglected food-producing agricultural sector.

Other support for the potential reversibility of the Latin American transition pattern may be offered by looking very briefly at a third group of countries, the potential future SICs of Asia, that is, Malaysia, Indonesia, and the Philippines. These countries have natural resource endowments and other characteristics which place them somewhere between the East Asian and Latin American SICs. Their performance with respect to growth and equity (see the Appendix Country Indicator Tables) has quite similarly been somewhat "intermediate," best for Malaysia, followed by Indonesia, and perhaps worst for the Philippines. With respect to phasing, they have essentially been following a Latin American SIC transition growth sequence, moving from a colonial pattern after World War II, to primary import substitution in the 1950s and to secondary substitution in at least the Philippines since then. As the East Asian SICs successfully mopped up their surplus labor and as their wages rose, they moved, one by one, into secondary import substitution/ export substitution during the late 1960s and early 1970s; there are clear signs, moreover, that the other Asian countries, Malaysia in particular, are currently making an effort to step into the labor-intensive export niche being vacated. Indonesia still seems to be doing somewhat less well in avoiding a Kuwait Effect coupled with adverse policy changes; and the Philippines, while it has the potential, is not as yet seriously in the running.

As Latin American policymakers ponder both the challenge and the opportunity arising from the East Asian historical example they may well—and in fact frequently [do]—cite the "specialness" of these cases, either in terms of favored access to capital and markets or a more favorable international environment generally in the 1960s as compared with the 1980s. Yet one must also add to the record of, say, Taiwan that it had to overcome substantial disadvantages, including not only the poverty of natural resources, but also two major economic/political upheavals followed by the continuous drain of high defense expenditures, and increasingly severe protectionist restrictions by the United States and Europe, accompanying its success in export substitution growth.

The niche in world trade labeled "labor-intensive manufactured goods" is, of course, not limited in size but expandable in terms of both variations in quality characteristics and markets, including among the developing countries themselves. In the final analysis, the question of whether Latin American SICs will be persuaded that a change in the direction of policy is both feasible and desirable depends as much on the capacity for political reform mongering as on the technical issues raised. But it is certainly necessary, if not sufficient, for such policymakers to be convinced that "moving back" toward a more agriculture- and labor-intensive, industry-oriented growth path is likely to enhance growth along with equity objectives more dependably than grafting export promotion policies onto a heavily encrusted import substitution base.

Appendix (*Editor's Note:* The following tables are four of the ten appendix tables that appeared in the original article.)

Table 9A.1   Country Statistical Indicators, East Asian SICs—South Korea

Indicators	1950	1960	1965	1970	1973	1974	1975	1976	1977
(1) Annual real per capita GNP growth rate (%)	2.4 (52-60)		3.2	7.8	8.3	5.6	6.4	11.0	9.0
(2) θ—% nonagricultural labor	20.3 (55)	41.9 (63)	41.7	45.3	—	—	49.7	50.6	51.5
(3) Savings/GNP	—	4.0	8.5	12.0	14.4	10.8	10.3	14.4	17.9
(4) Investment/GNP	9.5	11.3	15.7	26.8	26.0	28.5	28.0	24.7	28.9
(5) Gini coefficient	—	—	.27 (66)	37	—	—	—	—	—
(6) Income % of bottom 20%	—	—	9.4 (66)	7.1	—	—	—	—	—
(7) Agricultural X_a/X exports (%) as % of total exports	82.3 (52)	51.4	25.3	16.7	13.2	10.9	15.1	9.3	12.8
(8) Mineral exports (%) as % of total exports	11.2 (52)	8.3	22.7	8.3	8.5	14.2	7.9	7.8	6.2
(9) Manufactured exports (%) as % of total exports	6.4 (52)	40.3	52.0	74.9	78.1	74.5	76.8	82.6	80.9
(10) Annual total export (X) growth rate (%)	10.7	58.6	30.6	55.3	-0.8	7.3	13.6	19.3	
(11) Total exports/GNP	2.1 (53)	3.3	8.5	14.3	30.3	28.5	28.5	33.4	35.8

Source: U.N., *Commodity Trade Statistics, Statistical Papers,* Series D.

Table 9A.2   Country Statistical Indicators, East Asian SICs—Taiwan

Indicators	1950	1960	1965	1970	1973	1974	1975	1976	1977
(1) Annual real per capita GNP growth rate (%)	3.6 (51-60)		5.1	6.2	9.6	-1.1	0.9	9.8	6.8
(2) θ—% nonagricultural labor	37.3	43.9	46.3	55.6	62.8	63.1	63.4	65.4	66.2
(3) Savings/GNP	10.3	12.0	14.9	20.7	27.4	24.8	19.8	24.3	24.1
(4) Investment/GNP	12.2	17.6	18.0	23.5	28.3	31.1	32.7	30.7	29.1
(5) Gini coefficient	.56	.44 (59)	—	—	.29 (72)	—	—	—	—
(6) Income % of bottom 20%	2.9 (53)	5.6	7.8 (64)	—	8.8 (72)	—	—	—	—
(7) Agricultural X_a/X exports (%) as % of total exports	—	51.7 (62)	57.9	22.5	15.8	15.5	17.5	13.6	13.4
(8) Mineral exports (%) as % of total exports	—	2.1 (62)	0.4	0.7	0.3	0.3	1.1	1.3	1.6
(9) Manufactured exports (%) as % of total exports	—	46.2 (62)	41.7	76.8	83.9	84.2	81.4	85.0	84.9
(10) Annual total export (X) growth rate (%)	9.5	22.2	23.7	31.6	-10.9	1.2	49.6	11.6	
(11) Total exports/GNP	10.1 (51)	11.1	18.4	29.6	49.0	45.4	41.2	52.3	53.8

Source: Monthly trade figures, Taiwan Statistical Office.

Table 9A.3   Country Statistical Indicators, Latin American SICs—Brazil

Indicators	1950	1960	1965	1970	1973	1974	1975	1976	1977
(1) Annual real per capita GNP growth rate (%)		3.2	—	5.0	9.7	6.7	3.1	6.0	1.9
(2) θ — % nonagricultural labor	39.4	—	51.2	54.4	—	—	58.0	58.8	59.5
(3) Savings/GNP	—	17.0	18.4	17.4	20.5	20.1	15.2	15.0	14.9
(4) Investment/GNP	16.5	18.0	15.6	23.7	24.5	25.7	27.1	25.4	23.5
(5) Gini coefficient	—	.59	—	.65	—	—	—	—	—
(6) Income % of bottom 20%	—	3.5	—	2.8	—	—	—	—	—
(7) Agricultural X_a/X exports (%) as % of total exports	96.8 (54)	88.8	80.8	75.2	70.3	63.9	57.9	61.9	63.9
(8) Mineral exports (%) as % of total exports	2.1 (54)	7.9	11.7	14.3	10.0	12.0	16.7	15.7	12.3
(9) Manufactured exports (%) as % of total exports	0.8	3.3	7.5	9.7	17.9	22.3	23.3	20.8	23.0
(10) Annual total export (X) growth rate (%)		-0.4	6.7	9.9	28.0	10.1	0.5	8.9	9.3
(11) Total exports/GNP	8.3	7.4	7.3	6.6	8.1	8.0	7.5	7.4	7.8

Table 9A.4   Country Statistical Indicators, Latin American SICs—Mexico

Indicators	1950	1960	1965	1970	1973	1974	1975	1976	1977
(1) Annual real per capita GNP growth rate (%)		6.2	3.5	3.4	2.5	2.1	1.0	-1.0	—
(2) θ — % nonagricultural labor	42.2	45.6	49.7	54.8	—	—	59.5	60.4	61.3
(3) Savings/GDP	—	10.0	6.4	7.0	7.2	12.5	11.6	13.1	19.4
(4) Investment/GDP	15.7	18.3	18.9	21.3	22.4	23.4	24.7	24.6	23.0
(5) Gini coefficient	—	.54 (63)	—	.58 (69)	—	—	—	—	—
(6) Income % of bottom 20%	—	3.7 (63)	—	4.2 (69)	—	—	—	—	—
(7) Agricultural X_a/X exports (%) as % of total exports	53.5	64.1	64.7	48.8	42.6	40.8	38.1	42.1	—
(8) Mineral exports (%) as % of total exports	38.6	24.0	22.3	21.2	16.5	23.1	32.4	30.3	—
(9) Manufactured exports (%) as % of total exports	7.9	11.9	13.0	30.0	40.8	36.0	29.5	27.5	—
(10) Annual total export (X) growth rate (%)		0.9	5.9	1.7	9.3	7.9	-12.0	20.5	24.6
(11) Total exports/GDP	17.0	10.6	9.7	8.2	9.4	9.3	7.6	8.5	10.2

chapter ten

Import Substitution Policies, Tariffs, and Competition

Felipe Pazos

In the nineteenth century and the first three decades of the twentieth, Latin American countries followed completely liberal commercial and financial policies, which they were ultimately forced to change by the Great Depression and World War II. During the Great Depression, prices of primary products dropped precipitously and private capital flows, formerly very large during the twenties, ceased completely. Confronted with a drop in their current and capital external receipts, Latin American countries closed their economies and suspended payment on foreign debt in order to reduce the impact of the drop of external receipts on their internal economies. During World War II and the years immediately thereafter, the industrial countries were unable to keep up with Latin America's demand for manufactures and these countries had to produce industrial goods by, and for, themselves. Lack of supplies from abroad was a great incentive to produce locally, but, before establishing new plants, entrepreneurs requested a tariff to protect themselves against a renewed influx of foreign supplies at the end of the war. Thus, during the thirties and forties, circumstances forced our countries to follow a policy of domestic development.

By the end of the forties and beginning of the fifties, the United States, and the newly formed international organizations, pressured the Latin American countries to lower tariffs, but our governments firmly resisted. Resistance was based on a combination of narrow interests and lofty ideals, upon economic theory as well as on deeply felt political emotions. Naturally, pressures to open the economy were resisted by the entrepreneurs who had so recently established themselves during the previous two decades; but,

Reprinted with permission in abridged form from Felipe Pazos, "Have Import Substitution Policies Either Precipitated or Aggravated the Debt Crisis?" *Journal of Interamerican Studies and World Affairs* 27 (Winter 1985–1986).

more important than entrepreneurial interests were the ideas and feelings of political and intellectual leaders, for whom industrialization represented progress, stability, diversification, high wages and development. Above all, it meant economic independence, a logical culmination of the political libera-tion wrung from Spain a century before. Industrialization was more than an economic policy, it was a national goal, perhaps the most important of all national goals.

The role of economists was not to decide whether or not the goal should be pursued, but to demonstrate that it was obtainable, and to devise the ways and means to attain it. This was the task of Raúl Prebisch and the economists who worked with him, mainly, but not exclusively, on the staff of the Economic Commission of Latin America (ECLA) in the years im-mediately following the end of World War II.

From the very beginning, Latin American writings (Urquidi 1946; Pre-bisch 1949) maintained that industrialization was not only feasible, but necessary. Essential to economic development, went the reasoning, was the modernization of agriculture. It was assumed that, as the agricultural sector modernized, its productivity would multiply and produce a surplus of goods. Increased efficiency in production would render many of these work-ers redundant, forcing them either to emigrate in the search for work, or to seek employment in the newly created manufacturing industries. Since ag-ricultural exports could not be expanded, because basic commodities were already in oversupply, and since displaced workers were already saturating the overseas job market so that further increase in emigration appeared un-likely, industrialization at home became the necessary policy, the only pos-sible solution. Though hard to believe nowadays, this elementary reasoning was not understood in industrial countries, as shown by the fact that, in 1950, Jacob Viner, one of the great economists of all times, recommended that underdeveloped countries should abandon their ambition to industrialize and strive, instead, to attain the agricultural productivity of farmers in California, Iowa and Nebraska (Viner 1952). It defies the imagination to think of the consequences of Viner's advice had it been followed: 95 percent of the world labor force unemployed, or a world food surplus 19 times larger than total consumption, or a trade-off figure between the two situa-tions. It may be noted that Viner expressed these ideas in the course of argu-ing against Prebisch's thesis that poor agricultural countries should create a manufacturing industry.

Latin American economists did not repeat the List (1955) and Manoi-lesco (1929) contention that industry is intrinsically more productive than agriculture, but showed that the factorial terms of trade between agriculture (especially tropical agriculture) and industry have historically moved strongly against the former and, hence, that industry has a much higher eco-nomic yield and can pay much higher wages. In the international division of labor that has prevailed over the last two centuries, one group of countries produced and exported goods with high demand elasticity, while another group produced and exported goods with low demand elasticity. For the first group, an expanding market for its products promoted fast economic growth, high employment absorption, quick mechanization, and a rapid rise in wages. In the second group, the slow expansion of the market for its products retarded economic growth, checked employment absorption, discouraged mechanization, and kept wages stagnant. Countries that produced and exported primary products, the demand for which expanded at a rate of 2 or 3 percent per year, and whose populations grew at the same rate, could not raise their production per worker, nor their wages, except by producing goods with high income elasticity of demand, i.e., by establishing manufacturing industries.

Originally, it was believed that this process necessarily implied a secular deterioration of the merchandise terms of trade (Prebisch 1949; Singer 1950). Some economists from industrial countries tried to show, statistically, that this had not happened, in an attempt to prove that the international division of labor had not harmed the primary producing countries. However, deterioration of the merchandise terms of trade is not a necessary result of the process, owing to the rapid and progressive divergence in the productivity trend of the two types of goods. What the process does provoke is a deterioration in the factorial terms of trade, and such deterioration does not require very refined statistical methods to be proven.

For Latin America, industrialization was a policy needed to create employment and to raise the standard of living in primary producing countries. At the time, industrialization was identified with import substitution, since we did not believe that countries just learning to produce manufactures could export them to the world market in competition with mature producing nations. In this, we were thinking in the same way as the mercantilists, as Alexander Hamilton, as Friederich List and as all economists who, in the past, had ambitions to industrialize their countries, with the single exception of Japanese policy advisers and government authorities who opted for the most difficult road to industrialization.

Adoption of a strategy of import substitution, to be implemented primarily by means of tariff protection, involves costs. Some costs are more theoretical than real and have to be analyzed to reveal their relative insignificance, whereas other costs are real and cannot be ignored. These costs, both theoretical and real, are: (1) a less efficient allocation of resources; (2) a reduction in the real wages of workers currently employed; (3) distortion of price relationships which may hinder future exports (especially of manufactures); and (4) a relatively narrow scope for growth since import substitution possibilities are limited.

The first of the four mentioned types of costs would be real if the alternative to protection for development purposes was unlimited production for export of those goods in which the country has comparative advantages (natural or institutional), be they sugar, steel, textiles or shoes; but not if the alternative is unemployment, which is the worst of all possible allocations of resources. The second type of cost is real, but it is more than compensated by the fact that industrialization creates many new job opportunities in the modern sector and, therefore, a small reduction in the wages of the head of the family may be more than compensated by employment of [the spouse] and grown-up children in new jobs in manufacturing industries and services.

The third type of cost has not emerged or, at least, has not been high enough to impede the rapid development of manufactured exports that took place in the larger Latin American countries from the middle of the sixties to the initial years of the eighties. Distortion of the price structure, and the consequent hindrance to export of manufactures, was the expected effect of protection which I feared most; but, fortunately, it has not been significant, probably for reasons which are explained further on in this chapter.

The limited scope of import substitution has been criticized, not only by foreign economists, but also by Latin Americans, who have argued that development will stop when all the easy substitutions have been made; but "easy" is a relative term, and Latin American countries have been able to manufacture substitute goods progressively more difficult to produce, as their industrial ability has developed. It has been a process of learning by doing, in which production of "easy" substitute goods was preparation for the production of more complex ones, and so encouraged them to produce for export. In the course of this process, the import coefficient of the large Latin American countries has narrowed to a degree very near self-sufficiency. Table 10.1 shows that the import coefficient of Argentina in 1981 was substantially below that of the United States, while that of Brazil was only a little above it. Even if national account estimates in developing countries are subject to large margins of error, the figures in Table 10.1 show that the large countries of our region have narrowed their import coefficients excessively.

Export of Manufactures

In the late forties and early fifties, when ideas on development were taking shape, nobody believed that developing countries could export manufactures to the world market in competition with industrial nations. American and European economists were then strongly inclined to attribute underdevelopment to sociological, cultural, and anthropological factors, and could not even imagine that traditionally slow-working societies could produce goods in competition with the hard-working, technologically advanced modern countries. In Latin America, we could not reconcile protectionism with free competition abroad: since our industries needed protection to compete within our countries, obviously they could not compete outside in the world market.

A good example of our conviction that Latin America could only export primary products is the ECLA report entitled "Introduction to the Technique of Programming" (ECLA 1953), prepared in 1953, which estimates the value which basic variables would have to attain in order for Latin America to grow at a rate of 5.6 percent in the twenty-five-year period of 1955–1980. The document took exports as an exogenous variable entirely dependent upon the volume and value of primary products imported by the United States and Europe, which it estimated would expand at an annual rate of 2.2 percent. Based on that figure, the report calculated that, in order to attain the above mentioned rate of growth, Latin America would have to reduce its import coefficient from 16.4 in 1955, to 6.8 percent in 1980. The report fully recognized that such reduction would require an herculean effort, but it did not

Table 10.1   Import Coefficients, 1981 (relation of imports to GDP)

Latin American Country	Import Coefficient
Costa Rica	0.45
Panama	0.44
Honduras	0.40
Haiti	0.37
Nicaragua	0.28
El Salvador	0.28
Dominican Republic	0.22
Guatemala	0.21
Chile	0.19
Ecuador	0.17
Peru	0.16
Uruguay	0.16
Colombia	0.16
Venezuela	0.16
Brazil	0.11
Mexico	0.10
Bolivia	0.10
Paraguay	0.10
Argentina	0.06

Non-Latin American Country	Import Coefficient
Belgium	0.64
Netherlands	0.47
Norway	0.27
Sweden	0.26
Germany	0.23
France	0.21
U.K.	0.20
Japan	0.13
U.S.	0.09

Source: Computed from data of Tables 3 and 9 of the 1983 Development Report of the World Bank.

even explore the possibility of raising external receipts by exporting manufactures.

The authors of the report could not believe, nor could I at that time, that our infant industries would be able to compete with mature industries in the developed countries. It was entirely illogical to suggest that industries requiring protection at home would be able to compete abroad. We had forgotten the example of Japan in the twenties and thirties, or disregarded it as a feat that only Japan could accomplish; but while we were still thinking of it as something impossible Korea, Taiwan, Hong Kong and Malaysia started to export manufactures, and years later our own countries, especially Brazil, Argentina, Mexico and Colombia, did the same. The explanation seems to lie in several concurrent factors, of which the principal are the following: (1) low wages give a competitive advantage to developing countries in labor-intensive industries; (2) the efficiency of workers and managers in the more advanced developing countries is higher than was believed at the end of World War II and has increased rapidly since then; and (3) given the rapid pace of technological progress, the more modern machinery and equipment newly installed in developing countries have evidenced greater productivity than that of the average, but older, industrial plant in developed countries.

Owing to the above facts, and also to the great advance in industrialization achieved by Latin American countries, thanks to import substitution, the large countries of the region began to export manufactures by the middle of the 1960s and rapidly expanded these exports during the 1970s. Exports of nontraditional manufactures, by nine Latin American countries covered by a World Bank study, expanded at a rate of 17.5 percent between 1970 and 1977, increasing from an initial 23 percent of total exports to 35 percent in 1977 and to an estimated 40 percent in 1980. This rapid growth took place not only in large nations which have acquired a relatively high level of industrialization, such as Brazil (21.5 percent), Argentina (18.8 percent) and Colombia (16.9 percent), but also in smaller, less-developed countries, such as El Salvador (10.2 percent), Costa Rica (8.4 percent) and Guatemala (8.2 percent). Mexico achieved a very high rate of export for its manufactured products during the early 1980s (as well as in the latter half of the 1960s), but the boom in petroleum production had a negative effect on industrial exports owing to wage increases and to a weakening of promotion efforts. As a consequence, the average growth for the seven-year period was only 12.6 percent.

Since the industrial protection policy followed for several decades, in Latin America, should have fostered inefficiency in the production of manufactures, and in their increased price relative to the general price level, it might be thought that sale of these goods abroad would have required the concession of export subsidies in order to offset the effect of import tariffs;

but his did not really prove to be the case. In their very thorough study of Latin America's export of manufactures, Teitel and Thoumi conclude that export subsidies did not play a major role in the process:

> Summarizing the evidence about the incentive system in Argentina and Brazil during the 1970s does not support the hypothesis that manufacturing exports were caused by subsidies. Rather, the evolution and maturity of manufacturing appears to have been the main factor in bringing about export success. Of course, policies mattered in the sense that they were not as anti-export biased as they had been in the past, but exports seem to have essentially reflected long term real changes such as increased competitiveness due to economics of scale, learning by doing, and improvements in manufacturing and marketing techniques, and were not mainly generated by policies which would have made foreign markets only temporarily attractive (Teitel and Thoumi 1986).

Tariff Protection and Domestic Competition

According to Teitel and Thoumi the main factor in bringing about export success has been the evolution and maturity of Latin American manufacturing industry; but, if this is the case, how has this industry managed to mature in an artificial climate of protection presumed to foster inefficiency and high costs? The explanation seems to be that the negative effects of protection can be, and frequently are, offset by competition among domestic industries. If a tariff promotes production by many enterprises competing among themselves and if a good's supply and demand schedules are elastic, domestic prices should drop below the protected level and begin to approach, or even fall below, international prices, depending on a country's capability to produce such goods. If production costs should fall below international costs, the country may then become an exporter of a good that it formerly imported.

As far as I know, this effect, of domestic competition and of demand and supply elasticities on the price of protected goods, has not been taken into account by international trade theory, which works on the assumption that protected producers make full and permanent use of the protection granted to them to maintain prices far above those prevailing in the world market. This practice would, and should, prevent protectionist countries from becoming efficient exporters. However experience shows that this is not necessarily true; the United States and Germany developed their economies under a system of protection and went on to become leading world exporters; and, throughout the twentieth century, Japan, with a tightly protected market, has been an outstanding exporter.

To my knowledge, the fact that domestic prices may fall below the level of protection was first uncovered by William G. Tyler during his study of the

Table 10.2   Redundant Tariff Protection in Brazil, 1980-1981

Industry	Legal Tariff	Difference Between Domestic and Foreign Prices
Mining	27.9	-15.9
Nonmetallic minerals	107.5	-22.5
Metallurgy	54.3	3.0
Machinery	56.3	24.0
Electrical equipment	99.1	45.2
Transportation equipment	101.9	-16.7
Lumber and wood	125.3	-8.9
Furniture	148.2	20.0
Paper	120.2	-19.9
Rubber	107.3	-23.3
Leather	156.6	10.0
Chemicals	50.3	40.7
Pharmaceutical products	27.9	79.0
Perfumery	160.5	38.5
Plastics	203.8	14.3
Textiles	167.3	20.6
Apparel	181.2	24.2
Food products	107.8	-21.3
Beverages	179.0	-9.9
Tobacco	184.6	-3.6
Printing and publishing	85.5	18.1
Miscellaneous	87.0	73.9

Source: William G. Tyler,"Effective Incentives for Domestic and Exports: A View of Anti-Export Biases and Commercial Policy in Brazil, 1980-81" (mimeographed).

relative weight of incentives to production for the domestic market and production for export (Tyler 1983). Tyler compares the prices of a large sample of Brazilian goods of all types with the foreign price of such goods c.i.f. Brazilian ports, converted at the current exchange rate, and considers that the difference measures the "implicit tariff" which really protects the goods. As Table 10.2 shows, in all but one of the industries studied, the "implicit tariff" is less than the "legal tariff", generally much less; and, in nine out of the twenty-two industries sampled, it was negative. This means that, in most cases, producers utilized only a small part of the protection to which they were entitled and in many instances did not utilize it at all, letting their prices fall below foreign prices, probably due to export prohibitions or to export difficulties, either institutional or economic.

Tyler's findings have enormous theoretical and practical importance; they show why protection in Latin America has not fostered inefficient industries nor distorted the price structure.

References

Economic Commission for Latin America (ECLA). 1953. *Analyses and Projections of Economic Development: An Introduction to the Techniques of Programming,* New York: United Nations.

List, F. 1955. *Sistema nacional de economía política.* Madrid, Spain: Aguilar.

Manoilesco, M. 1929. *Theorie du protectionisme.* Paris: Marcel Giard.

Prebisch, R. 1949. "El desarrollo económico de México." *El Trimestre Económico* (January-March).

Singer, H. 1950. "The Distribution of Gains Between Investing and Borrowing Countries." *American Economic Review* (May): 473-485.

Teitel, S., and F. Thoumi. 1986. "From Import Substitution to Exports: The Recent Manufacturing Export Experience of Argentina and Brazil." *Economic Development and Cultural Change* 34, no. 3 (April).

Tyler, W. 1983. "The Anti-Export Bias in Commercial Policies and Export Performance: Some Evidence from the Recent Brazilian Experience." *Weltwirtschaftliches Archiv* 119:97-108.

Urquidi, V. 1946. "El progreso económico de México." *El Trimestre Económico* (January-March).

Viner, J. 1952. *International Trade and Economic Development.* New York: Free Press.

part six

Transnational Corporations and the Role of the State

Two fundamental and powerful institutions in modern Latin America are the transnational corporations and the state. In Chapter 11, Gary Gereffi and Peter Evans investigate the interaction between these two major actors and the evolution of the development models in Brazil and Mexico. Gereffi and Evans place these two countries in the "semi-periphery"—between the center and the periphery—and describe their economic growth processes as "dependent development." The easy stage of import substitution industrialization (ISI) described by Alexander in Chapter 8, here denoted as horizontal ISI, was initiated in Brazil and Mexico as a result of a balance-of-payments crisis. This was followed in the 1950s by vertical ISI (secondary, or "difficult," ISI) caused by another balance-of-payments crisis. In fact, balance-of-payments crises were, and continue to be, fundamental in forcing the Latin American economies to alter their previous paths of development. The impact of such "external disequilibria," then, must be understood if the evolution of development strategies in Latin America is to be grasped fully. In all of these changeovers of strategy, state policy has guided the economies onto their new paths of development.

An important difference between the horizontal and vertical stages of ISI is that the horizontal stage was accompanied by an expansion of the role of local capital and entrepreneurship in the economy while vertical ISI (which according to Ranis's typology in Chapter 9 arrived prematurely in Latin America), was accomplished only through greater transnational corporate investment. Given the technological backwardness of the region, only foreign investment seemed capable of producing the more sophisticated nondurable consumer, intermediate, and capital goods characteristic of this stage. The result of greater transnational corporate investment, however, has been the denationalization of production in Brazil and Mexico, as transnationals frequently entered the market by purchasing existing firms rather than through the creation of new production facilities. In this transition, the Mexican and Brazilian states, as well as other Latin American governments, have fostered and promoted a "triple alliance" among a domestic elite class, the transnationals, and the state itself, an alliance in which transnational direct foreign investment (DFI) comes to play a restraining and retarding role on national economic policy and development, according to Gereffi and Evans.

Indeed, the progressively negative impact of transnational investments in a country led Albert Hirschman, the "dean" of heterodox development economists who have studied Latin America, to recommend divestment of overseas control as the best policy for all participants in the international economy. In Chapter 12, Hirschman develops his case, which rests to an important extent on the adverse impact of DFI on the supply of local factors of production—entrepreneurship, capital, and skilled technicians—and the "institutional inertia" encouraged by an excessive reliance on foreign inputs. The loss of national economic sovereignty and a decline in the importance of local factors of production, points stressed by Gereffi and Evans in the previous chapter, grow with greater DFI, even when DFI results in the growth of output and income, to the detriment of the Latin American economies and to relations between the region and, especially, the United States. For these reasons, Hirschman makes a strong case for limiting DFI in Latin America, perhaps even unilaterally.

The readings in this section help to put DFI in a more complex perspective than is common to orthodox economics. DFI can provide important inputs to the development process in Latin América; however, an adverse impact on Latin America's income, production possibilities, and indigenous technological capacity is just as possible. These chapters provide further support for the structuralist and institutionalist argument that a laissez faire approach to development is a likely recipe for disaster. The complexities of Latin America's development problems and the place of the region vis-à-vis the more developed nations necessitate a more active and positive democratic state role in planning and directing the path of economic progress.

chapter eleven

Transnational Corporations, Dependent Development, and State Policy in the Semiperiphery: A Comparison of Brazil and Mexico

Gary Gereffi
Peter Evans

Introduction

Brazil and Mexico occupy distinctive positions in the structure of the capitalist world economy. They bear little resemblance to the classic model of a "peripheral" country: they are too industrialized, having many of the modern industries typically found only at the center of the world economy; they supply themselves with too large a share of the finished goods consumed domestically; their exports are too diversified and include too many manufactured items; and they have developed unusually strong states with sophisticated administrative apparatuses capable of promoting and protecting local interests. But neither do Brazil and Mexico possess the characteristics commonly associated with "developed" or "core" nations. Their gross domestic product per capita is far below that of the United States, Japan, or almost any of the countries of Western Europe; their distributions of income are highly skewed compared to those of the developed countries;[1] they are recipient rather than source countries of foreign investment; they are debtor rather than creditor nations; and they are on the receiving rather than the originating end of product innovation and new production techniques.

From the perspective of the world system approach to the study of development, the position of Brazil and Mexico between the core and periphery countries on a series of dimensions makes them members of the "semiperiphery" (see Wallerstein 1974a, 1974b, 1976; Chirot 1977). Member-

Reprinted with permission from Gary Gereffi and Peter Evans, "Transnational Corporations, Dependent Development, and State Policy in the Semiperiphery: A Comparison of Brazil and Mexico," *Latin American Research Review*, 16, no. 3 (1981):31-64.

ship in the semiperiphery implies both a definite *structural position* in the international division of labor and an historical *process of development* leading from the periphery to the semiperiphery.[2] This process of development in the contemporary period has been labeled "dependent development": "development" because it is characterized by capital accumulation and an increasingly complex differentiation of the internal productive structure, "dependent" because it is indelibly marked by the effects of continued dependence on capital housed in the current core countries (Evans 1979a).[3] As dependent development proceeds, direct foreign investment (DFI) plays an increasingly prominent role.[4]

The objective of this chapter is to analyze the role that direct foreign investment has played in the process of dependent development in Brazil and Mexico. We hope to demonstrate that membership in the semiperiphery entails, at least for these two countries, not only fundamental similarities in the sectoral distribution of DFI and in the behavior of transnational corporations (TNCs),[5] but also increasing convergence in the responses of the Brazilian and Mexican states to the contradictions raised by the predominant role of TNCs in their economies.

We feel that the existence of these commonalities argues strongly for the important effects on national development of structural position within the capitalist world economy, given the undeniable differences between the two countries. Not only is Brazil much larger than Mexico in both area and population, but the two have very different political histories as indicated most recently by the contrast between Mexico's unbroken civilian rule and Brazil's fifteen years of military control (see Eckstein and Evans 1978). Mexico's political and economic affairs have been deeply marked by its proximity to the hegemonic core power, the United States. Its long border with the United States has resulted in a particularly heavy flow of U.S. capital into Mexico, the creation of a large assembly (*maquiladora*) industry just south of the Texas border, and increased agricultural exports. The two semiperipheral countries also have very different resource endowments, with Brazil's iron ore, bauxite, and other minerals opening a set of possibilities quite distinct from those presented by Mexico's oil wealth.

The first aim of our project can be summarized in the form of a question: Does the evidence with regard to DFI in Brazil and Mexico support the idea that both countries have converged around a single model of dependent development and that both have consolidated a "semiperipheral" position within the capitalist world economy? The second aim of our project is to consider the available data on DFI in the two countries with respect to a number of questions relating to the impact of dependency on domestic actors in the semiperiphery. To what extent has the level of external control over the local economy been exacerbated by displacement of the national bourgeoisie? To what extent have these effects been counterbalanced by joint national-foreign ownership of TNC subsidiaries and effective state regulation of their behavior? What has been the role of TNCs in narrowing the range of required external inputs and in increasing the diversity and flexibility of Brazil's and Mexico's export offerings?

Our explanation of changes in the character and role of DFI in Brazil and Mexico assumes that endogenous political and economic forces are at least as important as external ones. The process of dependent development is the result of the interaction of TNC strategies with the political and economic strategies of local social classes and host country states. TNC strategies are conditioned by the world economic environment especially as it impinges on their home states and by the forces of oligopolistic competition in global industries. The strategies of local groups vis-à-vis DFI are primarily expressed through the policies and actions of the state apparatus. These are conditioned not only by the international context but also by an historically given configuration of class structure, ideology, and local productive base. The local class structure and productive base, in turn, are the outcome of previous interaction between foreign capital and local classes.

Our discussion of the evidence will begin with an historico-structural summary of four phases of DFI in Brazil and Mexico. In this section we hope to provide some sense of the political and economic chronology that accompanied changes in the role and character of DFI itself, as well as highlight the degree of convergence that had occurred by the mid-1950s. We will then try to use the more detailed data that are available for the 1960s and 1970s to elaborate on the themes that we feel are especially important in the last two phases.

An Historico-Structural Analysis of Foreign Investment in Brazil and Mexico

Both Brazil and Mexico began the century as classic peripheral countries, exporters of primary products. In both countries the primary product export phase was superseded by an emphasis on "horizontal" import substituting industrialization (ISI) during the Great Depression, a phase which focused on local production of consumer nondurables and the local assembly of consumer durables. By the mid-1950s, horizontal ISI was superseded by a phase of "vertical ISI" in which the emphasis was on internalizing all phases in the manufacture of consumer goods and integrating backward in the direction of intermediate products and capital goods. Finally, since the 1970s, the current phase is one with a threefold emphasis: the expanded local production of capital goods, diversified export promotion, and the increased importance of finance capital (loans) relative to DFI.

There is a rough correspondence between movement from one phase to another, changes in structural position within the world economy, and the emergence and consolidation of the process of dependent development. The transition from periphery to semiperiphery began with the horizontal ISI phase and was accomplished during the vertical ISI phase. Dependent development also began with the movement from horizontal to vertical ISI. The current capital goods/diversified exports/finance capital phase represents an attempt to consolidate semiperipheral status and lay the foundations for moving beyond it to "nondependent" development or even to core status.

The Primary Product Export Economy (1880–1930)

The primary product export phase had a different character in Brazil than it did in Mexico. In Mexico, mineral exports (silver, gold, copper, lead, zinc) were the most important sources of export earnings and, until the Mexican Revolution, mining was thoroughly controlled by foreign capital. United States capital was dominant, accounting for at least 60 percent of the total investment in Mexican mining (Wright 1971:54-55).[6] Minerals were not particularly important in Brazil. Coffee was king and the coffee plantations were run by Brazilians. Brazil was nonetheless extremely dependent during the primary export phase (Evans 1976)—its internal division of labor was narrow (Graham 1968; Dean 1969), forcing it to rely on British imports to provide almost all its manufactured goods, and its fortunes were determined to a frightening degree by fluctuations in the New York coffee market—however, there was not the same degree of direct foreign control over internal production in the export sector in Brazil that there was in Mexico.

Patterns of DFI in the two countries during the first phase were also different. Although British investors were preeminent in both Brazil and Mexico, in the latter there was an almost equally large amount of American investment. From the 1870s to 1912, Mexico attracted more U.S. direct investment than any other country in the world (Wilkins 1970:113), while in Brazil, non-British investments came from a variety of countries, with the United States playing only a minor role (ECLA 1965:17).

The sectoral distribution of DFI also diverged in this early period; although the majority of foreign capital in both Brazil and Mexico was invested in railways and government bonds (see Singer 1975; Rippy 1959; Vernon 1963; Lewis 1938; Wright 1971), the remainder was distributed differently in each country. Foreign capital was concentrated in mineral extraction for export in Mexico and gravitated to public utilities in Brazil. This is particularly clear in the case of U.S. DFI: 40 percent of U.S investment in Mexico in 1929 was in extractive industries, while extraction was a negligible category in Brazil; and public utilities accounted for half of U.S. DFI in Brazil and less than a quarter in Mexico (see Table 11.1).[7]

Another important contrast between the two countries in this initial phase lay in the differential importance of DFI relative to indirect foreign

Table 11.1   U.S. Direct Investment in Brazil, Mexico, and Latin America, 1929-1978

		A. Absolute Amounts (in U.S. $ millions)								
		1929	1940	1946	1950	1957	1963	1967	1973	1978
Extractive[a]	Brazil	—[b]	—[b]	—[b]	7	10	30	68	81	268
	Mexico	289	178	115	124	149	116	100	85	97
	L.A.[c]	1,524	866	913	1,148	1,673	1,093	1,277	1,194	1,664
Petroleum	Brazil	23	31	45	112	130	60	79	198	424
	Mexico	206	42	7	13	31	66	44	10	41
	L.A.	589	516	697	1,233	2,702	3,094	2,903	2,162	3,661
Manufacturing	Brazil	46	70	126	284	378	663	893	2,033	4,684
	Mexico	6	10	66	133	335	503	890	1,798	2,752
	L.A.	231	210	399	780	1,270	2,103	3,305	5,992	10,855
Public	Brazil	97	112	125	138	182	190	32	16	26
Utilities[d]	Mexico	164	116	112	107	134	25	27	31	22[e]
	L.A.	886	960	880	927	1,001	710	621	377	308
Other[f]	Brazil	28	27	27	110	128	185	256	544	1,770
	Mexico	18	12	16	38	90	197	281	454	800[e]
	L.A.	233	154	116	357	1,208	1,657	2,159	3,802	6,989
Total	Brazil	194	240	323	644	835	1,128	1,327	2,885	7,170
	Mexico	683	358	316	415	739	907	1,343	2,379	3,712
	L.A.	3,462	2,705	3,005	4,445	7,434	8,657	10,265	13,527	21,336

	B. Relative Proportions								
	1929	1940	1946	1950	1957	1963	1967	1973	1978
Brazilian investment as a proportion of total Latin American investment	.06	.09	.11	.14	.11	.13	.13	.21	.34
Mexican investment as a proportion of total Latin American investment	.20	.13	.11	.09	.10	.10	.13	.18	.17
Brazilian investment as a proportion of Mexican investment	.28	.67	1.02	1.55	1.13	1.24	.99	1.21	1.93
Manufacturing investment as a proportion of total investment in Latin America	.07	.08	.13	.18	.17	.24	.32	.44	.51
Manufacturing investment as a proportion of total investment in									
Brazil	.24	.29	.39	.44	.45	.59	.67	.70	.65
Mexico	.01	.03	.21	.32	.45	.55	.66	.76	.74

Source: U.S. Department of Commerce, *Survey of Current Business*, various years.

a Mining and agriculture.
b Included in "Other."
c Latin America refers to Latin American republics and does not include the Caribbean.
d Includes transportation.
e Estimated; data suppressed for reasons of disclosure.
f Includes trade, finance, insurance, and other.

investment (i.e., public loans). The amounts of DFI in the two countries were about equal, but Brazil had almost three times as many foreign loans outstanding as Mexico at the time of World War I (Baklanoff 1969:26; Wright 1971:54). Between World War I and the Great Depression, Brazil's loans doubled to equal DFI, while in Mexico debt remained a small fraction of DFI (Baklanoff 1969:26).[8]

Finally, DFI also played a different role in the transition from the primary product export phase to the horizontal ISI phase in each country. From the Mexican revolution to the beginning of the depression there was almost a complete halt in the growth of DFI in Mexico, except in the petroleum sector.[9] Investment in manufacturing, useful in making the transition to horizontal ISI, was growing in Brazil but not in Mexico. For example, by 1929, almost one-fourth of U.S. DFI in Brazil was in manufacturing (see Table 11.1), while this represented only 1 percent of U.S. DFI in Mexico. Available data indicate the same was true for non-U.S. investment as well; even as late as 1940, only 7 percent of overall DFI in Mexico was in manufacturing (Cinta 1972:177).

Horizontal Import Substituting Industrialization (1930–1955)

Horizontal ISI had its beginnings in both countries during the phase of primary product exports. In Brazil local textile manufacturers had begun to replace British imports as early as the turn of the century. In Mexico as well, manufacturing ventures sprang up during the mineral export phase of development. It was not, however, until the Great Depression made export-oriented growth untenable that horizontal ISI, which is to say the development of local manufacturing of light consumer goods, became the dominant aspect of development in the two countries.

The shock was particularly great for Brazil. Coffee prices collapsed and the massive public debt, which the country had built up in the process of trying to improve its urban infrastructure, became an overwhelming burden as public debt service soared to 43 percent of export earnings in 1932/33 (Baklanoff 1971:195). Sharp devaluations made local production more profitable, but British capital did not respond aggressively to the shift in the situation. Local capital in Brazil, especially from the coffee sector, played a strong role in the manufacture of the consumer goods that were the focus of horizontal ISI.[10] During the Depression there was even some "renationalization" of local manufacturing operations as, for example, when the Votorantim rayon mill was bought from the British by the Ermírio de Moraes group.

State policy reinforced the impact of external events. Getúlio Vargas gradually abandoned his faith in Brazil's agricultural vocation and began to pursue policies that supported horizontal ISI. State entrepreneurship in basic industries like steel helped ensure manufacturers a supply of locally available inputs while at the same time limiting foreign control in these strategic sectors. Vargas also helped ensure that there would be local demand for manufactured goods by artificially supporting coffee prices. In addition, he pressured foreign subsidiaries to increase local content and raised tariff barriers against imported manufactured goods.

State policy in Mexico was also important in moving the country out of the primary export phase, but with very different consequences as far as DFI was concerned. Cárdenas' nationalization of the petroleum industry in 1938 knocked the keystone out of the foreign-dominated export model, but it also reinforced investors' fears that Mexico might be serious about the socialist rhetoric inherited from the revolution. While the U.S. investors expanded their position in Brazil, replacing the retreating British as the principal source of DFI, U.S. investments in Mexico dropped by 50 percent between 1929 and 1946. Most of this drop was accounted for by the elimination of petroleum holdings, but the level of investments in other extractive industries also declined rapidly and DFI in public utilities fell as well (see Table 11.1). Not until the more probusiness regime of Miguel Alemán (1946–1952) did foreign investors begin to see Mexico with the same favor that prevailed during the reign of Porfirio Díaz.

Despite differences in domestic politics and investor reactions in the early part of this phase, the post–World War II segment of the horizontal ISI period saw the emergence of several trends that brought the pattern of ISI in the two countries closer together. First, the unchallenged world hegemony of the United States resulted in a North American dominance of Brazilian DFI that was similar to the Mexican pattern. North American (including Canadian) overseas investments reached a peak of over 70 percent of Brazil's total DFI in 1950 while European investments dropped to 25 percent (Baklanoff 1966:109). The importance of DFI relative to loan capital also peaked in a similar fashion in both countries during this period (ECLA 1965:122). Perhaps the most important and durable of the convergent trends was the strong assertion of the tendency toward a common sectoral distribution of DFI. As foreigners were pushed out of the primary export sector in Mexico, manufacturing investment continued to grow, making the Mexican sectoral distribution more like Brazil's and increasingly compatible with horizontal ISI.

Overall, the period of horizontal ISI appeared to be one of diminished dependency. Not only was the industrial strength of the local bourgeoisies increasing, but foreign investors seemed to be playing a more positive role. The effects of World War II and later the Korean War gave further reason for an optimistic perspective. With the demand for raw materials accelerated and the industrial capacity of core countries diverted to wartime production, Mexico and Brazil found new markets for primary exports and diminished competition from imports in their domestic markets.

Vertical Import Substituting Industrialization (1955–1970)
The year 1955 marked a turning point, both in these optimistic perceptions and in the development process of the two countries. The Korean War boom was over and demand for "traditional" Brazilian and Mexican exports had fallen. Mexico experienced a severe recession after the Korean War and by 1954 balance-of-payment pressures forced a 50 percent devaluation of the peso. Brazil confronted a fall in coffee prices in 1955 that left them 30 percent below their Korean War peaks while imports of machinery and equipment were up 60 percent over the late 1940s (Leff 1968:60; Bergsman 1970:30). Furthermore, by the standards of the early 1950s, inflation in both countries had assumed critical proportions. The clear message from both the external and the internal sectors was that a shift in development strategy was necessary.

Policymaking elites in Brazil and Mexico made the decision at this juncture to replace horizontal ISI by vertical ISI. The objectives of vertical ISI were to broaden the range of local production to include consumer durables, especially the automobile, and to build up local manufacture of the capital and intermediate goods that were causing the big drain on the balance of payments. The investments required were more technologically sophisticated and capital intensive than those required by horizontal ISI, thus making TNCs rather than local capital the most likely instrument. The TNCs were ready to respond; the growth of investment in the core countries, especially in the United States, no longer demanded all the resources at their command.

Political shifts within Brazil and Mexico helped open the way for new kinds of participation by TNCs. The shift was most dramatic in Brazil, where the nationalist thrust of Vargas' second administration (1951–1954) was brought to an abrupt end by his suicide. Kubitschek, who became Brazil's president in 1956, established a policy of rapid industrialization based on full participation by foreign private investors. In Mexico, President Ruiz Cortines (1952–1958), worried about Mexico's persistent balance-of-payment difficulties, inflation, and scarce public sector revenues, shifted gears in midadministration and moved to attract foreign capital rather than keep it at arm's length as before. In both countries, imports of machinery and equipment were subsidized in order to encourage manufacturing investment. These incentives were combined with high tariff walls and quantitative controls on imports of manufactured goods that essentially "closed the border" once local manufacture had been undertaken.

Local elites interested in development thus found common ground with many of the TNCs interested in global expansion. Local manufacture rose, imports as a percentage of total consumption fell, DFI burgeoned,[11] and local manufacturing became increasingly foreign-owned.[12] It is this initial period of the vertical ISI phase that has been characterized as "the internationalization of imperialism" (Evans 1976) or the "internationalization of the internal market" (Cardoso and Faletto 1979). Vertical ISI created the foundations for the "triple alliance" of state, TNC, and local capital. The vertical ISI stage marks the full blossoming of the process of "dependent development" and the final stages of transition from the periphery to the semiperiphery.

The tendency toward sectoral convergence that had begun in the horizontal ISI phase culminated in the vertical ISI stage. For example, by 1967, two-thirds of total U.S. DFI in both countries was concentrated in manufacturing, with most of the rest in service industries and finance. This concentration not only gave U.S. DFI in the countries a parallel configuration, it also sharply distinguished them from the overall Latin American pattern in which manufacturing investment accounted for less than one-third of total U.S. DFI (see Table 11.1).

Similarities in the distribution of DFI went beyond a concentration on manufacturing. The locus of TNC investments in the largest firms in the most dynamic industries in both countries produced a similar pattern of distribution *within* the manufacturing sector (see Table 11.2). Brazilian DFI was still more diverse in terms of its origins. But the dominant foreign presence in key sectors of the local industry that emerged as a result of vertical ISI forced both countries to confront dependency in the form of external control over the local productive apparatus. As Table 11.2 indicates, by the beginning of the 1970s, TNCs held about half the assets of the largest manufacturing firms in each of the two countries.

Table 11.2   Percentage of Assets of Largest 300 Manufacturing Firms in Brazil and Mexico Held by U.S. and Other Foreign TNCs: Selected Industries, 1972.

Industry	U.S. TNC Share		Other Foreign Share		Total Foreign Share	
	Brazil	Mexico	Brazil	Mexico	Brazil	Mexico
Food	2	20	30	6	32	26
Textiles	6	0	38	5	44	5
Metal fabrication[a]	4	48	21	8	25	56
Nonmetallic ores	11	—	11	—	22	—
Chemicals	34	54	35	14	69	68
Rubber	100	100	0	0	100	100
Nonelectrical machinery	34	36	40	58	74	94
Electrical machinery	22	35	56	25	78	60
Transportation equipment	37	70	47	9	84	79
Total manufacturing	16	36	34	16	50	52

Source: Newfarmer and Mueller (1975: 55, 108)

[a] Metal fabrication does not include primary metals in Mexico. Percentages for primary metals in Mexico are as follows: U.S. TNCs—31 percent; Other Foreign TNCs—10 percent; Total Foreign—41 percent.

In both Brazil and Mexico there were nationalist reactions to the de-nationalization that accompanied vertical ISI, but their character and impact on DFI were quite different. In Mexico, nationalist periods alternated with periods of conciliatory policies toward private capital in general and foreign capital in particular. López Mateos, like Ruiz Cortines, moved first in a more nationalist direction and then in a more conciliatory one. When López Mateos spoke of governing "on the extreme left with the Constitution" at the start of his term in December 1958, roughly $250 million from the Mexican private sector fled the country in a matter of days (Hansen 1971:169). In 1960 and 1961, spurred by López Mateos' various efforts to cut back the role of DFI in Mexico, capital flight continued, and was estimated to have reached a magnitude of well over $200 million (Wionczek 1967:240-241; Vernon 1963:122). With the Mexican peso near crisis and economic growth sluggish, López Mateos and top members of his administration assured the business sector of their esteem for and support of private enterprise.

Vertical ISI developed in Brazil under political conditions quite different from those that prevailed in Mexico. When Brazilian nationalism reached full flower during the brief regime of João Goulart (1962–1964), it was less under control and therefore much more threatening to capital both local and foreign. From an average of $115 million for the five previous years, DFI in Brazil practically dried up entirely in 1962, with a total inflow of only $9 million (Evans and Gereffi 1981:Table A-1). In April of 1964, on the verge of defaulting on its international debt payments, with negative per capita growth, inflation of over 100 percent, and mounting internal opposition, the Goulart government fell to a military coup headed by General Humberto Castello Branco (1964–1967). The military regime in Brazil was closer to Mexico's Porfiriato in political tone than anything that had appeared in the interim in either country, and its attractiveness to foreign investors was similar. By 1970, the annual flow of DFI into Brazil was again well over $100 million, bolstered by a substantial quantity of foreign public funds.

The political contrasts resulted in differences in the rate, distribution, and to a lesser extent, ownership of DFI, but the common outcome was in the end more important than the differences. Both countries ended up with an expanded and diversified manufacturing capacity, the leading sectors of which were largely controlled by foreign capital. In short, by the end of the vertical ISI phase, dependent development had become thoroughly established as the dominant mode of economic growth in both countries.

Diversified Export Promotion (1970–Present)
Diversified export promotion (1970–present)[13] emerged as the most recent phase in the evolution of dependent development for many of the same reasons that vertical ISI succeeded horizontal ISI. By the late 1960s, in both

Brazil and Mexico, vertical ISI alone proved incapable of resolving the problem of imbalanced economic relations with the external world. Chronic balance-of-payment deficits were growing larger and inflation was becoming worse in both countries. Something new was needed. At the same time, reduced levels of profits in the core and increased confidence in the profitability of manufacturing in the semiperiphery[14] made it possible to gain the cooperation of the TNCs in the promotion of manufactured exports.

The export promotion that characterizes this phase is fundamentally different from the export-oriented growth of the primary export phase. Increasing diversification rather than the quantitative expansion of a single commodity or a small number of commodities is its key feature and manufactured exports have been particularly prominent in this process. Between 1965 and 1972 the proportion of exports accounted for by manufactured goods doubled in Mexico[15] and more than doubled in Brazil (Kaufman 1979:236; Serra 1979:135). Primary product exports, even though they represented a smaller share, were expanded and diversified. In Mexico this meant maintaining its previous extraordinary export variety (no single product, with the exception of cotton for a few years, and oil very recently, has accounted for more than 10 percent of Mexico's exports in the postwar period); for Brazil this meant a decline in the share of coffee from 42 percent of exports in the mid-1960s to 13 percent in 1974.

While it does not entail the same dramatic implantation of new industries that accompanied vertical ISI, the export promotion phase does entail a significant transformation of the place of the semiperiphery in global TNC strategy. Brazil and Mexico are no longer seen simply as profitable domestic markets; rather they are treated as part of an overall strategy of "worldwide sourcing." TNC subsidiaries in the semiperiphery play a role more like that of facilities in the core, and yet at the same time their fate is more thoroughly determined by the plans of the parent, since most TNC manufactured exports from countries like Brazil and Mexico are "intrafirm" sales between affiliated corporate units (see Table 11.6). The markets in which these subsidiaries sell are now less under the potential political control of Brazil and Mexico and more under the administrative control of individual TNCs.

It is important, of course, to keep in mind that even more than in the case of horizontal and vertical ISI, the diversified export promotion phase is characterized by a complex set of features, not all of which are a direct part of export promotion. To begin with, vertical ISI efforts continue in this phase, especially in the capital goods sector. Changes in the structure of the capitalist world economy also affect the character of DFI at this juncture. The trend toward increasing U.S. domination of DFI which was evident in the immediate post–World War II period has now reversed itself. The new dispersion in sources of DFI reappeared first in Brazil, but, by the end of the 1970s,

Mexico, too, was moving in the direction of greater diversification among non-U.S. foreign investors (see Evans and Gereffi 1980:36). The relative importance of DFI and loan capital also shifted in this period, partly out of Brazil's and Mexico's attempts to solve balance-of-payment problems, but also because of the post-1973 explosion of Eurodollar funds.

Brazil entered the current phase with certain advantages in its relation to TNCs. Having apparently exorcised left-leaning nationalism, Brazilian military regimes had created the best possible investment climate for foreign private enterprise. In Mexico, President Luis Echeverría, while hardly a radical, was continuing to push the interests of the local bourgeoisie (as well as the state sector) by expanding the scope of Mexicanization and taking a generally nationalist stance in relation to DFI. The contrast in the attractiveness of the two countries for business was manifest. For example, in 1967, after the Goulart scare and the disruption of the coup, Brazil had slightly less U.S. DFI than Mexico. In 1976 at the end of Echeverría's regime, it had 80 percent more than Mexico—that is, $5.4 billion versus $3.0 billion (U.S. Department of Commerce, *Survey of Current Business*). The reaction of non-U.S. investors was similar.

As the 1970s drew to a close, however, the tendency toward convergence reasserted itself. By the time López Portillo entered the Mexican presidency in 1976, the costs of trying to pursue a more nationalist course were evident and movement toward a more conciliatory stance began. In Brazil, local capital was putting more pressure on the military and the technocrats to attend to their needs by taking a more nationalist line toward TNCs.

Reviewing the four phases, there is a common process of transformation in the nature of dependency: in each transition, balance-of-payment difficulties, caused in part by shifts in the international economy, along with domestic inflation and a lack of capital or needed technology, created pressures for change. The direction of change was determined by the interaction of TNC strategies and local state policies. Frequently there was a strong correspondence between what the state wanted from the TNCs and the latter's own global strategies. Although the changes in the *nature* of dependency are apparent, it is much harder to say whether there has been a change in the overall *level* of dependency. For Mexico, with its much higher degree of dependency in the Porfiriato and its greater nationalist thrust in subsequent periods, the movement may be in the direction of less dependency. For Brazil, the direction of change is less clear, and depends more on the relative importance assigned to dependency as generated by vulnerability to the external market and dependency as generated by external control over the internal productive apparatus.

TNCs in the Contemporary Semiperiphery:
Contrasts and Convergences Between Brazil and Mexico

By the 1960s, the salient issues between the TNCs and Brazil and Mexico were no longer those that are the focus of conflict in the real periphery. While the smaller countries of Latin America, with little DFI in manufacturing, might still have an interest in fighting the battles of horizontal ISI, Brazil and Mexico had to worry about the consequences of having won those battles. Having sketched the historical processes that brought Brazil and Mexico to this point, it is time to delve in more detail into the implications of dependent development for the shape of DFI, the behavior of TNCs, and the policy responses of semiperipheral countries.

Three dilemmas stand out for the semiperiphery and we will try to deal with each of these in turn. First, there is the question of whether an excessive price has been paid for dependent development in terms of increasing TNC control in the local economy—that is, the issue of denationalization. Second, there is the question of the continuing imbalance in Brazil's and Mexico's economic relations with the international capitalist economy. Finally, there remains the question of whether a primary concern with these two dilemmas has led both countries down a development path that impedes the resolution of the even more intransigent questions of welfare and equity.

Comparisons between Brazil and Mexico on these issues often focus on policy responses, contrasting Mexico's relatively greater emphasis on preserving local ownership with Brazil's more effective manipulation of TNC behavior. While there is some truth to this contrast, we will argue that it is overdrawn. Careful examination of the data suggests that Mexico has not protected the local bourgeoisie to the extent that it might appear on the surface and that Brazil has not been as effective at manipulating TNC behavior as some have claimed. We argue further that by the end of the 1970s it was more useful to see state policy in the two countries as having converged around a similar blend of ownership and behavioral controls.

TNCs and the Local Bourgeoisie: The Denationalization Issue
As Table 11.2 and discussions of the vertical ISI phase have shown, TNC dominance of leading industries is common to both countries. Available data indicate that the relative share of foreign firms was on the increase during the 1960s (Newfarmer and Mueller 1975:57; Malan and Bonelli 1977:34-35; U.S. Tariff Commission 1973:411). Findings of increasing denationalization are, of course, subject to at least two different interpretations. If TNC growth can be attributed to pioneering entrepreneurship in new industrial sectors that local capital was incapable of entering, then denationalization

can be seen as a price for broadening the internal division of labor and diminishing dependency in this sense. If, on the other hand, TNCs were concentrated in industries in which local firms previously had been operating, then the effects of denationalization are more negative.

To address this issue, we turn to data on the mode of entry of TNCs into Brazil and Mexico. Other things being equal, entry by acquisition is an indication of direct displacement of local capital, whereas a newly formed subsidiary is more likely to represent an expansion of the internal division of labor. Looking at Table 11.3, it appears that displacement of the local bourgeoisie became an increasingly important feature of U.S. TNC expansion after World War II.[16] During the vertical ISI period, acquisition gradually emerged as the predominant method of entry into both Brazil and Mexico and by the beginning of the diversified export promotion phase it was clearly the preferred strategy for a U.S. TNC trying to break into these markets.

What is peculiar about Table 11.3 is that it gives no indication whatsoever of the supposedly greater Mexican concern with the preservation of the local bourgeoisie. To be sure, the data precede in time Echeverría's famous "Mexicanization" law of 1973 and presumably evidence from the 1970s would look different,[17] but even in the 1950s and 1960s, Mexico appeared to be taking a tough stance on the question of local ownership. In the late 1950s, for example, Mexico restricted foreign ownership in basic and secondary petrochemicals, anticipating by more than a decade similar though less thoroughgoing moves on the part of Brazil. In 1961 legislation

Table 11.3   Acquisition as a Mode of Entry into Mexico and Brazil: Percent of New U.S. Manufacturing Affiliates Established by Acquisition (rather than formation or reorganization)

Date of Formation	Mexico		Brazil	
	Total Number of Newly Established Affiliates	% of New Affiliates Established by Acquisition	Total Number of Newly Established Affiliates	% of New Affiliates Established by Acquisition
Prior to 1945	35	9	28	0
1946-1950	18	6	11	9
1951-1955	18	11	22	22
1956-1960	54	39	36	33
1961-1965	60	43	16	38
1966-1970	77	64	46	52
1971-1973a	32	75	18	61
Total all periods	294	43	177	33

Source: Newfarmer and Mueller (1975: 69, 122)

a The terminal date for Mexico is 1972.

Table 11.4   Number and Size of Locally Owned Firms Acquired in Mexico and Brazil (acquisitions by U.S. TNCs, 1960-1972)

	Mexico				Brazil			
	Number of Firms		Value of Assets[a]		Number of Firms		Value of Assets[a]	
Size of Firm	Amount	%	Amount	%	Amount	%	Amount	%
Large firms[b]	13	10	$170	57	15	30	$248	85
Small firms	115	90	128	43	35	70	44	15
Total	128	100	$298	100	50	100	$292	100

Source: Newfarmer and Mueller (1975: 71, 124)

a Millions of U.S. dollars
b Large firms are those with assets greater than $5 million.

was passed requiring Mexicanization of the mining industry, and in 1967, while the Brazilian military was opening up mining to foreign firms, Mexico's last foreign-dominated mining activity—its large and profitable sulphur industry—came under majority Mexican ownership. If Mexicanization, or local equity participation and preferably majority control by nationals, was a consistent informal policy of Mexican regimes as a condition of foreign entry in the late 1950s and the 1960s, then why don't we see far fewer acquisitions in Mexico than in Brazil?

Part of the answer lies simply in the fact that U.S. TNCs account for about 50 percent of all acquisitions in Mexico, but only about 15 percent in Brazil (Vaupel and Curhan 1973:331, 334); thus, consideration of non-U.S. TNCs would increase the value of foreign acquisitions in Brazil relative to those in Mexico. If the data were adjusted to get an estimate of *all* acquisitions in the two countries, the total number and value of acquisitions in Brazil would be greater than in Mexico. Another insight into the differences between the countries is provided by reanalyzing the U.S. data: when large and small firms are separated, as in Table 11.4, it is clear that small firms accounted for a substantially higher proportion of U.S. acquisitions in Mexico than they did in Brazil; and, while the number of large firms acquired was about the same in both countries, the assets of the large firms acquired in Brazil amounted to $80 million more than the assets of the large firms acquired in Mexico.[18] In other words, large firms were much more likely to remain locally owned in Mexico. Mexicanization policies may not provide protection for the bourgeoisie in general, but they seem to provide greater protection for the large enterprises.

Further evidence that Mexico's relatively greater emphasis on ownership issues has in fact affected TNC behavior is provided by data on joint ventures (Table 11.5). TNCs are more likely to share ownership and much more likely to accept minority positions in Mexico than in Brazil. When a

Table 11.5   TNC Joint Ventures in Mexico and Brazil

A. Degree of Control by TNC		
	Mexico	Brazil
Wholly owned (95% +)	50%	61%
Majority owned (50% - 94%)	25%	27%
Minority owned (6% - 49%)	25%	12%
	100%	100%
	(339)	(315)

B. Nature of Other Owner in TNC Joint Ventures		
	Mexico	Brazil
Local private	52%	35%
Local state	1%	7%
Dispersed stock owners	35%	19%
Other foreign partner	12%	39%
	100%	100%
	(112)	(80)

Source: Vaupel and Curhan (1973: panel A, 272, 269; panel B, 313, 316)

Note: The direction of the differences between Mexico and Brazil is the same whether the data on U.S. and non-U.S. TNCs are analyzed separately, or combined as above.

distinction is made between sharing ownership with the local bourgeoisie or sharing it with other TNCs, the differences between the two countries became even more pronounced. Over half the partnerships in Mexico involve the local bourgeoisie as significant (i.e., nondispersed) owners; in Brazil, the most frequent kind of partnership involves other foreign partners more than the local bourgeoisie.

The data suggest a pattern similar to that indicated by Bennett and Sharpe's (1977) interpretation of Mexicanization. While Mexicanization has not lowered the participation of TNCs in the commanding heights of industry (Table 11.2), or prevented the displacement of certain segments of the local bourgeoisie (Table 11.3), it does seem to have limited the impact of TNC encroachments on the larger economic groups in Mexico (Table 11.4) and provided a better chance for some local capitalists to gain access to partnerships with TNCs (Table 11.5). Our data also seem consistent with the generally held interpretation that the largest local capitalists in Mexico are better connected to the state political apparatus than their Brazilian counterparts (cf. Domínguez 1979; Eckstein and Evans 1978; Kaufman 1977; and O'Donnell 1978).

Having argued for the contrast between Brazil and Mexico on the ownership issue, we should reiterate our contention that the difference is one of degree. Even during the apex of its legitimacy in the early 1970s, the Brazilian military was careful to limit foreign ownership in the most important and dynamic industrial sector of the decade, the petrochemical industry (see Evans 1979a:229-249). More recently, observers have noted that the Brazilian political *abertura* (opening) has had as one of its concomitants an increased emphasis on the protection of the local bourgeoisie (e.g., Evans 1979b; Domínguez 1979). There are a number of examples that support this view: the restriction of the minicomputer market to firms with majority local participation (*Business Latin America [BLA]* 1978:75, 218); the requirement that TNCs bidding on telecommunications contracts present "Brazilianization" plans (*BLA* 1979:61); and recent legislation that would bar state contracts with foreign controlled companies in the health care field (*BLA* 1980:154-155).

If the current trend toward political openness continues, we may expect future data on acquisitions and joint ventures in Brazil and Mexico to appear more similar. Even a complete convergence toward policies of shared ownership, however, is unlikely to eliminate the problem of denationalization. Some examples from the recent "nationalist" period in Brazil will serve to illustrate the intractability of the problem. Brazilian capital goods manufacturers are welded together in a powerful industry association, Associação Brasileira pelo Desenvolvimento de Industria de Base (ABDIB), and are known as the most politically effective sector of the local industrial bourgeoisie. Yet local capital goods manufacturers were among the hardest hit by recent government efforts to trim deficits by cutting the expenditures of state companies. One prominent member of ABDIB, Pedro Sanson, was forced to sell 80 percent of his company to a West German firm (*Latin America Economic Report [LAER]* 1979:172). Even worse, Brazilian planning minister Delfim Neto, often considered the best political friend of the local bourgeoisie, was forced by Brazil's failure to cope with inflation to come out with an economic package in the fall of 1979 that included the abolition of Brazil's Law of Similars. This law, which prohibited imports of capital goods being produced within Brazil, had been one of the keystones of the local industry's survival (see *Latin America Weekly Report [LAWR]* 1979:72).

The case of the minicomputer industry also illustrates the difficulties of implementing policies that will succeed in preserving local ownership of leading industries. Setting up Cobra as a Brazilian state-owned venture to produce minicomputers and excluding IBM from this market was considered to be an important nationalist initiative (cf. Evans 1979b; Domínguez 1979). Yet by 1979, Cobra was called a "resounding failure" that had "unwisely bought outdated and expensive technology" from its minority TNC partner, a U.S. company named Sycor (*LAER* 1979:207). Meanwhile, IBM continues to develop a successful line of mid-range computers that are potential competitors for the minicomputers produced by newly created, locally controlled joint ventures like Cobra (*LAER* 1979:68). From capital goods to minicomputers, it is clear that even with a convergence around supportive state policies regarding local ownership, the displacement of the domestic bourgeoisie will continue to be a major political issue in the semiperiphery.

Shaping TNC Behavior to Resolve External Imbalances
Just as denationalization has persisted as a problem for the semiperiphery despite the transformation in the nature of dependency, so has the question of external imbalances. Both Brazil and Mexico have waged a continuous and chronically unsuccessful struggle to balance their international accounts. TNCs, with their voracious appetites for imported inputs and their tendency to generate outflows of profits, royalties, and other service payments, are a part of the problem. On the other hand, as potential sources for fresh capital inflows, as potential producers of currently imported goods, and, most critically in the present phase of dependent development, as generators of export income, TNCs can also be part of the solution.

During the 1960s Brazil developed a reputation for effectively shaping TNC behavior comparable to Mexico's reputation as a defender of local ownership. The auto industry is often used as an example. Brazil started a program of local integration in 1956, six years before Mexico. By 1962 Brazil already required 99 percent local content by weight for passenger cars produced nationally. Mexico required only 60 percent local content and gave the companies more leeway by measuring the 60 percent in terms of proportion of direct cost rather than weight (Jenkins 1977:53; Bennett et al. 1978: 275). By the end of the 1960s, Brazil could boast of an integrated auto industry which, although totally foreign owned in the terminal (finished autos) sector, was a great success as far as import substitution was concerned.

By the beginning of the 1970s Brazil had discovered that the combination of profit remittances and imported capital inputs made the auto industry a drain on foreign exchange despite its advances in the area of import substitution. In 1972 the BEFIEX (Export Fiscal Benefits) program, which allows companies tax credits and other fiscal benefits if they agree to programs that would result in positive trade balances, was introduced with the auto industry as one of the main targets. Again, Brazil was remarkably successful. By 1977 the foreign auto companies operating in Brazil were exporting at a yearly rate of almost $700 million and creating a trade surplus of $300 million, a remarkable contrast to the deficit of almost $100 million they had generated just three years earlier (Müller and Moore 1978).

Brazil's success in this regard stood in contrast to the performance of the Mexican auto industry. In 1977 exports from Mexico's auto industry were about one-tenth of Brazil's auto exports (*LAER* 1978:212). The Mexican industry generated in that year a net trade deficit of $400 million, down from 1976's $600 million deficit but still discouraging in relation to the Brazilian surplus.

Brazil's greater success was not confined to the auto industry. For instance, if the export performance of U.S. TNCs in the two countries is examined for the 1960s and early 1970s, it is clear that, while both countries were able to expand the share of sales of manufactured goods going to export markets, Brazil did so more effectively. Mexico, given its proximity to the United States and the existence of the border industries program, began the period with a considerable advantage (see Table 11.6). Its manufactured exports were more than three times the magnitude of Brazil's in absolute terms in 1960 and also three times larger as a proportion of local sales. In the next six years, U.S. TNCs based in Mexico quadrupled their exports, but those in Brazil increased theirs nearly eightfold. In the next four years manufactured exports by U.S. TNCs in Mexico increased by a factor of six, but again, subsidiaries in Brazil increased theirs by a factor of eight. Thus, while no one could deny that Mexico was engaged in the promotion of manufactured exports, Brazil was far more successful at shaping the behavior of the TNCs in this direction.

During the late 1970s there were signs of convergence on this issue similar to those in policies relating to local ownership. In 1979 Mexico established a broad set of Brazilian-type incentives for firms that would undertake the local production of capital goods and balance their imports with exports. In what *Business Latin America* (1979:64) called "an encouraging sign of flexibility," reductions in import duties were made available to foreign-owned as well as locally owned firms as long as their export sales were sufficient to cover their import needs. The auto firms, provided with their own special set of incentives in 1977, were allowed to take advantage of this general scheme as well, and the number of products eligible for export tax rebates was increased from 300 to 800 (*BLA* 1980:43).

Again, as in the case of ownership policies, convergence in the area of export promotion should not be taken to indicate the end of the problems faced by semiperipheral countries. Mexico's attempt to take a stronger stand against TNCs in selected areas in the early 1970s resulted in an unexpectedly sharp investor reaction. From about 1973, when the Mexicanization law was

Table 11.6   Exports in Comparison to Sales for U.S. TNCs in Brazil and Mexico, Manufacturing Only: 1960, 1966, 1972 (in millions of U.S. dollars)

	Local Sales (1)	Total Exports (2)	Exports to Affiliated Companies (3)	Exports as % of Local Sales (2)/(1)	% of Exports that are Intracompany Sales (3)/(2)
1960					
Brazil	453	1.6	1.1	0.4	69
Mexico	413	5.4	3.0	1.3	56
1966					
Brazil	854	12.0	7.4	1.4	62
Mexico	1,164	22.2	16.6	1.9	75
1972					
Brazil	2,850	98.9	72.6	3.5	73
Mexico	2,689	137.1	112.7	5.1	82

Source: Newfarmer and Mueller (1975: 181-186)

passed, until the end of Echeverría's regime, Mexico was increasingly defined as a "bad investment climate,"[19] and the country suffered from a severe reduction of DFI, despite the fact that investors there were making high rates of return, comparable to rates in Brazil and about 50 percent higher than those of manufacturers in the United States (Connor and Mueller 1977:49-52).

What Echeverría was doing "wrong" from the viewpoint of TNCs can be inferred from the policies that López Portillo embarked on to "restore investor confidence" in 1977 and 1978. The government's 1977 policy was "decidedly recessionist." Its success in bringing inflation down was "paid for primarily by the growing number of unemployed and by the drop in the standard of living of those lucky enough to find work" (*LAER* 1978:85), but the International Monetary Fund (IMF), which conditioned new loans to Mexico upon such measures, was pleased. The correspondence between these policies and the ones Brazil embarked upon is hard to ignore. The sharp drop in the standard of living of the average Brazilian between 1964 and 1969 is well known, but it is important to keep in mind that this was not only a feature of the anti-inflationary "readjustment period." Between 1969 and 1977 productivity in Brazil increased by 70 percent while the real value of the minimum wage dropped by 20 percent (*LAER* 1978:144). The positive impact on profits is obvious, but in all likelihood the general "good intentions" implied by such policies are just as important in ensuring that a country is defined as a "good investment climate."

The implications of this analysis for the countries of the semiperiphery are somewhat grim. Mexico, one of the richest and best-behaved nations in the Third World, had only to stray slightly from the path of sound business practice to end up shifting the impact of TNC capital and profit flows from a positive $179 million in the 1960–1969 period to a negative $349 million in the 1970–1976 period. Since Echeverría was only mildly reformist in a Third World context, it would appear that the band of acceptable policy is exceedingly narrow and that the penalties for straying outside it are strict and swift.

While the Echeverría period demonstrated the limitations within which semiperipheral countries must work, Brazil's experience in the late 1970s showed that even the most generous policies toward DFI may not resolve the problem of external imbalances. After a decade of carefully constructed export incentives Brazil still finds itself with unfavorable trade balances. Worse still, incentives have only partially changed the role of TNCs in generating current account balance-of-payment deficits.[20] Rapidly growing flows of DFI thus have been insufficient to solve Brazil's balance-of-payments problems, and the incentives used to attract them contributed to driving Brazil's inflation rate back up to the levels associated with the Goulart period by the end of the decade (nearly 80 percent in 1979). It was estimated that for 1979, government subsidies to industry and agriculture cost $10 billion or about 5 percent of Brazil's GDP (LAWR 1979:73). Looking at the costs and benefits of its incentives to the TNCs, one had to wonder whether Brazil was shaping the behavior of the TNCs or vice versa.

The BEFIEX program in the auto industry is a good example of the dubious balance of costs and benefits. To begin with, the TNCs were able to make higher profits producing cars in Brazil and exporting them than they could have made manufacturing them in the United States, Europe, or Japan, so increased production for export was hardly a sacrifice on their part. Added to the general profitability of these operations were the generous BEFIEX subsidies. Among other benefits, the companies were allowed an export credit for taxes they normally would have paid on their domestic production (state sales tax and industrial products tax). Together these two credits amounted to 30 percent of the value added portion of export sales. Put crudely, the Brazilian government was paying the companies an extra 15 to 20 cents for every dollar's worth of goods they sold abroad. For the TNCs there is no question that the "trade-off" is positive; for Brazil the equation is more doubtful.

There is another aspect of Brazil's export promotion that seems even more disturbing in the long run. Most of the growth of TNC manufactured exports is represented by "intracompany sales" between a TNC's affiliated members. For instance, Table 11.6 shows that by 1972 almost three-fourths of U.S. TNC manufactured exports from Brazil were intracompany sales and over four-fifths of those from Mexico. In many cases, there is really only one customer for the product being exported. Sales of Pinto engines, for example, depend entirely on the fortunes of a single TNC customer (the parent, Ford Motor Company) and the administrative decisions of that customer as to where these engines will be made. Thus, it is the TNC, and not Brazil or Mexico, who generally has the final word on the export "market" and local production. Export promotion, which seems like a victory for semiperipheral countries because it further transforms their position in the international division of labor, appears to increase dependency when viewed from a perspective that focuses on control.

In addition to all its other problems, and perhaps most seriously of all, export promotion must face the retaliatory responses of the TNCs' home governments. In 1979, for example, Fred Bergsten told the Brazilians that taxes on their textile exports to the United States would be increased to a level of 37 percent by 1980 (*LAER* 1979:34). The effects of this policy are likely to be severe. In 1979, when the U.S. government raised its duties to the level of 17 percent, Brazil's textile exports to the United States began to drop immediately (*Gazeta Mercantile*, São Paulo, 18 May 1979).

Export promotion must be viewed, then, not as another victory over dependency so much as another transformation in a continuing struggle with dependency, one that is likely to see new strategies in the not too distant future. It is perhaps ironic that Delfim Neto, who had begun the 1970s formulating incentive programs, ended the decade in December of 1979 by announcing that his system of subsidies for manufactured exports was being dismantled (*LAWR* 1979:73).

The limits to export promotion in the less developed countries (LDCs) are more generalized than those defined by Mexico's or Brazil's relations with the core countries. To combat the inflationary impact of higher oil bills, most core countries are adopting restrictive fiscal and monetary policies that are geared to slow economic growth. Stagnation in the core erodes the best markets for LDC manufactured exports and depresses the prices of their primary-product exports at the same time. According to Morgan Guaranty Trust Co., a downturn in the industrial world as severe as the 1974-1975 recession would produce an impact on LDC trade balances equivalent to a $25-a-barrel increase in the price of OPEC oil (*Newsweek* 1980:74-75).

Prospects for the Future Evolution of
Foreign Investment in the Semiperiphery

Brazil and Mexico show both the extent to which fundamental changes in the role of foreign investment are possible and the strictness of the limits created by dependent development. Time and again during the process of dependent development in the two countries, presidents have discovered the constraints imposed by the necessity of maintaining a "good investment climate." From Cárdenas in the 1930s to the initial years of López Mateos' regime to the Echeverría period, the flow of DFI to Mexico declined immediately whenever a president sounded too nationalistic or too concerned with the problems of labor and the poor. Brazil saw the flow of DFI decline in the nationalistic period of Vargas' second presidency (1950-1954) and drop off even more dramatically during the experiment with a more left-leaning nationalism under Goulart. Each time, the tenor of the regime has been reversed and positive relations with the TNCs have been recovered, but the limits have been demarcated anew. The semiperiphery is simply not free to explore a welfare-oriented version of capitalist development.

Under friendly regimes, however, DFI has proven to be much more flexible than early theories of the "development of underdevelopment" (Baran 1957; Frank 1967) would have predicted. Both Mexico and Brazil succeeded in building diversified, sophisticated, and internationally competitive industrial economies, in large measure on the basis of DFI. Given the strong parallels in the evolution of DFI in the two countries, the pattern may represent a general trend rooted in the nature of the capitalist world economy as well as in the social structures of the two countries under consideration here, and should not be dismissed as fortuitous or idiosyncratic.

Like the behavior of the TNCs, the behavior of the Mexican and Brazilian states has shown many parallels. The convergence of state policies has been particularly evident in the most recent period. As the 1970s progressed, the blend of measures oriented toward trying to protect local ownership and trying to induce TNC behavior that would improve external imbalances became remarkably similar in the two countries. In neither case, however, were the policies adopted real solutions to the basic dilemmas of denationalization and external imbalance. The semiperiphery continues to be a locus for transformation rather than a setting for stable solutions.

Important changes in the structure and role of DFI are still underway. Perhaps best publicized is the growth in loan capital relative to DFI. By the end of the 1970s, foreign debt in Brazil and Mexico had ballooned out of all proportion to DFI. In Mexico, the predominance of debt to DFI was related to the difficulty of attracting new TNC investments during the Echeverría period; debt tripled between 1970 and 1976 while DFI increased by only 50 percent (Weinert 1977:123). Brazil had no problem attracting DFI, but debt mounted at an even faster rate than in Mexico (Malan and Bonelli 1977:34,38).

The explanation for the skyrocketing of foreign debt is complex. It depended on international liquidity relating to the availability of "petrodollars" from OPEC nations and the relative stagnation of investment opportunities in the developed countries, as well as on mounting balance-of-payment problems in Brazil and Mexico. It also depended in part on the foundation of good relations with TNCs that had been built up through the growth of DFI. Not only did the TNCs themselves contract or vouch for some of the debt, but their strong presence in Brazil and Mexico made these countries seem more reliable than others less thoroughly tied to international capital. For instance, the extent of this relative attractiveness can be seen from the fact that together Brazil and Mexico accounted for one-half of all loans to LDCs made by the twenty-one largest North American banks (Baird and McCaughan 1979:83).

Whether increased reliance on loan capital represents a diminution in the degree of dependency or an increase is even more difficult to sort out than the reasons for the increase. Effects on external imbalances and effects on control of the internal productive apparatus are both hard to judge. For Mexico during the Echeverría period, the willingness of bankers to lend when TNCs were reluctant to engage in DFI represented an important extra degree of freedom. However, the long-run implications of loan capital for external imbalances are more negative. DFI generates profit remittances but the original investment itself does not have to be repaid. Loans require both interest payments and amortization. For Brazil, whose debt has now surpassed $50 billion, interest payments are running over $3 billion per year and amortization of debt requires about $5 billion per year (*LAER* 1979:60). According to Delfim Neto, this means that Brazil will have to borrow about $15 billion a year for the next few years. It is not surprising, therefore, that Delfim is trying to persuade TNCs to transform some of their loans to subsidiaries into equity (*LAWR* 1979:44).

As far as control over the internal productive apparatus is concerned, it is usually the case that investors expect more of a say over what their money is used for than do lenders. On the other hand, lenders may attempt a generalized kind of control over national policy that is rarely attempted by investors. In cases where they felt their loans were in jeopardy, like Peru (see Stallings 1979) and Argentina (see Frenkel and O'Donnell 1979), international lenders, under the leadership of the IMF, have succeeded in imposing a whole gamut of fiscal, monetary, and economic policies on the receiving nations. Whether countries as important to TNCs as Brazil and Mexico would be subjected to the same strenuous belt tightening as countries like Peru and Argentina remains to be seen. Nonetheless, it seems clear that the lender will play an increasingly important role in shaping the nature of dependent development in the next decades.

A second emerging feature of dependent development in the 1980s is also reminiscent of earlier periods of dependency. Having accelerated the growth of manufactured exports to the limit, both Brazil and Mexico are again looking to extractive industries to help them resolve external imbalances. In Brazil, there has been a resurgence of DFI in extractive industries; for example, between 1973 and 1978 the amount of U.S. DFI in extractive industries tripled, growing at a more rapid rate than investment in manufacturing (see Table 11.1). At the same time, soaring bills for imported oil led Brazil to reverse the thirty-year ban on the exclusion of foreign oil companies from exploration. By 1978 U.S. investors had more capital invested in the petroleum industry in Brazil than they did in Venezuela. For Mexico, the expansion of extractive investments carried with it no equivalent expansion of DFI. In this instance, U.S. DFI in extractive industries in 1978 remained below the levels of the 1960s and about one-third of the 1929 level (see Table 11.1). Petróleos Mexicanos' good fortune in the area of oil exploration has generated sufficient revenues for investment so that there is no need to look for assistance from foreign companies; thus, DFI in petroleum was also below the levels of the 1960s. Whether other more general forms of divergence emerge between the two countries based on Mexico's oil bonanza and Brazil's increasing dependence on foreign oil remains to be seen. The fact that Mexico's current account continues to be in deficit despite oil exports, and the experience of Venezuela, which found no panacea for its economic or social problems in oil reserves, both suggest that future differences between Mexico and Brazil may be less than expected. Nonetheless, the future evolution of the two countries will provide a significant experiment in the relative importance of oil in the process of dependent development.

The third important change in DFI, which is prefigured in the data for the 1970s, is the least dramatic but may well prove to be the most important. If we look at total U.S. DFI, the share of manufacturing in both countries seems to have reached a peak around 1973, although this is more apparent in Brazil. At about that time, investments in the service sector began to accelerate, reaching a proportion of total U.S. DFI by the end of the decade comparable to that held by manufacturing at the beginning of the horizontal ISI phases (see Table 11.1). If the growth of the service sector TNCs is a significant future trend in DFI in the semiperiphery, then students of dependent development will be faced with a new series of intellectual challenges. Arguments over the effects of DFI are framed in terms developed to analyze the manufacturing sector. Issues like appropriate technology, employment effects, and oligopolistic pricing require some rethinking before they can be applied to the analysis of the service sector.

Overall, the safest prediction for the shape of future phases of DFI in Brazil and Mexico is that they will have the same general character as past phases. DFI will continue to adapt to changes in state policy and changes in the structure of semiperipheral economies, flowing into new areas while perhaps being replaced by state and local capital in some of its traditional strongholds. The technology and expertise of TNCs will contribute to the construction of ever more differentiated and sophisticated economies in both countries. Still, problems of dependency will persist. The local bourgeoisie will find itself continually threatened by displacement, though the sectors in which it is displaced may shift. External imbalances will continue to be a chronic problem, though the nature of the imports, exports, and service payments that are included in the imbalances will change. The two states will continue to devise new policy instruments to deal with the new forms these problems will take, and will probably find that their policies continue to converge around the same sorts of attempted solutions. Finally, the welfare possibilities of capitalism will continue to lie outside of the policy boundaries that are compatible with either country continuing its success in attracting DFI.

Notes

1. In 1978, the GDP per capita of Brazil and Mexico was roughly the same—$1,200. This is equivalent to one-sixth the 1978 per capita income of the Organization for Economic Cooperation and Development (OECD) countries of North America, Western Europe, and Japan (Inter-American Development Bank 1980:104). Per capita income in Brazil and Mexico is spread extremely unevenly among the population (see Reynolds 1978:1012), and longitudinal data show that the distribution of income

in both countries is growing still more skewed in favor of the rich versus the poor over time.

2. Most of the contemporary members of the semiperiphery, such as Brazil, Mexico, Argentina, Iran, Egypt, Nigeria, South Africa, India, and Indonesia, ascended from classically peripheral positions in the relatively recent past. This is only one route to the semiperiphery, however. Another route, less common, is decadence and decline on the part of a center country (e.g. Spain and Portugal). Our concern here is limited to the ascendant members of the semiperiphery.

3. Dependency and nondependency are relative concepts that must be interpreted in the context of a country's overall position in the capitalist world economy. Dependency implies vulnerability to the external economy and a significant degree of external control over the local productive apparatus. Nondependency, on the other had, means diminished external determination of the course of a country's development. It means having an internal productive structure that is capable of producing a broad range of goods and that also is locally owned and controlled to a substantial degree, especially the "leading sectors" in terms of capital accumulation and sectors where considerable market power is exercised by the major firms. (For a thorough discussion of the notions of dependency and nondependency, see Gereffi 1980: Chapters 2-4; for their application to the case of Mexico's steroid hormone industry, see Gereffi 1978).

4. Foreign investment is of two main types: direct and indirect. Direct foreign investment refers to the acquisition or control of productive facilities outside the home country. Control is generally thought to mean at least a 25 percent participation in the share capital of the foreign enterprise, although the published U.S. Department of Commerce data are based on equity holdings as low as 10 percent. There are two kinds of indirect foreign investment: (a) international portfolio investment, which refers to the purchase of securities issued by foreign institutions without any associated control over or management participation in them; and (b) public loans to foreign countries. Portfolio investments typically take the form of bonds, whereas direct foreign investment entails holding equity. Although both direct and indirect foreign investment in Brazil and Mexico will be discussed in this paper, our primary concern is with the former.

5. Transnational corporations may be defined as any business enterprise engaging in direct foreign investment in production facilities spanning several national jurisdictions. The parent firm of the TNC and its network of affiliates are bound together by common ties of ownership, they draw on a common pool of human and financial resources, and they respond to some sort of common strategy.

6. The extent of foreign domination in Mexico during the reign of Porfirio Díaz (1876–1910) is astonishing. By the end of Díaz's rule, foreigners probably owned one-fourth of the country's total land area and accounted for two-thirds of Mexico's total investments outside agriculture and handicrafts (Wright 1971:59; Vernon 1963:43).

7. Our data on U.S. DFI are generally more comprehensive and span a greater period of time than our data on non–U.S. DFI; we have, therefore, used U.S. data in most of our tables. However, we have consulted a variety of sources that contain data on both U.S. and non–U.S. TNCs (ECLA 1965; Vaupel and Curhan 1973; Newfarmer and Mueller 1975; Fajnzylber and Martínez, Tarragó 1976; United Nations 1978), and find them to be consistent with the U.S. data, unless otherwise noted.

8. Following the revolution, foreign loans were virtually impossible to obtain in Mexico for a decade or two, since the postrevolutionary administrations refused to acknowledge the external debts of their predecessors. Service payments on the public debt were suspended for over fifteen years until an adjustment of Mexico's general external debt was negotiated in 1942, and of its railroad debt in 1946 (Wright 1971:72). With these settlements, Mexico's external credit was reestablished, and the Mexican government increasingly sought foreign loans to help finance the country's economic expansion.

9. For instance, from 1911 to 1929, U.S. investment in petroleum jumped from $20 million to $206 million, while the overall stock of U.S. DFI in Mexico rose very little—from $616 to $683 million (Wright 1971:54, 77). The foreign-owned oil companies escaped major property damage because of their location along the coastal periphery of the country and by paying for protection. Their production expanded substantially throughout the revolution. By 1921, Mexico had become the second largest oil-producing country in the world; its output of 193 million barrels amounted to a quarter of the world's total (ibid.:62).

10. The existence of locally controlled capital in the primary export sector gave Brazil an advantage in the development of horizontal ISI. Liquid capital from the sale of coffee found its way into new import-competing industrial enterprises. Government subsidies to the coffee sector further added to its supply of capital, thus increasing the incentives for coffee planters to invest in industry. The result was that industrial production in Brazil fell off less than 10 percent in the early depression years and by 1933 had regained its 1929 levels (see Baer 1965:22-24).

11. Beginning in 1955, DFI began to pour into the Brazilian and Mexican economies at an almost unprecedented rate. In the six-year period marking the tenure of Brazil's President Kubitschek (1956–1961), $674 million in DFI were attracted into Brazil, an annual average of over $110 million. During the six years prior to 1955, which include the nationalist reign of Getulio Vargas, DFI in Brazil averaged less than $8 million per year. Similarly in Mexico, the average flow of DFI from 1955 through 1958 was $115 million, compared to an annual flow of less than $70 million in 1952–1954, the first three years of the Ruiz Cortines sexenio. (The data are taken from Evans and Gereffi 1981: Table A-1.)

12. In absolute terms, the value of foreign investment as a proportion of total investment in Brazil and Mexico appears relatively small. Net foreign capital inflows of all types into the two countries in the 1950–1965 period amounted to only 8 to 12 percent of total gross investment in each economy, with this proportion being somewhat higher for the manufacturing sector alone (Leff 1968:75; Wright 1971:78, 93; Vernon 1963:113). The importance of DFI is considerably increased, however, when one takes a more disaggregated view of these economies, focusing on their leading sectors and the largest firms in these sectors. In Brazil, the estimated share of total growth produced by foreign firms in the 1949-1962 period was 34 percent in manufacturing and 42 percent of all industrial growth deriving from import substitution (Morley and Smith 1971:128, 130). Foreign firms accounted for 35 percent of Mexico's overall industrial production in 1970, and for more than half of the industrial production in some of the more modern and strategic sectors (such as chemicals, electrical and other types of machinery, and transportation equipment). Among the 290 largest firms operating in Mexico, TNCs account for 45 percent of their industrial output and for over two-thirds of production in the modern and strategic sectors

(Fajnzylber and Martínez Tarragó 1976:159, 165).

13. In Brazil this phase actually began a bit earlier, around 1968.

14. Data from a survey of 179 of the biggest U.S. manufacturers located in Brazil and Mexico, gathered by the U.S. Senate Subcommittee on Multinational Corporations, indicate that the overseas operations of these TNCs were very profitable. After-tax earnings of foreign affiliates amounted to 16.1 percent of direct investments in equity and long-term debt in 1972, and broad earnings (after-tax earnings plus royalties, payments for management services, and other intangibles) amounted to 20 percent. Consolidated net (after-tax) earnings of these TNCs for their domestic and foreign operations together were only 12.7 percent (Newfarmer and Mueller 1975:41).

15. In Mexico this tendency has been further stimulated by the "border industry" program which assembles component parts from the U.S. for reexport using lower-cost Mexican labor.

16. While we have no comparable data on the evolution of acquisitions by non–U.S. TNCs, it appears from overall data (Vaupel and Curhan 1973:331, 334) that non–U.S. TNCs are, in the aggregate, as prone to entry by acquisition as are U.S. TNCs.

17. Evidence presented by Newfarmer and Mueller (1975:68) suggests that there was indeed a sharp drop in the number of TNC acquisitions as a result of the 1973 law.

18. This conclusion is reinforced by a look at the relative size of non–U.S. TNCs in Brazil and Mexico. Non–U.S. TNC subsidiaries in Brazil are substantially larger—more than double the size in sales, on the average—than non–U.S. TNC subsidiaries in Mexico. This differential is far greater than for U.S. TNCs—whose subsidiaries in Brazil are only one-third larger than those in Mexico (Fajnzylber and Martínez Tarragó 1976:206). If this difference in subsidiary scale is reflected in the scale of acquisitions in the two countries, we would expect non–U.S. TNC acquisitions to be concentrated even more heavily on large firms in Brazil than are the U.S. TNC acquisitions shown in Table 11.4.

19. In addition to concern over ownership policies, TNCs found Echeverría insufficiently tough on labor. *Business Latin America* complained that "labor is one area where companies are fighting a losing battle to keep costs down." Taxation policies were also considered negative. In his first year in office Echeverría hit the companies with reduced depreciation allowances, a new limit on their ability to deduct advertising expenses, higher taxes on technical fees, and an increase in the gross mercantile revenue tax (*BLA* 1970:10). While taxes amounted to 46 percent of pretax earnings in Mexico in 1972, they amounted to only 21 percent in Brazil (Newfarmer and Mueller 1975).

20. According to CACEX, the foreign trade department of the Bank of Brazil, adding together the deficits of only nineteen TNC subsidiaries in 1977 was sufficient to produce a trade gap of $661 million, roughly four times larger than the gap calculated by the U.S. Bureau of Economic Analysis for all U.S. TNCs in 1970.

References

Baer, Werner. 1965. *Industrialization and Economic Development in Brazil*. Homewood, Ill.: Richard D. Irwin.

Baird, Peter, and McCaughan, Ed. 1979. *Beyond the Border: Mexico and the U.S. Today.* New York: North American Congress on Latin America.

Baklanoff, Eric N. 1966. "Foreign Private Investment and Industrialization in Brazil." In *New Perspectives on Brazil,* edited by Eric N. Baklanoff, 101-136. Nashville, Tenn.: Vanderbilt University Press.

————. 1969. "External Factors in the Economic Development of Brazil's Heartland: The Center-South, 1850–1930." In *The Shaping of Modern Brazil,* edited by Eric N. Baklanoff, 19-35. Baton Rouge: Louisiana State University Press.

————. 1969. "Brazilian Development and the International Economy." In *Modern Brazil: New Patterns and Development,* edited by John Saunders, 190-214. Gainesville: University of Florida Press.

Baran, Paul. 1957. *The Political Economy of Growth.* New York: Monthly Review Press.

Bennett, Douglas; Blachman, Morris J.; and Sharpe, Kenneth. 1978. "Mexico and Multinational Corporations: An Explanation of State Action." In *Latin America and the World Economy: A Changing International Order,* edited by Joseph Grunwald, 257-282. Beverly Hills, Calif.: Sage Publications.

Bennett, Douglas, and Sharpe, Kenneth. 1977. "Controlling the Multinationals: The Ill Logic of Mexicanization." Unpublished manuscript.

Bergsman, Joel. 1970. *Brazil: Industrialization and Trade Policies.* New York: Oxford University Press.

Business Latin America (BLA). Various Issues.

Cardoso, Fernando Henrique, and Faletto, Enzo. 1979. *Dependency and Development in Latin America.* Berkeley: University of California Press.

Chirot, Daniel. 1977. *Social Change in the Twentieth Century.* New York: Harcourt Brace Jovanovich.

Cinta, Ricardo. 1972. "Burguesía nacional y desarrollo." In *El perfil de México en 1980,* vol. 3, edited by Instituto de Investigaciones Sociales, Universidad Nacional Autónoma de México. México D.F.: Siglo XXI.

Connor, John M., and Mueller, Willard F. 1977. *Market Power and Profitability of Multinational Corporations in Brazil and Mexico.* Report to the U.S. Senate, Committee on Foreign Relations, Subcommittee on Foreign Economic Policy. Washington, D.C.: Government Printing Office.

Dean, Warren. 1969. *The Industrialization of São Paulo, 1880–1945.* Austin: University of Texas Press.

Domínguez, Jorge I. 1979. "National and Multinational Business and the State in Latin America." Unpublished manuscript.

Eckstein, Susan, and Evans, Peter. 1978. "The Revolution as Cataclysm and Coup: Political Transformation and Economic Development in Brazil and Mexico." In *Comparative Studies in Sociology* 1, edited by R. Tomasson, 129-155. Greenwich, Conn.: JAI Press.

ECLA (Economic Commission for Latin America). 1965. *External Financing in Latin America.* New York: United Nations.

Evans, Peter. 1976. "Continuities and Contradictions in the Evolution of Brazilian Dependence." *Latin American Perspectives* 3, no. 2 (Spring):30-54.

————. 1979a. *Dependent Development: The Alliance of Multinational, State, and Local Capital in Brazil.* Princeton, N.J.: Princeton University Press.

————. 1979b. "Shoes, OPIC, and the Unquestioning Persuasion: Multinational Corporations and U.S.–Brazilian Relations." In *Capitalism and the State in U.S.– Latin American Relations,* edited by Richard R. Fagen, 302–336. Stanford, Calif.: Stanford University Press.

Evans, Peter, and Gereffi, Gary. 1980. "Inversión extranjera y desarrollo dependiente: Una comparición entre Brasil y México." *Revista Mexicana de Sociología* 42, no. 1 (January-March):9–70.

————. 1982. "Foreign Investment and Dependent Development: Comparing Brazil and Mexico." In *Brazil and Mexico: Patterns in Late Development,* edited by Sylvia Ann Hewlett and Richard S. Weinert. Philadelphia, Penn.: Institute for the Study of Human Issues. All the tables in this article are also contained in Evans and Gereffi 1982.

Fajnzylber, Fernando, and Martínez Tarragó, Trinidad. 1976. *Las empresas transnacionales: Expansión a nivel mundial y proyección en la industria mexicana.* México: D.F.: Fondo de Cultura Económica.

Frank, André Gunder. 1967. *Capitalism and Underdevelopment in Latin America: Historical Studies of Chile and Brazil.* New York: Monthly Review Press.

Frenkel, Roberto, and O'Donnell, Guillermo. 1979. "The Stabilization Programs of the International Monetary Fund and Their Internal Impacts." In *Capitalism and the State in U.S.–Latin American Relations,* edited by Richard R. Fagen, 171–216. Stanford, Calif.: Stanford University Press.

Gereffi, Gary. 1978. "Drug Firms and Dependency in Mexico: The Case of the Steroid Hormone Industry." *International Organization* 32, no. 1 (Winter):237–286.

————. 1980. "'Wonder Drugs' and Transnational Corporations in Mexico: An Elaboration and a Limiting-Case Test of Dependency Theory." Ph.D. dissertation, Yale University.

Graham, Richard. 1968. *Britain and Modernization in Brazil: 1850–1914.* Cambridge: Cambridge University Press.

Hansen, Roger D. 1971. *The Politics of Mexican Development.* Baltimore, Md.: Johns Hopkins University Press.

Inter-American Development Bank. 1980. *Annual Report, 1979.* Washington, D.C.: Inter-American Development Bank.

Jenkins, Rhys Owen. 1977. *Dependent Industrialization in Latin America: The Automotive Industry in Argentina, Chile and Mexico.* New York: Praeger Publishers.

Kaufman, Robert R. 1977. "Mexico and Latin American Authoritarianism." In *Authoritarianism in Mexico,* edited by José Luis Reyna and Richard S. Weinert, 193–232. Philadelphia, Pa.: Institute for the Study of Human Issues.

————. 1979. "Industrial Change and Authoritarian Rule in Latin America: A Concrete Review of the Bureaucratic Authoritarian Model." In *The New Authoritarianism in Latin America,* edited by David Collier, 165–253. Princeton, N.J.: Princeton University Press.

Latin America Economic Report (LAER). Various Issues.

Latin America Weekly Report (LAWR). Various Issues.

Leff, Nathaniel H. 1968. *Economic Policy-Making and Development in Brazil, 1947– 1964.* New York: John Wiley and Sons.

Lewis, Cleona. 1938. *America's Stake in International Investments.* Washington, D.C.: The Brookings Institution.

Malan, Pedro S., and Bonelli, Regis. 1977. "The Brazilian Economy in the Seventies: Old and New Developments." *World Development* 5, nos. 1/2 (January-February):19-45.

Morley, Samuel A., and Smith, Gordon W. 1971. "Import Substitution and Foreign Investment in Brazil." *Oxford Economic Papers* 23, no. 1 (March):120–135.

Müller, Ronald E., and Moore, David H. 1978. "Brazilian Bargaining Power Success in Befiex Export Promotion Program with the Transnational Automotive Industry." Paper prepared for the United Nations Center on Transnational Corporations.

Newfarmer, Richard S., and Mueller, Willard. 1975. *Multinational Corporations in Brazil and Mexico: Structural Sources of Economic and Noneconomic Power.* Report to the U.S. Senate, Committee on Foreign Relations, Subcommittee on Multinational Corporations. Washington, D.C.: Government Printing Office.

Newsweek. 1980. "A New LDC Debt Crunch." 26 May, 74–76.

O'Donnell, Guillermo A. 1978. "Reflections on the Patterns of Change in the Bureau-cratic-Authoritarian State," 13, no. 1:3–38.

Reynolds, Clark W. 1978. "Why Mexico's 'Stabilizing Development' Was Actually De-stabilizing (with Some Implications for the Future)." *World Development* 6 (July-August):1005–1018.

Rippy, J. Fred. 1959. *British Investments in Latin America: 1824–1949.* Minneapolis: University of Minnesota Press.

Serra, José. 1979. "Three Mistaken Theses Regarding the Connection Between Indus-trialization and Authoritarian Regimes." In *The New Authoritarianism in Latin America,* edited by David Collier, 99–163. Princeton, N.J.: Princeton University Press.

Singer, Paulo. 1975. "O Brasil no contexto do capitalismo mundial, 1889–1930." In *Brasil republicano: Estructura de poder e economia,* edited by Boris Fausto. História Geral da Civilização Brasileira, tomo 3, vol. 1. São Paulo: Difusão Europeia do Livro.

Stallings, Barbara. 1979. "Peru and the U.S. Banks: Privatization of Financial Rela-tions." In *Capitalism and the State in U.S.–Latin American Relations,* edited by Richard R. Fagen, 217-253. Stanford, Calif.: Stanford University Press.

United States Department of Commerce. 1929–1978. "U.S. Direct Investment Abroad, Sales of U.S. Affiliates." In *Survey of Current Business.*

United States Tariff Commission. 1973. *Implications of Multinational Firms for World Trade and Investment and for U.S. Trade and Labor.* Report to U.S. Senate, Committee on Finance. Washington, D.C.: Government Printing Office.

Vaupel, James W. and Curhan, Joan P. 1973. *The World's Multinational Enterprises.* Boston, Mass.: Harvard University, Graduate School of Business Administration, Division of Research.

Vernon, Raymond. 1963. *The Dilemma of Mexico's Development.* Cambridge, Mass.: Harvard University Press.

Wallerstein, Immanuel. 1974a. "Dependence in an Interdependent World: The Lim-ited Possibilities of Transformation Within the Capitalist World Economy." *African Studies Review* 17, no. 1 (April):1–26.

———. 1974b. *The Modern World System: Capitalist Agriculture and the Origins of the European World-Economy in the Sixteenth Century.* New York: Academic Press.

————. 1976. "Semi-Peripheral Countries and the Contemporary World Crisis." *Theory and Society* 3, no. 4:461-484.

Weinert, Richard S. 1977. "The State and Foreign Capital." In *Authoritarianism in Mexico,* edited by José Luis Reyna and Richard S. Weinert, 109-128. Philadelphia, Pa.: Institute for the Study of Human Issues.

chapter twelve ═══════════════════════════════

How to Divest in
Latin America and Why

Albert O. Hirschman

The [U.S.] President, in 1940, [recounted] that when he had visited Rio de
Janeiro in 1936, President Getúlio Vargas had told him that the bus lines in
the capital were owned in Montreal and Toronto, and had asked: "What
would the people of New York City do if the subways were all owned in
Canada?" Roosevelt's reply had been: "Why, there would be a revolution."
The President went on to say that he thought that, when foreign capital
went into a Latin American country, the country should gain control of the
utility or other business after the investment had been paid off in a period
that might be set at twenty-five or thirty years. Thus, the country could look
forward to gaining ultimate control of utilities and perhaps other foreign-
financed corporations through having what Roosevelt called "an option on
the equity."

Bryce Wood

The dispute between Peru and the United States over the expropriation of
the International Petroleum Company is only one of a monotonously long
list of incidents and conflicts which call into serious question the wisdom of
present institutional arrangements concerning private international investment. This chapter will discuss the principal weaknesses of these arrangements, with particular emphasis on political economy rather than on economics proper, and will then survey a number of ways in which current
institutions and practices could be restructured. It is written against the back-
drop of rising nationalism and militancy in the developing countries, particularly in Latin America, and of an astounding complacency, inertia, and
lack of institutional imagination on the part of the rich countries.

The basic position adopted here with respect to foreign private investment is that it shares to a very high degree the ambiguity of most human

Reprinted with permission from Albert O. Hirschman, *A Bias for Hope* (New
Haven: Yale University Press, 1971).

inventions and institutions: it has considerable potential for both good and evil. On the one hand, there are the celebrated and undoubted contributions of private international investment to development: the bringing in of capital, entrepreneurship, technology, management and other skills, and of international market connections, all of which are either wholly lacking in the poor countries, or are in inadequate supply given the opportunities and programs for economic development. On the other hand, foreign investment brings not only the dangers of economic plunder and political domination which are the stock-in-trade of the various theories of imperialism, but a number of other, more subtle, yet serious effects and side effects which can handicap the development efforts of countries placing prolonged and substantial reliance on private investment from abroad. The picture that has sometimes been painted of the career of foreign investment is that at one time, long ago, the negative aspects predominated: there was sheer exploitation of human and natural resources as well as crude power play in the early free-wheeling days, when capital followed the flag or was, on the contrary, the "cat's paw of empire"; but this unfortunate phase has been outgrown, so it is widely thought, with decolonization, with the worldwide assertion of national sovereign states and their taxing powers, and with the desire, on the part of modern foreign investors, to perform as "good corporate citizens" of the host country and as "partners in progress." Unfortunately, this edifying story of human progress is incomplete and one-sided. It can, in fact, be argued that certain negative aspects of foreign investment do not only continue to coexist with the positive ones, but typically tend to predominate over them as development proceeds, at least up to some point. These are the just-mentioned "more subtle" effects and side effects that will now be briefly explained.

Private Foreign Investment—An Increasingly Mixed Blessing

The positive contribution of foreign investment to an economy can be of various kinds. In the first place, it can supply one of several missing factors of production (capital, entrepreneurship, management, and so forth), factors, that is, which are simply and indisputably not to be found in the country receiving the investment. This is the situation often prevailing in the earliest stages of development of a poor country. More generally, foreign investment can make it possible for output to increase sharply, because it provides the recipient economy with a larger quantity of comparatively scarce (if not entirely missing) inputs.

Another contribution of foreign investment, conspicuous in relations among advanced industrial countries and inviting often a two-way flow, is of a rather different nature: it can have a teaching function and serve to improve the quality of the local factors of production. By on-the-spot example and through competitive pressures, foreign investment can act as a spur to the general efficiency of local enterprise. This effect is likely to be particularly important in economic sectors which are sheltered from the competition of merchandise imports from abroad. Such sectors (services, industries with strong locational advantages) appear to expand rapidly at advanced stages of economic development. If foreign investment is successful in enhancing the quality of local enterprise, then its inflow will be providentially self-limiting: once the local business community achieves greater efficiency, there will be fewer openings for the demonstration of superior foreign techniques, management, and know-how. But what if local businessmen, faced with overwhelming advantages of their foreign competitors, do not respond with adequate vigor and, instead, deteriorate further or sell out? This is, of course, the nub of recent European fears of the "American challenge." I cannot deal here with this problem, but the fact that it exists has interesting implications for the topic at hand.

If foreign investment can fail to improve and may even harm the quality of local factors of production, then the question arises whether it may also, under certain circumstances, lead to a decrease in the quantity of local inputs available to an economy. In other words, could the inflow of foreign investment stunt what might otherwise be vigorous local development of the so-called missing or scarce factors of production?

This question has been little discussed.[1] The reason for the neglect lies in the intellectual tradition which treats international investment under the rubric "export of capital." As long as one thinks in terms of this single factor of production being exported to a capital-poor country, it is natural to view it as highly complementary to various local factors—such as natural resources and labor—that are available in abundance and are only waiting to be combined with the "missing factor" to yield large additional outputs. But, for a long time now, foreign investors have prided themselves on contributing "not just capital," but a whole bundle of other valuable inputs. In counterpart to these claims, however, the doubt might have arisen that some components of the bundle will no longer be purely complementary to local factors, but will be competitive with them and could cause them to wither or retard and even prevent their growth.

The possibility, and indeed likelihood, that international trade will lead to the shrinkage and possibly to the disappearance of certain lines of local production as a result of cheaper imports has been at the root of international trade theory since Adam Smith and Ricardo. This effect of trade has been celebrated by free traders through such terms as "international specialization" and "efficient reallocation of resources." The opponents of free trade have often pointed out that for a variety of reasons it is imprudent and harmful for a country to become specialized along certain product lines in accordance with the dictates of comparative advantage. Whatever the merit of these critical arguments, they would certainly acquire overwhelming weight if the question arose whether a country should allow itself to become specialized not just along certain commodity lines, but along factor-of-production lines. Very few countries would ever consciously wish to specialize in unskilled labor, while foreigners with a comparative advantage in entrepreneurship, management, skilled labor, and capital took over these functions, replacing inferior "local talent." But this is precisely the direction in which events can move when international investment, proudly bringing in its bundle of factors, has unimpeded access to developing countries. In the fine paradoxical formulation of Felipe Pazos: "The main weakness of direct investment as a development agent is a consequence of the complete character of its contribution."[2]

The displacement of local factors and stunting of local abilities which can occur in the wake of international investment is sometimes absolute, as when local banks or businesses are bought out by foreign capital; this has in fact been happening recently with increasing frequency in Latin America. But the more common and perhaps more dangerous, because less noticeable, stunting effect is relative to what might have happened in the absence of the investment.

As already mentioned, foreign investment can be at its creative best by bringing in "missing" factors of production, complementary to those available locally, in the early stages of development of a poor country. The possibility that it will play a stunting role arises later on, when the poor country has begun to generate, to a large extent no doubt because of the prior injection of foreign investment, its own entrepreneurs, technicians, and savers and could now do even more along these lines if it were not for the institutional inertia that makes for a continued importing of so-called scarce factors of production which have become potentially dispensable. It is, of course, exceedingly difficult to judge at what point in time foreign investment changes in this fashion from a stimulant of development into a retarding influence, particularly since during the latter stage its contribution is still ostensibly positive—for example, the foreign capital that comes in is visible and measurable, in contrast to the domestic capital that might have been generated in its stead. One can never be certain, moreover, that restrictions against foreign investment will in fact call forth the local entrepreneurial, managerial, technological, and saving performances which are believed to be held back and waiting in the wings to take over from the foreign investors. Nevertheless, a considerable body of evidence, brought forth less by design than by accidents such as wars, depressions, nationalist expropriations, and international sanctions, suggests strongly that, after an initial period of development, the domestic supply of routinely imported factors of production is far more elastic than is ever suspected under business-as-usual conditions. If this is so, then the "climate for foreign investment" ought to turn from attractive at an early stage of development to much less inviting in some middle stretch—in which most of Latin America finds itself at the present time [late 1960s].

The preceding argument is the principal economic reason for anticipating increasing conflict between the goals of national development and the foreign investment community, even after the latter has thoroughly purged itself of the excesses that marred its early career. The argument is strengthened by related considerations pertaining to economic policymaking, a "factor of production" not often taken into account by economists, but which nevertheless has an essential role to play. In the course of industrialization, resources for complementary investment in education and overhead capital must be generated through taxation, the opening up of new domestic and foreign markets must be made attractive, institutions hampering growth must be reformed, and powerful social groups that are antagonistic to development must be neutralized. The achievement of these tasks is considerably facilitated if the new industrialists are able to speak with a strong, influential, and even militant voice. But the emergence of such a voice is most unlikely if a large portion of the more dynamic new industries is in foreign hands. This is a somewhat novel reproach to foreign capital, which has normally been taken to task for being unduly interfering, wire-pulling, and domineering. Whatever the truth about these accusations in the past, the principal failing of the managers of today's foreign-held branch plants and subsidiaries may well be the opposite. Given their position as "guests" in a "host country," their behavior is far too restrained and inhibited. The trouble with the foreign investor may well be not that he is so meddlesome, but that he is so mousy! It is the foreign investor's mousiness which deprives the policymakers of the guidance, pressures, and support they badly need to push through critically required development decisions and policies amid a welter of conflicting and antagonistic interests.

The situation is in fact even worse. Not only does policymaking fail to be invigorated by the influence normally emanating from a strong, confident, and assertive group of industrialists; more directly, the presence of a strong foreign element in the dynamically expanding sectors of the economy is likely to have a debilitating and corroding effect on the rationality of official economic policy making for development. For, when newly arising investment opportunities are largely or predominantly seized upon by foreign firms, the national policymakers face in effect a dilemma: more development means at the same time less autonomy. In a situation in which many key points of the economy are occupied by foreigners while economic policy is made by nationals it is only too likely that these nationals will not excel in "rational" policy making for economic development; for, a good portion of the fruits of such rationality would accrue to nonnationals and would strengthen their position.[3] On the other hand, the role and importance of national economic policymaking for development increase steadily as the array of available policy instruments widens, and as more group demands are articulated. Hence the scope for "irrationality" actually expands as development gains momentum. That its incidence increases as well could probably be demonstrated by a historical survey of tax, exchange rate, utility rate and similar policies that were aimed directly or indirectly at "squeezing" or administering pin pricks to the foreigner, but managed, at the same time, to slow down economic growth.

The preceding pages have said next to nothing about the direct cost to the capital-importing country of private international investment nor about the related question of the balance-of-payments drain such investment may occasion. While these matters have long been vigorously debated, with the critics charging exploitation and the defenders denying it, the outcome of the discussion seems to me highly inconclusive. Moreover, undue fascination with the dollar-and-cents aspects of international investment has led to the neglect of the topics here considered, which, I submit, raise issues of at least equal importance and suggest a simple conclusion: strictly from the point of view of development, private foreign investment is a mixed blessing, and the mixture is likely to become more noxious at the intermediate stage of development which characterizes much of present-day Latin America.

Hence, if the broadly conceived national interest of the United States is served by the development of Latin America, then this interest enters into conflict with a continuing expansion and even with the maintenance of the present position of private investors from the United States. Purely political arguments lend strong support to this proposition. Internal disputes over the appropriate treatment of the foreign investor have gravely weakened, or helped to topple, some of the more progressive and democratic governments which have held power in recent years in such countries as Brazil, Chile, and Peru. Frictions between private investors from the United States and host governments have an inevitable repercussion on United States-Latin American relations. In a number of cases such disputes have been responsible for a wholly disproportionate deterioration of bilateral relations. The continued presence and expansion of our private investment position and our insistence on a "favorable investment climate" decisively undermined, from the outset, the credibility of our Alliance for Progress proposals. Land reform and income redistribution through taxation are so obviously incompatible, in the short run, with the maintenance of a favorable investment climate for private capital that insistence on both could only be interpreted to signify that we did not really mean those fine phrases about achieving social justice through land and tax reform.

If these political arguments are added to those pertaining to economics and political economy, one thing becomes clear: a policy of selective liquidation and withdrawal of foreign private investment is in the best mutual interests of Latin America and the United States. Such a policy can be selective with respect to countries and to economic sectors and it ought to be combined with a policy of encouraging new capital outflows, also on a selective basis and with some safeguards.

Notes

1. Important exceptions are the articles by J. Knapp, "Capital Exports and Growth," *Economic Journal* 67 (September 1957):432-444, and by Felipe Pazos, "The Role of International Movements of Private Capital in Promoting Development," in John H. Adler, ed., *Capital Movements and Economic Development* (New York: St. Martin's Press, 1967).

2. Pazos, "International Movements of Private Capital," 196. A. K. Cairncross expresses the same thought in discussing the contribution of foreign-owned branch plants and subsidiaries to economic development: "Their very power to break all the bottlenecks at once . . . can be, from the point of view of the host country, their most damning feature" (*Factors in Economic Development* [London: George Allen and Unwin, 1962]. 181).

3. For some interesting remarks along these lines, see Hans O. Schmitt. "Foreign Capital and Social Conflict in Indonesia," *Economic Development and Cultural Change* 10 (April 1962):284-293.

part seven

Development and the Technological Imperative

As already has been stressed in a number of chapters, the role of technology and its relation to the institutional and ceremonial structure are fundamental to the institutionalist and structuralist understanding of Latin America's past development and its contemporary problems. In Chapter 13, James Street considers the potential for development based on the future application of technology to the Latin American economies, one of the last "great frontiers." The problem, he argues, is that there is a whole array of "past-binding" institutions that is inappropriate to the pressing growth needs of the region, that acts as a brake on both the development and application of the required technology. Such institutions include the transnational corporations, of course, but also ceremonial behavior such as the superficial consumption patterns of the small domestic elites who emulate, for status and other reasons, the wasteful consumption behavior of the more advanced center countries. For Street, as for most institutionalists, more, better, and technologically appropriate education is essential, although not the only factor, if these barriers are to be broken through and the full potential of Latin America's development is to be realized.

chapter thirteen

The Technological Frontier in Latin America: Creativity and Productivity

James H. Street

Latin America as a Great Frontier

Latin America is one of the world's last great frontiers. *Frontier* is used here in the sense in which C. E. Ayres incorporated it in his theory of economic progress. "A frontier," he says, "is a penetration phenomenon."[1] It is a region that offers the space for expansion of population in movement, for a rupture with old institutions, and for the application of techniques brought from other regions to achieve an accelerated rate of development.

In terms of land space and relative sparsity of population, Latin America is one of the few remaining regions of the world where a major population expansion and a massive utilization of resources can take place. Most areas of Europe and Asia are already heavily populated. The inner reaches of the Soviet Union, northern Canada, and central Australia, although they will no doubt continue to grow, are constrained by formidable climatic limitations. Sub-Saharan Africa appears to have a considerable growth potential, but must overcome ancient tribal and colonial traditions that weigh heavily on the development process.

Latin America, particularly in portions of Brazil, Argentina, Colombia, and Mexico, still possesses large zones of relatively isolated, underpopulated, and unexploited land space. Over half the region contains fewer than two inhabitants per square mile, and large additional areas contain fewer than twenty-five inhabitants per square mile.[2] For the immediate future,

Reprinted in abridged form from the *Journal of Economic Issues* 10 (September 1976) by special permission of the copyright holder, the Association for Evolutionary Economics.

however, many of these zones are unlikely to form poles of attraction. These include much of the great Amazon basin, the dry Andes, the bleak areas of southern Argentina and Chile, and desert areas on the Pacific coast, in the Chaco, and in northern Mexico.

Nevertheless, with improved techniques, the conditions of habitability can change markedly. Before World War II, areas of Mexico such as the dry, prehistoric lake bed of the Laguna in the state of Durango and equally arid lands in Sonora could support only a sparse and insecure population. During drought periods, often extending several years, entire villages of farmers left their homes, many to enter migrant labor streams in the United States. But in recent years, vast tracts have been brought under intensive cultivation with water supplied by dams, tube wells, powerful pumps, and cement-lined irrigation systems, all requiring the application of advanced engineering. These areas now offer secure and stable employment for money wages, and Mexico has acquired an important source of export earnings. Such expansion may ultimately be limited by the capacity of underground aquifers, yet it illustrates the scope of technology for the enlargement of resources.[3]

As a consequence of the rising interest in frontier development, a few years ago the Inter-American Committee for the Alliance for Progress (CIAP) conducted a survey to locate regions in South America that remain underdeveloped because of such factors as natural barriers, soil limitations, or endemic disease. CIAP identified nine major regions with developmental potential and a number of subsidiary zones with special concentrations of known resources. These are obvious targets for a determined effort to open the internal frontier, and future development planning must overcome the specific obstacles that have impeded the earlier growth of these resource areas.[4]

In addition to providing room for expansion, a frontier has a second characteristic, as Ayres has noted: It becomes infiltrated by new migrants from other zones who bring with them new knowledge. This process is occurring in many parts of Latin America as interior roads are constructed and colonization takes place. The region has long been oriented overseas as a consequence of traditional trade and cultural connections, but the focus is visibly shifting inward. The recent extensive construction of trunk highways in Brazil has initially encouraged ribbon colonization along these routes, but the interior dispersion of population is likely to continue as new growth centers are formed. A single cross-country road accompanied by a new hydroelectric development in eastern Paraguay has profoundly affected the drift of population within that country. Even smaller countries, such as those of Central America, obtained penetration roads and feeder connections to the Pan American Highway during the short-lived availability of exceptional outside assistance under the Alliance for Progress. These have opened access to previously remote communities and encouraged forms of commercial intercourse that are indispensable to the regional integration movement.

Colombia and Mexico are among the few countries that in this half of the century have made significant advances in the use of the railroad, which is still the basic carrier of freight wherever rails have been laid. The adoption of a common gauge for its disconnected lines and the bridging of the Magdalena River—a project that took nine years—has enabled Colombia to operate an integrated rail system for the first time.[5] At about the same time Mexico opened a cross-country line of commercial importance from Presidio, Texas, via Chihuahua to Topolobampo on the West Coast.[6] This railway passes through exceedingly rugged terrain and required the construction of seventy-two mountain tunnels. Under the impact of the oil crisis, Brazil is also returning to the building of railways to accomplish national economic integration.

The opening of new routes of transport, a process that has been accelerating since mid-century, is certain to reduce the isolation of the interior of Latin America and will bring new groups into contact with each other.

All students of Ayres are aware of the importance he attached to a third aspect of the frontier: It permits a continuity of technological transfers, while at the same time fostering a detachment from previous institutional controls.[7] Latin America, through its overseas connections, has long had contact with European and, more recently, North American influences, and it has become a substantial borrower of foreign technology. Yet its traditional institutions of concentrated landholding, paternalistic labor control, speculatively biased investment, and overcentralized administration have impeded the structural transformation necessary for a fully industrial society. Whether the surging population movements now under way will have any appreciable effect on the loosening of institutional controls remains to be seen, but such an outcome would probably require a significant qualitative shift in attitudes and educational processes.

Ayres emphasized the possibilities for cross-fertilization at the frontier.[8] Given the increased cultural contact, new combinations and adaptations of preexisting elements are almost certain to occur. Two literal instances in the field of applied genetics may be cited. Norman E. Borlaug, the Nobel laureate who performed his early experiments in plant hybridization in Iowa, sought to utilize differences in growing seasons in Mexico to produce two successive crops of wheat a year in order to speed up his breeding trials.[9] Discovering that some varieties were less sensitive to the length of day in determining their maturing and fruiting, he was able to select those with the least photosensitivity and thus shorten the plant life cycle. By this means he was able to shift the determinant of the period of maturity from an environmental influence to an inherited, stable one. From this discovery came an important application, incorporated in the Green Revolution, that increased the number of crops that could be grown annually under subtropical conditions both in Latin America and Asia.

More recently, plant breeders at Cornell University, cooperating with Mexican investigators at the International Maize and Wheat Improvement Center at El Batán, have crossed North American with Caribbean varieties of corn to develop plants resistant to the European corn borer.[10] These experiments are significant because they suggest possibilities for increasing international collaboration among scientific investigators wherever institutional barriers do not stand in the way.

The horizontal land frontier in Latin America must ultimately come to a close, but beyond that, as Frederick Jackson Turner foresaw in the United States toward the end of the last century, there extends the vertical frontier of internal development.[11] The vertical frontier is, of necessity, largely technological. Montague Yudelman has pointed out, for example, that for a considerable time Latin America has chiefly depended upon expanding land use to increase agriculture production.[12] Only one-third of the total increase in farm output in the period 1948–1964 could be attributed to higher yields and hence to the employment of more intensive cultivation and new techniques for increasing yields per hectare; two-thirds of the increase in output stemmed from bringing new land under cultivation. (In the case of cereals, higher yields contributed only one-fourth of the increase.)

The ratio of gains from increased yields to those from the expansion of cultivation will clearly have to shift in the direction of greater intensity and the greater application of new techniques as the density of population mounts. Since improvement in yields requires time for research and time for the dissemination of knowledge, it must be phased in with the continued spatial expansion.

This change in conception of the rural frontier is critically important. The long political contention over the desirability of land reform has obscured the nature of what is involved. Latin America requires not only a change in the way land is controlled and operated, but also a sharp rise in agricultural productivity, and hence a widespread and continuing revolution in methods of production.

A region that in terms of resources should be one of the major food surplus areas of the world is becoming increasingly dependent upon other regions to supply its deficiencies. According to a recent report of the Inter-American Development Bank, "The considerably changed composition of Latin American exports and imports in 1972 indicates that the region was unable to supply its own home needs for basic foodstuffs such as wheat and wheat flour, barley, rye and even corn. As a result of the drop in Argentine corn production, Latin America changed from an exporter to a net importer of this crop in 1972.[13] While 1972 was not a very good crop year, the statement reveals the precarious relation of domestic food production to the region's consumption needs.

Two Latin American countries illustrate the difference in rural development trends. Thirty years ago Argentina accounted for 80 percent of the world's exports of corn and half the exports of beef, and was the second largest exporter of wheat. Today, while it continues to depend upon agricultural exports for more than 70 percent of its foreign exchange, this richly endowed country has neglected its agricultural sector and is a steadily diminishing factor in the world market for food. Because of the natural fertility of its soil, the level of corn yields in Argentina in 1935–1939 was higher than in the United States.[14] By 1960–1962, however, largely as the result of genetic research and plant breeding, U.S. yields had increased so rapidly relative to the slight Argentine improvement that they were more than double those in Argentina. Also by contrast, Mexico, which has steadily augmented its technical capacity to produce foodstuffs, increased its corn yields by 52 percent, while Argentine yields increased by only 7 percent during this period.[15]

The improvements in Mexican wheat yields are even more impressive. The level of Mexican wheat yields in 1935–1939 was below those of the United States and Argentina, but by 1960–1962, average yields exceeded those of both countries. Mexico actually trebled its wheat yields between 1948–1952 and 1964–1965.[16] As a result, the country has been able to export appreciable quantities of wheat, except in unusually dry years, and the total value of its agricultural exports has tended to climb over the long term.[17] According to Yudelman, "There can be little doubt that one important factor in these differential growth rates in corn and wheat yields has been the sustained high quality of research in producing new varieties of wheat and corn in Mexico and the United States."[18] The technological frontier in Latin America has, of course, many other aspects than increasing food production in relation to an exploding urban population, but none is more critical.

Technological Transfers and Domestic Creativity

Perhaps it is foolhardy to be sanguine about the prospects for exploiting the technological frontier in Latin America: certainly the literature on internal development and technological transfer is overwhelmingly pessimistic. Raúl Prebisch and his associates in the Economic Commission for Latin America were for a time enthusiastic supporters of the strategy of import substitution as a means of internal development. They recognized the crucial importance of domestic research and development to the efficient operation of local agriculture and industry, and they encouraged a vigorous search for ways of promoting the international transfer of technology.[19]

Later they became disillusioned with import substitution, believing that the urban middle class market for domestic products would soon become saturated, and that the resistance of vested interests would not permit the redistribution of income necessary to expand internal markets to reach the lower classes and the rural population. In some cases, import substitution merely shifted the demand for finished goods to imported raw materials, complex equipment, and industrial know-how.

Osvaldo Sunkel, a close associate of Prebisch in the Structuralist School, initially devoted his attention to a study of the internal bottlenecks that have blocked or distorted a process of balanced growth in Latin America. Increasingly he has turned to external factors that he now considers predominant. Sunkel believes that the technology necessary for development, and the means of its continual improvement, are lodged in the control of the multinational corporations, and a qualitative shift in its availability has occurred.[20] Previously, Latin American industrialists could obtain the processes they needed through simple franchises or licensing agreements. Governments simultaneously could promote industrial progress through public financing of local enterprise, whether state operated or private. Occasionally, new industries would enter with immigrant entrepreneurs.

In the recent period, however, Sunkel believes that international capitalism has become much more highly organized, and governments work hand-in-glove with multinational corporations to dominate weaker economies. Research and development are centralized in the home country, and foreign users are obliged to buy complete packages of entrepreneurship, management, skills, design, technology, financing, and marketing organization at oligopoly or monopoly prices. Even domestic brainpower, government credit agencies, import substitution policies, and other preferential arrangements are coopted for the benefit of foreign firms. The result is increasing dependency and a widening of the technological gap.[21]

Jorge M. Katz, who has made intensive studies of the transfer of foreign technology to Argentine industry, shares Sunkel's view of the futility of stimulating domestic research and development as a means of restoring a degree of parity.[22] Katz considers that the only remedy for this form of technological dependency is for the national government to intervene and use its strength in bargaining with foreign corporations. By using its oligopsony power, the government might hope to reduce the cost of borrowing techniques and processes, a habit that he believes is now unavoidable and irreversible.

David Felix has offered another explanation for the widening technological dualism that persists between Latin America and the industrial countries. "Underdevelopment," he says, "is essentially a condition of enduring incapacity to modify and disseminate technology on a broad scale."[23] This incapacity he attributes to the circumstance that the main world sources of innovation have undergone a significant qualitative shift from Period I, running from the 1860s to the 1920s, to Period II, from the 1920s to the present. During the earlier period, it was possible for major innovations to be introduced by lone inventors engaged in "empiricist tinkering and learning by doing." (Thomas Alva Edison typified such an inventor.) In the latter period, inventive research has become more formalized and systematic. It requires a high degree of theoretical training in pure science and the careful design of experiments to ensure the probability of precise, planned results. Characteristically, this process requires team organization and is highly responsive to calculated investment, which may be carried out by private or public agencies.

"Latin American countries," according to Felix, "though eager borrowers of imported technologies, have been institutionally out of phase in both periods."[24] In an illuminating historical review of the earlier period, he describes the complex economic dualism of the village economy and the overseas trade that impeded the progressive growth of local artisanship and agricultural skill. At a higher organizational level, similar cultural factors led to the displacement of local entrepreneurship by foreign capital in such promising domestic enterprises as the Argentine meat export trade and Chilean nitrate and copper mining.[25] As a result, Latin America lost the opportunity to become an effective participant in the earlier—and easier—phase of innovational development and was seriously handicapped in entering the more recent phase.

The latter phase coincided, in the more advanced countries of the region, with the adoption of policies for import substitution industrialization. Felix believes that the rapidity with which the new import substituting industries must introduce new products to maintain their market leads biases these firms against investing in domestic technological creativity.[26] Both local firms and foreign subsidiaries find it easier and more profitable to draw on the international pool of product innovation than to try to enter the expensive game of domestic research and development. He sees no immediate solution for the trend toward increasing technological dualism and economic dependency, although in another essay he suggests that a concentration on biological research might be one area in which Latin America could still reap important gains in agriculture, forestry, and pest control.[27]

These gloomy assessments of Sunkel, Katz, and Felix must be taken seriously, as they are based on close observations of hard realities. Yet, there are grounds for believing that the prospect may not be as hopeless as it seems. These grounds rest upon the cumulative and unpredictable nature of technology itself.

In his Nobel laureate lecture, Simon Kuznets commented that "a technological innovation, particularly one based on a recent major invention, represents a venture into the partly unknown, something not fully known until the mass spread of the innovation reveals the full range of direct and related effects. . . . The effects of such ventures into the new and partly unknown are numerous. Those of most interest here are the *surprises,* the unexpected results, which may be positive or negative."[28]

In the 1930s, few in the United States foresaw the economic and social transformation that would later take place in the agricultural South, largely through a cluster of innovations in methods of cotton production, the shock effect of World War II on institutional arrangements, and the entry of diversified industry into various parts of the region.[29] Previously, southern institutions had been highly resistant to change, and innovation was not characteristic of southern agriculture; yet, under the impact of new conditions, in only two decades major modifications in the structure of the regional economy were achieved. A similar process may be under way now in the more receptive regions of Latin America, of which Mexico seems to be one.

Material technology, it must be remembered, is not a single package, but a multitude of discrete elements, a storehouse from which it is possible to select useful parts and to reassemble them into a set of techniques adapted to earlier stages of development and to local circumstances. Seymour Melman, in his studies of industrial decision making, has taken a similar view: "Technology, within the limits set by nature, is man-made and hence variable on order. If one wants to alter our technologies, then the place to look is not to molecular structure but to social structure, not to the chemistry of materials but to the rules of man, especially the economic rules of who decides on technology."[30]

It is doubtful that the intense competition that has taken place under import substitution to introduce a greater variety of consumer goods, in a frantic effort to keep up with the outside world, is the best contribution that modern technology can make to emerging Latin American society. Everyone who has observed the operation of the "demonstration effect" in Latin America is aware of the waste of resources involved in attempting to duplicate the immense range of superficial goods of the more "advanced" countries, which in Latin America serve only the need for conspicuous consumption of a minor elite. It would clearly be more helpful to direct policies toward basic research in improving productivity in food and other high priority goods. A number of sources of such innovation are not exclusively in the control of the multinational corporations, but flow through the relatively open channels of research by universities, foundation supported institutes, and government. Other innovations can be acquired in relatively competitive markets.

In this connection, the explorations of Dilmus James in the transfer of obsolescent but still serviceable industrial and farm equipment to less developed countries warrant further consideration.[31] The mechanical revolution in North American agriculture was disseminated partly in this fashion, and there are instances of industrial firms in Japan and Latin America that similarly built up domestic know-how and market capacity. The development of "appropriate" technologies particularly suited to use in village economies being investigated by Allen Jedlicka and others also has interesting possibilities.[32]

The Role of Education on the Technological Frontier

There is an element of Yankee ethnocentric superiority in assuming that the techniques of innovation and adaptation cannot be learned by other peoples, especially when their survival depends upon it. Ayres has affirmed that "a technically sophisticated community can and will equip itself with the instrumentalities of an industrial economy. There is no instance of any such community having failed to do so. Conversely, an ignorant and unskilled community cannot advance except by acquiring knowledge and skills."[33]

Kuznets, who has also emphasized the transfer of useful knowledge in fostering economic growth, has suggested that, in the case of the less developed countries, "the later the entry the higher the initial rates of growth should be, reflecting the existence of a greater stock of technological and social innovation to choose from and the pressure of greater backwardness."[34]

The role of functional education in Latin America is to create a forcing bed in which the acceleration of experimentation, innovation, and adaptation will take place. It is clear that prevalent educational institutions in Latin America have been very deficient in this regard.

The habituation to tool using and technical problem solving is an activity that must go on at many levels. We ordinarily assume that training must be received through formal education—in the elementary and secondary schools, the colleges and universities, and the foundation or government sponsored research institutes. Equally vital, of course, are the vocational schools, apprentice training programs in private industry, and industrial research and development laboratories.

Yet, the development of technological attitudes and skills begins from infancy in play activities; this fact is now well understood in industrial societies, but is rarely acted upon in societies with a different cultural formation. There is perhaps no greater cultural difference between children who grow up in Latin America and those in the United States than in the degree to which the latter begin in infancy to play with "educational" toys—building blocks, puzzles, and simple tools—and proceed through adolescence to the Tinker Toy, the Erector set, the chemistry set, the home-made radio, and often the home microscope and astronomical telescope. The typical North American childhood is littered with artifacts to excite the curiosity, to be manipulated and understood, and to be used with some end in view. This environment is, of course, made possible by the preexistence of an industrial culture and by the wide diffusion of higher incomes. In Latin America these circumstances do not prevail; yet, there is also a marked difference in the expression of cultural attitudes, which has shaped much of the educational system.

Two factors apparently account for the Latin American pattern of education: the authoritarian form under which it developed while under Catholic church control, and which has carried over into the secular education, and the composition of social classes during the formative period. Authoritarian education took the form of rote learning; the child was catechized rather than encouraged to think and explore in new ways. Today, even in such an advanced country as Argentina, rote learning has survived as a common mode of instruction. In a perennial search for national identity, children are taught to memorize names of past leaders and dates of historic events, with little perception that they are living in a time of dynamic growth to which the earlier episodes have little relevance. James Scobie has ably described the two-class system which existed in Argentina at the beginning of the maximum growth period about a century ago. Class disparities actually widened with national prosperity. Despite a promising beginning in popular and scientific education under Domingo Faustino Sarmiento, Argentine schooling soon lapsed into a traditional pattern. "This education remained oriented toward the classics, the humanities, and philosophy, and it emphasized theoretical discussion rather than applied experimentation. Even medical students learned anatomy from texts, not from dissection, and future engineers rarely got any practical training until after they had received their degree."[35]

Both the upper class—the *gente decente*—and the aspiring members of the lower class—the *gente de pueblo*—saw educational opportunities in the same light, as training for the well-paid and socially prestigious professions of medicine and law. "There existed, in effect, no middle ground in the Argentine educational system. The *gente decente* benefited from the elitist educational structure that prepared their children for 'leadership.' Parents from the lower strata who by dint of savings and sacrifice pushed a child into *colegio* training had no desire to settle for 'trade school' education."[36] Technical education had little appeal and received little support, and this condition has changed only moderately in recent times.

The pattern described by Scobie came to prevail quite generally in Latin America, but there have been notable exceptions, and the current revolution in popular education in some of the rural districts of Mexico owes its origins to one of these. This was the movement begun by the Swiss educator, Enrique C. Rébsamen, in the state of Veracruz in the 1880s.[37]

Rébsamen was a disciple of Johann Heinrich Pestalozzi and, like him, believed that a child learned best by using his own senses and by discovering things for himself. This was a novel idea in Mexico at that time, and one that antedated the Deweyan revolution in education in the United States.

Rébsamen thought of education as a functional process in which pupils should be exposed directly to the materials, plants, and animals of their natural environment from their earliest years. They were taught to appreciate these elements as features of natural history, as sources of esthetic satisfaction, and as materials for practical use. Thus prepared, the child was expected to make better functional use of the resources at hand in his own community.

Rébsamen attached to his classrooms an array of shops and laboratories in which children worked with their hands in the arts, crafts, and sciences. Additions to rural schools were built by the children themselves under the guidance of their teacher-craftsman, and each school was surrounded by gardens, orchards, and livestock pastures as a self-sufficient enterprise. Rébsamen's principal achievement was the founding of a normal school at Jalapa that has perpetuated and recently given a rebirth to his educational principles, so clearly related to the needs of a developing economy.

Interest in Rébsamen's approach was vitiated by the circumstance that the national educational leaders of his time, the celebrated *científicos* associated with the regime of Porfirio Díaz, although they professed an enthusiasm for the promotion of science and technology, had no genuine interest in popular education or the advancement of the Mexican lower classes.[38] The positivist movement concentrated on order and progress derived from abroad. President Díaz, although a *mestizo* himself, had a great admiration for the ingenuity of foreigners, and he encouraged them to direct the expansion of railroads, mining, and petroleum development with scant employment opportunities for the indigenous and *mestizo* population except as menial workers. Thus no educational foundations were laid for an effective participation by Mexican craftsmen and technicians in the development of their own resources.

After the bloodiest period of the Mexican revolution, leaders sought to consolidate their gains under President Alvaro Obregón in the early 1920s. Popular education received a great impetus when Obregón made available an ample budget to his energetic minister of education, José Vasconcelos, who had great confidence in the capacities of the indigenous masses. He began a vigorous campaign against illiteracy, and within four years he established almost 1,000 new schools in rural villages.[39] These were of a new type, which he called *La Casa del Pueblo* (The House of the People). They featured basic education in reading, writing, arithmetic, and folk culture, but they also laid stress on practical instruction in sanitation, scientific agriculture, and other useful arts. Vasconcelos's famous *anexos* provided for the education of adults as well as children and sought to make the school the village cultural center through the introduction of electric lighting, sewing machines, mills for grinding corn, and other useful equipment that would ensure the support of the villagers who were thus benefited.

Aside from resistance from the *cacique* and the *curandero,* the local chieftain and the medicine man, Vasconcelos's principal problem was to find teachers who were themselves literate and who had the versatility and political skill necessary to effect a social transformation. The isolation of the villages and the general poverty militated against popular education, but the foundations were laid. Later, under President Lázaro Cárdenas, an ambitious plan was undertaken to select the brightest adolescents from every village and send them to the National School of Agriculture at Chapingo, from which they were expected to return to their own villages and instruct their compatriots in improved methods of farming, using the local dialect or language. Some youngsters succumbed to the bright lights of Mexico City and never returned, but others became the new leaders of rural Mexico.[40]

The Mexican revolution in popular education, although hampered by a contentious bureaucracy that has maintained traditional methods in many districts, marches on.[41] It is particularly vigorous in Veracruz, where the Escuela Normal Superior Enrique C. Rébsamen has produced hundreds of dedicated teachers who have made it their mission to bring functional education and practical versatility to the most remote corners of the state. Many of these schools can be reached only on horseback, and building materials have had to be brought in on the backs of villagers. Often the initial teaching must be in Maya, Nahuatl, or Totonaco, before the children can be weaned to the common instructional language of Spanish.

It is impressive to visit the local post offices before the beginning of each school term and find them filled with textbooks labeled "The Property of the Mexican People." Opponents of these government-issued books sometimes charge that they are written for ideological indoctrination, yet it must be borne in mind that these are the first free and readily available textbooks that have ever reached the hands of masses of Mexican children. Only when school libraries become available will those who have barely learned to read be able to sort out and compare ideas from a diversity of sources. It is at this level that general education must begin in rural Mexico, in the impoverished districts of Mexico City, and indeed throughout most of marginal Latin America.

Mexico is not alone in experiencing a revolution in popular education. Notable strides have also been made in Costa Rica, Guatemala, Panama, and a few of the South American countries. Too often, however, the expenditure of funds remains concentrated in the offices of the Ministry of Education, and the mode of instruction follows traditional patterns that ultimately lead to functional illiteracy as children drop out of school in the early years. Where there is so little direct acquaintance with the artifacts of a material culture, learning-by-doing in schools and laboratories is an indispensable substitute.

Mexico is also making progress at higher levels of education. The number of technical schools has increased in recent years, and the universities are giving more attention to fields of pragmatic value and to the beginnings of graduate study and research. Outstanding among these institutions are El Colegio de México, a graduate center; the Instituto Politécnico Nacional and some divisions of the Universidad Nacional Autónoma de México (UNAM), which are also beginning to offer graduate work; and the Instituto Tecnológico y de Estudios Superiores de Monterrey, with its emphasis on engineering. A relatively new institution in the field of management training is the Instituto Panamericano de Alta Dirección de Empresa (IPADE). Despite occasional manifestations to the contrary, students in these institutions appear to be shifting their interest from ideological issues to developing the personal skills needed to take part in the direction of new enterprises that offer promising career opportunities. This interest has had significant effects in upgrading the quality of instruction and drawing attention to technically useful subjects never before offered in the universities.

Mexico is still deficient in mass secondary education, in formal vocational education and apprenticeship training, and in industrial research such as that carried on at the Centro Internacional para el Mejoramiento de Maíz y Trigo (CIMMYT), and at the Instituto Mexicano de Investigaciones Tecnológicas (IMIT).

Genuine education at the graduate level, involving collaborative research between professors and graduate students, is still relatively uncommon in Latin America. Brazil has recently launched a major effort to develop domestic graduate training through a government agency for the Coordination of the Formation of Higher Level Personnel (Coordenação do Aperfeiçoamento de Pessoal de Nível Superior [CAPES]). The Fundação Getúlio Vargas, a semiautonomous research agency, also conducts graduate instruction in economics and in public and private administration. The foundation incorporates perhaps the largest body of well-trained social scientists in the region.

Conclusion

Ayres has said that "the process of economic development is indivisible and irresistible."[42] While, in general, one must recognize that Latin America has a long way to go before it will be a significant contributor to the world storehouse of technological innovations, some of the more advanced countries such as Argentina, Brazil, Colombia, and Mexico are at the adaptive stages of their use of foreign techniques, as Canada has been for a longer period.[43]

The pressures to develop the internal technological frontier are building up inexorably in Latin America. The urban explosion, as we have seen, promises to bring about the long overdue penetration of the domestic frontier, both spatially and in terms of vertical resource development. Population is beginning to flow into previously poorly exploited zones, and a knowledge of what has been done in the more successful colonizations will inevitably be carried to some of the less developed communities.

The familiar institutional resistance emphasized by the structuralists cannot be minimized, yet enough positive instances within the region and the culture demonstrate that the crust of custom can be broken, and, in the very critical case of agriculture, lagging productivity can be overcome. It is well within reasonable expectations that Latin America can ensure its own self-sufficiency in foodstuffs and become once more a major source of food supply to more densely populated areas of the world.

Beyond this, the problems of industrial diversification are also subject to a multifaceted attack by intelligent, well-prepared Latin Americans, working with foreign collaborators where necessary. Such collaboration should be promoted, rather than rejected. Dependency theory has in some respects become a "cop-out" that reinforces a cultural fatalism no longer appropriate to a changing Latin America.

In view of these pressures, a more effective system of education, at all levels, is critically important to the development process and should receive the highest priority in long-range planning. Such education would change basic attitudes from the acceptance of prevailing practices to the consideration of feasible alternatives and the systematic solution of problems. It is becoming clearer to a new generation that the stereotypes of traditional political polarities, whether liberal versus conservative, clerical versus anti-clerical, or Marxist versus anti-Marxist, are largely irrelevant to the constructive needs of the growth process. Instead, creativity becomes the key to productivity.

Fortunately, there are already implanted in the culture, as we have seen, significant elements of a functional—as opposed to a ceremonial—approach to education. The concept of the technological frontier in its full Ayresian significance should be conveyed to the generation that has the prospect of opening that frontier.

Notes

1. C. E. Ayres, *The Theory of Economic Progress,* 2d ed. (New York: Schocken Books, 1962), 133-154.

2. Rawle Farley, *The Economics of Latin America* (New York: Harper and Row, 1972), 28-29, 318, 348.

3. See Farley's description of the development plan for the Guayana district of Venezuela as another indication that "spatial obstacles and regional unbalance are not necessarily permanent characteristics of the economic landscape." *Economics,* 59.

4. These regions include the Darien Gap of Panama; two wet, tropical lowland areas in Colombia; the East Andean piedmont; the Campo Cerrado; the Gran Chaco and the Gran Pantanal; the Río de la Plata drainage system; the Rio de Janeiro, São

Paulo, Buenos Aires axis; and the Guiana complex. *The Frontiers of South America*. Document presented at a meeting of the Inter-American Committee on the Alliance for Progress, Washington, D.C., 3-6 October 1966 (Washington, D.C.: Pan American Union, 1967). Cited by Farley, *Economics,* 152-157.

5. *New York Times,* 29 May 1961, 23; and 13 August 1961, 27.

6. Ibid., 19 April 1961, Pt. X, 1; and 26 November 1961, 44.

7. Ayres, *Economic Progress,* xviii, 136-154.

8. Ibid., 137.

9. E. C. Stakman, Richard Bradfield, and Paul C. Mangelsdorf, *Campaigns Against Hunger* (Cambridge, Mass.: Belknap Press, 1967), 84-85, 274-275.

10. *New York Times,* 3 January 1975, 20.

11. Frederick Jackson Turner, *The Frontier in American History* (New York: Henry Holt and Co., 1920), 219-221; 244-247; 311-323.

12. Montague Yudelman, *Agricultural Development in Latin America: Current Status and Prospects* (Washington, D.C.: Inter-American Development Bank, October 1966), 38-46. "Changes in yields per hectare may be interpreted as an indirect measure of the extent to which modern agricultural technology has been applied on a large scale to the region. During the last five years, a comparison of average yields from 1965–1967 with those of the period 1970–1972 shows no very significant changes vis-à-vis the yields in the more developed countries and Latin America's own expectations." *Economic and Social Progress in Latin America.* Annual Report 1973 (Washington, D.C.: Inter-American Development Bank, 1974), 16.

13. Ibid., 16.

14. *Foreign Agricultural Economic Report,* no. 25 (Washington, D.C.: U.S. Department of Agriculture, April 1965), 43. Cited by Yudelman, *Agricultural Development,* 45.

15. Ibid., 44.

16. Ibid., 45; Farley, *Economics,* 169. See also Stakman, Bradfield, and Mangelsdorf, *Campaigns,* 90-91.

17. *Economic and Social Progress in Latin America.* Annual Report 1973, 254-255.

18. Yudelman, *Agricultural Development,* 45.

19. Raúl Prebisch, *Towards a Dynamic Development Policy for Latin America* (New York: United Nations, 1963), 3-20, 36-43. See also Raúl Prebisch, *Change and Development—Latin America's Great Task.* Report submitted to the Inter-American Development Bank (New York: Praeger Publishers, 1971), 191-215.

20. Osvaldo Sunkel, "The Pattern of Latin American Dependence," in *Latin America in the International Economy,* edited by Victor L. Urquidi and Rosemary Thorp (London: Macmillan, 1973), 3-25.

21. An earlier theoretical study of the technological dependence of the less developed countries also reaches quite pessimistic conclusions. See Meir Merhav, *Technological Dependence, Monopoly, and Growth* (Oxford: Pergamon Press, 1967), especially 199-203.

22. Jorge M. Katz, "Industrial Growth, Royalty Payments and Local Expenditures on Research and Development" and "Discussion" following, in Urquidi and Thorp, eds., *Latin America,* 197-232.

23. David Felix, "On the Diffusion of Technology in Latin America" (Paper presented at the Conference on Diffusion of Technology and Economic Development, Bellagio, Italy, 21-26 April 1973), 6.

24. Ibid., 10.

25. Ibid., 20-59. See also James H. Street, "The Domestication of Science and Technology in Latin America" (Paper presented at a meeting of the Latin American Studies Association, San Francisco, California, 16 November 1974), 12-19.

26. Felix, "Diffusion," 16.

27. David Felix, "Technology and Social-Economic Development in Latin America: A General Analysis and Recommendations for Technological Policy," Consultant document prepared for the United Nations Economic Commission for Latin America, revised, November 1974 (mimeo), 111.

28. Simon Kuznets, "Modern Economic Growth: Findings and Reflections," *American Economic Review* 63 (June 1973):252-253.

29. James H. Street, *The New Revolution in the Cotton Economy* (Chapel Hill: University of North Carolina Press, 1957), 91-171.

30. Seymour Melman. "The Impact of Economics on Technology," *Journal of Economic Issues* 9 (March 1975):71.

31. Dilmus D. James. *Used Machinery and Economic Development* (East Lansing: Division of Research. Graduate School of Business Administration, Michigan State University, 1974).

32. Allen Jedlicka, "Comments on the Introduction of Methane (bio-gas) Generators in Mexico with an Emphasis on the Diffusion of 'Back-yard' Generators for Use by Peasant Farmers," A brief for the Commission on International Relations, National Academy of Sciences, 10 September 1974 (mimeo). Note also the work being carried on at Puerto Peñasco, Mexico, by scientists from the University of Arizona in collaboration with associates at the University of Sonora on the growth of vegetables and seafood under controlled environmental conditions in arid zones, using very little water. Merle H. Jensen and Hamdy M. Eisa, "Controlled-Environment Vegetable Production: Results of Trials at Puerto Peñasco, Mexico." Environmental Research Laboratories, University of Arizona, Tucson, 1972, mimeographed.

33. Ayres, *Economic Progress,* xxi. (See Chapter 4.)

34. Simon Kuznets, *Modern Economic Growth: Rate, Structure and Spread* (New Haven: Yale University Press, 1966):29.

35. James R. Scobie, *Buenos Aires: Plaza to Suburb, 1870–1910* (New York: Oxford University Press, 1974):222-223.

36. Ibid., 224.

37. Juan Zilli, *Historia de la escuela normal veracruzana* (Tacubaya, México: Editorial Citlatepetl, 1961):9-82

38. Although a free compulsory primary education law was passed in Mexico in 1891, "on the eve of the Revolution the Mexican literacy rate was still only about 20 percent." Felix, "Diffusion," 54.

39. Hubert Herring, *A History of Latin America from the Beginnings to the Present,* 2d rev. ed. (New York: Alfred A. Knopf, 1961):364-366.

40. The current training of skilled agronomists in the field by the use of improved methods of communication is described by Allen Jedlicka in "The Acquisi-

tion and Use of Technical Knowledge by Mexican Farmers of Limited Resources" (Paper presented at the joint meeting of the Southwestern Social Science Association and the Association for North American Economic Studies, San Antonio, Texas, 29 March 1975).

41. The following account of recent developments in Mexican popular education is based on personal observation by James H. Street and John W. Street on several visits to Mexico from 1965 to 1970 and on a series of unpublished reports by the latter.

42. Ayres, *Economic Progress,* xviii.

43. See. W. Paul Strassmann, *Technological Change and Economic Development: The Manufacturing Experience of Mexico and Puerto Rico* (Ithaca: Cornell University Press, 1968); and Loretta G. Fairchild, "A Comparison of Foreign and Domestic Firms in Monterrey, Mexico: Performance and Sources of Technology" (Paper presented at a Conference on Science and Technology Policy in the Developing Nations, Cornell University, Ithaca, New York, 5 March 1975). For the Canadian case, see O. J. Firestone, *Economic Implications of Patents* (Ottawa: University of Ottawa Press, 1971), especially Chapter 7.

part eight

Employment, Unemployment, and the Informal Economy

The problems of the nature of employment, the extent of unemployment and underemployment, and the informal economy are all intimately related to the unequal distribution of income (and power) and the extreme levels of poverty that characterize almost all the economies of Latin America and the Caribbean. William Glade, in Chapter 14, considers the relation between the type and pattern of development strategies pursued in Latin America and the levels of observed employment and unemployment. Glade describes the "technological unemployment" that has resulted from the shift from horizontal import substitution industrialization toward vertical (secondary, or hard) ISI, which uses borrowed, capital-intensive technology in manufacturing. Such technology unfortunately utilizes relatively little labor in relation to Latin America's abundant supply. Low labor requirements in manufacturing have been compounded by the weakness of the employment-generating capacity of agriculture as a result of the neglect this sector has suffered during the ISI strategy. Glade suggests some useful, and perhaps necessary, policies to improve the use of labor and to reduce unemployment. These include agrarian reform, limits on conspicuous consumption by the elite class, and other changes in government policies that are worthy of further analysis and discussion.

Víctor Tokman, a labor specialist for the United Nations Economic Commission for Latin America (ECLA), provides in Chapter 15 an elaboration and extension of Glade's analysis. Tokman argues that Latin America and the Caribbean suffer from "premature tertiarization"— that is, from a service sector that has grown larger than would seem to be warranted by the overall level of economic development. In particular, the informal (or underground) economy has shown no tendency to diminish in size as it did in the center countries on their path of economic development. The informal sector, including the underground sector, which now absorbs about 30 percent of Latin America's labor on average, is typically characterized by low-productivity, low-income occupations like those of street vendors, very small household shop owners, and backyard manufacturers. In addition, there is a whole range of illegal activities, some of which, like drug-trafficking, are extremely lucrative.

Tokman dispenses with the argument that Latin America has become urbanized too rapidly or that population growth has been excessively rapid and that these factors account for higher unemployment and underemployment. He shows that the urbanization trends and population growth patterns in Latin American are quite similar to those that occurred in the center countries during comparable periods of development. What is different in the Latin American experience is the relatively more limited labor absorption capacity of the manufacturing (secondary) sector compared to the labor absorbing growth of manufacturing in the center during its earlier period of development. This limited absorption capacity explains, in Tokman's view, the premature and persistently impoverishing growth of the tertiary sector.

Tokman also demonstrates that Latin America has not suffered from low levels of saving or investment, which is one explanation advanced for the weaker employment generation in Latin America's manufacturing sector. The actual problem, according to Tokman, is rather different and more complex. Because the Latin American countries are late developers and borrowers of technology from the center, especially through the intervention of transnational corporations, the levels of investment relative to gross national product that were adequate for the center countries in the past now are no longer sufficient to generate equivalent levels of employment. The greater capital intensity of production today creates relatively fewer jobs per dollar of investment. To obtain the same labor absorption capacity in manufacturing as the center did in the past, *given the existing composition of technology,* Latin America would need substantially greater shares of its total income and output devoted to investment than was the case in earlier times. This insufficiency of labor utilization in manufacturing is worsened, as other readings have noted, by the poor performance of agriculture, which has barely increased its productivity and uses labor very inadequately. Once again, the weakness of technological progress in Latin America is revealed as a hurdle that must be overcome, a hurdle that requires the elimination of fundamental institutional obstacles to progressive change and development.

chapter fourteen

The Employment Question and Development Policies in Latin America

William P. Glade

The Employment Impact of Current Development Policies

While it might be argued that efforts to promote general economic expansion in the hemisphere contain an ultimate answer for the employment problem, a closer examination of both the general design of development policy and the particular policy instruments which have been used to promote economic growth leads to doubts that a satisfactory relationship between growth of GNP and growth of employment will be automatically obtained. In fact, there is some basis for believing that a number of policies and institutions tend to influence the economy-wide choice of capital-intensive techniques, partly because of their effects on primary and intermediate input prices.

For one thing, industrialization along import substitution lines has played a fairly central role in the overall development strategies of many of the larger Latin American countries, and this in itself raises the possibility that a large part of the employment problem originates in the problem of technological dualism which has been discussed by such writers as R. S. Eckaus and Harvey Leibenstein.[1] Moreover while industrialization was especially rapid in the 1940s and 1950s, there has been a distinct change in the character of industrial development since the late 1950s. In the earlier periods of industrialization, the growth of manufacturing activity was concentrated in such fields as textiles, food and beverages, and other nondur-

Reprinted in abridged form from the *Journal of Economic Issues* 3 (September 1969) by special permission of the copyright holder, the Association for Evolutionary Economics.

able consumer goods, many of which were labor-intensive types of operations. Consequently, as these industries were established and expanded, their growth created jobs for a considerable number of workers, while the income of these workers, in turn, helped to expand the markets for the kinds of simpler consumer goods these industries were producing. To the extent that these types of goods were widely consumed, particularly among the lower-income groups of the population, the rise in the associated marketing or distribution activity also opened up new employment opportunities in the labor-intensive tertiary sector.

By the mid-1950s, however, the major dynamism had gone out of these fields, and industrialization shifted into such activities as the production of more elaborate consumer durable goods and basic industrial goods. For the most part, the production technologies employed in these newer fields have been borrowed almost intact from the industrialized nations in which they were originated, comparatively little attention having been devoted to examining the possibilities of modifying and adapting them to the very different factor endowment and factor prices which obtain in the borrowing milieu.[2] The weakness of competition—because of protectionist policies and the prevalence of monopoloid and oligopoloid structures in domestic markets—has generally served to exempt many of these firms from the necessity of seeking the most efficient types of production technologies for their own production environments. Among a sizable number of these newer firms, however, foreign ownership, in whole or in part, is present, and with it access to the international capital market. Consequently, for these firms the supply price of capital often does not reflect domestic factor market conditions (where capital is relatively scarce and dear) so that their microeconomic level decisions may even lead rationally in the direction of greater capital intensity on this basis alone.

Particularly may this be the case if we consider that it is not solely the internationally transferred capital—capital goods or production technology—which contributes to the level of productivity in these foreign-linked enterprises. Of great importance too are the concomitantly transferred organizational structures, the social technology of management systems and the like which determine the way one organizes, lays down channels of communication, and arrives at decisions. There is, admittedly, an insufficient amount of empirical information available on the actual production functions of foreign operations, with such functions defined to include organizational inputs as well as capital and labor. But one element which might contribute to maintaining fixed functions of high capital intensity derives from the cross-culturally transferred organizational arrangements. Without conscious adaptation, they simply do not permit great flexibility in the feasible combinations of capital and labor inputs. A shift to other, less familiar, factor combinations may be perceived as involving higher opportunity costs.[3]

Something of the sort, for example, seems to be involved in the observed preference of the World Bank and similar institutions for large capital-intensive projects which are easier to plan and control than less capital intensive undertakings.[4]

In any event, whatever the cause, it appears that that portion of the industrial sector which has exhibited the most dynamism in recent years has had very different implications for the employment situation when contrasted with the earlier phase. To be sure, labor productivity tends to be relatively high, if only artificially so because of administered prices, in these newer fields, and wage levels there are correspondingly higher than in older industries. Yet, for the most part, they are much more capital-intensive than the earlier types of industries, so that their establishment and subsequent expansion have not increased the employment opportunities in manufacturing at anything like the rate which prevailed up to, say, the mid-1950s. Serving much more limited markets, the new industries' effect on associated expansion in tertiary-sector employment has probably been less as well. At the same time, the kinds of jobs available in the new industries have skill requirements far higher than those which many of the new entrants into the urban labor market possess, a circumstance which encourages a resort to increased capital intensity as a means of economizing on skilled labor.[5] Since, moreover, many of these newer industries cater to higher-income clientele, which is augmented only slightly by the employment generated in the industries themselves, they contribute relatively less than did the earlier industrial growth to a general broadening of the national market. For a number of reasons, it may be supposed that many of these newer industries will reach the limits of their rapid growth stage much sooner than did the older industries, so that it would be misleading to expect the new wave of industrialization to provide much of an answer to the employment problem over the years ahead.[6] Indeed, to the extent that regional economic integration should accelerate the process of technological modernization in the older, and hitherto protected, industries, it is conceivable that increased technological unemployment might result in the same period.[7]

A second macrostructural feature of contemporary Latin America which raises problems for the employment level stems from the widespread relative neglect of the agricultural sector. In this case the failure to introduce meaningful institutional and other reforms has apparently been a factor in driving people out of the depressed rural regions into the cities, where they arrive with few skills of the sort which would facilitate their absorption into the urban employment structure. At least a portion of these migrants might well have found productive employment in the countryside had public investment been geared along Nurksian lines to transforming rural labor into rural capital, into raising the production possibilities of the agricultural sector by labor-intensive construction projects to build dams, irrigation and drainage systems, farm-to-market roads, rural schools, erosion control schemes, land-clearing schemes, and the like—some of which projects would also have served to increase the supply of cooperant land factors. At the same time, the institutionally conditioned distribution of rural income has tended to inhibit the growth of national markets for the kinds of manufactures and services which have generated many of the new jobs in the past several decades, thereby restricting the labor absorptive capacity of the urban sector, while the neglect of agricultural productivity has apparently been a factor in raising food prices in urban markets, producing a consequent upward pressure on industrial sector wages and encouraging employers to respond by replacing men with machinery in an effort to cut the wage bill.

Unfortunately, now that more thought is at last being given to programs for agricultural development, some of the new ideas under consideration offer scant promise of relieving unemployment, particularly those which aim at replicating the large-scale, capital-intensive, corporate style of agriculture practiced in the United States.[8] While this latter approach to agricultural modernization might conceivably be more compatible with the existing land tenure system, at least so far as concerns the large holdings, it is doubtful that it will be politically and socially tolerable or, indeed, really very economic if all social costs be taken into account. More difficult, institutionally speaking, but in the long run probably more feasible even from an economic point of view would seem to be an alternative route of rural modernization patterned somewhat after the Japanese experience, one in which a more progressive, labor-intensive type of agricultural technique would serve both to raise rural productivity and to enhance the employment opportunities of the rural sector.[9]

Related to the emphasis on industrialization and the neglect of the agricultural sector is a third macrostructural policy choice which has tended to compound the difficulties of maintaining reasonable levels of employment, particularly among the unskilled and semiskilled. Where export sector activities have suffered from discriminatory taxation and/or a discriminatory manipulation of exchange rates, the result has often been to been to discourage the expansion of output and employment in fields in which the comparative international advantage has depended, in part, upon extensive use of labor factors. Granted that the adverse employment repercussions stemming from this source are more significant in the case of agricultural exports than in mineral export industries, the importance of the former in the overall pattern of Latin American exports is such that the implications of development policy framed on the basis of export disincentives can hardly be overlooked.

A fourth problem at the macroeconomic policy level, one suggested by the previous reference to Nurkse's concept of capital formation, relates to the general inability or disinclination to institute the kinds of fiscal reforms which would enable the Latin American governments to accelerate public or social investment programs without recourse to inflationary techniques of finance. Any curtailment of the existing levels of conspicuous consumption, with their usual high import component, would probably be justifiable from the standpoint of releasing resources for more productive alternative uses, such as employment-creating outlays, just as a reduction of the possibilities for capital exportation currently enjoyed by the moneyed classes might be desirable on the grounds of fostering greater domestic capital formation. But from an employment perspective, there are even additional values. To the degree that social investment programs redistribute income downward, they tend to broaden the home market for the kinds of items in which Latin American manufacturing industries have accumulated some production competence already, thereby renewing the dynamism of the industries which formerly played such an important role in adding to the supply of jobs. Beyond this, however, it is clear that a public investment program of the sort which is needed to meet the most pressing economic and social needs of the day in most countries would involve a considerable emphasis on construction activity—the building of roads and highways, education and health centers, popular housing, urban water systems, and so on—in which there are considerable possibilities for utilizing labor-intensive production techniques effectively to absorb larger numbers of unskilled and semiskilled workers into the employment structure.[10]

Besides these four general or macrostructural policy questions, the much-discussed problem of Latin American inflation is also germane to the issue because of its effects on the character of investment decisions. Quite apart from the inducement it has provided for capital flights, and the relation it has to the consequent lowered rates of national investment and associated increases in employment, inflation has functioned as a tax on liquid assets. Since labor-intensive methods of production tend to require relatively heavy current assets as contrasted with fixed assets, and since investments in fixed capital may often be financed on credit, the impact of inflationary expectations may well have been that of encouraging firms to incur debts, the real burden of which declines through time, particularly where the rate of inflation is high. The differential impact of inflation on fixed variable segments of the cost structures of enterprises, in other words, would seem to be such that employment has suffered from the consequent biasing of investment decisions at the firm level. This in turn leads to a consideration of other policy repercussions which are manifested chiefly at the microeconomic level of operations.

At the microeconomic level of decisionmaking, one can identify a number of policies which seem inappropriate to a context in which employment objectives should loom large. For example, in most Latin American countries the labor and social legislation is such that the incidence of fringe benefits on the total labor cost in industry is high in relation to straight hourly wages, as much as 50 percent or more, in some instances. As a result, employers "tend to favor the payment of overtime rather than the recruitment of new workers for whom they would have to pay all the fringe benefits." Legally prescribed rules make severance difficult and costly and also increase the reluctance of employers to hire workers if, subsequently, it should be desirable to discharge any of them. Here, increased capital intensity carries the advantage of a greater flexibility in decisionmaking.

Fringe benefit costs are also high because of the prevailing Latin American practice of financing social programs by what are, in effect, taxes on payrolls rather than through taxes on net business income.[11] While such practices may conceivably be justified on the grounds that employers might directly provide social services where needed more efficiently than could the public administrative apparatus, it is obvious that the policy of tying the tax obligation to the size of the wage bill rather than to net income tends to increase the supply price of labor while leaving the supply price of capital unaffected. Thus, the existing labor and social legislation tends to bias business decisions against the employment of labor factors and to favor their replacement by capital. In all probability, the same set of circumstances also operates to discourage a more widespread use of multiple shifts as a technique of modifying the capital-labor mix in a direction favorable to employment objectives.

Additional distortion of business decisions regarding the factor mix, again in a direction unfavorable to the employment of labor, has been fairly common as a result of other prevalent policies. Very often, for instance, internal inflation has coexisted with fixed exchange rates and, from an international point of view, overvalued currencies. Since much of the capital equipment used in Latin American industry is imported, the effect of this foreign exchange policy has generally been to cheapen the supply price of imported capital inputs at the very time that labor costs were rising. While this alone would tend to encourage the displacement of labor by capital, the effects have on many occasions been accentuated when, under multiple exchange rate systems, preferentially low rates have been given for the importation of machinery and equipment. To be sure, the practice of favoring importation of capital items through preferential foreign exchange rates has been pursued with the intention of stimulating industrial growth rather than reducing employment, but from the standpoint of employment policy the negative impact of such a policy can hardly be ignored.

It should be noted that the same employment-diminishing side effects also inhere in a number of the other industrial promotion techniques common to the area. Here and there, for example, tax reduction inducements designed to encourage new investment seem to be based largely, or even entirely, on new investments in fixed capital rather than on new investments in fixed and working capital combined, the latter of which includes the wage bill. Few, if any, of the countries base tax reductions on employment created, while accelerated depreciation rates, where used as an industrial incentive, also lower the cost of fixed capital relative to labor. In the same manner, the low-interest loans frequently offered by development banks to new industries as a technique of subsidizing their inception are, more often than not, extended for the purchase of capital equipment and/or the construction of physical plant; much less frequently is this special low-cost credit made available for working capital purposes such as the financing of payrolls. In both cases—the tax inducements and the development loans—the manner in which the investment incentive is provided tends not only to raise the inducement to invest but also to influence the investment choice regarding factor proportions in a direction prejudicial to the employment of the labor factors of production.

The foregoing is intended to be a suggestive rather than exhaustive listing of the employment aspects of contemporary development policy in Latin America. The fact that employment policy, as such, has been so evidently peripheral to most Latin American policymaking and that, even when it has been mentioned, it has not entailed a systematic examination of the employment consequences of the policies actually being pursued, a number of which are of questionable value in this regard, suggests that serious efforts to moderate the impact of population growth on the working class population lie almost entirely in the future. Furthermore, little in recent experience would support the view that the existing framework of policy formation in Latin America is adequate to the task. For reasons which lie beyond the scope of this chapter, the most salient feature of the policymaking machinery which has functioned in the period under review has been, in plain terms, its rather consistent capacity to dodge the issue, or, perhaps, to bury it amid a preoccupation with other matters.

Notes

1. R. S. Eckaus, "The Factor Proportions Problem in Underdeveloped Areas," *American Economic Review,* 45 (September 1955); and H. Leibenstein, "Technical Progress, the Production Function, and Dualism," *Banca Nazionale del Lavoro Quarterly Review* (December 1960).

2. Relatively little use, for example, seems to be made of the kinds of subcontracting and other practices which enabled Japanese industry to develop on the basis of a technological dualism that tended to enhance the employment aspects of growth. See S. Broadbridge, *Industrial Dualism in Japan: A Problem of Economic Growth and Structural Change* (London: Frank Cass, 1966). At the same time, however, it must be conceded that the cost of search for means of adapting imported industrial technologies to the Latin American factor situation may not be negligible,

given the dearth of the kinds of engineering and other skills needed for this task.

3. To illustrate one of several possibilities in this respect, the shortage of middle-level supervisory skills required for effective management of a larger labor force (possessing fewer skills) works to bias the choice against relatively labor-intensive techniques.

4. For a discussion of this point, see Andrew Shonfield, *The Attack on World Poverty* (New York: Random House, 1960):15-16, 124-130. More broadly, if it is reasonable to assume that larger-scale enterprises may generally (at least in many fields) tend to be more capital intensive than smaller-scale ones, the distinct edge which the former usually enjoy over the latter in access to loan capital again leads to an antiemployment bias in the allocation of capital.

5. This situation, of course, simply underscores the point that labor is not a homogeneous commodity and that, whereas unskilled labor is abundant, skilled labor (the type of input germane to the choice of factor mix) is scarce. Few governments provide direct subsidies linked to labor-training costs.

6. For two articles examining this development, see "The Growth and Decline of Import Substitution in Brazil," *Economic Bulletin for Latin America* 9, no. 1 (March 1964):1-60; and "Structural Changes in Employment Within the Context of Latin America's Economic Development," *Economic Bulletin for Latin America* 10, no. 2 (October 1965):163-187. See also the *Economic Survey of Latin America* (New York: U.N., 1966):50, 63.

7. Even without integration and its stimulus to technological modernization, the displacement of artisan production has been a source of technological unemployment. "The relative reduction in artisan employment as against factory employment is one of the factors most responsible for the failure of Latin American manufacturing as a whole to absorb much of the increase in the labor force." United Nations Economic Commission for Latin America, *The Process of Industrial Development in Latin America* (New York: U.N., 1966):40.

8. Typical of the new perspective in agrarian modernization is L. H. Berlin, "A New Agricultural Strategy in Latin America," *International Development Review* 9, no. 3 (September 1967):12-14. That this may be, in part, a function of the particular institutional context of the lending process (as Shonfield observed) through which credit-administration costs are reckoned is suggested by Warren J. Bilkey, "The Dominican Beef Case: Two Approaches to Stimulating Industry in a Developing Country," *International Development Review* 8, no. 1 (June, 1966):19-22.

9. A provocative discussion of the possibilities of this approach (with reference to India) is found in Morton Paglin, "'Surplus' Agricultural Labor and Development: Facts and Theories," *American Economic Review* 55, no. 4 (September 1965):815-834.

10. There are, of course, still other developmental values to such a program, among them the ability of the construction industry to draw upon resources which are largely internally available, the external economies generated by infrastructure, the use of construction employment to "prepare" workers for industrial employment in terms of skills and discipline, and the probable usefulness of popular housing as an "incentive good." Further, by expanding and modernizing the educational system, governments could do much to increase the supply of trained workers to industrial and other employers. The failure to do much along this line in the past has

forced employers either to assume the additional expense of training their workers on the job (with consequent higher costs of production, higher prices, and narrower markets) or to seek to overcome the skills bottleneck by replacing labor with automated processes of production.

11. A typical example of this may be taken from the Peruvian case in which employers assume responsibility for maternity benefits for female workers and must provide free elementary school for the children of workers when the workers' families live adjacent to the establishment and when the school-age dependents of the workers number more than thirty.

chapter fifteen

Unequal Development and the Absorption of Labor

Víctor E. Tokman

The purpose of this chapter is to offer some conceptual elements for interpreting the process of absorption of labor in Latin America during the past thirty years, in the light of the available information provided by the Regional Employment Program for Latin America and the Caribbean (PREALC 1981).

The current regional interpretations may be associated in one way or another with the work of Raúl Prebisch and other authors connected with ECLA, who draw attention to the low level of absorption of labor and associate it with various factors inherent in Latin American development. These interpretations have been changing over time, and those which we call here the ideas of the 1960s are clearly distinguishable from those of the 1970s.

The former arose as an implicit reaction—since they were not made explicit in any of the studies published—to certain distortions which were appearing in the behavior of the labor absorption process. These distortions were defined in relation to what should have occurred according to a supposed normal model of growth. The implicitly accepted normal model postulates three basic trends associated with growth. The first is the transfer of population from rural to urban areas; the second is that the secondary sectors (particularly manufacturing) become the most dynamic ones as regard absorption of labor; and the third refers to the growing degree of homogenization resulting from the reduction in the intersectorial differences in productivity (between agricultural and nonagricultural and between tertiary and secondary).

Reprinted in abridged form from the *CEPAL Review* 17 (August 1982), a publication of the United Nations Economic Commission for Latin America.

In order to analyze the historical validity of the normal model in other countries of the world, one may refer to two pioneer works by Clark (1951) and Kuznets (1957). Both studies, but especially the second, analyze the changes in the sectoral distribution of the product and of employment, and the differences in productivity. For this purpose, they review the available information for many countries and make comparisons of the position in a number of countries in a given year (around 1947) or of the changes which have occurred in a single country through time (from the middle of the nineteenth century until around 1950).

This analysis makes it possible to test empirically the validity of two of the expected trends, but not the third. There appears to be a clear association between the transfer of labor to the nonagricultural sectors and growth, and differences in productivity tend to decrease as countries develop. This behavior is observed both in comparisons between countries and over time. However, it is not so clear what role the secondary sectors have played historically in the absorption of labor. The country analysis reaffirms the normal model by indicating a growing absorption of employment in nonagricultural activities and, within these, mainly in the secondary sector. The analysis over time, however, shows that the tertiary sectors are the ones which absorb the greatest proportion of the labor displaced from agricultural activities, while the secondary sectors show asystematic behavior, with expansion in some countries and contraction in others, albeit in general a lower growth rate than in the tertiary sector.

Studies by Prebisch (1970) and ECLA (1965) analyzing the evolution of the structure of employment in the region until the end of the 1960s show two anomalous trends. In the first place, there is a premature urbanization resulting from the high rates of rural-urban migration, and in the second place, there is a structural deformation in the direction of a premature tertiarization of the nonagricultural labor force, given the inability of the secondary sectors, particularly manufacturing, to absorb it. In turn, this behavior results from three main factors: first, the dynamic insufficiency which leads to a slow expansion of the Latin American economy; second, the effect of technological change, which has meant the use of increasingly capital-intensive techniques, and finally, the need to absorb a high proportion of the labor now employed at low levels of productivity in the artisanal sector of manufacturing.

The most recent works by Prebisch (1976, 1978 and 1981, *inter alia*) probe more deeply into dynamic insufficiency, examining the process of appropriation and use of the surplus and maintaining that the use of inadequate technology resulting from delayed industrialization is another basic explanatory factor. Finally, these studies identify structural heterogeneity (analyzed by various authors, but particularly Pinto, 1970) as another important variable in explaining the behavior of employment in the region. This concept, as opposed to previous ones, brings out not only the intersectoral differences but also the intrasectoral ones. It should be noted that the emphasis previously placed on the two basic distortions—premature urbanization and structural deformation—are abandoned in this approach.

This chapter explores the relevance of the abovementioned explanatory factors for the period 1950-1980. For this purpose, comparisons are made with developed countries—particularly with the United States during the significant periods—in order to determining what factors are specific to the Latin American situation. The methodology used in the analysis does not, of course, imply accepting that there is a single process of development at the world level, but on the contrary makes it possible to paint a more precise picture of the characteristics of what Prebisch has called "peripheral capitalism."

Basic Structural Anomalies

Migrations and Premature Urbanization
One of the most outstanding characteristics of the development of the employment situation in Latin America during the past thirty years has been the rapid rate of migration from rural areas to the cities. Thus, in 1950, 55 percent of the labor force was engaged in agricultural activities, while in 1980 it is estimated that only 35 percent worked in this field. Although the transfer of population from rural to urban areas is to be expected as normal behavior when countries are growing, it is noteworthy that there was a premature manifestation of this phenomenon during the 1960s.

In order to assess whether the transfer of population from the country to the city was extremely rapid or occurred during a very brief period, we may examine the experience of some developed countries which showed similar demographic behavior, such as the United States, the Scandinavian countries and Japan. (The countries of Western Europe displayed types of demographic growth and thus labor growth which are not comparable with those of the Latin American countries).

Table 15.1 shows clearly that the experience of the region does not display very different characteristics from those of the United States, Sweden or Japan in respect to its population, labor, and spatial mobility dynamics. The thirty years that it took Latin America for the percentage of agricultural labor to drop from 55 percent to 35 percent is a similar period to that required for similar evolution to occur in the United States (between 1870 and 1903), and Sweden (between 1891 and 1920). Similarly, the three developed countries included in the table took twenty years—as did Latin America—to increase the proportion of nonagricultural labor from 45 percent to 58 percent.

Table 15.1 Population Dynamics and Migrations

	Latin America	United States	Sweden	Japan
Percentage of labor force working in agriculture				
(i) 55%	1950	1870	1891	1920
(ii) 42%	1970	1890	1912	1940
(iii) 35%	1980	1903	1920	n.d.
Number of years between (i) and (iii)	30	33	29	n.d.
Number of years between (i) and (ii)	20	20	21	20
Annual population growth[a]	2.8	2.0	0.7	1.2[b]
Annual growth in labor force[a]	2.4	2.7	1.5[c]	1.6[b]
Annual growth in urban labor force[a]	3.7	3.7	3.1[c]	2.9[b]

Source: Latin America: information provided by PREALC. United States: Lebergott (1964). Sweden and Japan: Colin Clark (1951).

[a] Between (i) and (iii).
[b] Between (i) and (ii).
[c] Between (ii) and (iii).

An analysis of the table also makes it possible to examine the relative validity of the argument which explains Latin America's limited labor absorption capacity by the rapid growth of its population. Although it has been confirmed that the region's population growth rate is the highest of all the countries considered, the differences diminish when referring to the labor force, which is the relevant concept in an analysis of the employment situation. Indeed, during the comparison period the United States showed higher labor force growth rates than those recorded in the Latin American countries.

Structural Deformation and Premature Tertiarization

According to the current theories, premature urbanization was partly the cause of a deformation in the sectoral distribution of labor among nonagricultural activities. Thus, both ECLA (1965) and Prebisch (1970) draw attention to the insufficient labor absorption of the secondary sectors (industry, mining and construction), and particularly of manufacturing. According to various studies, among them the abovementioned ones by Kuznets and Clark, in proportion as the average income of a country increases, there is likely to be a reduction in the share of agricultural labor and an increase in the importance of employment in the secondary sectors is likely to be more rapid during the first stages of development.

Contrary to expectations, the information analyzed by ECLA going up to 1965 showed a reduction in the share of manufacturing employment in nonagricultural employment. Thus, the 1965 ECLA report indicates a reduction in the share of manufacturing employment from 35.4 percent in 1925 to

27.1 percent in 1960, while Prebisch (1970), dealing with the participation of the secondary sector, shows a drop from 35 percent to 31.8 percent and estimates a level of 30 percent for about 1970.

Table 15.2, made up from PREALC figures, confirms that the secondary sector is not increasing its share in nonagricultural labor, since it decreased from 42 percent to 40 percent between 1950 and 1970 and then apparently stabilized at that level. This behavior too, however, is similar to that shown by the United States, Japan and Sweden (in one of the available estimates) in the relevant comparison period: indeed, these countries showed greater reductions than in Latin America during periods of equal duration. It should be noted that the highest level reached by the countries compared exceeds the Latin American level which can partly be attributed to the differences in technologies between the periods considered. We will return to this point later.

In addition to looking at the results of the above comparison, it is worth reviewing the conclusions of the studies which suggested that a given behavior for the structure of employment could be predicted. Thus, as pointed out earlier, Kuznets reaches different conclusions when he analyzes the information over time (thirty to forty years) for twenty-eight countries; although it is true that there is a reduction in the share accounted for by agricultural employment in the total as income grows, the secondary sector does not show such consistent behavior as in the international comparisons. In five countries, the share of the secondary sector in the total decreases, and in another five the increases are very small. Finally, the proportion of the labor force in tertiary activities grew in all the countries, and in most of them it did so more rapidly than employment in the secondary sectors.[1]

Table 15.2   Absorption of Labor in the Secondary Sector[a] (as a percentage of nonagricultural labor)

	1950[b]	1970[b]	1980[b]
Latin America	42.0	39.7	40.3
United States	50.0	47.4	41.5
Sweden[c]			
(i)	36.4	50.0	53.8
(ii)	62.2	63.2	57.8
Japan	49.0	36.9	

Source: Latin America: information provided by PREALC. United States, Sweden and Japan: Kuznets (1957).

[a] Including manufacturing, mining and construction.
[b] Time periods are similar to those defined in Table 15.1. Latin America 1950 corresponds to United States 1890, to Sweden (i) 1891 and (ii) 1900, and to Japan 1920. Latin America 1970 corresponds to United States 1890, to Sweden 1912 and 1924, and to Japan 1940. Latin America 1980 corresponds to United States 1903 and to Sweden (i) 1920 and (ii) 1938.
[c] The estimate for (i) corresponds to data from Colin Clark (1951); the estimate for (ii) corresponds to data from J. Svennilson, cited by Kuznets (1957).

The behavior of manufacturing is the main factor determining the evolution observed in the secondary sector, and this gave rise to a series of interpretations which highlight the insufficiency of the manufacturing sector in the creation of employment. The international comparison shows, however, that, like the entire secondary sector, the share of industrial employment went down slightly from 1950 to 1970 and stabilized around 28 percent of the nonagricultural labor force as from the latter year. This drop is lower than that recorded in the United States between 1870 and 1903, and the level of the coefficient is on average similar to that of the developed countries after the 1920s, which again suggests the influence of delayed industrialization on the absorption of labor.[2]

Explanatory Factors

Dynamic Insufficiency and Accumulation Capacity
The deformation of the structure of employment generated by the low relative capacity of manufacturing to absorb labor would appear in turn to be partly the result of insufficient accumulation capacity. The imitation of the consumption patterns of the central economies leads, according to Prebisch, to the consumption of that part of the surplus which should be used for expanding productive capacity, thus reducing the possibilities for increasing production and employment; this process is known as dynamic insufficiency.

In order to examine to what extent dynamic insufficiency has been a determining factor in the evolution of the employment situation in Latin America in the past thirty years, we should take another look at the international comparisons, particularly with the United States in the relevant period.

In the first place, the growth of the product of Latin America on average exceeded that of the United States in the period when the latter country was experiencing internal migrations of the same magnitude as those which occurred between 1950 and 1980 in Latin America (Table 15.3). In the second place, the investment coefficient in the two cases is practically equal. The selected period in United States economic history shows the highest rates of the past century and a half, since after 1920 the investment coefficient did not rise above 15 percent there. In addition, it should be remembered that the United States is the country which had the highest investment rates in the world, both during the period between the middle of the nineteenth century and World War I and from the end of the nineteenth century until around 1960, which were the years analyzed by Kuznets (1961). Thus, if this comparison suggests anything it is that Latin America seems to be showing a similar dynamism to that displayed by the United States in the past, so that it is necessary to decide what meaning is to be assigned to dynamic insufficiency.

Table 15.3   Capacity for Accumulation and Growth of the Product: Latin America and the United States

| | Latin America | | | United States | |
Years	Growth of the Product[a]	Investment Coefficient[b]	Years[c]	Growth of the Product[a]	Investment Coefficient[b]
1950-1960	5.1	20.5	1869-73/1877-81	6.5	18.9
1960-1970	5.7	20.0	1882-86/1892-96	3.3	22.3
1970-1980	5.7	24.0	1891-1901/1902-06	4.5	23.0
1950-1980	5.5	21.5	1869-73/1902-06	4.8	21.4

Source: Latin America: ECLA. United States: product: Kuznets (1956); investment: U.S. Department of Commerce, Bureau of the Census (1960).

[a] Annual growth rate of the gross domestic product at constant prices.
[b] Ratio between gross fixed investment and the gross domestic product, both at constant prices.
[c] The periods corresponding to the growth rates of the product do not correspond exactly to those of the investment coefficient, due to problems in the original presentation of the data. The first subperiod of the product corresponds to 1869-78/1879-88; the second to 1879-88/1889-98; and the third to 1889-98/1899-1908. The total corresponds to 1869-78/1899-1908.

The evidence of the past three decades indicates that there are limitations to the interpretation of the problem in terms of dynamic insufficiency, at least as regards absolute dynamism, so that it is necessary to look more closely at the absorption of labor by occupational category and the differences in productivity, both between sectors and within some sectors. The first is necessary because it can more precisely reflect the particular situation of employment in Latin America, and the second because it enables us to analyze the cost involved in the creation of production jobs.

Structural Heterogeneity

The Informal Sector   Perhaps the most significant phenomenon in the employment situation in Latin America is the presence of an informal urban sector which not only absorbs a considerable share of the urban labor force but also does not seem to show any signs of decreasing. Many studies deal with this subject from very different angles (see, for example, PREALC 1978), but it is not appropriate to analyze them here. It is enough to point out that this sector is made up of activities which are quite easy to enter, require little capital and organization, and are associated generally with small units of production. These characteristics result on average in low levels of productivity per person and a low capacity for accumulation.

Table 15.4 shows the size and evolution of employment in the Latin American informal sector and compares it with the behavior shown in the United States in the relevant period. It can be seen, first, that the informal sector accounts for about 30 percent of the urban labor force in the region and that this level has remained practically the same during the past three decades. It should be noted that in about 1900 the United States registered a similar share for this sector, but unlike the situation in Latin America there was a clear tendency for this sector to decline in the twenty years under consideration. This situation occurs both in the informal nonhousehold sector and in the household services sector.

Moreover, as shown in Table 15.5, there are appreciable differences in the sectoral distribution of informal employment. If we observe the sectoral importance of own-account workers (considered as a suitable proxy), we note that the levels are almost similar for the urban total, but in Latin America they are distributed equally between the industrial and services sectors, whereas in the United States these workers are concentrated mainly outside industrial activities. It also confirms that there is a clear asymmetry in the trend, which in the case of the United States appears in all the sectors.

The above comparative analysis suggests at least three conclusions which are useful in interpreting the evolution of the employment situation in Latin America. The first is that the size of the urban informal sector seems to be associated with the beginnings of intense migratory processes, and is not a feature peculiar to the region. The second highlights the difference in evolution, since in Latin America the sector persists almost without decreasing while in the United States it was gradually absorbed by the urban modern sectors. Finally, the sectoral distribution brings out an additional difference, since Latin America shows a relatively high level of informal activity in its industrial sector, while this level is low in the United States. These two latter characteristics are among the peculiarities of the employment situation in the region which show that, while the United States has been resolving the problem of its informal sector, the region has been incapable of doing so in the past thirty years, and that the Latin American industrial sector must deal with an additional task compared with the situation faced at the corresponding time by [North] American industry.

. . .

Table 15.4 Urban Informal Sector: Latin America and the United States[a]

	Latin America				United States		
Years	Nonhousehold Informal Sector[b]	Household Services	Total	Years	Nonhousehold Informal Sector[c]	Household Services	Total
1950	20.0	10.5	30.5	1900	23.2	10.4	33.6
1970	19.8	9.6	29.4	1910	18.9	8.2	27.1
1980	20.8	9.0	29.8	1920	14.8	5.4	20.2

Source: Latin America: PREALC (1981). United States: Lebergott (1964).

[a] Percentages of the non-agricultural labor force.
[b] Including own-account workers, except professionals and technicians, plus unpaid family members.
[c] Including own-account workers plus unpaid family members.

Table 15.5   Own-Account Workers by Sectors: Latin America and the United States

	Latin America				United States		
Years	Total[a]	Urban[b]	Manufacturing[c]	Years	Total[a]	Urban[b]	Manufacturing[c]
1950	26.4	19.2	22.1	1900	34.0	22.2	7.2
1960	29.9	20.9	23.1	1910	29.4	18.1	6.0
1970	28.1	19.0	20.7	1920	26.2	14.1	4.4
1980	n.d.	19.9	n.d.	1930	23.1	13.4	3.3

Source: Latin America: information provided by PREALC. United States: Lebergott (1964).

[a] Own-account workers as a percentage of the total labor force.
[b] Urban own-account workers as a percentage of the urban labor force.
[c] Own-account workers in manufacturing, as a percentage of the labor force of that sector.

Access to Capital and Employment at Low Levels of Productivity

The fast growth of the labor force, the rapid rate of migration from rural to urban areas, and the sectoral distribution of employment in urban activities do not seem to have been specific to the region. This calls into question the capacity of these variables for explaining the employment situation, although they were undoubtedly assigned an important role in many of such interpretation efforts particularly those made by ECLA in the 1960s.

We have found confirmation of what various diagnostic studies have pointed out as the truly special feature of the employment situation in the region: the existence and permanence of a significant contingent of the labor force in activities which in PREALC studies are called "informal" and in studies by Prebisch are described as activities of the "lower-productivity technical levels" and "lower strata". It is possible to add new factors to this diagnosis, as it is not the relative size of the informal sector at the beginning of the comparison period which is a distinguishing feature of urban employment, but rather the differences in productivity per person which exist between informal activities and the remaining urban activities, and their asymmetrical sectoral distribution. There are also major differences in inter-sectoral productivity, a particularly striking case being the extremely low agricultural productivity. This picture of sharp inter and intrasectoral productivity differences makes up what Aníbal Pinto rightly calls "structural heterogeneity," which is ultimately the main differentiating element in the prevailing situation.

The existence of major differences in productivity at different levels has a clear implication for the dynamics of job creation. It is harder, in terms of resources, to absorb migrants and reconvert urban informal employment into modern employment than it was for the developed countries to do so in the past. The result is that the absorption of employment in the modern urban sectors, despite its intensity by the standards of past international experience (Tokman 1981) is relatively insufficient for the purposes of decreasing the population employed in the informal sector and reducing the degree of heterogeneity.

The reasons why the differences in productivity in Latin America are greater than those in the United States are to be sought in two areas: first, in the nature of technological change, and second, in the structure of the ownership of capital and the unequal access to this capital.

The first aspect is connected with the fact that Latin America entered the process of industrialization quite late. This implies the advantage of having access, without incurring the costs of research and development and technological obsolescence, to technologies which yield greater productivity, but in turn it has the disadvantage that the creation of jobs becomes more costly. The technological change originating in the central countries tends to increase the productivity of resources, but by making more intensive use of capital than of labor. The result is that, generally speaking, the possibilities for growth are greater for a given amount of resources, but on the other hand there is a lower degree of labor absorption.

In addition, the differences in productivity are related to the distribution of wealth and access to this wealth. Thus, the lower relative productivity of the agricultural sector is largely explained by the greater concentration of land ownership, while the differences in the distribution of urban wealth are perpetuated by the existence of mechanisms which restrict access to capital for those who do not already possess some wealth.

Some partial data help to illustrate the differences in the concentration of wealth. The Gini coefficient for land distribution in Latin America was 0.843 around 1950 and remained almost unchanged between that year and 1970 (OAS-IASI 1975). The same indicator of land concentration shows that in the United States in 1900 the figure was 0.572; around 1910 it dropped to 0.529, and in 1920 rose to 0.588.[3] The situation in manufacturing is apparently similar. Comparing ten Latin American countries with five Western European countries around 1960, Meller (1978) concludes that the concentration in the Latin American countries as a whole, and individually, is systematically greater than in the European countries as a whole and individually. In addition, evidence presented by Lagos (1966) for Chile shows that the fifty largest manufacturing firms generated 38 percent of the value added in 1957; in comparison, the same number of firms generated between 17 percent and 25 percent of the industrial value added in the United States between 1947 and 1970.

The mechanisms which restrict the access to capital are related, *inter alia,* with the segmentation of the international capital market, the absence or segmentation of the domestic capital market, the preference for investment in enterprises connected with the owners of the capital, and biases in public investment. The existence of such restrictions, as well as the initial concentration, generates and tends to perpetuate a differentiation in the productive structure as regards capital intensity, which is true both between sectors (agricultural versus industrial) and within the same sector (formal versus informal enterprises).

Insufficient Absorption and Strategic Options

The higher cost associated with the creation of employment in the sectors with the highest productivity theoretically implies the need to increase investment and consequently also the saving necessary to finance it. Given the limits observed in the utilization of the surplus, which are in keeping with the prevailing distribution of income and the consumption habits derived from imitative capitalism, the result is what Prebisch calls "dynamic insufficiency." This interpretation, which is correct in its theoretical supposition, points up, however, only one aspect of the solution to the problem, i.e., the expansion of the capacity to accumulate.

An increase in investment would make it possible to accelerate the transfer of persons from low-productivity activities to those of higher productivity. Besides being costly economically, however, this solution inevitably implies prolonged adjustment periods. In addition, its feasibility does not seem clear when we take into account that the empirical evidence of the past thirty years suggests that the investment made by the region is among the highest in the world, and is in fact similar to that made by the United States in comparable historical periods. Nevertheless, it would be worth exploring the possibility of changing the composition of investment with a view to creating reproductive capital rather than consumptive capital (to use Prebisch's terminology).

It is thus necessary to emphasize the reasons for this greater need for accumulation which according to the analysis are basically the characteristics associated with modern technology and the existing differences in productivity. This would imply a need for some complementary action to deal with the factors determining the greater cost of creating jobs. On the one hand, the pursuit of a more suitable selection of technology would make it possible to absorb more labor without affecting efficiency, either through changes in the composition of production, promotion of plants of a certain size, or changes in the relative prices of the factors of production.

On the other hand, productivity gaps could be narrowed by raising the prevailing levels in the most backward sectors, especially agriculture and the informal urban sector. This would make it necessary to deconcentrate capital (land, in the case of agriculture) and to act upon the determining factors of the segmentation of the capital market which help to perpetuate the original status quo situation.

Notes

1. Almost all the developed countries cited as evidence of the "atypical" behavior of Latin America are also in this position. Among them are England from 1841 to 1951; France from 1866 to 1950; Germany from 1882 to 1933; and Italy from 1871 to 1954 (Kuznets 1957).

2. The share of manufacturing employment in nonagricultural employment in Latin America in 1970 (28.4%), which was maintained in the following ten years, was similar to that of the United States in the 1920s and of France in the late 1930s, and slightly lower than that of England in this century.

3. These coefficients were prepared from information provided by the United States Department of Commerce, Bureau of the Census (1975). In 1974 the Gini index for the total of land, including forests, was 0.726, and if limited to cultivated land, 0.605.

4. The countries included were Argentina, Chile, Colombia, Costa Rica, Ecuador, Mexico, Paraguay, Peru, Uruguay, Venezuela, Germany, Belgium, France, Holland, and Italy.

References

Clark, C. 1951. *The Conditions of Economic Progress.* London: Macmillan.

ECLA. 1966. *The Process of Industrial Development in Latin America.* New York: United Nations.

Garcia, N. 1981. *Empleo manufacturero, productividad y remuneraciones, por tamaño de establecimiento, México 1965–1975,* Monografías sobre empleo series, no. 18 Santiago: PREALC.

Kuznets, S. 1957. "Quantitative Aspects of the Economic Growth of Nations:II. Industrial Distribution of National Product and Labour Force." *Economic Development and Cultural Change.* Chicago: University Research Center on Economic Development and Cultural Change.

———. 1961. "Quantitative Aspects of the Economic Growth of Nations: VI. Long-term Trends in Capital Formation Proportions." *Economic Development and Cultural Change.* Chicago: University Research Center on Economic Development and Cultural Change.

Lagos. R. 1966. *La industria en Chile: Antecedentes estructurales.* Santiago: Universidad de Chile, Instituto de Economía.

Lebergott, S. 1964. *Manpower in Economic Growth: The American Record Since 1980.* New York, McGraw-Hill.

Meller, P. 1978. *El patrón de concentración industrial de América Latina y de Europa Occidental,* Notas técnicas series, no. 5. Santiago: CIEPLAN.

OAS-IASI. 1975. *América en cifras 1974. Situación económica. Agricultura, ganaderia, silviculutura y pesca.* Washington: OAS.

Pinto, A. 1970. "Naturaleza e implicaciones de la 'heterogeneidad estructural' de la América Latina." *El Trimestre Económico,* (January-March).

PREALC. 1978. *Sector informal: Funcionamiento y políticas.* Santiago: PREALC.

———. 1981. Dinámica del subempleo en América Latina, Santiago: PREALC.

Prebisch, R. 1970. *Change and Development: Latin America's Great Task.* Report submitted to the Inter-American Development Bank, Washington, D.C.

————. 1976. "A Critique of Peripheral Capitalism." *CEPAL Review,* no. 1.

————. 1978. "Socio-economic Structure and Crisis of Peripheral Capitalism." *CEPAL Review,* no. 6.

————. 1981. "The Latin American Periphery in the Global System of Capitalism." *CEPAL Review,* no. 13.

Pryor, F. L. 1972. "An International Comparison of Concentration Ratios." *The Review of Economics and Statistics.*

Ramos, J. 1980. *Capital Market Segmentation, Underemployment and Income Distribution.* Monografías sobre empleo series, no. 16. Santiago: PREALC.

Tokman, V. E. 1981. "The Development Strategy and Employment in the 1980s." *CEPAL Review,* no. 15.

U.S. Department of Commerce, Bureau of the Census. 1975. *Historical Statistics of the United States. Colonial Times to 1970.* Washington, D.C.: Department of Commerce.

part nine

Inflation, Monetarism, and the IMF

Without doubt, the debate between monetarist and structuralist economists has been most intense regarding the issue of inflation. Monetarists argue that inflation is caused by improper government policy: subsidies to lower the cost of food and other basic goods; large central government budget deficits; closed economies with high levels of tariff protection; overvalued exchange rates; and uncontrolled growth in the money supply. Such policies are often blamed by monetarists on the influence, well intentioned but wrong-headed, of structuralist and other heterodox economic advisors.

Monetarists, known also as the Chicago School, see an easy solution to inflation: get government out of economic affairs. Let the market (Adam Smith's invisible hand) direct the economy; the visible hand of government should be minimized and severely restricted (with one very telling exception—wage levels need to be repressed, at least initially, and government performs this task). According to the monetarist view, without the burden of government interference, which distorts prices and market incentives, output will grow as more food and other products are brought to market, and prices will fall, or at least rise more slowly. Hence, "getting prices right," particularly by opening the economy to international competition through tariff reductions, and drastically reducing government's role in the economy become the keys to both greater production and lower inflation.

Structuralists, however, understand inflation quite differently. They blame it on rigidities, or bottlenecks, in markets, particularly in agriculture where a backward land tenure system—characterized by many small peasant farms and relatively few absentee-operated haciendas—is not very responsive to price signals. Technically, structuralists believe supply in many markets to be quite price inelastic; output does not react strongly or rapidly to changes in market prices. Thus inflation will be one of the costs of economic growth (and the corresponding increase in demand for food and other products) until the backward institutional structure of agricultural and other markets where bottlenecks exist (banking and finance, for example) can be altered. But this can be only a long-term strategy. For structuralists, then, the problem of inflation is not one primarily of government interference in markets, but of uneven and incomplete development in the productive structure that makes inflation one of the unfortunate side effects of economic growth.

During the 1970s and 1980s, monetarists had a chance to apply their policies rigorously in a number of countries where institutionalist strategies had predominated. Alejandro Foxley, in Chapter 16, argues that the Chicago School's "shock treatment" for curing inflation, which was applied in Chile, Argentina, and Uruguay to the fullest extent, could be administered fully only by repressive, undemocratic military governments that were not sensitive to, or even interested in, the devastating impact of the monetarist experiment on wages and living conditions for the poorest in their societies. (This point also was made in Chapter 2 by Street.) Foxley demonstrates, however, that even by the monetarist criteria—reducing balance-of-payments deficits and inflation and increasing economic growth—the "radical conservative" policies of the monetarists met with failure. Inflation continued and growth lagged; endogenous money supply growth continued unabated; and real incomes and output declined. Democratic regimes, when they returned to power in Argentina and Uruguay in the early 1980s, were left with the shambles of failed monetarist policies and thus with raging inflation.

In other countries in Latin America, monetarism has made its appearance under another influence, as James Street details in Chapter 17. Because of balance-of-payments crises and the debt disaster (discussed more fully in Part 10), many countries in Latin America found themselves short of the foreign currencies required to purchase imports or to service their debts. Having no other apparent alternative, these countries turned to the International Monetary Fund (IMF) for necessary loans to meet their external obligations. The IMF, however, attaches "conditionality" to most of its loans. Conditionality means that countries must meet, or at least try to meet, certain austerity rules as a condition for borrowing (for example, reducing government spending by eliminating subsidies). IMF conditionality in most respects is indistinguishable from the monetarist shock treatment applied by military governments in the Southern Cone, except that now it is thrust upon governments from the outside by an influential international lending institution that cloaks its income-reducing policies in the technical language of economists and "sound" banking policies.

As Street argues, the effective outcome of IMF/monetarist austerity measures is to restructure radically the Latin American economies in ways that destroy much of the remedial function of government in societies where income, power, and justice are distributed unequally. What the IMF/monetarist restructuring promises for Latin America is not the "magic of the marketplace" as a means to economic efficiency and rapid growth, but a restoration of a traditional system of class discrimination and power concentration that may work well for a tiny, but vocal and powerful, elite, but that is devastating in its impact on the great majority of poor people in the region. Street's chapter makes clear, too, that there is an important moral component in the structuralist and institutionalist perspective on the least-cost way to reduce inflationary pressures that is lacking, or at best minimized, in orthodox monetarist policies.

chapter sixteen

Latin American Experiments in Neo-Conservative Economics

Alejandro Foxley

An Historical Perspective on Inflation

A Latin American perspective on the problem of inflation and economic stabilization must begin by referring to the two main currents that have influenced the thinking about inflation since the 1950s: structuralism and monetarism. The interest is not purely academic. In fact, as will be shown further on, both schools of thought have deeply influenced the design and application of stabilization policies in Latin America. By contrasting theoretical conception and historical experience, we can learn something about the effects of policies conceived under radically different assumptions.

The subject is of interest not only to Latin Americans. The so-called "new inflation" in developed countries and the subsequent discussion as to why the traditional monetary-fiscal approach has failed in bringing it down within a reasonable period of time have resulted in increasing attention to the structural factors behind the inflationary forces prevailing in developed countries today.[1] The parallel with debates in Latin America in the late 1950s and 1960s is striking, as Hirschman and Diamand have pointed out.[2]

The structural approach asserts that the roots of inflation are imbedded in the economic structure. This is characterized in developing countries by resource immobility, market segmentation, and disequilibria between sectoral demands and supplies. As growth proceeds, the economy is prone to develop extended bottlenecks since the changes in demand associated with higher income levels are not followed by an adequate supply response.

A characterization of the main bottlenecks includes the supply of food products, the availability of foreign exchange, the rigidity in the tax and ex-

Reprinted with permission from *Latin American Experiments in Neo-Conservative Economics* (Berkeley: University of California Press, 1983).

penditure structure of the government, the inability to raise enough internal savings, and the supply of various intermediate inputs, whose relative scarcity varies depending on the country's resource base and in some cases on the level of development achieved.[3] We refer to inputs like fuels, fertilizers, transport facilities, credit availability, and so on.

According to the structural view, a stabilization policy that does not recognize the existence of such bottlenecks is doomed to failure. It may reduce one disequilibrium (the rate of inflation) but at the expense of creating other disequilibria: excess capacity, unemployment, and concentration of income and wealth. The main thrust of a structuralist stabilization policy then lies in doing away with the bottlenecks that are forcing the economy to go through inflationary cycles. Almost by definition, this is basically a long-run policy since structural disequilibria can be eliminated only by a reallocation of investments. Thus, controlling inflation is necessarily a gradual process.

The structuralist view of stabilization is not only gradual and rather long run, but it is also part of a reformist or, in some historical cases, revolutionary process of change. According to this view, deep institutional reforms are needed if bottlenecks are to disappear. Land reform, tax changes, and state intervention in various areas of economic activity are required if the roots of inflation are to be eliminated. All these changes would negatively affect the income of those who control the scarce resources where bottlenecks originate: the owners of land and those who control key raw materials or exports. Resources extracted from these sectors would be channeled to the state. They would provide the basis for sustaining productivity increases and income redistribution in the lagging, poorer segments of the economy. Structural reforms would produce a progressive income redistribution in the long run.

By contrast, the monetarist view is generally thought to be short term and favoring a rapid control of inflation. In a somewhat ambiguous but revealing statement, a monetarist has asserted that "the monetarist is a structuralist in a hurry." According to this view, inflation is negative for efficient growth. It also produces negative income distribution effects mainly through the presumably regressive "inflation tax." Thus, the monetarist approach to stabilization is consistent with a strong preference for zero inflation. The shorter the period before this goal is achieved, the better. In this sense, a "shock treatment" approach to stabilization is more desirable than a gradual adjustment to equilibrium.

The monetarist approach is usually focused on the use of a few policy instruments: control of money supply, reduction of the government deficit, exchange rate devaluation, freeing of prices, and eliminating subsidies. These instruments are assumed to produce neutral distributive effects as a consequence of the application of a uniform "rule" for all economic agents: the working of a free price system.

These were roughly—and in a very summary form indeed—the views on stabilization prevalent in the 1950s and 1960s in Latin America and which were tested in various countries and political circumstances. The late 1950s saw the application of monetarist programs in several countries, including Chile in 1956–1958, Argentina in 1959–1962, Bolivia in 1956, Peru in 1959, and Uruguay in 1959–1962. The results of these experiences have been compared and described by many authors.[4] The policies applied followed rather closely the orthodox package: monetary and credit contraction, reduction in public expenditures, a fall in real wages, exchange rate devaluation, increases in utility rates, and elimination of subsidies and price controls.

The short-run results of the policies were judged to be, on the whole, unsuccessful. While typically the inflation rates decreased for a short period, production at the same time fell, unemployment went up rapidly, and the income share of wage earners deteriorated.

The structuralists' turn in applying their policies came in the 1960s and early 1970s. A good example is the stabilization program during the Frei administration in Chile. The idea was to stabilize the economy gradually and at the same time undertake those long-term reforms needed to overcome the basic bottlenecks in the agricultural, external, and fiscal sectors. At the same time, income redistribution was an explicit policy objective. This was to be achieved by (1) land reform, (2) the reorientation of public developmental programs toward small producers, (3) increasing expenditures in housing, health, and education, and (4) generous wage policies. After six years, the results show an inflation rate stabilizing around 30 percent a year, moderate growth, and significant gains in labor participation in the national income.

The relatively high rate of inflation at the end of the reformist structuralist experiment was only an external sign of a problem that is inherent in this type of stabilization package: in order to be successful, it needs to advance consistently in three fronts: price stability, structural reforms, and income redistribution. The balance is precarious. It may easily be disrupted by dissatisfied pressure groups (organized labor in the case that we are examining). If, for example, wage increases get out of line, this is bound to be reflected in a higher rate of inflation than was originally programed.

Besides the monetarist and structuralist experience, one finds another type of stabilization policy in the populist regimes in Latin America. These programs typically apply extended price controls while at the same time expanding wages, government expenditures, and the money supply. The Perón administrations in Argentina (1946–1952 and 1973–1976) and the Radical party government (1963–1966) are adequate illustrations of populist policies. As can be easily predicted, detailed price controls and large increases in expenditures make up for an inconsistent policy package. After a brief initial success in redistributing income toward wage earners and moderating the rate of inflation, the imbalances generated by the policy result in accelerating inflation and a regression in the initial distributive gains.

The "New" Stabilization Policies of the 1970s and 1980s

The 1970s witnessed a return to prestructuralist policies, with some important new features as will be described later. The failure of populist experiences brought about not only a full reversal in economic policies but the breakdown of the democratic political system in many countries. One factor in this breakdown was "the low propensity of policymakers to defer to normal economic constraints" when implementing stabilization policies during the populist experiences.[5] This was one of the elements leading to high inflation, extended bottlenecks in production, scarcity of basic goods, and losses in real income for almost all groups in society. The result was that wrong economic policies reinforced the political instability of the regimes and contributed to their replacement by authoritarian military governments.

As a reaction to the previous experience, these governments chose to apply strictly orthodox policies as they were heavily influenced by the modern monetarist approach. At the same time they reversed the previous trend toward increased economic and political participation by excluding workers and workers' organizations from decisionmaking mechanisms both in the political and economic spheres.

It would seem on the surface that as far as stabilization policies are concerned, the process had come full circle, back to the approach to stabilization of the late 1950s. Although, in fact, many of the policies being applied today in several Latin American countries bear strong resemblance to those of the 1950s, there are at least two new components that must be taken into account.

One is a political component: orthodox policies are being applied today by authoritarian military governments. This seems to solve what the monetarists saw as the reason for the previous failures: the premature reversal of the policies, caused by the adverse reaction of the social groups most affected, mainly the workers and the "partial" application of the package.

Obviously, an authoritarian government should have no problem in "disciplining" its workers and in controlling the political and social environment in such a way that a sustained application of a consistent stabilization policy is possible. Thus, authoritarianism is presented almost as a requisite for the success of the orthodox economic policies.

The second new element in the orthodox policies of the 1970s was their strong long-term component. Monetarism is usually associated with short-term adjustment policies, and their degree of success is judged accordingly. In their present version in Latin America, the orthodox policies put a heavy emphasis on changing the more fundamental ways in which the economy works. In a curious parallel to structuralist thinking, inflation is increasingly viewed as the result of an economic system that does not work.

Solving the problem of inflation requires a radical transformation of the economy. This involves such "structural" changes as reducing the size of the public sector, reorienting the surplus to the private capitalist sector, creating private capital markets, opening up the economy to free trade, and redefining the participation of private enterprise vis-à-vis labor organizations in decisionmaking mechanisms. Thus, the original problem, inflation, is "escalated" to a generalized malfunctioning of the economy.

In this sense, it could be argued that the new stabilization policies in Latin America are a form of structuralism using orthodox instruments. Obviously the direction, content, social support, and alliances behind it are entirely different. To give one example: while the structuralism of the sixties was incorporating the poorer masses of workers and peasants to the benefits of the system, the main aim of the new structuralism of the 1970s was to "modernize" the economy by incorporating it into the world economy and by favoring free market, probusiness policies. If this required excluding workers from political and economic participation, then this was a task that had to be undertaken.

In short, the two new elements in the recent stabilization policies in Latin America seem to be (1) the political framework within which they are applied (authoritarianism), and (2) the heavy emphasis on a long-term transformation of the economy as a condition for price stability.

The Turn Toward Radical Economic Policies

The new stabilization policies of the 1970s in Latin America were characterized by being applied by authoritarian military governments that emphasized a deep transformation of the economy and social and political institutions in order to solve the economic problems, inflation being the one given the highest priority.

We will explore some of the factors that may explain these changes. The changes are twofold. One is an initial turn toward economic orthodoxy, not necessarily a radical one, that accompanied the change in political regime. The existence of large disequilibria in most markets accentuated by ill-conceived populist policies provided a fertile ground for a reactive approach to economic policy that almost necessarily reflected a higher degree of orthodoxy. This entailed an enlarged role for the market, a higher priority for fiscal discipline, and a move toward the elimination of restrictions on foreign trade.

But this was not the only change. If a comparison is made of economic stabilization policies by right-wing military regimes in the 1960s and the 1970s, one will observe a noticeable radicalization in the policies of these regimes in an orthodox and conservative direction. How can this turn toward more radical policies be explained?

First I will deal with the conditions for the emergence of right-wing authorization regimes and hence of orthodox policies and then enumerate the factors behind the radicalization of economic policies in the 1970s and 1980s. Then I will illustrate the mild, rather heterodox, policies of the 1960s by describing some features of Brazilian policies. A third section picks up the previous themes in an attempt to provide a reasonable hypothesis as to why the economic policies evolved in the 1970s in a more radical conservative direction. Finally, I will deal with the way changes in the international economy influenced these events.

Change in Political Regime

There is widespread agreement that no single cause can explain the change in political regime and in economic policies that several Latin American countries have undergone since the 1960s. The turn toward political authoritarianism and economic orthodoxy began with Brazil in 1964 and was followed by Argentina in 1966. It received new impetus in the 1970s with Chile, Uruguay, and again with Argentina, which in 1976 initiated a new phase of political and economic changes in a conservative direction under an authoritarian regime.[6]

Recent literature that explores the origin of political authoritarianism stresses a mixture of economic and political factors behind the change in regime. A slowing down of economic growth accompanied by increased inflation and economic instability lead to a crisis of confidence in the economic system both by key domestic actors (workers, businessmen) as well as by foreign investors. To the extent that the countries choose to pursue and perhaps accentuate the same economic policies that led to the slowdown, the crisis is aggravated. Political factors are also present. The mobilization of popular groups and the strength of labor organizations create a pervading feeling of threat to business groups and eventually to the military as well. An open, competitive political system allows these conflicting forces to clash until a generalized political stalemate and crisis develop.

Conditions are ripe then for a regime, a coalition, or a policy change or for all of them to occur simultaneously, in which case the authoritarian regime emerges. The new regime represents a new coalition of the military and the more internationalized sector of the business community. It also represents a new approach to economic policies as a response to the inherited economic crisis. The questions that now arise are why this economic crisis developed and what were the factors behind it. We shall now explore these in more detail.

It is no mystery that import substitution industrialization (ISI) had run into trouble by the mid-1960s in those countries in Latin America that had most consistently followed these policies in the postwar period. As Hirschman has convincingly argued, the problem was not so much that of a supposed exhaustion of ISI but rather that the mechanisms used to promote it had run their course and were proving to be an expensive and inefficient way of pushing ISI strategies.[7]

Relative prices had been extensively used as a means of financing indus-trialization in Latin America. High protection for industry vis-à-vis agricul-ture, an overvalued domestic currency, and import controls made it possible to transfer resources away from the primary sectors to manufacturing. The policies led to periodic balance-of-payments problems, and inflation be-came a permanent feature. Through inflationary public expenditures the government was able to take command over resources without resorting to taxation. These resources were then used to finance industrial projects or the provision of infrastructure and social services required by the rapid pro-cess of industrialization.

As balance-of-payments problems become more recurrent, thus pre-venting the economy from fully using its productive capacity, inflation accel-erates. In the face of slower growth and higher inflation, redistributive prob-lems acquire enhanced importance. Antagonistic and mutually inconsistent redistributive objectives by various social groups substitute for the less con-flictive global development goals. Whatever one group is going to gain, another one must lose. The economy enters more and more into a zero-sum situation where the various social and economic groups perceive the others as a threat. The political system is strained, and social conflict escalates.[8]

At this point a revision of conventional policies was urgently needed in order to increase efficiency, stimulate growth, reduce economic instability, and enhance the possibilities of an equitable distribution of income. A more significant use of market signals as resource allocation criteria, a realistic ex-change rate that would allow balanced external accounts, and a more consis-tent effort toward export growth were obviously needed, as well as doses of fiscal and monetary restraint on the part of government.

A few countries in Latin America in the 1960s like Colombia and Vene-zuela were able to move in the required direction without changes in their political system. Chile initiated that process under the Frei administration, but it was not continued under Allende. Other countries like Brazil and Argentina suffered a breakdown of the political regime instead and em-barked on what was at the time a profound revision of economic policies. It was thought that orthodox stabilization measures were required in order to solve the economic problems.

In sum, in the 1960s several countries in Latin America were facing se-vere economic problems and social and political tensions. These phenomena were not as serious as they were to become in the 1970s. Even so, partly as a result of economic problems and partly out of a political crisis, some coun-tries like Brazil in 1964 and Argentina in 1960, after a military coup, attempted to turn their economic policies toward orthodoxy. The Brazilian experiment lasted only three years and evolved by 1967 toward a mixed package with strong heterodox components. The Argentinian stabilization policy of 1967 was never a case of pure orthodoxy but a mild blend of partial orthodoxy and "desarrollismo." By contrast, similarly authoritarian governments in Chile after 1973, Uruguay after 1974, and Argentina after 1976 followed a more radical course in their policies.

We believe that this is related to four concurrent factors. One was the existence of a much larger disequilibrium in the economy when the new experiments were initiated in the 1970s as compared with the 1960s. Second was the presence of a deeper, more extended political crisis than had been the case in the 1960s. Third was that the degree of threat posed by the populist or socialist coalition that anteceded the military regimes in the 1970s was perceived as being much greater than previously. The fourth originates in the changes that were occurring in the international economy.

It is our contention that in the 1970s most of these factors worked in the direction of reinforcing the feeling of the military that a very serious emergency was being faced and that it required tough solutions. Considerations about the cost of the policies in terms of output losses, unemployment, or regressive social impact became secondary.

Given this climate, it is not surprising that a more radical course was followed particularly when one compares equivalent cases in the 1960s, such as the Brazilian policies after 1964 or the economic stabilization scheme of Argentina between 1967 and 1970.

In contrast to the more radical versions of the 1970s, the 1960s policies look more pragmatic. They seem to have been less influenced by ideological fervor and adjusted more flexibly to the particular conditions or constraints faced by the economies at the time. At the same time, the policy design was more responsive to possible negative side effects of the policies such as recessionary tendencies. Before returning to the more recent cases, we shall illustrate this argument by drawing on the Brazilian economic policies after 1964.

Brazilian Policies After 1964 Revisited

Brazilian economic policies after the military coup of 1964 represented a turn toward orthodoxy.[9] Reductions in the fiscal deficit, in the expansion of money supply, and in real wages became a high priority, as well as the elimination of extended subsidies and nonmarket restrictions to trade. A gradual reduction of external tariffs was part of the orthodox policy package, as well as a liberalization of regulations affecting foreign investment. However, from the beginning the stabilization policy had some nonorthodox components. Price controls and credit incentives were used in order to curb inflationary pressures. The government took an active role in order to sustain an acceptable level of economic activity. Public investment was used as a countercyclical instrument. Opening up to trade—a typical component of orthodox economic programs—was pursued in a gradual manner so that high unemployment would be avoided. Even monetary and fiscal policy, after a first phase that lasted up to 1967, became mildly expansionary. This proved to be consistent with a reduction in the rate of inflation and high gross domestic product (GDP) growth rates.

Heterodox components in Brazilian policies reflected an early recognition of some structural constraints that were present in the Brazilian economy. Adapting the policies to these constraints was essential to the success of the policies. Let us illustrate this with two examples: trade policies and investment policy.

The structural constraint affecting the external sector was the low relative importance of external vis-à-vis domestic demand. The constraint affecting the level of economic activity was the traditionally high share of total investment performed by the public sector. We will discuss the importance of both factors.

If exports represent a low share of total output, a policy of rapid and drastic opening up of the economy to trade may imply losses in production and employment in the import substitution sectors that will be much higher than any conceivable expansion originating in exports. Even if exports do grow very rapidly, as was the case in Brazil, their relative share in GDP cannot compensate for the output loss elsewhere in the economy.

On the other hand, the reallocation of resources away from import substitution industries and toward the export sector is a slow process. It requires capacity expansions in the export activities. It also requires that the necessary complementary investment in infrastructure be forthcoming. This process takes more time than the fall in output and employment in the import substituting sectors. Thus, an almost unavoidable effect of rapid tariff reduction is to generate a large recession in the economy. If this is accompanied by contractionary fiscal and monetary policies, these negative effects will be reinforced.

What the previous reasoning implies is not that the shift to the new policies would not be possible. Given the relative size of the external sector and provided the government has some preference for less recession and unemployment, what it means is that a better transition path is a slow one. And this was the course followed by Brazil in the 1960s. The opening up to foreign trade through tariff reductions took place in Brazil only in the fourth year of the stabilization policy. During 1967, the tariff reform which, in any case, was quite moderate (see Table 16.1) was implemented by bringing tariffs down to an average of 41 percent. In addition, tariff reductions were not uniform. Internal production of durable and nondurable consumer goods continued to enjoy a high degree of protection after the reform. Average nominal tariffs in these sectors were reduced only to 116 percent and 56 percent, respectively, at their lowest point (in 1967). What these figures indi-

Table 16.1 Tariffs: Brazil (percentages)[a]

	1966	1967	1969
Nondurable goods	152	56	82
Durable consumer goods	260	116	176
Intermediate goods	76	36	45
Capital goods	60	40	40
Manufacturing sector	114	49	67
Agriculture	83	32	32
Average for the economy	98	41	53

Source: A. Fishlow, "Foreign Trade Regimes and Economic Development: Brazil," *National Bureau of Economic Research* (n.d., mimeo).

[a] These are nominal rates plus extra charges (such as deposits required previous to importing) and surtax rates on certain imported products.

cate is that Brazilian industry was allowed to adapt gradually to the new conditions without severe repercussions in industrial production.

On the other hand, the development pattern pursued by Brazil, consistent with these tariff reductions, represented an effort to pursue a balanced growth of industry oriented to the domestic sector and toward exports. It consisted in taking advantage of the existing capacity to expand the durable goods sector, construction activities, the capital goods sector—all mainly oriented to the domestic market—and exports. This pattern can be observed in Table 16.2. What it meant in practice was that the strategy of gradually opening up the economy did not result in large output losses or high unemployment because of the compensating role played by the expansion of industry oriented to the domestic market. A reasonable balance was achieved between stabilization goals, opening up to trade objectives, and high employment.

A second constraint facing policymakers, besides the high importance of domestic vis-à-vis external demand, was the predominant role played by public investment in Brazil. This was recognized, and in fact public investment played a significant countercyclical role. This was another sign of a movement away from rigid orthodoxy in the Brazilian case. The share of

Table 16.2 Industrial Growth and Exports: Brazil (rates of growth, percentages)

	1965-1967	1967-1970
Durable consumer goods	13.4	21.9
Nondurable consumer goods	3.6	9.7
Capital goods	4.5	13.7
Intermediate goods	10.8	13.7
Exports	5.9	10.7

Sources: M.C. Tavares and L. Belluzo, "Notas sobre o proceso de industrialização recente no Brasil" (Paper presented to the U.N. Economic Commission for Latin America [CEPAL] meeting on industrialization in Latin America, Oct. 1978; in CEPAL, "Políticas de promoción de exportaciones," vol. 5 Santiago, 1978).

public investment in the total had been historically high. It was likely that private investment would go down during the stabilization phase, as in fact it did. Instead of retreating and leaving the investment function to the private sector as the more radical version of orthodoxy in the 1970s would dictate, the public sector stepped in and increased its programs.

In fact, during the first phase of the stabilization program, the government was faced with a difficult option: either it waited for the domestic private sector to gain confidence and invest or the government would take an active role, providing the resources and undertaking the new projects needed to stimulate the economy out of the recession. It is clear from Table 16.3 that the option taken was the last one. It can be seen that public investment played an important role from the very beginning of the stabilization program. Government investment rose 7.9 percent and that of state enterprises 70.5 percent during 1965. This trend was maintained in the following years, with the exception of 1966, when fiscal balance became a high priority goal.

In sum, flexibility and early recognition of structural constraints were features of the post-1964 Brazilian economic policies. These characteristics explain the low doses of orthodoxy in the stabilization package and the relatively mild economic recession that accompanied it. An equivalent stabilization experience in Argentina between 1967 and 1970 during the military government of Onganía shows similar features.

Why the Economic Policies Are More Radical in the 1970s and 1980s

Why was this restraint not so in Chile and Argentina in the 1970s and 1980s? As was suggested before, several factors were present that pushed in the direction of more radical and rigid orthodox policies. These were related to (1) the magnitude of the inherited economic disequilibria, (2) the intensity of the political stalemate and crisis, (3) the degree of threat to existing institutions as perceived by the private sector, which, in turn, was a function of the depth of the transformation of the economy and society in a socialist direction, and (4) the effect of changes in the international economy.

The initial economic conditions in Argentina and Chile in the 1970s were much worse than any comparable situation in the 1960s. Inflation in Argentina was running at monthly rates close to 30 percent in 1976 whereas a decade earlier, when Onganía took power, that had been the rate of inflation for the whole year. Indeed, things had turned for the worse after the 1960s in Argentina. The Chilean economy was in no better shape during 1973. Yearly inflation was also at the three-digit level, markets were seriously disrupted, generalized scarcity of basic goods coexisted with extended black markets, and production was falling.

Table 16.3 Fiscal Deficit and Public Investment: Brazil

Year	Investment (annual growth rate, %)	
	Federal, States and Municipalities	State Enterprises
1963	-7.9	-17.3
1964	5.2	11.7
1965	7.9	70.5
1966	-4.6	4.9
1967	17.3	22.6
1968	0.6	11.7
1969	16.1	24.9
1970	11.7	25.0

Sources: For the federal government deficit: A. Foxley, "Stabilization Policies and Stagflation: The Cases of Brazil and Chile," in A. Foxley and L. Whitehead, eds., *Economic Stabilization in Latin America: Political Dimensions* (Pergamon, 1980); for public investment: estimates of J.R. Wells, quoted in ibid. The estimate includes the federal government, *autarquias*, state governments, municipalities, and state enterprises (*autarquias* are decentralized government agencies).

It would be naive to explain this drastic economic deterioration in Argentina and Chile as simply a result of wrong economic policies although these certainly played a significant role. Monetary, fiscal, and wage expansion coexisting with controlled prices, negative real interest rates, and fixed exchange rates could not but generate large sectoral imbalances that would be ultimately reflected in rampaging inflation, the breakdown of large parts of the productive system, and a generalized scarcity of essential goods.

In a sense, these inadequate policies reflected, at least in part, a rather desperate attempt to rescue political and economic experiments that had sought to solve the old problems of slower growth, higher inflation, and distributive contradictions from a radical populist and socialist perspective. After a long succession of the most diverse economic-political formulas that had been attempted in Argentina and Chile in the 1950s and 1960s in order to break the economic deadlock and political immobility, the Perón and Allende governments were showing the enormous failure of yet two more experiments.

But this time the economic crisis had been concurrent with a deep crisis in the political system. Political participation was on the rise. The popular sectors had been establishing a powerful claim on resources in the form of increased income shares and enlarged access to public services, housing, and property ownership. They were also pressing for increased access to and influence over political institutions, the media, the universities, and various means of cultural expression.

This "threatening" presence of the masses resulted in a rapidly escalating social conflict that generalized to all levels of political and social activities. The private sector reacted by withdrawing resources for investment.

The more radical the schemes pushed by the government, the larger the withdrawal. Since the economy was in disarray and not growing, it was increasingly difficult to meet the needs of redistributing income and increased capital accumulation without resorting to more drastic (and more antagonistic) redistributive policies—like expropriation of assets—or to the easier expedient of more inflation. These processes eventually led to the breakdown of the political and institutional system and gave way to new authoritarian regimes.

The new military governments imposed a rigid and drastic economic program as a reaction to "economic chaos." It constituted a complete reversal of previous policies, and its objective was not only to bring the economy back to equilibrium but also to discipline the economic and social groups until they adhered to a new rationality.

At this point the main task of the policymakers was to make the policy package a credible one. To achieve this, the government had to apply—with no vacillation or concessions—the policy that had been decided upon as the best one to deal with the situation. One must go all the way with the orthodox economic package, irrespective of how the situation evolves or how the policies affect the population. The most clear example of this approach is provided by the Chilean stabilization policies after 1973.

What are the most critical problems as perceived by policymakers at this stage? One is the balance-of-payments deficit and the other is low investment. For both problems to be solved without resorting to active government intervention—something radical orthodoxy will try to avoid—it becomes essential to restore the confidence of the business community and international financial centers. They will provide badly needed capital that will finance the trade deficit and raise investment.

In order to restore the confidence of these groups and make the economic program credible as a long-term solution to the country's problems, the new policies must conform to certain rules. These rules of "sound economic management" are perfectly codified by the international financial community, including the International Monetary Fund (IMF), large private international banks, and business groups. They consist of reducing the rate of expansion in money supply, eliminating the fiscal deficit, devaluing domestic currency, deregulating prices and private sector activities, and opening up the economy to free trade. Given such an explicit codification of what constitutes sound policies, the restoration of confidence requires strictly abiding by them. In doing so, the economic policies acquire a distinct orthodox flavor.

Why do they also become more radical in a political sense? The depth of the transformation of the economy in a noncapitalist direction previous to the crisis forces a new dimension into the orthodox policies. If there was expropriation of assets and land in the previous economic scheme, the new policies will almost certainly seek not only to reverse the trend but to proceed to privatize as many public enterprises and public sector activities as possible. Dismantling the public sector may seem the most effective way to ensure that the socialist "threat" will not be repeated. More generally, it is likely that the deeper the previous transformation, the greater the emphasis will be in the new economic policies on long-term transformation in the opposite direction. In these cases, the orthodox short-term stabilization scheme will be indissolubly married to a radical, long-term conservative project. Again the Chilean case provides the best example of this.

. . .

The Evolution from Conventional to Open Economy Monetarism

Monetarist stabilization policies in countries like Chile, Argentina, and Uruguay in the second half of the seventies represented a clear, simple, if somewhat rigid set of measures whose principal virtue was its coherence with respect to a powerful and robust body of theory. This corresponded to monetarism as popularized by Milton Friedman and other Chicago School economists. Inflation was "always and everywhere a monetary phenomenon," and its cure must be found in the contraction of money supply, in the elimination of the fiscal deficit, and in setting the "prices right," including currency devaluation when needed. As has been argued before, this was the basic policy framework behind Latin American monetarism in the 1970s.

However, when the policies are evaluated more carefully, we find at least two other theoretical frameworks. One of these represents a change in emphasis to cost pressures and inflationary expectations as sources of inflation. It is claimed that built-in indexing is at least partly responsible for the perpetuation of inflation. Policies then shift toward the gradual deindexation of critical prices: the exchange rate, public utility rates, and wages. The main effort of the government is put in enforcing rigid deindexation rules and in trying to increase the credibility of the gradual disinflationary targets. Monetary contraction continues to play a role but not the central one. Indeed, the "new" stabilization theory reflects to a large extent the frustrations of policymakers in trying unsuccessfully to enforce strict monetarism.

A third theoretical framework appears when the economy has advanced to deregulating trade and external financial flows. In the open economy, money supply is an endogenously determined variable. Why is money supply endogenous? The two main components of the monetary base are loans to the national treasury and changes in reserves. Of these, the first one is irrelevant once the fiscal deficit has been brought under control. The change in international reserves, on the other hand, is an endogenous variable. It depends on the size of the trade deficit and on external capital flows, which are regulated by the difference between international and domestic interest rates, adjusted by expected devaluation of domestic currency. At the same time, if the economy is fully open and all goods are tradable internationally, the domestic price level is just a function of international prices and the exchange rate.

This new theoretical framework, referred to as the monetary approach to the balance of payments, has replaced the more conventional form of monetarism. This new framework became a useful device to justify a marked change in the approach to stabilization. In the Latin American experience, this change occurred in the middle of the stabilization effort, 1978 in Argentina and 1979 in Chile. Where previously the control of money supply was the critical variable, now it was irrelevant; fixed exchange rates replaced the crawling peg as the optimal exchange rate policy; reserve accumulation was not considered a problem for monetary policy; quite the contrary, it allowed for a smooth adjustment of domestic inflation rates to external inflation.

How was this policy reversal justified within the new theoretical framework? According to the new paradigm, once we are dealing with an open economy, the process of economic adjustment is substantially modified. Suppose that, for a given exchange rate, the monetary authority decides to reduce domestic credit expansion. This action, essential in the conventional monetarist approach for the closed economy, will not be effective now. To be sure, credit restriction will have a contractionary effect on money supply, but the adjustment of the economy to monetary contraction will be different. Given a certain demand for real cash balances reduction in money supply will result in an excess demand for money. Two effects will follow. The first is a rise in domestic interest rates that will attract an inflow of foreign capital. This will increase net reserves and expand money supply, partly compensating for the previous reduction. A second effect will occur because the public, in the face of scarce money, will try to replenish its desired level of cash balances by withdrawing money from transactions. This will make expenditures and income fall. The contraction in monetary income will in turn affect imports. A lower demand for imports will reduce the trade deficit, also increasing net reserves and thus having an additional expansionary effect in money supply. The mechanism will operate automatically until the original equilibrium is restored.

This policy action was futile. Money supply adjusted automatically to the original rate of expansion. Domestic prices did not go down (or the rate of increase did not go down). In fact, the theory predicts that domestic prices will not grow faster than external prices except for movements in the exchange rate. The process of adjustment may be slow if there remain internal sources of money creation like a significant public sector deficit. But once this has been eliminated, the internal rate of inflation should converge to the international rate unless devaluations occur. Since policymakers favor automatic adjustment in the economy at this stage and an "equilibrium" rate of inflation equal to external inflation, a strong preference develops for a fixed exchange rate policy.

. . .

In sum, orthodox stabilization programs in Latin America in the 1970s and 1980s broadly represented the evolution of monetarist ideas. The old monetarism for the closed economy that had been in vogue in Latin America in the late 1950s, as well as during the first phase of the more recent stabilization policies, gradually gave way to open economy monetarism with its emphasis on the automaticity of the adjustment process. The transition from the old to the new approach was not an easy one. It required frequent adjustments. Mistakes were made, and policy actions did not often correspond to what was needed.

Policy Performance

We will now describe some macroeconomic results of several countries' experiences: Chile after 1973, Argentina after 1976, Uruguay from 1974, and Brazil in the period 1964–1967. Obviously the policies undertaken by these various governments have some similarities and several differences. They all share a monetarist origin irrespective of their different degrees of incorporation of nonorthodox elements in the policy package. Of the cases covered, Chile is by far the more orthodox, with Brazil at the other extreme. Stylized results suggest the following:

1. A resilience of the inflation rate despite sustained stabilization efforts: in three of the four cases considered, it takes between four and five years to bring the inflation rate to a level around 40 percent a year; and in the Argentinian case, after four years it was still around 150 percent.[10]
2. The coexistence of high inflation with recession during an equivalently long period (notice that in two of the four cases—Argentina and Chile—GDP per capita actually fell in real terms).
3. Unemployment went up sharply in at least two of the four cases, the extreme case being Chile where the rate of unemployment even went up between three and four times the historical rates.
4. Wages fell between 20 percent and 40 percent in real terms in all four cases.
5. The family income distribution, when available, showed a deterioration in the income share of the poorer and a significant gain for the higher quintile.

. . .

Notes

1. See F. Modigliani, "The Monetarist Controversy or Should We Forsake Stabilization Policies?" *American Economic Review* (March 1977).

2. A. Hirschman, "The Social and Political Matrix of Inflation: Elaborations on the Latin American Experience," *Brookings Project on the Politics and Sociology of Global Inflation,* Oct. 1978 (mimeo); M. Diamand, "Toward a Change in the Economic Paradigm Through the Experience of Developing Countries," *Journal of Development Economics* 5 (1) (March 1978).

3. See C. H. Kirkpatrick and F. I. Nixson, "The Origins of Inflation in Less-Developed Countries: A Selective Review," in M. Parkin and G. Zis, eds., *Inflation in Open Economics* (Manchester University Press, 1976); O. Sunkel, "La inflación chilena: Un enfoque heterodoxo," *El Trimestre Económico* (October 1958); A. Pinto, *La inflación, raíces estructurales,* Serie de Lecturas *El Trimestre Económico,* no. 3 (1973).

4. For comparative reviews of the policies see CIDE, "Papel de las politicas de estabilización," *Economía de América Latina* (September 1978), O. Sunkel, "El fracaso de las políticas de estabilización en el contexto del proceso de desarrollo latinoamericano," *El Trimestre Económico* (October 1963), and R. Thorp, "Inflation and the Financing of Economic Development," in K. Griffin, ed., *Financing Development in Latin America* (Macmillan, 1971).

5. The quotation is from A. Hirschman, "The Turn to Authoritarianism in Latin America and the Search for Its Economic Determinants," in D. Collier, ed., *The New Authoritarianism in Latin America* (Princeton University Press, 1979).

6. For an illuminating analysis of this phenomenon, see G. O'Donnell, *Modernization and Bureaucratic Authoritarianism* (Institute of International Studies, University of California, Berkeley, 1973); J. Linz and A. Stepan, eds., *The Breakdown of Democratic Regimes in Latin America* (Johns Hopkins University Press, 1978); and D. Collier, ed., *The New Authoritarianism in Latin America* (Princeton University Press, 1979).

7. A. Hirschman, "The Political Economy of Import-Substituting Industrialization in Latin America," in his *A Bias for Hope* (Yale University Press, 1971). Also see Chapter 8.

8. A. Hirschman, "The Turn to Authoritarianism."

9. See A. Foxley, "Stabilization Policies and Stagflation: The Cases of Brazil and Chile," in A. Foxley and L. Whitehead, eds., *Economic Stabilization in Latin America: Political Dimensions* (Pergamon, 1980). Detailed references to studies on Brazilian economic policies, on which my own comparative study was based, are given in Foxley's article.

10. Grouping all cases together is not totally fair, given the differences in the initial conditions—inflation in Brazil and Uruguay was about 90 percent vis-à-vis more than 300 percent in Argentina and Chile.

chapter seventeen ══════════════════════════

Values in Conflict: Developing Countries as Social Laboratories

James H. Street

Like a father welcoming home his prodigal son, Jacques de Larosière, [former] managing director of the International Monetary Fund, in an address at an annual meeting of the Fund, singled out Mexico as a model of correct policy in dealing with the international debt crisis. Praising the austerity program adopted by the newly elected government of President Miguel de la Madrid Hurtado in December 1982, Larosière said that the Mexican problem had been dealt with "in a very efficient way, not only by the creditors and the financiers, but more importantly, by the Mexican authorities and the Mexican people."[1]

During the same meeting, Jesús Silva Herzog, Mexico's [former] secretary of finance and public credit, an erstwhile radical economist, was chosen by *Euromoney* magazine as "Finance Minister of the Year," and feted with a champagne party for bankers and financiers in Washington. Silva Herzog modestly remarked that Mexico's economic performance undoubtedly pleased foreign bankers more than it did Mexican housewives, but he promised that under the belt-tightening program things would get better by next year.[2]

Antonio Ortíz Mena, president of the Inter-American Development Bank, also congratulated Mexico on having selected the "only way" to cope with its $80 billion external debt and return to a path of sustained development.[3] Officials of the World Bank and the United States government likewise expressed hearty approval.

With such a concurrence of knowledgeable experts on the remedy, it would appear that Mexico cannot fail in its restorative efforts. Mexico has become another "showcase" country, a social laboratory that will demon-

---

Reprinted from the *Journal of Economic Issues* 18 (June 1984) by special permission of the copyright holder, the Association for Evolutionary Economics.

strate what orthodox economic policy, pervaded by monetarist conceptions, can do.

The irony of foreign approval of Mexico's economic success during the past year [1982–1983] is that it was expressed in a period of extreme distress for the mass of the Mexican people, as the cost of living doubled during the year. The Global Development Program co-authored by President de la Madrid before he assumed office has been halted in its tracks, and unemployment is the highest known in years.

One of the requirements of the austerity program imposed by the International Monetary Fund as a condition for receiving a package of financial aid was the elimination of government subsidies. As a result, the price of corn tortillas, a staple of life among the common people, doubled in a single day, and continued to rise throughout the year. Other basic foodstuffs sold at reduced prices by the government through Conasupo, its national network of food distribution outlets, have also soared in price, while milk was virtually unobtainable in normal channels of distribution in Mexico City by September 1983.

The [U.S.] government, in response to the emergency faced by the government of President José López Portillo in August 1982, made $1 billion available in Commodity Credit Corporation loans to permit Mexico to buy U.S. surplus food on a concessionary basis. U.S. officials later amplified this credit to $1.7 billion over the year to enable Mexico to increase its imports of beans, another staple of consumption among masses of poor people who occupy the vast slums of Mexico City.[4]

The U.S. government thus finds itself in the paradoxical position that it has shown great generosity in providing vast quantities of food, produced under subsidized conditions in the United States, to meet the emergency in Mexico, but it upholds policies under which such food must be sold at market prices beyond the reach of most hungry Mexicans.

Moreover, the restrictions imposed by the IMF on Mexico have led the government to abandon a program for attaining self-sufficiency in food production through improvements in domestic agriculture because this program likewise was construed as requiring a proscribed subsidy. The Mexican Alimentation System (known by its Spanish acronym as SAM) would have required an expenditure of $4 billion in the Mexican rural economy over three years in order to extend the techniques of the Green Revolution to the production of corn, beans, rice, wheat, soy beans, and sorghum on peasant farms, with the aim of meeting national requirements in these basic crops by 1985. The SAM program was also intended to improve standards of rural nutrition and increase money incomes among small farmers so that they could be effective participants in the national economy.

The authorities of the IMF do not appear to take into account that Mexico's federal income tax does not effectively reach the upper income levels. Nor does it have an adequate social security system that provides old age pensions and other cash benefits to large excluded groups. Hence it cannot redistribute income in ways normally available in the industrial countries. The Conasupo food distribution system was devised as one of the few effective means by which some of the income generated by greatly increased oil exports in recent years could be redistributed in real terms, to the common people. After all, under the Mexican constitution, it is their patrimony that helps to supply oil for the strategic reserve of the United States as a form of payment in kind for food imports.

Thus in accepting intervention in its internal policies by the International Monetary Fund, the Mexican government must give up efforts to redistribute real income among the great majority of its population and it must desist from programs to feed its own people from domestic sources. These are heavy costs, and along with other restrictions on public investment imposed by the fund, they raise the question of whether this is indeed the path to economic recovery and growth for Mexico.

A Conflict of Values

The rigid application of policies such as those of the IMF in developing countries gives rise to a profound conflict of values. The asserted values of orthodox economics in maximizing consumer satisfaction, insuring efficiency in the use of resources, and, particularly in monetarist theory, eliminating the sources of inflation, are well ingrained in the thinking of IMF experts and frequently expressed in public statements as the ultimate justification for their policies. Some 45 countries among the 146 members of the fund are now subject to such rules.

However, there are also social values imbedded in the concept that sovereign peoples have the right and responsibility to select their own paths to development, especially when many of the pressures that fall upon them are exogenous. The energy crisis has deeply affected the entire world economy, but since the international community has found no way to limit the oligopoly power of the Organization of Petroleum Exporting Countries, much of the burden of adjustment has fallen on the oil-consuming countries. Alleviation of their balance-of-payments deficits requires these countries to expand their export earnings, but the terms of trade for the non-oil developing countries since the first oil shock in 1973 appear to have entered a period of long-term deterioration. The terms of trade for these countries fell in five of the eight years from 1974 to 1981, and a further decline of 12 percent is estimated to have taken place in 1982 [though there has since been some recovery for many countries due to lower oil prices, for most the terms of trade index remains below the 1980 level].[5]

For the international monetary authorities to insist that the entire burden of adjustment be borne by the lower income groups in the less developed countries is to pose the question, By whose values and by whose authority are these decisions made?

The Standardization of Orthodoxy in the Southern Cone

Mexico is not the first of the developing countries to be selected as a social laboratory. At least three countries in South America—Argentina, Chile, and Uruguay—and, in most respects, a fourth—Brazil—have been so regarded in the last decade. The record is one of almost unrelieved failure. It is highly significant that these massive and prolonged experiments in social engineering have required severely coercive enforcement by unconstitutional authoritarian governments and have, in every instance, been carried out against the public will. When, in December 1983, an elected Argentine government recovered its constitutional powers, one of its first acts was to demand an amelioration in the terms of IMF conditionality.

Although monetarist stabilization programs have been in effect from time to time in Latin America since the 1950s, the comprehensive, radical programs of the 1970s relied more heavily on military repression to prevent a premature reversal of unpopular politics; and they sought to achieve sweeping changes in the structure of the economy to reestablish an unrestricted free-market system.[6] The elements of extreme economic orthodoxy became standardized in the Southern Cone during this period.

Beginning in September 1973, Chile was the first of the Southern Cone nations to become a testing ground for radical stabilization policy. The Chilean program was applied with exceptional consistency and ideological fervor, since, by an unusual circumstance, a large cadre of Chilean economists was available who had received their entire advanced training at a single institution, the University of Chicago. Headed by Minister of Economy Sergio de Castro, they were selected to staff the ministries and the universities and became known locally as "the Chicago boys." The intellectual mentors of this group were Milton Friedman and Arnold C. Harberger, who made public statements in Santiago to lend academic support to the "shock treatment" they prescribed for Chile's ills.[7] The shock treatment, which consisted of an abrupt reduction in aggregate demand and an intensification of structural changes such as the privatization of all industrial and financial enterprises and the elimination of protective tariffs, has been maintained with only minor modifications for the eight years since 1975.

Shortly after the beginning of the Chilean experiment, a similar military coup occurred in Uruguay in 1974, and two years later a junta took over the elected government in Argentina. In each case, the military government instituted a monetarist stabilization policy that, in the case of Uruguay, is still in effect and, in the case of Argentina, was pursued vigorously for five years, after which it fell into disorder. Brazil had also earlier adopted orthodox stabilization policies after the assumption of power by the armed forces in 1964, but the application of these policies has been less rigid than in the Southern Cone countries and has been influenced by significant structural differences.

While differing in detail and in timing, the radical monetarist policies of Chile, Uruguay, and Argentina have been remarkably similar in their general characteristics. These have been delineated as a standardized strategy in independent studies by Alejandro Foxley and David Felix.[8]

In each of the three cases, the economic authorities began with an attack on inflation, which was conceived of as stemming, mainly if not exclusively, from monetary sources. Fiscal deficits were reduced by cutting back public investment and social services, and the prices of public services were raised to increase revenue. Monetary expansion was curbed while bank credit was largely reserved for the private sector. Interest rates were allowed to rise in real terms in order to draw flight capital back into the domestic financial system and improve efficiency in the allocation of resources. (This proved to be one of the major mistakes in the monetarist strategy, as the policy stimulated the speculative use of credit.)

At the same time exchange rates were manipulated by minidevaluations and export taxes were removed, while protective measures, such as tariffs, quantitative restrictions, and exchange controls, were removed on the import side. These actions were intended to stimulate competitive efficiency on the part of local industry. Simultaneously, state enterprises were returned to private hands whenever feasible, sometimes at knockdown prices. Nevertheless, the military juntas refused to privatize enterprises considered part of the national patrimony or as of strategic significance. These included the nationalized copper mines of Chile and YPF, the state petroleum entity, and Fabricaciones Militares, the defense industry of Argentina.

The initial aims of the stabilization programs were set out as short-term emergency measures to curb inflation and to eliminate deficits in the balance of payments. However, as time went on, it became evident in each instance, as Foxley has shown, that the authoritarian governments of the Southern Cone had larger ends in view.[9] They intended nothing less than a fundamental restructuring of society to establish centralized forms of control and to redistribute income according to a hierarchical scheme that had strong appeal to the most conservative elements in the society.

Thus, while the official ideology constantly stressed the virtues of the free market, the concept was not applied to the labor market, where trade unions were restricted, collective bargaining was eliminated or severely curtailed, and wages were controlled. Foxley points out that the fact that real wages declined did not mean that there were no cost-push pressures in the economy. "Strong cost-push pressures originated in price deregulation, exchange rate devaluations, and financial sector liberalization. These pressures were perpetuated by strong inflationary expectations and widespread indexation schemes."[10] Monetary policy alone had little effect on these forces.

The monetarist view that inflation invariably arises from monetary sources and is propagated by excess consumer demand stemming from irresponsible government responses is thus seen as theoretically inadequate. The failure of monetarist policies, even when carried to the extreme, to eliminate inflation in the Southern Cone countries bears witness to the structuralist contention that inflation is a complex phenomenon arising from many causes.

It is doubtful, even under the best of circumstances, that an untrammeled free market would insure distributive justice without adequate fiscal controls. Yet the authoritarian governments of Argentina, Chile, and Uruguay clearly could not trust the distribution of income to the free market; the wage sector, affecting the great majority of the population, had to be held under continuous control. The long-term goal of establishing a permanent redistribution of income by social classes therefore provides the major explanation for the fierce determination with which the authoritarian governments have resisted a return to democratic institutions.

When considering the basic conflict of values that these strategies represent within the Southern Cone, one must not overlook the fact that most of the leading monetary and financial authorities in the world and a number of prominent academic economists not only countenanced the contractionary economic policies that were applied, but raised no objections to the coercive means that were used to make them effective. Only late in the day, for example, did Milton Friedman make some effort to dissociate himself from the extreme authoritarianism of the government of General Augusto Pinochet in Chile.[11]

Eventually, as the emergency phase of monetarist policies intended to curb inflation and correct balance-of-payments deficits stretched out ineffectually into the decade, "the Chicago boys" and their counterparts in Argentina and Uruguay overreached themselves, their respective economies began to fall apart, and the very business and financial community whose interests they intended to serve was subjected to severe shock.

In part, the crisis stage of the Great Experiment can be attributed to an excessive willingness of the local ministries of finance and of key business firms to accept the outside help generously extended by the International Monetary Fund, foreign commercial banks, and other agencies at a time when world interest rates were at their peak.[12] Ultimately the accumulation of external short-term debt became unmanageable and led to complaints that the onerous service charges on the debt did not actually represent free-market rates, but were the result of irresponsible fiscal policy on the part of the government headed by President Ronald Reagan. Jacques de Larosière has recently joined in this complaint.[13]

Despite this effort to find an exogenous explanation for the failure of monetarism in Latin America, it must be recognized that the main cause of the collapse of the industrial sector in these countries, carrying with it the virtual destruction of the banking system, was the decision to open each economy to the unfettered winds of free trade. Orthodox economics, of course, places great store by the Heckscher-Ohlin model, in which the benefits of comparative advantage insure the efficient allocation of resources among all trading partners. However, the economies of the Southern Cone achieved most of their existing industrial capacity under regimens of import substitution, with no provision for the gradual elimination of protection. Furthermore, because their traditional exports are limited in diversity, they are exceptionally vulnerable to the swings of the world market engendered by recessions in the advanced industrial countries.

To open such economies suddenly to the impact of world competition was predictably to create havoc among domestic industries, increase the levels of unemployment, and impair the local banks that had financed these operations. It was the accumulation of business bankruptcies and the virtual collapse of the financial structure in Argentina in 1981 that brought down the monetarist regime of Minister of Economy José Martínez de Hoz after five years of unparalleled free-market discipline. And it was the eight hundred-odd bankruptcies and attendant financial disorders of Chile in 1982 that sealed the fate of the Chicago experiment.[14] When the business and financial community could no longer see advantages in an economy drastically restructured in the mold of nineteenth-century free trade, authoritarian government lost a major pillar of support.

The Record of Economic Performance and Its Prognosis

After nearly a decade of monetarist experimentation in the Southern Cone, inflation continued to rage, reaching 433 percent in Argentina in 1983, and forcing down real income in Chile and Uruguay as relentlessly as before. In each country, the payments problem can be met only by inducing foreign banks to increase their lending sufficiently to cover the interest in arrears on past debt, with no assurance that the outstanding principal can ever be renegotiated on a manageable basis.

From a longer range view, the problem is even more acute, since neither country has in place a strategy for growth to overcome a succession of liquidity crises. Monetarist theory provides no strategy for growth, as the structuralists have long pointed out. On the contrary, the imposition of conditionality has persistently retarded growth, and now that this policy has been generalized to most of the developing countries of the world, it threatens to bring stagnation to the network of international trade such as we have not seen since the "beggar thy neighbor" days of the Great Depression. What the world needs is a growth model, not a model for further general contraction.

To return to the opening theme of this article: In light of the record, is Mexico, which is now embarking on another Great Experiment in austerity, well served to accept the advice of the international banking and financial community? Must a country give up sovereign control over its own destiny because the mainstream of economic thinking persists in believing there is no other way? This is the conflict of values between economic orthodoxy and the pragmatic experience that defines common sense.

The instructive cases of the failures in the Southern Cone suggest that, sooner or later, the decisions shaping a basic strategy of growth will be taken out of the hands of the "mainstream" economists and the coercive governments who offer their people as guinea pigs in social laboratories that they were never entitled to claim.

Notes

1. Leonard Silk, "Monetary Fund Chief Is Firm About Demands on Debtors," *New York Times,* 16 October 1983, 1, 16.

2. *Mexico City News,* 2 October 1983, 6.

3. Luis Acevedo, "Pese al costo social, es necesario el ajuste: BID," *Uno Más Uno* (México, D. F.), 29 September 1983, 1, 8.

4. Eugenio Laris Alanis, secretary of urban development and public works of the State of Mexico, estimates that 600,000 new migrants arrive each year to swell the population of Mexico City and its environs, which now numbers more than 18 million inhabitants. Most of the new arrivals find scant employment, housing, or water and sanitation services. "Cities Lacking Sufficient Housing, Water Services Growing Dynamically on the Perimeter of Mexico City," *Mexico City News,* 3 October 1983, 1.

5. Moshin S. Khan, and Malcolmn Knight, "Sources of Payments Problems in LDCs," *Finance & Development* 20 (December 1983):2-5.

6. Alejandro Foxley, *Latin American Experiments in Neo-conservative Economics* (Berkeley: University of California Press, 1983):9-23. Also see Chapter 16.

7. Jonathan Kandell, "Chile, Lab Test for a Theorist," *New York Times,* 21 March 1976, IV, 3.

8. Foxley, *Latin American Experiments,* 149-201; David Felix, "On Financial Blowups and Authoritarian Regimes in Latin America," Working Paper no. 60, Washington University, St. Louis, Mo. October 1, 1983, 5-18.

9. Foxley, *Latin American Experiments,* 2-6, and passim.

10. Ibid., 199-201.

11. In a telephone interview in September 1983, Milton Friedman clarified his position. "Some have charged that Dr. Friedman has supported the military junta. Contrariwise, the Nobel Prize-winning economist holds that the maintenance of free markets in Chile requires the abolition of the military government. A fundamental principle of juntas, he noted, is rule from the top down. Free markets work from the

bottom up." David R. Francis, "Friedman: Chilean Advisors Erred," *Christian Science Monitor* (Eastern edition), 27 September 1983, 9.

12. Private bank borrowing in Chile soared from $147 million in 1977 to $2.7 billion in 1981; in the initial period Chilean borrowers had to pay premiums as much as 2 percent over the London Inter-Bank Borrowers Rate (LIBOR). Observers who marveled at the "Chilean economic miracle" at this time took little notice of this exceptional source of support. Paul E. Sigmund, "The Rise and Fall of the Chicago Boys in Chile," *SAIS Review* 3 (Summer-Fall 1983):41-58.

13. Jacques de Larosière, in a speech on "The Domestic Economy and the International Economy—Their Interactions," to the American Enterprise Institute, Washington, D.C., 5 December 1983. Quoted in "Heightened Global Cooperation Advocated by Managing Director," *IMF Survey* 12, no. 23, (5 December 1983):379-382.

14. José Pablo Arellano and others, *Modelo económico chileno: Trayectoria de una crítica* (Santiago: Editorial Aconcagua, 1982).

part ten

The Debt Disaster:
Causes and Solutions

The debt crisis, which can be dated from August 1982 when Mexico declared a moratorium on its debt payments, has caused the worst economic collapse in Latin America since the Great Depression. In all countries, per capital income levels by the mid-1980s had fallen back to levels first attained in the 1970s. In Peru and Argentina, the deterioration was even worse, as income slipped back to 1960s levels. Throughout the period, poverty, income distribution, and living standards have worsened, especially for the poorest. Further, it has proven impossible for Latin America to repay its current debt obligations *and* simultaneously achieve economic growth. This conflict between debt servicing and the need for greater economic growth has dominated the increasingly antagonistic renegotiation process, which, since 1982, has pitted the center and its financial institutions against the Latin American periphery.

Chapter 18, by James Dietz, considers the history of debt accumulation in Latin America, a buildup that preceded the first oil price hike of 1974. However, as part of a net-oil-importing region, most Latin American countries were hard hit by the Organization of Petroleum Exporting Countries' (OPEC) action that dramatically increased their need for foreign exchange if imports, and economic growth, were not to be severely curtailed. This shortfall in financing, however, was overcome in the short run by the "recycling" of petrodollars through the private international banks, such as Chase Manhattan and Citibank, which increased their loans to Latin America, thus averting an immediate economic crisis for most countries.

Unfortunately, debt accumulation as a means of sustaining growth, particularly when used in unproductive ways, as it was in so many instances, was revealed to be an illusion (as it always was) when the

world economy was thrown into recession in the early 1980s as a consequence of anti-inflationary U.S. policies. With the recession and its
accompanying decline in export possibilities, the private international
banks shut Latin America off from the loans that it had come increasingly to depend upon.

Dietz also considers how the debt crisis might be resolved once it
is conceived of as a long-term growth problem and not just as a short-
term liquidity crisis, which is how the IMF and bankers have tended to
view the problem. There may be important lessons in the East Asian
debt and development experience, and these are reviewed, but Dietz
counsels caution in attempting to apply models where the initial conditions, especially the institutional structure, are inappropriate for
such a transfer. Dietz offers some positive suggestions for needed institutional reform and structural change that, if implemented, could
help to make the Latin American economies more dynamic, productive, and equitable. What is certain, however, is that a real resolution of
the debt disaster will require a transformation of the existing economic and power relations, not only between Latin America and the
center countries, but within Latin America as well.

chapter eighteen

Debt and Development: The Future of Latin America

James L. Dietz

> The challenge to North American institutionalism and Latin American struc-
> turalism, . . . is the urgency of formulating development strategies superior
> to those of conventional doctrine. Twenty years have gone by in which the
> goals of expansion and development should have replaced the aims of con-
> traction and stagnation (Street 1983:309).

Renegotiation of Latin America's debt since 1982 may have led to the illusion
that the problem period has passed. At best, the crisis is under control; at
worst, this is only the calm before the storm, lulling too many in the developed world into complacency, while those paying the real costs of adjustment are forced beyond all reasonable limits of sacrifice. The challenge is to
turn the ideological tables against the orthodoxy that has, until now,
weighed heavily, if not exclusively, in defining the debt problem and in providing solutions acceptable to principal vested interests, in this instance the
international banks and the International Monetary Fund (IMF) (Dornbusch
1985:167).[1] The affected countries in Latin America are slowly attempting to
come to terms with a "resolution" to the debt crisis that concentrates its burden on but a segment of the principals, and the poorest at that, generously
granting that they actually *were* beneficiaries of the debt accumulation in
the first place.

Increasingly, there is wider awareness that the costs of the current solution to the debt problem are much too high. Though the facts are now well
known, they bear repeating (see Table 18.1). After more than a decade of
growth rates that exceeded the industrial and U.S. average, in the 1980s Latin
America's income suffered a historical reversal. From 1980 to 1985, the aver-

Reprinted in abridged form from the *Journal of Economic Issues* 20 (December 1986) by special permission of the copyright holder, the Association for
Evolutionary Economics.

Table 18.1   Growth of Real Output, 1967-1985[a] (percent from preceding year)

	Average 1967-1976[b]	1978	1980	1981	1982	1983	1984	1985[b]
Industrial Nations	3.7	4.1	1.3	1.6	-0.2	2.6	4.9	—
United States	2.8	5.0	-0.3	2.5	-2.1	3.7	6.8	2.2
Latin America (excluding Cuba)	5.9	4.1	5.3	0.4	-1.5	-2.5	3.2	2.8

	Individual Countries, Growth of Gross Domestic Product						
	Average 1971-1980	1981	1982	1983	1984	1985[b]	Cumulative 1980-1985
Argentina	2.4	-6.7	-6.3	3.0	2.0	-3.0	-10.9
Brazil	8.6	-2.0	1.4	-2.7	4.8	7.0	8.4
Chile	2.8	5.2	-13.1	-0.5	6.2	2.0	-1.7
Mexico	6.6	8.3	0.0	-5.2	3.5	3.5	9.8
Peru	3.5	3.7	-0.2	-12.0	4.4	2.0	-2.8

	Growth of Gross Domestic Product Per Capita						
Argentina	0.8	-8.2	-7.8	1.4	0.4	-4.5	-17.7
Brazil	5.9	-4.2	-0.9	-4.9	2.5	4.8	-3.0
Chile	1.0	3.6	-14.4	-2.1	4.5	0.2	-9.1
Mexico	3.5	5.4	-2.6	-7.6	0.9	0.7	-3.6
Peru	0.9	1.0	-2.7	-14.3	1.8	-0.4	-14.6

Sources: International Monetary Fund (1985: Table 1, 205); Inter-American Development Bank (1985: Table 1, 152); González (1986: Table 2, 107; Table 3, 108).

[a] For industrial nations and the U.S., gross national product; for Latin America, gross domestic product.
[b] Preliminary.

age real growth rates of per capita income in Argentina, Brazil, Chile, Mexico, and Peru were negative, and per capita income levels have been turned back a decade to those prevailing in the 1970s, or, for Peru and Chile, to pre-1970 levels (Table 18.2). Real gross domestic investment in Latin America declined by 32.5 percent between 1980 and 1984, clouding the prospects for future growth (Inter-American Development Bank 1985: Table 5, 389). Further, a net capital outflow from Latin America to the developed countries existed during the period 1981–1985, amounting to an estimated $108.9 billion (Organization of American States 1986:ii). Whatever real aggregate income gains might have occurred as a result of the debt buildup have now been fully erased by recession and the debt adjustment process. Such setbacks could not be more ill-timed; they come during a cycle in which most of the Latin American republics—Chile stubbornly remains an exception—have returned to civilian rule and are promising and experimenting with new democratic forms of political participation that are not only sensitive to popular pressures, but are fragile and weak.

Latin Americans have begun searching for solutions to the debt crisis that define the limits of repayment in a development, and not a strictly financial or accounting, context (Concenso de Cartegena 1986; Organization of

American States 1986). This, of course, is contrary to the IMF, orthodox approach, which has been to first put Latin America's "financial house in order" and to see the debt fully serviced. Austerity and hardship, lamentable though they may be, are the costs following from the imprudent borrowing and the bloated public sectors characteristic of the Latin American economies. The orthodox view is rejected by Latin American structuralists, however, who long have stressed the need to understand Latin America's reality differently (Street 1967). They now are joined by scholars in the United States and elsewhere influenced by their theories, all of whom are forcing a rethinking of the debt crisis. It is to such an understanding that this chapter is addressed.

Redefining the Problem

The IMF/orthodox perception essentially has considered the debt crisis to be a liquidity problem (Cline 1985). With reactivation of the Organization for Economic Cooperation and Development (OECD) economies and the necessary internal and external liberalization in Latin America—"getting the exchange rate and other prices right," reducing the fiscal deficit, reducing money supply growth—Latin American economic growth is expected to resume, and the short-term difficulties encountered in servicing the debt will be overcome. Hence, bridge loans and other accounting sleight-of-hand, which until now have characterized the renegotiation process, make sense to enable the economies to weather what is seen as a temporary phenomenon due to the business cycle and to correctable but ill-advised public policy suggestions attributable, mostly, to the influence of the United Nations Economic Commission for Latin America (ECLA) and other structuralist economists. With the problem defined as short run and caused by mismanagement and excessive government interference in the economy, the orthodox recommendations all but suggest themselves.

Structuralists view the crisis in a much longer time frame, and as generalized, rather than limited to a few debtor nations. The real debt problem is not illiquidity, in this alternative view, but insolvency or, better, structural barriers which, given the uses to which borrowed funds were put, sub-

Table 18.2   Gross Domestic Product Per Capita (1982 dollars) in Selected Latin American Countries

Country	1960	1970	1980	1984
Argentina	$1,586	$2,065	$2,223	$1,929
Brazil	710	1,006	1,783	1,626
Chile	1,413	1,735	1,878	1,674
Mexico	1,104	1,575	2,228	2,086
Peru	814	1,051	1,142	978

Source: Inter-American Development Bank (1985: Table 3, 388).

stantially limit repayment possibilities, renewed OECD growth or not. It is useful to remember that much of the debt in Latin America was incurred in the 1970s by nonelected, nondemocratic governments that borrowed not only for productive (foreign exchange-producing or saving) investments, but also to finance nonproductive military expenditures (Argentina, for example), to rollover short-term debt, or to finance capital flight.[2] Nondemocratic governments too often privatized the benefits of the debt accumulation to a military or other elite; the repayment costs, however, are socialized to the entire population, particularly the least well-off. There would seem to be, on this count alone, a strong argument for a more comprehensive understanding of the real barriers to debt repayment and, hence, for a wider sharing-out of the costs of debt reduction beyond the debtor countries.[3]

There is a further argument to be made for a redistribution of the costs of debt readjustment that can help to focus our discussion on where the burden ultimately should be placed. The great growth in debt accumulation was, of course, a post-1970 phenomenon (Table 18.3) spurred, and made possible, by the OPEC oil price increases in 1973–1974 and 1979–1980.

Higher energy prices should have forced all oil-importing nations to make adjustments in their import bills through a reduction in oil or other imports, in line with the expected growth of future exports. But immediately reducing energy or other productive imports—capital, technology, and intermediate goods—meant slower rates of growth of aggregate production and income. There emerged another (short-term) option, of course, and that was to borrow externally the funds necessary to finance the higher import bill, an option made even more viable by the availability of loanable funds because of OPEC itself. Borrowed funds, however, were not used simply to ease the transition to a new import mix, but also to continue the growth and consumption behavior of the past. Petrodollars received by the OPEC countries were deposited in the private international banks and recycled back to the oil importers, only to begin the triangular circuit again. All of this helped to maintain OPEC prices and demand, the OPEC cartel, and hence the need for even more debt longer into the future. This extensive borrowing option, however, would not have been open to Latin America if the private international banking system had not been so autonomous, unregulated, and irresponsible. The desire of Latin American governments to prolong economic growth, to arm their militaries, and to finance current consumption (often via the public sector), however, conveniently converged with the profit-making interests of the banks, awash with excess liquidity.

No one seriously doubts now that the Latin American countries as a group overborrowed. It ought not to be in doubt that, besides the profits made by the private international banking system, which seriously overlent,

Table 18.3   Total Disbursed Debt[a] (millions of dollars)

	1975	1979	1980	1981	1982	1983	1984 [b]	1985 [b]
Latin America	75,393	184,193	229,054	279,697	314,360	336,230	360,410	368,000
Argentina	6,026	19,668	27,065	32,276	36,680	40,718	47,800	50,000
Brazil	23,344	51,482	64,631	74,051	83,206	91,613	102,039	101,930
Chile	4,854	8,484	11,084	15,542	17,153	17,654	18,946	19,580
Mexico	16,900	40,800	52,652	75,496	82,450	86,516	96,700	97,700
Peru	4,066	7,166	8,839	8,844	10,356	11,592	13,364	13,750

Sources: Inter-American Development Bank (1984: Table 1, 12 for 1975-1983); González (1986: Table 15, 111 for 1984 and 1985).

a Includes total public and private debt, including short term.
b Figures not exactly comparable due to different source.

the OECD nations also benefited from Latin America's debt. The Latin American countries were able to keep their levels of import purchases from the developed countries at a high level, and hence their debt accumulation contributed to offsetting, to an extent, the downturn in the developed countries set in motion by the higher oil prices. Further, international corporations in Latin America were able to make higher profits than would have been the case if adjustment had been forced on Latin America by tighter lending practices or by real structural adjustment to higher oil prices, and larger flows of repatriated profits were recorded as a result (which added to the need for further debt accumulation as current account balances worsened).

In effect, then, the petrodollar recycling process, which the private international banking system initiated and promoted, worked, at least in terms of short-run aggregates, to the benefit of the three major actors: the Latin American countries (and their governing elites), the banks, and the OECD countries. The costs of the debt crisis, however, are not being distributed in proportion to these benefits, but are rather concentrated predominately in the debtor nations. On this basis, too, there is a strong case to be made for a wider and more equitable sharing of the costs of debt readjustment among all parties, as part of the redefinition of the debt problem within a development context (for a related discussion, see Guerguil 1984:156-158).

Disaggregating Reasons for Debt Accumulation
To begin to resolve the debt crisis it is essential to understand the reasons underlying its accumulation. Table 18.4 shows year-to-year external borrowing, the amount of which depended upon overall country financing requirements. These needs were increased by payments for foreign factor services (including amortization), for foreign nonfactor services (insurance, shipping, tourism), and when central government deficits were financed externally. The need for external debt accumulation was reduced by direct foreign investment inflows and positive net transfers.

What is evident from the table is that, first and significantly, the major countries adjusted their *merchandise* trade balances fairly rapidly to higher oil prices. Merchandise trade surpluses were the rule by 1979 and thus did not contribute to additional debt buildup. On the other hand, nonfactor service payments grew rapidly, thus leading to a deficit on the trade and services account; and amortization and investment income outflows increased spectacularly, with the greatest growth occurring in interest payments on external debt (about 70 percent of foreign income outflow in 1982). It is also clear from the table that an increasing proportion of new debt was being used for little more than servicing past debt and for external payments to direct foreign investment, that is, it never even entered productive uses. The rapid growth of service payments was due to two factors: very high and variable rates of interest which, since 1979, have averaged above 15 percent, and the dramatic change in the term structure of the debt. In 1975, 14.7 percent of the total debt was short term (less than one year). By 1980, this had risen to 24.1 percent (Inter-American Development Bank 1984: Table 1, 12). This shift toward debt with shorter maturities has severely exacerbated the payback problem by accelerating servicing needs, as amortization of short-term debt is added on to medium- and long-term servicing requirements.

The orthodox solution for servicing the debt, given the debt structure, the outflows due to foreign investments, and the paucity of current external

Table 18.4   Borrowing and Use of Funds—Selected Countries[a] (millions of dollars)

Year	External Borrowing	DFI	MTB	FY	NFS	A
1974	12,489	1,493	-288	-5,394	-2,205	-2,785
1975	12,025	1,915	-5,080	-6,300	-3,093	-3,360
1976	13,466	464	-1,473	-7,333	-3,017	-4,066
1977	15,312	1,390	385	-8,884	-3,232	-6,505
1978	24,683	2,043	-1,684	-11,229	-4,402	-10,582
1979	30,346	3,798	1,780	-16,101	-5,796	-14,462
1980	41,896	4,124	116	-22,019	-7,600	-12,841
1981	44,657	5,477	630	-33,748	-10,611	-12,871
1982	28,207	4,569	10,992	-40,565	-9,008	-11,878
1983	19,452	2,737	31,524	-31,671[b]	-5,153	-8,083
1984	16,905	2,672	38,758	-32,935[b]	-4,452	——
1985	——	——	34,310	-31,990[b]	-4,520	——

Sources: Inter-Amercian Development Bank (1984: Table 11, 34-35; Table A.1.02, 72; 1985: Table I-2, 22); González (1986: Tables 12 and 13, 118).

[a] Argentina, Brazil, Chile, Colombia, Mexico, Peru, and Venezuela.
[b] Net flows.

DFI = Direct foreign investment
MTB = Merchandise trade balance
FY   = Foreign income outflow (profits + interest)
NFS = Balance of nonfactor services
A   = Amortization of debt

debt financing, is to generate expanding trade surpluses, which is precisely what the Latin American countries have done. This, however, has occurred predominately through reductions in imports, which fell by 44.8 percent from 1981 to 1984 (Inter-American Development Bank 1985: Table I-2, 22) due to the decline in living standards precipitated by austerity measures. Trade surpluses have not resulted from expansion of exports; in fact, in 1985, for all of Latin America, exports actually declined in value by 5.7 percent.[4] Harry Magdoff has referred to this situation as "the trap of debt peonage," which pushes the Latin American countries to try to export more and import less in the hope that a point will be reached when it finally will be possible to again attract foreign capital and loans to cover the current account deficit, even though this only can prolong and deepen the debt cycle (Magdoff 1986:8).

Restructuring the Latin American Economies: What Is Desirable?

Structuralists and institutionalists have pointed to the different realities in the Latin American economies that suggest caution in attempting to apply neoclassical models and remedies. Given the imperfection and incompleteness of markets and the pervasiveness of noncapitalist behavior patterns, neoclassical tools are at best partial aids to understanding the complexities of Latin America's economic life. One significant factor, reflecting on the nature of the overall productive structure of the Latin American debtors, has to do not with the volume of debt per se, but with high debt-to-export ratios, which measure, imperfectly to be sure, the payback capacity of a country.

Comparisons between the East Asian and Latin American economies have, for some time now, been the rage; unlike most fads, however, this comparison may be instructive if conducted carefully. Jeffrey Sachs has argued that the major differences between debtor nations in the two regions, and for the presence of crisis in Latin America and its virtual absence in East Asia, has to do with the nature of the trade regime as revealed in the debt-to-export ratio and in differential debt-service ratios (Table 18.5). The high ratios for Latin America (though they have been declining for Mexico and Peru) relative to East Asia indicate to Sachs and others a structural imbalance that makes short-run attempts to service the debt inappropriate (see also Dornbusch [1985]). Latin America's debt problem, in other words, is not one of simple illiquidity.

The explanation for the different debt-to-export ratios seems, but only seems, easy to find. Latin America's development model since the 1930s, in the familiar "stylized version," has been based to a large degree upon import substitution industrialization, while East Asia's has depended (increasingly) on its export orientation (Bradford 1986:117). In 1965, with the exception of Malaysia, which was already quite open, the countries shown in Table 18.5

Table 18.5   Debt/Export and Debt-Service Ratios

	Debt Ranking 1981[a]	Debt/GNP 1981	Debt/Exports	Degree of Openness[b] 1965	Degree of Openness[b] 1983	Debt Service[c]
Latin America						
Argentina	10	31.6	334.7	.08	.13	214.9
Brazil	1	26.1	298.7	.08	.08	132.6
Chile	22	47.6	290.0	.14	.24	153.3
Mexico	2	30.9	258.8	.09	.20	161.8
Peru	14	44.7	223.5	.16	.21	122.2
East Asia						
Indonesia	4	24.1	87.1	.05	.25	n.a.
Malaysia	20	27.8	51.8	.44	.54	16.9
South Korea	3	27.6	76.6	.09	.37	90.1
Thailand	17	25.7	103.1	.18	.22	58.1

Sources: Sachs (1985: Table 4, 533; Table 5, 537); World Bank (1983: Table 16, 178-179); also see Inter-American Development Bank (1984: Table 1, 12; Table 11, 34-35) for debt service ratios for other years.

[a] Based on public sector debt only.
[b] Exports/gross domestic product.
[c] As a percent, average 1980-1983; includes interest and amortization on long- and medium-term debt and all short-term debt (which is due in one year, by definition).

had roughly similar degrees of openness, as measured by exports as a share of gross domestic product. However, by 1983, there was a clear distinction between the regions (with the exception of Thailand), as the growth in the degree of openness in East Asia increased substantially relative to Latin America. Thus, Sachs concludes, roughly comparable debt accumulation in the two regions, as measured by the debt/gross domestic product ratio, has not resulted in a debt crisis in East Asia because it was accompanied by the expansion of exports, which have contributed the necessary foreign exchange to service the debt. On the other hand, Latin America's import substitution strategy did not save enough foreign exchange or generate a rapidly rising export share, and thus the income required to repay the debt did not materialize as quickly as the debt. The underlying reason for this difference in trade regimes is to be found, it is argued, in the nature of state policy and in the weight given to exports in East Asia's development models and to a particular kind of import substitution in Latin America based on a faulty model fostered by earlier structuralist and Economic Commission for Latin America thinking. The message—and it is one being pushed from all sides—is that Latin America must shift from its so-called inward-looking model to an outward orientation similar to the East Asian model.

There is, unfortunately, far too much misunderstanding about the actual historical development in the two regions, which may lead to incorrect public policy and, for Latin America, a resurgence of crisis if this advice is followed blindly. Gustav Ranis, however, has provided a useful typology for comparing the Latin American and East Asian experiences that can help to orient our thinking about them (Ranis 1981 and Chapter 9 in this volume).

Both Latin America and East Asia began to industrialize via primary import substitution ("easy" or horizontal import substitution industrialization [ISI]), in which domestic production replaced imports of nondurable consumer goods. The East Asian countries passed through this stage later, and in at least half the time as the Latin American economies. Following the stage of primary import substitution industrialization, the largest Latin American countries began to pursue secondary ("hard" or vertical) import substitution in which some consumer durables (automobiles, for example) and some capital and intermediate goods began to be produced behind protective trade barriers.

After completing the easy import substitution industrialization stage, however, the East Asian economies began a process of primary *export* substitution; that is, they began to export some nondurable consumer goods, to a great extent produced by national capitalists, which began to replace primary agricultural exports in importance. In the process, their economies became more open, and more importantly, the share of manufactured goods to total exports reached an (unweighted) average of 82.9 percent for Taiwan and South Korea in 1977 (compared to less than 30 percent for Brazil, Mexico, Argentina, and Colombia). It is worth noting, however, that Malaysia, a "good" East Asian performer by the measures of Table 18.5, had but 15.2 percent of its exports in manufactured goods and nearly 60 percent in agricultural products, making it much closer, on these variables, to the Latin American countries [Appendix Tables, Chapter 9]. Thus it can be questioned whether the message should be that it is *manufacturing* exports that make the difference to the East Asian model's better handling of debt accumulation.[5]

Latin America, according to Ranis's typology, moved beyond hard import substitution industrialization to a further stage combining continued secondary import substitution industrialization with export *promotion*. Export promotion, Ranis explains, is "the selective encouragement of particular industries or even firms by administrative action in order to 'push out' exports in the absence of a general change in the structure of protection, or market liberalization." (Ranis 1981:212). In other words, Latin America's more limited increase in manufacturing exports was achieved only through the addition of more controls—for example, domestic content requirements for automobiles—combined with incentives to export *without* any basic changes in the secondary import substitution industrialization controls, without a fundamental opening of the economy to the international sector, and without the replacement of older exports by a new export structure.

The East Asian current "superexporters" stage of development involves secondary import substitution industrialization and *secondary export substitution,* as more complex consumer goods, as well as capital and intermediate goods, are produced not only for domestic use but, increasingly, for export, substituting for the less complex (primary) manufactured exports. Ranis suggests that this progression—primary import substitution industrialization→primary export substitution→secondary import substitution industrialization with secondary export substitution—is a more natural evolution than the Latin American model, which "skipped" over the primary export substitution stage and is now promoting exports rather than substituting new exports for traditional ones. Ranis argues that it was the primary export substitution stage that allowed the East Asian countries to successfully shift labor from agriculture to industry without substantial wage increases; to use labor-intensive industries to generate high employment levels and to avoid unemployment; and to institutionalize a learning process that created a dispersion of skills among workers and the spread of entrepreneurial talent that facilitated the later shift into the higher productivity, higher wage stage of secondary import substitution industrialization and secondary export substitution. Having skipped the primary export substitution stage, however, the Latin American countries moved directly, and prematurely, to secondary import substitution industrialization with its higher wages and lower levels of employment generation; and these two forces have contributed to the greater employment and income distribution problems of Latin America relative to East Asia.

Applicability of the East Asian Model to Latin America

Ranis's analysis is helpful for understanding some of the differences between the East Asian economies and those of Latin America (remembering that there are "Latin American" East Asian economies, for example, the Philippines). The important question is, What exactly is the lesson to be learned? Is it that the Latin American countries should try to adopt the East Asian-type model or, more simply, that a greater level of exports is called for to supersede the debt crisis and to prevent its recurrence? Or is it something else altogether?

An important message of the above typology is that import substitution, be it primary or secondary, is an important and complementary part of any development strategy, including the expansion of exports. There has been an overabundance of criticism of Latin America's import substitution industrialization, which is compared unfavorably to the export performance of the East Asian economies. It is essential to keep in mind that import substitution industrialization was also integral to the East Asian model and to the learning process in production for East Asian workers and entrepreneurs; it is not an absolute deviation or an inappropriate policy choice per se, as the tone of so much of the criticism of Latin America's import substitution industrialization has sometimes implied.

The question of the applicability of the East Asian model, however, needs to be considered very cautiously. Latin America (and the Third World, in general) has been inundated with other-world models from its modern inception. The Economic Commission for Latin America economists, whatever failings we might now find, at least were groping for a strategy, if not a model, that fit Latin America's reality. They rejected, and reject, the too-often uncritical offering of other-world models to be grafted onto a very different economic and social context. On this basis alone, there is an a priori suspicion about the East Asian model's usefulness in the Latin American *context* unless there is a convincing case to be made that the underlying realities of the two regions are similar enough to justify model borrowing. There are, in this context, some significant differences.

The East Asian economies, it can be argued, evolved as they did not because of perfect foresight as to the best path to be followed, but because the institutional and economic power structures permitted and, perhaps, forced the particular transformation we now identify as the "East Asian model." Speaking generally, landed interests, and hence the significance of primary agricultural exports to income generation, were weakened in East Asia through forced and fundamental agrarian reforms (assisted by real resource barriers and by the United States in South Korea and Taiwan). In Latin America, despite a much longer experience with industrialization, landed interests remained strong, and they continue to exert a retarding force on more fundamental change, just as C. E. Ayres suggested backward social hierarchies tend to do wherever they are encountered (Ayres 1978:xxvi-xxviii; also see Chapter 4). The continued high levels of primary agricultural exports from Latin America may thus be less a reflection of the strength of the international division of labor in forcing such production upon the region, as is often argued, and more a result of the power of the entrenched landed elite and related classes that wish to protect their special interests against the wider transformation of social production that a broader-based industrialization strategy, based on a prior agrarian transformation, would necessarily imply. In fact, one observer has suggested that it is not the export success of the East Asian countries that should be emphasized, but the success of their agrarian revolutions in laying the groundwork for industrialization and fundamental class transformations (Mellor 1986:68).

Further, while the real importance of international corporations in East Asia's development model is frequently ignored or downplayed, their dominant role in key sectors, and their integration into the national economies cannot be so conveniently overlooked in Latin America where national capitalists have been displaced and their growth blocked. Exports from subsidiaries of U.S.-based international corporations have very often been prohibited or severely restricted so as to not create competition with the parent or other subsidiaries. These restrictions have thwarted the potential for the manufacturing export substitution stage (primary or secondary) more characteristic of the East Asian model. This, of course, has nothing to do with Latin America's levels of protection or overvalued exchange rates, which are so often fingered for Latin America's weak export performance, but with the *internal* policies of international corporations, which have been conceived to protect market shares and profitability and to avoid competition that directly threatens their worldwide sourcing and distributing networks.[6]

Differences in labor between the two regions also are significant. More skilled and educated in East Asia than in Latin America, labor also has been more docile, less unionized, and more repressed and, until recently, earned lower and slower-growing wages (Ranis 1981: Table 4, 213, provides comparative evidence for South Korea and Mexico). The distribution of income is generally better in the East Asian countries (average Gini coefficient = .40) than in Latin America (.56), with the average relative income share of the poorest 20 percent in East Asia being 85 percent larger (7.6 percent [excluding Malaysia] versus 4.1 percent) [Ranis, Appendix, Tables, Chapter 9; World Bank 1985, Table 28, 228-229]. Latin America, however, cannot now create a docile labor force simply to follow a model, since this would require levels of repression or a retrogression in social mores and values unacceptable as part of any meaningful strategy for development (in fact, this cost to the East Asian "success" ought to be reconsidered), and to the extent that these characteristics of the labor force are important, wholesale application of the East Asian model is made more dubious (Tessitore 1984:26, 52).

The *real* lessons to be learned from the East Asian experience are, however, more fundamental than simple model-typology comparison alone. In fact, looking at the models first is to get the correct order of analysis backward, not to mention that such a view is static and ahistorical when what is desperately demanded is a dynamic and flexible approach to future, not past, development possibilities. Models of development function only given certain institutional parameters that either preexist or are, or can be, introduced with model implementation. It is to the institutional structure—or better, to an understanding of the retarding effects of ceremonial behavior—that attention to change needs to be focused, not on the model type (Ayres 1978: Chaps. 8, 9). In Latin America this means particular attention to the social and class structure of the agrarian sector that continues to debilitate social and economic progress and that must be revolutionized if new, and more just, patterns of development are to follow.[7]

The fundamental differences in the paths of the stages of development in the East Asian and Latin American models, then, can be traced to the constant tension between technological progress and ceremonialism, between the push for change and the retarding forces of backward institutions and structures—with the latter stronger and more deeply imbedded in Latin America than in East Asia—and not just to wrongheaded, misguided policymaking which, in the orthodox view, has "distorted market forces and economic decisionmaking." It is the power of ceremonial institutions, including the international corporation and the interests of the privileged classes, that has resulted in "bad" policy and that has delineated the possible stages of development *rather* than the reverse sequence, the "normal" mode of analysis (Tessitore 1984: 32, 46, 52-53, 55-57). What Latin America most needs is a more dynamic, progressive, and flexible institutional order so that the region's economies can more easily respond to, and shelter themselves from, the international market. This is easy to say, of course. How to get such change is another matter, as the failure of the Alliance for Progress and land reform attests. The debt crisis has, however, like crisis periods in Latin America's past, perhaps provided an opening for the beginnings of fundamental change *if* the crisis is responded to as an opportunity for progressive change and *if* the institutional structure can be made to be more responsive to the needs for such change.

Debt Dynamics and Institutional Change
The need for adjustment to the debt accumulation of the past decade is unassailable. What is critical is the nature of the adjustment. Until now, the IMF/orthodox strategy has been to tinker with phenomenal causes of the crisis—central government fiscal deficits, overvalued exchange rates, trade barriers—without getting at the underlying structural and institutional forces which have engendered such outcomes in the first place. This recipe for social and economic instability, however, has provoked a response out of the crisis it has fomented. Democratic governments have emerged across the region to replace military regimes and dictators, and while it would be naive to believe that such leaders, coming as they do from the elite class, are more disposed by nature to fundamental change than in the past, it is now perhaps possible that, by the force of events, some of them will be forced to oversee and even initiate long-term structural transformation that can open new paths to development, though such a redirection is far from assured. Repressive reaction to see that debts are paid on time and that the economies are restructured along neoclassical guidelines, as the IMF would like, remains a strong contender, though a weakened one, as the spread of "debt fatigue" among the countries shows no sign of diminishing. Nor do remedial measures from the center (like the timid Baker Plan with its minimal additional financing of $3.1 billion) nor a resurgence of OECD growth offer much real hope for the means to muddle through.

But before such changes can begin to pursued or, better, as part of the

process of moving toward restructuring their institutional and class structures, a real resolution of Latin America's debt crisis must be sought. Of all
the proposals for coming to grips with the crisis, there is one that promises
to permit growth to take place, for the debt to be reduced significantly, and
for fundamental institutional reform to have a chance to be initiated.

Debt Reduction and Institutional Reform

There has been no shortage of proposals for relieving Latin America's debt
burden, from a new allocation of Special Drawing Rights (SDRs), to debt-for-
equity swaps, to lower interest rates, to repayments linked to export earnings, and so on.[8] Nearly all these proposals, however, require the private
international banks (or their governments) to initiate the policy. Further,
most do not solve the problem, but simply postpone the day when the debt
will ultimately come due. It is, in fact, the inordinate amount of debt owed
to the private international banks (82.1 percent in 1981) that makes an old,
orthodox solution to large debts—write downs—virtually impossible.
Further, some proposals, like the debt-for-equity swap, would increase the
penetration of foreign capital into critical sectors of the region's economies
at a time when the reverse is desirable. Other than unilateral debt repudia-
tion, there has been but one proposal that puts the decision of truly relieving
the debt burden (that is, correcting the debt-to-export balance and reducing
current account imbalances) into the hands of the Latin American debtors
themselves.

David Felix has suggested that the Latin American countries make use
of the externally held assets of their citizens to service the debt (Felix 1985).
Given the magnitude of capital flight (equal to about 50 percent of the gross
capital inflow in Mexico, 65 percent in Argentina, and 137 percent in Venezuela over the period 1978–1982 alone) into foreign bank accounts and the
buildup of equity in land owned in the United States and elsewhere by Latin
American nationals, Felix estimates there are at least $180 billion in Latin
American assets outside the region, or roughly half the region's total debt
(Felix 1985:50; see also Ayittey 1986). Felix asks:

> Can the privately owned foreign assets be mobilized for debt servicing?
> Let's first dispose of a spurious theological objection. To do so would not
> be to administer a death blow to capitalist property rights. Coercive mobili-
> zation even has a slight patina of orthodoxy; it was used in the past by major
> capitalist countries in duress. During World War I, Britain and France, the
> two leading international lenders of the laissez-faire era, compelled their
> nationals to register their foreign securities with the Treasury, which liqui-
> dated them as needed, paying the owners in local currency bonds, the
> foreign exchange being used to help cover current account deficits (Felix
> 1985:50).

From many perspectives, this proposal is ingenious. First, it recognizes the absurdity of continued large net outflows of capital from Latin America, as a result of capital flight and debt servicing, by reducing both. Second, as Latin American governments require their citizens to exchange their assets abroad (above some minimum level) for locally issued bonds, foreign exchange funds would be made available for servicing debt without the need to repress imports, to pursue ill-conceived export expansion, or for the need for new debt to roll over old. Billions of dollars would be released each year from debt service uses for potentially productive development purposes. Elements of the elite class in Latin America would be "hurt" by such a policy, of course, but that is precisely the idea. These are citizens who have, to a great extent, avoided the costs of the debt crisis and its current resolution and who are content to see the problem treated as one of liquidity. They hope that the future will be more or less like the past, a past from which they have gained in their privileged positions. What *is* desired is a shift of the burden to those more able to bear it and who share, as a group, major responsibility for the debt accumulation by their past actions.

Felix notes that foreign banks could be induced to assist the Latin American countries in identifying assets of their nationals (a task facilitated in the United States by the 1970 Bank Secrecy Act) by the decision of the Latin countries to limit any outflow of foreign exchange to service the debt to some limit, say 10 percent or less, of export earnings. The remainder of the debt service would be paid from whatever funds have been nationalized and set aside for this purpose (in an escrow account in the United States, Felix suggests). "The account would offer the banks the double prospect of avoiding new bailing-in lending and of belatedly collateralizing their existing Latin American loans, strong inducements for working with the debtor governments in tracking down foreign assets to build up the accounts" (Felix 1985:51).

With the cost to future capital flight substantially raised, additional funds would be reinvested in Latin America, causing perhaps some forced growth in confidence in the Latin American economies on the part of the elite, who would need to make their money work for them at home rather than in a "safe-haven" abroad.

What are the chances of such a proposal gaining adherents? Obviously they are better in some countries than in others. Peru, which already has capped its interest payments at 10 percent of exports, and whose workers have suffered grievously from the debt crisis, might be a very likely candidate. (In 1985, Peruvian workers' *real* wages were 40 percent below their 1980 level and 50 percent below the 1975 level [González 1986: Table 6, 111].) So, too, might Argentina. Both these countries, particularly Peru, have presidents with a substantial popular power base—fundamental if such a strategy is to have some possibility of implementation. Though Mexico does not fit this description, the size of its debt and the size of the external assets of its nationals may eventually make this an attractive solution (this proposal is not a solution for Brazil, however, which has had minimal capital flight).

Institutional Change

Implementing Felix's proposal could go far in removing the current burden of debt from the poorest, while opening the door for accelerated economic growth. By itself, however, it would not reorient the direction of the Latin American economies, though it may be that any country pursuing such a policy of asset nationalization might be more sympathetic to fundamental reform, as well. It is hoped that a close examination of the East Asian model will convince policymakers that the lesson of that experience is not to be found in the need for export growth, but in the need for an alteration of Latin America's institutions, their responsiveness to change, and the necessity for the inculcation of a value orientation conducive to national integrated development. If this lesson is learned, there is a chance for truly profound change emerging from Latin America's debt crisis.

What sort of transformation would be desirable in Latin America? To begin with, it is important to accept a basic needs or a "redistribution before growth" strategy that focuses on growth with a purpose: one that directly improves the lives and assures the social, political, and economic participation of the poorest majority (Streeten 1982; Adelman 1986). The basic needs approach recognizes the worth of all human life and the right of all to a decent and dignified existence—values with which institutionalists would have no disagreement. In improving the stock of human resources and the productivity of the poorest, the basic needs approach, like that of the institutionalist, recognizes that true development is not a simple function of the accumulation of capital or the saving rate, but is first and foremost a function of human talents, skills, and values operating within a permissive institutional framework.

Other changes, difficult but necessary, can be listed:

- Income distribution should be improved through more progressive income tax systems and more efficient tax collection and, as part of a basic needs or redistribution strategy, a larger social wage for the poorest.
- Agrarian transformation should be designed to improve agricultural production for domestic use, the demand for which will grow with income redistribution and the success of the basic needs/redistribution strategy in extending the size of the market (Adelman 1986:58-64; Mellor 1986). At a minimum, land taxes must be implemented on a wider scale to penalize speculative and unproductive ownership and

to reward use, especially for local consumption. A reduction in the power and influence of the landed elite is as much a goal of such transformation as the expansion and redirection of production.

- Production and ownership of capital by nationals should be encouraged and stimulated by the state in as many forms as possible for value-added reasons to assist in correcting the balance of payments, and for minimizing external technological dependence reasons, via small businesses, cooperatives, self-help organizations, joint state-private corporations, and so on. The production of *basic commodities* that, in turn, enter into the production of as wide a range of other goods as possible should be closely studied and planned (Thomas 1974:196-201). Foreign capital should not be discouraged per se, but foreign investment should be accepted only within an overall plan and only when such firms can contribute to furthering national development in ways domestic firms cannot (or cannot yet). In other words, foreign capital should be treated with an awareness of the contribution it can make to a well-conceived plan, and with respect for the pitfalls that overreliance on a laissez faire approach to foreign investment can bring.

- Universities should be granted real autonomy in an atmosphere of respect for academic freedom. Intervening in the universities must be understood as destructive to the process of technological creativity and inquiry necessary for more autonomous development (Street 1983).

- Regional trade and integration should be approached again with the realization that therein lie real possibilities for more equal competition and, if properly executed, for a widening of the growth and development paths for small and large nations, rich and poor. The Third World, in general, could benefit from closer relations—trade, financial, and otherwise—to counter the concentrated power of the center countries.

Exports should not be fetishized, even for smaller economies. The issue is not whether to export, but the how, the what and the timing. As Streeten has pointed out, an export-oriented strategy can be as ill-conceived and inefficient as any inward-looking economic model (Streeten 1986). Greater attention to equitable planning, with an eye both to efficiency *and* to new class structures and values conducive to both growth and development, is what Latin America requires over the future, not lectures on what markets can do. Invoking the East Asian "Gang of Four" as showing what the market can do no longer convinces; the essential role the state has played in these economies is now too well known. What is key is the degree of complementarity between the state and the private sector, with the state performing key organizational and planning functions (Bradford 1986). In thinking about these issues, particularly to determining the proper role of the internal market, domestic production, and the role of agriculture. Clive Thomas's book,. though written for other purposes, deserves serious attention in Latin America if the profound transformations so necessary are ever to have a chance of success (Thomas 1974).

Notes

1. Martine Guerguil writes: "The tendency to make adjustments in line with the perception of the banking system, rather than with the real situation of the debtor, has been characteristic of almost all the renegotiation process" (Guerguil 1984:149). Harry Magdoff argues that the IMF now plays the role, particularly in Latin America, that U.S. military interventions did in the past: guaranteeing the repayment of debt by restructuring economies to serve bankers' interests (Magdoff 1986:2-3). President Alan García of Peru has expressed the same view (Falcoff 1986:15).

2. Rudiger Dornbusch notes: "Some major borrowers incurred their debts in the very act of financing capital flight by domestic residents. Hence, at least in accounting terms, the external debt is matched by holdings of external assets" (Dornbusch 1985:339). Capital flight can only be estimated; typically it is "measured" by the statistical discrepancy in the balance-of-payments accounts. We will return to this issue below.

3. This is not to suggest, however, that there has been no distribution of the debt burden. As John Cavanagh et al. remind us, the decline in Latin American imports in the early 1980s as a result of the austerity programs has affected export industries in the United States, costing many workers their jobs and joining them with the poorest in the debtor nations in footing at least some of the costs of the excessive lending (Cavanagh et al. 1985).

4. Arguments supporting "export pessimism" have been given a boost by the Reagan administration's plans to "exclude imports from the more advanced developing countries," including Brazil and Mexico, by denying their current duty-free status under the Generalized System of Preferences in retaliation for "unfair" competition (Murray 1986:22). Debtors asked to export more and to import less in order to pay their debts are justified in balking at additional sacrifice when the developed countries seem bent on demanding of others what they themselves seem unwilling to bear—free trade.

5. Hollis Chenery makes a similar observation in his comment on Ranis's article (Chenery 1981).

6. See Felipe Pazos for a refutation of the thesis blaming Latin America's levels of protection and overvalued exchange rates for its weak export performance (Pazos 1985–1986).

7. It can be argued, as does Gustav Ranis, that Latin America's abundant natural resource endowment actually has acted as a brake on institutional change rather than as a blessing (Ranis 1981:215-216). The existing class structure was not constrained by resource limitations, and thus, the landed elites could maintain their lifestyles without pushing for technical change. The backwardness of Spain in the colonial

period has been explained in a similar way; colonial wealth, being too easily obtained and too abundant, blocked change instead of facilitating it.

8. See Guerguil (1984:152 ff) for a useful summary.

References

Adelman, Irma. 1986. "A Poverty-Focused Approach to Development Policy." In *Development Strategies Reconsidered*, ed. John P. Lewis and Valeriena Kallab, 49-65. New Brunswick, N.J.: Transaction Books for the Overseas Development Council.

Ayittey, George B.N. 1986. "The Real Foreign Debt Problem." *Wall Street Journal,* 18 April, 30.

Ayres, C.E. 1978. *The Theory of Economic Progress.* 3d ed. Kalamazoo, Mich.: New Issues Press.

Bradford, Colin I., Jr. 1986. "East Asian 'Models': Myths and Lessons." In *Development Strategies Reconsidered*, ed. John P. Lewis and Valeriena Kallab, 115-128. New Brunswick, N.J.: Transaction Books for the Overseas Development Council.

Cavanagh, John et al. 1985. *From Debt to Development.* Washington D.C.: Institute for Policy Studies.

Chenery, Hollis. 1981. "Comments on 'Challenges and Opportunities Posed by Asia's Superexporters.'" *Quarterly Review of Economics and Business* 21 (Summer):227-230.

Cline, William R. 1985. "International Debt: From Crisis to Recovery?" *American Economic Review* 75 (May):185-190.

Concenso de Cartagena. 1986. "Declaración de Montevideo: Propuestas de emergencia para las negociaciones sobre deuda y crecimiento." *Comercio Exterior* 36 (January):77-80.

Dornbusch, Rudiger. 1985. "Policy Performance Links Between LDC Debtor and Industrial Nations." *Brookings Papers on Economic Activity* 2:303-368.

Falcoff, Mark. 1986. "Peruvian President Gnaws Away His Northern Lifeline." *Wall Street Journal,* 28 March.

Felix, David. 1985. "How to Resolve Latin America's Debt Crisis." *Challenge* 28 (November-December):44-51.

González, Norberto. 1986. "Balance preliminar de la economía latinoamericana en 1985." *Comercio Exterior* 36 (February):105-124.

Guerguil, Martine. 1984. "The International Financial Crisis: Diagnoses and Prescriptions." *CEPAL Review* 24 (December):147-169.

Inter-American Development Bank. 1984. *External Debt and Economic Development in Latin America.* Washington, D.C.: Inter-American Development Bank.

————. 1985. *Economic and Social Progress in Latin America. External Debt: Crisis and Adjustment.* Washington, D.C.: Inter-American Development Bank.

International Monetary Fund. 1985. *World Economic Outlook, April.* Washington, D.C.: International Monetary Fund.

Lombardi, Richard. 1985. *Debt Trap: Rethinking the Logic of Development.* New York: Praeger.

Magdoff, Harry. 1986. "Third World Debt: Past and Present." *Monthly Review* 37 (February):1-10.

Mellor, John W. 1986. "Agriculture on the Road to Industrialization." *Development Strategies Reconsidered,* ed., John P. Lewis and Valeriena Kallab, 67-68. New Brunswick, N.J.: Transaction Books for the Overseas Development Council.

Murray, Alan. 1986. "Third World Export to U.S. Will Be Curbed." *Wall Street Journal,* 2 April.

Organization of American States. 1986. *The Economy of Latin America and the Caribbean.* Washington, D.C.: Organization of American States.

Pazos, Felipe. 1985–1986. "Have Import Substitution Policies Either Precipitated or Aggravated the Debt Crisis?" *Journal of Interamerican Studies and World Affairs* 27 (Winter):57-73.

Ranis, Gustav. 1981. "Challenges and Opportunities Posed by Asia's Superexporters: Implications for Manufactured Exports from Latin America." *Quarterly Review of Economics and Business* 21 (Summer):204-226.

Sachs, Jeffrey D. 1985. "External Debt and Macroeconomic Performance in Latin America and East Asia." *Brookings Papers on Economic Activity* 2:523-573.

Street, James H. 1983. "The Reality of Power and the Poverty of Economic Doctrine." *Journal of Economic Issues* 17 (June):295-313.

————. 1967. "The Latin America 'Structuralists' and the Institutionalists: Convergence in Development Theory." *Journal of Economic Issues* 1 (June):41-62.

Streeten, Paul. 1982. "A Cool Look At 'Outward-Looking' Strategies for Development." *The World Economy* 5 (September):159-169.

Tessitore, John, ed. 1984. *Asia Development Model and the Caribbean Basin Initiative* (workshop summary). Washington, D.C.: Council on Religion and International Affairs.

Thomas, Clive Y. 1974. *Dependence and Transformation.* New York: Monthly Review Press.

World Bank. 1983. *World Development Report, 1983.* New York: Oxford University Press.

————. 1985. *World Development Report, 1985.* New York: Oxford University Press.

Appendix Table   Latin America and the Caribbean: Key Indicators

Country	Annual Growth of GNP (%)			Accumulated Change in GNP (%) 1981-1986[a]	GDP per Capita, 1985[a] (1984 dollars)	Life Expectancy at Birth, 1984 (years)	Infant Mortality Rate, 1984 (under age one, deaths per 1000 births)
	1984	1985	1986[a]				
Latin America[b]	3.2	2.7	3.4	5.9	1,782	—	—
Oil Exporters	2.5	1.8	-1.9	1.6			
Bolivia	-0.9	-1.7	-3.5	-14.5	840	53	118
Ecuador	4.5	4.3	1.5	14.8	1,222	65	67
Mexico	3.5	2.7	-4.0	4.6	2,248	66	51
Peru	3.8	1.6	8.5	5.0	1,055	59	95
Trinidad and Tobago	-6.6	-3.1	—	—	2,837	69	22
Venezuela	-1.1	-0.6	1.5	-7.6	2,451	69	38
Non-Oil Exporters	3.7	3.2	6.5	8.3			
Argentina	2.2	-4.4	5.5	-7.2	1,971	70	34
Barbados	3.6	0.2	—	—	—	73	—
Brazil	4.8	8.2	8.8	18.7	1,852	64	68
Colombia	3.6	2.6	5.0	17.7	1,243	65	48
Costa Rica	7.9	0.9	3.0	4.0	1,708	73	19
Cuba[c]	7.3	4.8	2.5	45.7	—	75	16
Chile	6.0	2.4	5.0	3.7	1,817	70	22
El Salvador	1.4	1.4	-0.5	-11.1	771	65	66
Guatemala	0.0	-0.9	0.0	-6.0	1,216	60	66
Guyana	5.8	1.8	—	—	720	65	—
Haiti	0.4	3.5	-1.5	-3.2	320	55	124
Honduras	3.1	1.4	2.0	5.5	719	61	77
Jamaica	0.0	-5.4	—	—	1,701	73	20
Nicaragua	-1.4	-2.6	0.0	5.0	845	60	70
Panama	-0.4	3.3	3.0	15.4	2,218	71	25
Paraguay	3.3	4.0	1.0	13.8	1,777	66	44
Dominican Republic	0.5	-2.0	0.5	9.0	1,225	64	71
Uruguay	-2.4	0.5	5.0	-11.7	2,208	73	29
United States	6.8	2.2	—	—	15,390	76	11

Continued

Appendix Table continued

Sources: Inter-American Development Bank, *Economic and Social Progress in Latin America, 1986 Report* (Washington, D.C.: IDB, 1986), Table 3, p. 394; ECLA, "Balance económico y conferencia extraordinaria," *Comercio Exterior 37* (February 1987), Table 1, p. 117; World Bank, *World Development Report 1986* (Washington: World Bank), Table 1, pp. 180-181; Box A.1, p. 243; Table 27, pp. 232-233.

GNP stands for Gross National Product.
GDP stands for Gross Domestic Product.

a   Estimated data
b   Excluding Cuba
c   Refers to global social product

Contributors

James L. Dietz is professor of economics and Latin American studies at California State University, Fullerton. He is author of *Economic History of Puerto Rico,* as well as numerous articles on Latin America and the Caribbean.

James H. Street is professor emeritus of economics at Rutgers University, New Brunswick, New Jersey. Among his many publications on Latin American development are *Urban Planning and Development Centers in Latin America* (with Guido G. Weigend) and *Technological Progress in Latin America: The Prospects for Overcoming Dependency* (contributor and editor with Dilmus D. James).

Robert J. Alexander is professor of economics at Rutgers University, New Brunswick, New Jersey. He has published a great many volumes dealing with virtually all the countries of Latin America, including *Agrarian Reform in Latin America* (Macmillan, 1974) and *A New Development Strategy* (Orbis, 1976).

Clarence E. Ayres was professor of economics at the University of Texas, Austin, from 1930 to 1961. He is recognized as one of the leading contributors to the institutionalist economic tradition. His books include *The Theory of Economic Progress, The Industrial Economy,* and *Towards a Reasonable Society,* among others. Professor Ayres died in 1972.

Peter Evans is professor of sociology at Brown University. His book, *Dependent Development: The Alliance of Multinational, State, and Local Capital in Brazil* (Princeton University Press, 1979), has become one of the most influential in Brazilian studies published in recent years.

Alejandro Foxley is president of the Center for Latin American Economic Research (CIEPLAN) in Santiago, Chile. He is a frequent lecturer and visiting professor at major universities in the United States and is currently associated with the Kellogg Institute at Notre Dame University.

Gary Gereffi is associate professor of sociology at Duke University. He has written and published widely on Mexico and the role of transnational corporations in economic development.

William P. Glade is professor of economics and former director of the Institute of Latin American Studies at the University of Texas, Austin. His research has been focused on Mexico.

Albert O. Hirschman is professor emeritus at the Institute for Advanced Study at Princeton University. His many books include *A Bias for Hope, The Strategy for Economic Development,* and recently, *Rival Views of Market Society.* He was the 1986 recipient of the Kalman Silvert Award of the Latin American Studies Association.

Joseph L. Love, professor of history at the University of Illinois, Urbana-Champaign, recently has conducted research on the history of intellectual ideas. He is the author of *Rio Grande do Sul and Brazilian Regionalism* and *São Paulo and the Brazilian Federation.*

Felipe Pazos is economic advisor to the president of the Central Bank of Venezuela. He also founded and served as first president of the Central Bank of Cuba.

Gustav Ranis is Frank Altschul Professor of International Economics at Yale University and is former director of the Yale Economic Growth Center and a distinguished contributor to the orthodox theory of economic development, particularly the Ranis-Fei dual sector model.

Paul Streeten is director of the World Development Institute and professor of economics at Boston University. He was formerly, among many other positions, special advisor to the Policy Planning and Review Department of the World Bank. He has written widely on the basic needs approach and alternative development strategies.

Víctor E. Tokman is director, Regional Employment Program for Latin America and the Caribbean (PREALC) of the UN Economic Commission for Latin American and the Caribbean in Santiago, Chile. He has written extensively on issues related to Latin American labor, particularly in the *CEPAL Review.*

Index

Academic freedom, required for economic progress, 13, 16–25, 29, 29–30, 67, 71, 289
Agriculture: education in, in Mexico, 211; imitative of U.S., 222; land distribution, and development, 61–62, 114–115, 122–124, 126, 148, 200–201, 221–222, 237, 283, 284, 288–289; neglected, 115, 138–139, 144, 217, 218, 221–222; technical progress, 110, 202–204, 207–208, 262. *See also* Center-periphery thesis; Products, primary; *and specific commodities*
Advertising, 121–122
Alemán, Miguel, 165
Allende Gossens, Salvador, 23
Alliance for Progress, 78, 109–110, 196, 201, 285
American Association of University Professors (AAUP), 16, 25
American Economic Association, 10
Amin, Samir, 78, 91, 92
Antigua, 2
Aramburu, Pedro Eugenio, 19
Argentina: 54–73; agricultural development, 60, 61, 203–204; balance of payments, 83–84, 86; debt repayment, 82, 287; economic orthodoxy and authoritarianism, 249, 250–251, 254–255; economic growth before World War I, 7, 44, 55–56, 80–81; economic history, 106; education, 61, 63–64, 65, 67, 71, 109, 209; end of import substitution, 127; exchange controls during Depression, 81; founding of central bank, 80; government intervention in economy, 83; grain exports, 60, 81, 204; import capacity, 83; import coefficient, 150; income, per capita, 273–274; industrialization, 84–85, 86; inflation, 58; manufactured exports,

152, 281; meat exports, 60, 81, 204, 206; monetarist policies and, 25–29, 242, 246, 259, 264–267; monetary crisis, 86; monetary policy, 85; open lands, 200–201; populist policies, 246; repression of free inquiry, 18–22, 67, 71; stagnation, 54, 56–57, 67–68, 69–71; tariff structure, 94–95n12; trade with Great Britain, 62, 63, 81–82
Asian, East, model: 116; applicability to Latin America, 142–146, 272, 282–285, 289; debtor countries, compared with Latin American, 279–280; primary export substitution, 134–135, 281–282; SICs, 128–129, 130–133, 134–136. *See also* Hong Kong; Japan; Korea, South; Taiwan
Australia, 83
Authoritarian governments. *See* Military regimes
Auto industry, 137, 176, 177, 179
Ayres, Clarence, as institutional economist, 54, 59, 61, 63, 102, 109, 112, 200, 201, 202, 208, 212

Baer, Werner, 99n68
Bairoch, Paul, 99n68
Balance of payments, 9, 83–84, 85, 86, 196, 250, 263
Basic needs strategy, 14–15, 33, 38–41, 288
Bergsten, Fred, 179
Boenninger, Edgardo, 23
Branco, Humberto Castello, 168
Brazil: 2, 288; agriculture, 144; and center-periphery thesis, 78; direct foreign investment—history and role, 160–170, future of, 180–183; economic history, 37, 57, 106, 112, 143; end of import substitution, 127; exports of manufactured goods, 142, 145, 152, 281; highways, 201; IMF and, 114n17; import coefficient, 150; income—distribution,

304302   *Index*

209
Saving, and investment, 11–12n1, 218
Semi-industrialized countries (SICs),
    introduced, 128–130
Semiperiphery, members of, 160, 184n2
SICs, introduced, 128–130
Singapore, 130, 135
Singer, Hans, 76, 90, 91, 104, 149
Scobie, James, 209
Silva Henríquez, Raúl, 23
Silva Herzog, Jesús, 261
Social change: finding means of inducing,
    111–112; and investment, 255;
    movement of peoples and, 47–48. *See
    also* redistribution *under* Income
Social class, 4–5, 47, 65, 119
Spain, 3–5, 108, 109
Statistics, need for accurate, 106
Stroessner, Alfredo, 18, 24–25
Structuralism: as accurate description, 105–
    106; achievements, 108; challenge to, 29,
    140–142, 143–144, 145–146; and debt
    crisis, 274–275, 275–277; diagnoses, 107;
    gaps in theory, 108–112; vis-à-vis IMF,
    26; and inflation, 241–242, 244–245; vis-
    à-vis orthodoxy, 10, 11, 102–105, 274–
    275; program in Chile, 246; recent
    orthodox form of, 247–248; studies,
    106–107; as system of ideas, 101; and
    technological dependency, 205, 213. *See
    also* Center-periphery thesis; Import
    Substitution Industrialization; Prebisch,
    Raúl
Sunkel, Osvaldo, 106, 109, 113n11, 205
Superintendency of Development of the
    Northeast (SUDENE), 94n2
Surplus, economic, 92
Sweden, employment structure, 230–231,
    232

Taiwan, 130, 135, 139, 142, 145, 152, 281, 283
Tariffs: Argentine, 94–95n12; Brazilian, 154,
    252–253; Latin American, 147, 153–154;
    U.S., 82
Technology: Argentine, 62–65; dynamic
    insufficiency, 229, 233–234, 238;
    dependency and transfers, 13, 25, 202–
    208; process of development, 43–44, 46–
    52, 110–111. *See also* Inventions and
    innovations
Teitel, S., 153
Textiles, 164

Thoumi, F., 153
Trade: danger of permanent disequilibrium,
    86; equilibrium theories, 87; and factor-
    price equalization, 91–92; free, 5–6;
    restrictions, 83–84; terms of, 89, 91–92,
    103–104, 104, 148–149, 263. *See also*
    Center-periphery thesis; Comparative
    advantage; Exports; Tariffs; Unequal
    exchange
Tugwell, Rexford G., 111
Tyler, William G., 153–154

Underground economy, 217–218, 234–235,
    236–237
Unemployment: 36; inflation and, 409–410;
    monetarist policies and, 259; population
    growth and, 218; technological, 217, 219
Unequal exchange, 78, 79, 84, 92, 93
United Nations, 88–89
United States: as creditor, 82, 261, 262, 266–
    267; DFI in Latin America, 9, 162, 164,
    165, 167, 173; employment structure,
    230–231, 232, 234–235; import
    coefficient, 76–77, 88, 90, 150; innovative
    example of southern cotton production,
    207; investment history, internal, 233–
    234; low propensity to import, 86; trade
    with Argentina, 81, 86; and trade cycle,
    87
Universities and technical schools: Argentine,
    21, 61; Catholic—of Chile, 23, of
    Paraguay, 25; Mexican, 211–212;
    National—of Asunción, 17, 24–25, of
    Buenos Aires, 19, 20, 79, of Montevideo,
    24. *See also* Academic freedom
Urquidi, Victor, 106
Uruguay: monetarist theories and, 25–29,
    242, 246, 264–266; orthodox policies
    and, 249, 251, 259; repression of free
    inquiry, 18, 24; stagnation despite
    literacy, 109

Values, social: fostering evolution of society,
    52–53, 112; and imposition of economic
    orthodoxy, 263–264, 268
Vargas, Getúlio, 164, 165, 166, 180, 185n11,
    191
Vasconcelos, José, 210–211
Veblen, Thorstein, 16, 46, 47, 48, 50, 102, 109
Venezuela, 127, 213n3, 250
Videla, Jorge Rafael, 20–21
Villarreal, René, 28

About the Book

Presenting a major alternative to orthodox, monetarist economic analysis—and one supported by a preponderance of Latin American economists—this text provides a consistent institutionalist and structuralist perspective on Latin America's development problems. The major sections of the book touch on fundamental areas of concern: development versus economic growth; the institutionalist and structuralist mode of analysis; import substitution versus export development strategies; the role of transnational corporations and the state; technological change; employment and unemployment; inflation; and debt. Section introductions by the editors raise key issues and suggest solutions to the problems explored. The book is designed for use both as a core textbook and in tandem with other texts on Latin American economics.